CANADIAN MONETARY, BANKING AND FISCAL DEVELOPMENT

# CANADIAN

# MONETARY, BANKING

## AND

# FISCAL DEVELOPMENT

R. CRAIG McIVOR M.A., Ph.D.

*Professor of Economics*
*McMaster University*
*Hamilton, Ontario*

TORONTO

THE MACMILLAN COMPANY OF CANADA LIMITED

1961

*To MARION*

# FOREWORD

The prominence given fiscal and monetary policy questions in the national elections of early 1958 revealed very clearly the new importance which highly technical economic matters have attained in public discussion in Canada. The energy with which politicians hammered away at these themes reflected not only widespread interest in how business recession might be ended but also great concern over the tight-money policy which had been applied in the immediately preceding boom. Many Canadians found it perplexing that the central bank, a public agency set up to promote economic growth, should have abandoned its long-standing, cheap-money policy for one of monetary restraint. The modification of private business plans which had to be made as a result aroused some resentment, and the uneven impact of credit restrictions brought charges of discrimination. Moreover, confusion as to the relation of these policies to the recession which followed was widespread. Any well-rounded programme to counter serious recession must include both public works and tax cuts, yet, in the election, each major political party chose half of such a programme and disparaged the other half. Canadians were thus confronted with the necessity of making up their minds on matters which are complicated in theory and on policies which are hard to apply successfully. Since the spectres of unemployment and of inflation are not likely soon to be exorcised from the Canadian scene, discussion of the most appropriate means of combating them is likely to be even more of the stuff of Canadian politics in the future than it has been in the past.

If we are to handle these matters well, both in the day-to-day conduct of fiscal and monetary policy and occasionally at the ballot box, Canadians generally must become much better informed on the issues involved. This implies both some knowledge of the theory of such matters and of the institutions through which policy is carried out. Unfortunately, even in its popular versions, the theory is not easy and an appreciation of how our monetary and fiscal institutions may be expected to behave in particular situations is to be obtained mainly from a study of their history, of how they have come to be what they are. Theory is likely to remain the preserve of the student. Fortunately, however, when an expert surveys economic history, many of the conclusions of theory are made plain in his analysis of past experience. Indeed, such studies are perhaps the most impressive and interesting garb in which the conclusions of economic analysis can be set before the general reader.

This is one of the most important reasons for giving Dr. McIvor's study of our monetary and banking history an enthusiastic welcome and hoping it will be widely read. Not only does his book provide a well-organized and authoritative account of this branch of our economic history, but it is written in an easy and engaging style which bears the reader safely over some treacherous theoretical shoals and quickly along more placid but somewhat less inspiring stretches in our monetary history. While some knowledge of economic theory will undoubtedly increase the general reader's appreciation of the rich fare set before him, very much can be gained without it, given a reasonable effort of attention.

The author's two greatest services, however, will likely prove to be to university students of economics and to his professional colleagues. Not even university libraries are able to provide more than a few students with full access to the professional literature, to say nothing of the source material of which much use has been made in this book. The understanding of this branch of economic study will therefore be greatly enriched by the classroom use of this scholarly study. To sustain the interest of students in the more abstract and complicated reaches of economic theory is not an easy task for the teacher. Dr. McIvor's book makes it possible to discuss the theory in closer relation to the actual problems with which generations of Canadians have wrestled with varying degrees of success. He deserves the gratitude of the general reader, the student and the professional economist for the effort and skill he has lavished on their enlightenment.

F. A. KNOX

Queen's University,
Kingston,
April, 1958.

# PREFACE

The decision to undertake the following study is explained not only by the writer's general interest in Canadian monetary, banking and fiscal development, but also by the fact that he bears some responsibility for teaching this subject to undergraduates. It is in this latter connection that the comparative neglect of such an important phase of Canada's economic development has given rise to substantial and obvious difficulties.

It is true that by way of illustrating or complementing the theoretical aspects of his subject, the Canadian instructor in "money and banking" may guide his students with considerable care through the complex evolution of various foreign monetary and banking systems. However, confronted by a lack of adequate and readily available Canadian reference material, he must often dispose of comparable developments in his own country in a somewhat more fragmentary and much less satisfactory manner. As a result, his students are likely to gain neither a real understanding of contemporary developments nor the ability to view them in proper perspective. Such limitations are particularly unfortunate in view of the central position and steadily increasing importance accorded to monetary and fiscal techniques as instruments of control in the Canadian economy. It is hoped that the following study, by providing some generally useful background material, may help to bridge a gap which has long been apparent in this area. Several sections of the work are appreciably indebted to earlier and rather widely scattered writings, and an attempt has been made to render appropriate acknowledgment of these studies.

The existence of a close interrelationship among the three areas specified in the title of this study is immediately apparent. This is particularly so in the case of money and banking where, under our existing institutional arrangements, the functions of commercial banking and money-creating are inextricably interwoven, and where our chartered banks provide the economy with all but a small proportion of its available stock of money. The emergence of government fiscal policy as a force of major economic importance has occurred only in relatively recent times, but here also, its inseparable connection with monetary and banking policies will be readily apparent.

In an attempt to present the subject most effectively, an historical approach has been adopted, within which it is hoped that both institutional and theoretical developments have been appropriately related. In most of the periods discussed, the evolution of Canadian commercial banking has been selected both as the principal point of focus and the central point of departure. Although the subject of non-commercial banking is significant to the student of Canada's financial organization, and although its development presents features of peculiar interest, it does not fall directly within the scope of this present work, and this aspect of the Canadian capital market is therefore accorded only secondary attention.

I wish to acknowledge particularly the encouragement and invaluable assistance provided by Professor Frank A. Knox of Queen's University, who read the entire manuscript in its earlier stages. Because of his continuing interest, the shortcomings of the present study are undoubtedly substantially less than would otherwise have been the case. To Dr. Duncan A. MacGibbon, my former colleague at McMaster University, I am indebted for painstaking criticism of many details of the analysis, out of which a more readable text has emerged. Apart from expressing my appreciation for the unfailing co-operation provided by officials of the national and several provincial archives in making available manuscripts and other essential sources, I must thank Mr. Peter Lowe of Winnipeg, a former General Manager of Alloway and Champion, for his personal assistance in clarifying the role of private banking in Canadian financial development.

I am also much indebted to Mr. S. R. Noble, for more than two decades an Assistant General Manager of the Royal Bank of Canada and latterly Vice-President and General Manager of the Industrial Development Bank. Although the authorities of the day were hostile to such "radical" notions, Mr. Noble waged a sustained and, among his colleagues, almost single-handed battle for deliberate monetary expansion in the early depression years in Canada. In view of his intimate association with the banking problems and personalities of those days, his clarification and interpretation of the events of those difficult years have been invaluable. In addition, he has granted the writer access to personal files which shed much light on the earliest serious (but not generally known) efforts to establish a central bank in Canada at the end of World War I.

The completion of this work would not have been possible without the generous financial assistance provided by McMaster University, the Canadian Social Science Research Council and the Institute for Economic Research, conducted by Queen's University. Under the auspices of the last organization, summer research was made possible in Kingston on two different occasions. To all of the foregoing, to Miss Freda Harris of McMaster University, whose continuing secretarial services have been most helpful, and to Miss Winifred Eayrs of the Macmillan Company of Canada for her skilful editorial guidance, I gratefully acknowledge my indebtedness.

R. CRAIG MCIVOR

McMaster University,
Hamilton,
Spring, 1958.

# CONTENTS

# Contents

CHAPTER IV: THE CANADIAN MONETARY SYSTEM AND CHARTERED BANK EXPANSION BEFORE 1914      64

CHAPTER V: EARLY MONETARY AND BANKING DEVELOPMENTS IN WESTERN CANADA      86

Macdonald's Bank founded in 1859—first full-fledged bank in West—its brief but useful existence.

Entry into British Columbia of Bank of British North America; establishment by royal charter of Bank of British Columbia.

Founding (1879) and subsequent operations of Alloway and Champion, private bankers.

Later arrival of "eastern" chartered banks in Western Canada.

Contribution of private banks to early Western development—some other private banks.

## Contents

Two years of continuous monetary restraint in Canada—some basic problems encountered.

The problem of appropriate timing of central bank action.

Lag in the effectiveness of tighter money—chartered banks' securities liquidations.

Bank of Canada suggestions concerning use of chartered banks' savings deposits.

The Bank's use of "moral suasion"—limitations of non-statutory measures of control.

Non-bank sources of credit in Canadian economy as obstacles to effective monetary control.

Restrictions on Canadian monetary autonomy arising from close ties with the U.S. economy.

Problem of maintaining general acceptability and support for a credit squeeze.

Continuous restraint and its discrimination against small business.

General contribution of monetary control to curbing of inflation.

Necessity for the complementary use of monetary and fiscal techniques.

# TABLES

## CHAPTER I

# LESSONS FROM THE
# MONETARY DIFFICULTIES OF NEW FRANCE

THE fundamental features of modern commercial banking in Canada had already been established by the time of Confederation, despite the fact that some important differences were to be found among the banking systems which had evolved in the several provinces. It is scarcely necessary to emphasize that like all social institutions, banking is evolutionary, and does not appear full-blown upon the economic scene. Banks ". . . simply afford an easier, more effective and generally less costly manner of rendering services which are already performed in more or less primitive fashion."[1] It is therefore important, in tracing the early development of Canadian banking, to note not only the type of service which it was generally thought could be performed more adequately by the introduction of banking institutions, but also the environmental circumstances which gave rise to the features of banking peculiar to the several provinces. These regional differences persisted until 1867, when responsibility for the control and regulation of banking and currency in the new Dominion was assigned to the federal government.

It will subsequently be noted that a most important source of agitation for the establishment of banking institutions in British North America was the widespread dissatisfaction with the means of payment which existed at the time of the British conquest. The most frequently voiced complaints centred about the scarcity of currency, by which was almost always meant "hard" money, and the remedy was generally thought to lie in the direction of paper-money issues. These complaints were by no means new, having long been heard both in Canada before the conquest, and in the thirteen colonies to the south. It was true that in both of these areas the quantity of specie in circulation was seriously limited, for with neither gold nor silver mines, domestic supplies of hard money necessarily originated externally. A hard-money circulation was consequently something of a luxury, and it is not surprising that the solution to existing monetary difficulties should have been sought through the issue of paper currency. In actual fact, it was often the scarcity of some particular component of the circulating medium which represented the immediate source of exchange difficulties, and frequently it was the sudden withdrawal of specie or paper money which caused the disturbance.

Many of these complaints, however, appear to have been based on the wide-

[1]Adam Shortt, "The Early History of Canadian Banking", in the *Journal of the Canadian Bankers' Association*, IV, p. 129.

spread misconception that an abundance of paper currency constitutes a remedy for the relative scarcity of capital which is always characteristic of the pioneer economy. The fact was not generally recognized that improvement in the colony's economic condition rested not primarily upon an expansion of the quantity of money, but upon the expansion of its productive capacity and real output, and particularly upon the development of some extractive export staple. In the case of New France, the staple most readily saleable in European markets, and which therefore became the chief means of payment for European goods, was beaver fur.[2]

Because exchange difficulties in the primitive economy of New France gave rise to monetary developments, the effect of which continued to be felt for many decades, and from which some very useful lessons may still be learned, we shall begin with a brief review of this early period.

The monetary history of New France was influenced to some extent by the mercantilistic restrictions which were applied to the colony's economic development by the mother country. It was influenced to a much greater extent by the fundamental economic conditions which prevailed in the colony, and which no amount of legislation was capable of changing. The earliest attempts to develop the colony via royal paternalism, exclusive trading companies, import and export monopolies, etc., were not effective. Apart from the temporary nature of such royal concessions, which encouraged a policy of limited outlay and quick returns by those currently in favour, the fur trade soon became the backbone of the colony's economic development, and this circumstance was fatal for the establishment of any settled agricultural community.[3] The concessionaires who sought wealth from the fur trade were simply not interested in furthering settlement, for this would have destroyed, and ultimately did destroy, the basis of their trade. The entire history of the fur trade in North America has been well described as a "retreat in the face of settlement". Relatively unimportant and incidental to fishing until near the end of the sixteenth century, the fur trade after 1600 became ". . . the line of contact between a relatively complex civilization and a much more simple civilization".[4] The economic history of New France centred on this ever-changing relationship between the Indian and the European, with its disastrous consequences for the former.

One of the most persistent features of this historical development was the problem of securing a satisfactory medium of exchange. The circulation of specie was a luxury which could ill have been afforded and devices to prevent

[2]See H. A. Innis, *The Fur Trade in Canada* (New Haven: Yale University Press), 1930.
[3]A. R. M. Lower, *From Colony to Nation* (Toronto: Longmans, Green and Company), 1947, p. 19: "Fur was a kind of mine product like Spanish gold, and it had much the same effect on those who sought it as mining does: it induced a hectic, gambling spirit which had its colorful side and threw off infinite incidental activity with all sorts of political repercussions but it did not generate the plodding solidity of an agricultural society."
[4]H. A. Innis, *op. cit.*, p. 12. The heavy overhead costs incidental to the conduct of the fur trade were an important cause of its rapid growth.

its removal, such as its legal overvaluation in the colony, were invariably unsuccessful.[5] The establishment of a distinctive Canadian coinage was also suggested at various times, but was never carried out. Such a coinage would not have been acceptable to colonial merchants for the precise reason that it would have been incapable of circulating in France. But typical of such proposals were those made by Talon, the Intendant, in 1663 and 1671.[6] A brief experiment in 1721, limited to copper coins, was unsuccessful.

Lacking domestic supplies of the precious metals, the colony's sources of specie, apart from the small amounts brought out by the early traders and colonists, were to be found (1) in the proceeds of the export trade, which centred about one staple commodity, beaver fur, (2) in the money sent out by the French government to finance its colonial expenditures such as militia, civil government, etc., and (3) in funds transferred from France by religious orders for the establishment and support of missionaries in the colony, of whom the most important in early times were the Sulpicians and Jesuits. In connection with the specie proceeds from the sale of furs, an illicit traffic developed in the late seventeenth century between the traders of New France and those in the British colonies to the south. This resulted in a substantial inflow of foreign coins to New France, many of which were worn and light-weight. They were mostly Spanish, of which the silver dollar and its fractions were most common, but they included both Portuguese and English denominations. This circumstance did little to further the success of the government's numerous attempts, as in 1681, to establish by law the relative values of the various denominations of specie.[7] Because the colony was poor and its capital scarce, its demand for imports from the mother country was great, relative to its limited export capacity, and as a result, its commodity balance of trade was chronically unfavourable.

Because the maintenance of a domestic specie circulation was impracticable in this rudimentary economy of New France, barter exchange was widespread, and beaver, moose and other skins were widely used as media of exchange until the mid-seventeenth century. At one stage, wheat was made legal tender, at current market rates. In view of its fluctuating value, it was a poor standard. The Indians also used wampum as a means of payment. This took the form of small cylinders or tubes, about three-quarters of an inch long, made from sea-

[5]See Board of Historical Publications, Canadian Archives, *Documents Relating to Canadian Currency Exchange and Finance During the French Period* (Ottawa: King's Printer), 1925, I, 3-7, 37. The orders of 1654, 1661, 1662 and 1672 were typical examples of this economically unsound procedure. Coins imported from France had their values in the colony raised by one-third, relative to their values in France. The result was invariably a corresponding rise in colonial prices, which rendered such measures ineffective.

[6]See *ibid.*, pp. 9, 33.

[7]In view of the worn and light-weight condition of the specie which did circulate in the colony, the edict of 1681 provided that foreign coins should be exchanged by weight. See *ibid.*, p. 51. This was a most cumbersome and generally impracticable procedure. The edict also provided for the customary one-third increase in value of the French coins.

shells. The early value of the blue pieces was one sou or halfpenny, and of the white pieces, two sous or a penny. Because of the scarcity of specie, wampum remained legal tender until 1670, and continued to be used by the colonists until after 1700, and by the Indians themselves for another century. Its value was early reduced and eventually destroyed by cheap glass imitations from Europe.[8]

After the Company of One Hundred Associates gave up its trading monopoly in 1645, the need for a more definite standard of value became more urgent, and the importance of money in Canadian trade began to increase. The inefficiencies of a cumbersome system of barter gradually gave way to a greater freedom of exchange, as money prices were established for the most important commodities. It was at this time that bills of exchange were first employed to obviate the risk, cost and inconvenience of transferring specie between France and the colony, particularly in large transactions between parties of established credit. But for domestic trading purposes, coinage was still required.

A major development in the currency difficulties of New France was the introduction of "card" money in 1685. This experience is worthy of note not only because of the economic lessons involved, but because it influenced the attitude of the French Canadians toward all paper money for many years after the British conquest. The first appearance of card money in New France stemmed from the financial embarrassment of the local administration, and was intended to provide a source of temporary funds, rather than an addition to the means of payment of the colony. The depletion of the French treasury by costly European warfare had reduced the amount of financial aid which the mother country could provide for the support of her colony at a time when the outlay required for its military protection was becoming greater. Furthermore, the revenues accruing to the colonial administration from the fur trade were becoming increasingly uncertain because of interference from the English and the Indians and because of the illegal activities of the coureurs-des-bois. As a result of these circumstances, the Intendant, De Meulles, had encountered serious financial embarrassment by June, 1685. Funds and goods for the support of the colony during the current year had not arrived from France, and having tapped all private sources of funds for the maintenance of the troops, De Meulles resorted to an issue of paper money which, having been obtained by cutting playing-cards in pieces, became known as "card" money.[9] Backed by the sound credit of the

---

[8]See P. N. Breton, *Histoire des Monnaies et Jetons du Canada* (Montreal: P. N. Breton and Co.), 1894, p. 10.

[9]See R. M. Breckenridge, "The Paper Currencies of New France", in the *Journal of Political Economy* (Chicago: University of Chicago Press), 1893, I, pp. 410-18. Here the first issue of card money is characterized as "(a) an anticipation of remittances from France, (b) backed by the intendant's personal pledge of repayment, and (c) endowed with the quality of legal tender". A detailed account of the card money of New France may be found in Board of Historical Publications, *op. cit.*, pp. XXXIII-LXXXIX. See also Adam Shortt, "Canadian Currency and Exchange Under French Rule", *Journal of the Canadian Bankers' Association*, V, pp. 385-401, and VI, pp. 1-22, 147-65, 233-47.

local administration, this limited issue immediately became an addition to the circulating medium, and one which was accepted without question until the arrival of funds from France in the autumn, at which time the issue was redeemed. This experiment was repeated several times before 1690, with the issues in each instance being subsequently called for payment in specie. However, it was found that although the issue of 1690 was called during the following year, a considerable quantity remained in circulation. This of course provided a corresponding amount of specie for expenditures by the government, on whom the significance of the development was by no means lost. It was in this same year that "treasury notes" were first issued in Canada, as a temporary substitute for the other paper obligations (card money) of the colonial government.[10]

While officials in France understandably disapproved of the use of card money by the colonial authorities, since it represented a ready means for incurring a large colonial debt, it was nevertheless inevitable that its use would become increasingly widespread. Furthermore, the annual specie remittance from France frequently did not arrive before the departure of the last ship in the autumn for the mother country, with the result that the colonial merchants who held large quantities of temporarily irredeemable card money were unable to order their supplies for the following spring. This difficulty was in part overcome by permitting the holders to exchange this money for bills of exchange drawn on the French treasury. This procedure, which enabled the importers to avoid the cost and risk of remitting specie, was entirely sound, but the home treasury was most reluctant to sanction its general use.

Since card money could ". . . neither increase the supply of goods nor enable the merchants to purchase further goods from France, . . . prices rose steadily with the increasing issue of the card money, and ended in special prices where payment was made in this new currency".[11] It should be noted that two separate phenomena were involved here, the first being that of rising prices associated with the increasing quantity of money, the second that of the discrepancy between the value of specie and the value of paper money, stemming from the limited usefulness of the latter type.

Delays and losses in the annual transfer of specie to the colony led to substantial additions to the amount of card money outstanding between 1690-1700, but up to the latter date the depreciation of the card money had not been due to any failure of annual redemption. In subsequent years, as the French treasury became progressively unable to finance the needs of the colonial administration, deficits were met regularly by the additional issue of card money. Such funds as could be allocated to colonial needs began to be held in France, and were

---

[10]See Shortt, in *J.C.B.A.*, LI. Some of the holders of the card money issue of 1690 presented it for redemption before the annual supply of specie had arrived from France. The Intendant accepted this money and issued temporary notes in return, to be redeemed when the specie arrived.  [11]Shortt (ed)., *Canada and Its Provinces*, II (Sec. I, Pt. II), p. 497.

drawn upon by bills issued in Canada. But the deteriorating position of the French treasury brought increasing difficulty and delay in the honouring of such bills, and finally outright refusal, so that colonial merchants would no longer accept such a means of payment, preferring the colony's own card money. From 1708-13, appropriations to meet colonial expenses were discontinued entirely, by which time any specie which had previously remained in the colony had disappeared in payment for imports. It was, of course, impossible, in the absence of French financial support, to retire any of the previous issues of card money, and in fact, the Intendant had no choice but to issue new cards to the full amount of his financial needs. The total amount outstanding at the end of 1713 was approximately 1,600,000 livres, of which until 1711 the highest denomination had been four livres.[12] To meet the greater financial needs of the Intendant at the latter date, cards of 50 and 100 livres were issued.

The first episode in the history of card money in New France ended with a declaration in 1717 by the French government (the state of its treasury now having taken a turn for the better) which provided for the redemption of all outstanding issues at one-half of face values, a provision which seems to have corresponded very closely with the existing basis of their circulation. The redemption was effected by means of bills of exchange on the French treasury, which were liquidated in specie over a period of some two years. An edict which strictly forbade the issuing of card money for all time served to delay its reappearance for almost ten years, during which decade (1719-29) specie became the sole circulating medium of the colony.

The rapid depreciation in the value of the card money of New France following 1708 arose from the fact that promises to redeem the successive issues out of future funds had remained unfulfilled. This phenomenon well illustrates the necessity for maintaining the ready convertibility of non-standard paper money issues, if they are to circulate at their nominal value. Debtors were the one group in the colony who reaped a fortuitous gain from the continuous depreciation of card money, and we shall have occasion to note again the historical importance of such groups, whose support for and influence upon "cheap money" policies should not be underestimated.

One of the most unfortunate results of the currency experiences of New France may well have been the precedent established for later colonial experimentation. The disastrous currency inflation in many of the "American" colonies in the late seventeenth century and the eighteenth century illustrates this point. By a series of legislative enactments in 1741, 1751 and 1764, Britain succeeded

---

[12]In the French money-table of the seventeenth and eighteenth centuries, 12 deniers=1 sol (sou), 20 sols=1 livre, 3 livres=1 écu (crown). In 1670, the *livre tournois* (i.e., *monnaie de France*) was the unit of account, and contained 9.2 grams of silver, 11/12 fine. As already noted, various unsuccessful legislative attempts were made to retain specie in the colony by establishing artificially high values at which it should be accepted there (*monnaie de pays*), in terms of its value at home.

in curbing many of the excesses associated with colonial paper-money issues, but the last of these three measures unfortunately coincided with the advent of depression in the colonies, and the adverse economic effects of this monetary restriction were grossly exaggerated in the public mind, thereby fanning the political flames of revolt.

If it had been possible to maintain the convertibility of card money at all times, either in specie or in bills of exchange honoured by the French government, depreciation vis-à-vis these other forms of money would not have occurred. Failing this, the heavy dependence of the rudimentary colonial economy upon the exports of the mother country made it impossible to circulate domestic currency at its nominal value. While the fundamental colonial need was the expansion of its productive capacity, the economic and political philosophy which prevailed in the mother country was calculated to retard rather than facilitate this accomplishment.

In the interval between 1719 and 1729, when paper money was not in circulation, the impossibility of retaining specie in the colony was again demonstrated. To finance imports from France, specie was invariably returned there at the earliest possible time, and former complaints about the scarcity of a circulating medium were renewed. In addition, such time-honoured suggestions as the provision of a purely colonial coinage incapable of exportation, and the over-valuation of coins in Canada (this time by one-fourth), again appeared. An actual development, by no means historically unique, was the extensive appearance of notes issued by private individuals, to supplement the inadequate means of payment.[13] The extent of their circulation varied with the reputation of their source, but a growing belief that such issues should be controlled by the government rather than by private interests led to a petition to that effect, which was favourably received. While one may well be surprised at the view of the French government that "no remedial measure seemed more suitable than the establishment of a card currency", there is some evidence that the earlier unfortunate experiences were, for the moment, not entirely ignored.

In 1729, an issue of 400,000 livres of new card money was authorized, the issue to be legal tender, receivable for all goods sold by the government, and redeemable only by bills of exchange on the French treasury. This new card money differed radically from earlier issues. In particular, (1) it was used solely for currency, losing the quality of evidence of debt in anticipation of royal remittances; (2) it was re-issuable; (3) the issue was vested in the King rather than in colonial officials; (4) it was not convertible into specie.[14]

---

[13]See Board of Historical Publications, *op. cit.*, p. 581. Beauharnois, the governor of New France, wrote in 1728 that "the trafficking in personal notes is very dangerous and gives rise to frightful usury, the ill effects of which are only too visible". He urged the reintroduction of card money as a remedy for the scarcity of currency. The issue of small notes by local merchants had also occurred in 1683, just before the first issue of card money by the Intendant, De Meulles.   [14]See Breckenridge, *op. cit.*, pp. 418-23.

Two additional media of exchange appearing at this time were the "orders" on the Quebec treasury, issued by military commanders at frontier fortifications and outlying posts, in payment for various services and supplies purchased locally, and treasury receipts, issued by the administration at Quebec when there was a temporary deficiency of card money or bills of exchange with which to redeem "orders" when presented. First drawn for irregular amounts, the orders were later issued in standard denominations, while the treasury receipts, intended as evidence of temporary debt, were themselves circulated as notes. The established centres of commerce, e.g., Quebec, Montreal and Three Rivers, therefore had three types of paper money circulating at one time, all of equal validity.

The authorized amount of card money, although increased by successive stages between 1729 and 1749 to 1,000,000 livres,[15] performed its exchange functions most acceptably, and its depreciation in terms of specie was avoided by maintenance of its convertibility into bills on France. With confidence re-established, the colonists began to hoard it, rather than present it for redemption, with the result that the administration frequently complained of a shortage of card money for meeting its obligations, and urged the authorization of further issues for this reason. The home government, while reluctantly providing for the expansion already mentioned, frequently preferred to aid the local administration by shipping additional specie.

The monetary history of New France from 1749 to the time of its capitulation to the British in 1760 displays features which differ only in degree from those of earlier times. The necessity for the enormous issues of paper money in the closing years of the French régime lay in the fact that the colony was either engaged in war or preparing for war the whole time. In the Seven Years War, the French government viewed its North American struggle with the English as part of a much broader plan, and waged its campaign on a scale not only far beyond the resources of its colony, but far beyond its own willingness and ability to support. This period admirably illustrates the fact that in time of war, nations have invariably found it necessary to dilute their means of payment in the course of financing their war requirements.

While France met its heavy colonial expenditures with reasonable regularity as long as her military campaign fared well, the local administration found it necessary to expand its paper money issues very rapidly after 1755. Since the maximum issue of card money legally authorized had remained at 1,000,000 livres, Bigot, the able but corrupt Intendant, had several years earlier devised a new type of paper issue known as an "ordonnance", signed by himself and limited in amount only by the willingness of the community to absorb it.[16] This

---

[15]The ordinances of 1729, 1733 and 1742 had provided for the issue of 720,000 livres of card money. The ordinance of 1749 sanctioned a further issue of 280,000 livres, bringing the total to 1,000,000 livres. The 1749 issue ranged in denomination from 24 livres to 7s. 6d.　[16]See Breckenridge, *op. cit.*, p. 425.

paper was simply a transferable promise to pay, unauthorized by the French government, forced upon the public as legal tender, not payable in specie, and with redemption in card money problematical and finally impossible. With its increasingly prodigal issue, and its difficulties of convertibility into either card money or bills of exchange, it depreciated rapidly in terms of specie. A similar fate befell the existing card money, as bills of exchange on France became both scarce and subject to increasing delays in payment. Specie sent out with French troops soon disappeared into the private hoards of the peasants and tradesmen, where some earlier supplies had found their way. This specie reappeared a few years later under the British régime, when it became a common means of payment in Lower Canada.

It is estimated that by 1760, there were outstanding 34 million livres of ordonnances and 7 million livres of cards and local treasury bonds.[17] In addition to these 41 million livres of paper obligations in the colony, the debt of the French government included from forty to fifty million livres of bills of exchange still unpaid in France. This paper had continuously depreciated to the point where by 1760 it was regarded as practically worthless. This was the inevitable outcome of its uncontrolled issue and its inconvertibility, developments which could scarcely have been avoided in the light of the grossly inadequate financial support which the French treasury was able to provide for its colony during those critical closing years.[18]

The paper money orgy caused widespread suffering and loss to habitant and tradesmen alike, and particularly hard hit were those who in the earlier years had carefully hoarded the card money which had been re-established on a sound basis. In view of the official British declaration after 1760 that all French issues of any kind were considered worthless, any distinction between the older card money hoarded by the peasants and the later issues of ordonnances tended to disappear, the former descending to the level of the latter. However, in discussing the terms of peace, the possibility of the partial redemption of the outstanding mass of paper money became known in certain quarters. In particular, the British merchants in the colony began to accept it from the uninformed populace on a speculative basis and at a very heavy discount.[19] Large quantities were acquired in this manner, and after lengthy negotiations between the British and

---

[17]When the Quebec officials found themselves unable to redeem the ordonnances in card money in the autumn, they issued "bonds" to the holders, payable in cards after twelve months.

[18]See Board of Historical Publications, *op. cit.*, pp. 831 ff.

[19]For some time preceding the fall of French Canada, trade had been almost entirely in the hands of officials who managed it for their exclusive benefit. With no open markets for the country's produce, government officials purchased it with the depreciating and ultimately almost worthless paper money. Upon the British conquest, these officials returned to France, and the colony was left with no mercantile class. The British troops were followed by traders from the Atlantic colonies of New York and Massachusetts. The wholesale trade was thus developed by the English, while the retail and domestic trade remained predominantly French.

French governments, influenced by the intrigues of the various interested parties, the issues outstanding in Canada at the time of the capitulation were reduced to one-quarter of their face value and redeemed on that basis.[20] This was the concluding episode in the monetary history of New France, and one which provided little comfort for the inhabitants, who suffered serious loss in the outcome.[21]

Throughout the history of the colony, monetary developments were inseparably bound to the chronically unfavourable balance of trade with the mother country. An extremely rudimentary economic organization meant that exports were necessarily specialized, and this circumstance was not lessened by the mercantilistic atmosphere in which the development of the colony was undertaken. Even at the close of the French régime, exports consisted mainly of furs, while imports ranged over the diverse needs of the colonists, even to a partial supply of food.[22] The demand for goods from France being at all times relatively great, the fundamental difficulty of domestic exchange lay in the fact that specie could not be retained in circulation in the colony, for there was a continuous shortage of means of payment acceptable in France.

While it is true that the issuing of card money as a means of easing colonial financial difficulties was carried to great lengths in New France, neither the practice nor the conditions prompting it were peculiar to that part of French Canada. Prior to the capture of Port Royal by the British in 1710, the local commander, finding that his supply of ready money was inadequate, wrote to the home government that such a state of affairs ". . . obliges me to follow the example of Canada, in making use of card money, without which I would not have been in position to have the work carried on".[23] This issue of 1705 was strongly condemned by the King, as was a further issue of 1707, but since the aggregate amount of card money put into circulation did not exceed a few thousand livres, and since it had all been retired by 1708, the experiment was not of great significance. In this period, the Acadians had little external trade, and their monetary needs related to domestic dealings. Whatever small supplies of French silver and gold coins were brought to Nova Scotia by French officials soon disappeared into the hoards of the natives.

Having succeeded in withdrawing all card money from circulation, for the value of which he had given his personal notes in exchange, the local commander

---

[20]*Ibid.*, pp. 1005-13; see also pp. 973-7 for a short summary of "the origins of the paper money and its condition in 1762".

[21]Canadian Archives, *John Lee Collection, 1827-1865, Letter Regarding Canada Bills*: In this letter, the details of liquidation and the conditions and terms governing the redemption of the outstanding bills of exchange on France, and of the cards and ordinances are to be found.

[22]For a brief exposition of the obstacles to agricultural development in New France, see F. W. Burton, "The Wheat Supply of New France", in *Transactions of the Royal Society of Canada*, Section II, 1936.

[23]Board of Historical Publications, Canadian Archives, *Documents Relating to Currency, Exchange and Finance in Nova Scotia, 1675-1758*, pp. 13-14.

10

could then justly complain that ". . . as there is no coined money in this country, these individuals are continually bringing these notes back to me, to be broken up into numerous sums for the requirements of their business, and that is no small employment".[24] Following 1710, the British garrison at Annapolis Royal was supported largely through sterling bills which the governor discounted with Boston merchants, receiving payment in colonial currency. Because of frequent delay or non-payment of the governor's bills in London, public credit and the rates of exchange were often seriously depressed.[25] The colonial currency which was introduced to the area by the garrison at Annapolis reflected economic conditions in the pioneer colonies along the Atlantic seaboard. It contained a small proportion of French, Spanish and Portuguese coins obtained principally from the New England trade with the West Indies, but the bulk of the circulating medium was colonial paper money, in this particular instance being "Boston bills". In later years, the paper money issues of many of the thirteen colonies became excessive, resulting in its depreciation to the point of being worthless, an accomplishment which even Bigot could not have surpassed in the closing years of New France.

This situation led Britain to intensify some earlier attempts at legislative control of the situation by decreeing, in 1764, that all further issues of paper money in the colonies were to be banned. This measure was undoubtedly sound, but it aroused widespread antagonism in the colonies, since, as noted above, it came just at the advent of a depression. It is probable that more people considered themselves injured by this restriction than by any other economic restraint imposed by Britain in this period.

Elsewhere in Nova Scotia, the importation of specie from England was one method employed to finance the needs of the settlement at Halifax after its founding in 1749. The difficulties encountered in keeping a metallic currency in circulation are not surprising, in view of the colony's unfavourable balance of trade. For, just as in New France, any specie available for domestic exchange was represented largely by light-weight foreign coins, and the whole exchange problem was aggravated by the fluctuating rates between sterling and foreign coins, sterling and colonial paper, London bills and specie, London bills and colonial paper, and among the various colonial currencies themselves. As was to be the case at a much later time, ". . . the price of money was partly determined by reference to rates of freight and insurance on specie, which, to a degree, determined whether [external] payment by bills of exchange or by exporting specie would be the more economical".[26] In this early period, the colony suffered from both economic and political disorganization, and its future was very uncertain indeed.

[24]*Ibid.*, p. 15.
[25]Thus, for example, in 1726 ". . . exchange between Boston money and sterling was at 200% advance at Canso, and at 150% advance at Annapolis Royal." *Ibid.*, p. xxvii.
[26]See *ibid.*, p. XLIII.

## CHAPTER II

# EARLY CURRENCY AND EXCHANGE
# IN BRITISH NORTH AMERICA

BECAUSE of the flood of paper money in the closing years of the French régime in Canada, specie had gone into hiding and paper was the sole medium of exchange. That "hard" money hoards were substantial is indicated by a contemporary observer who wrote that ". . . the farmers in Canada cannot be possessed of less than one million pounds sterling in specie; they hoard up their money to portion their children; they neither let it out at interest nor expend it in the purchase of lands".[1] This characteristic of the French Canadian was undoubtedly an important factor contributing to the beginnings of banking in Canada.

The fallacious view that a scarcity of capital could be remedied by an abundance of currency seems to have been held by no less a personage than Governor Murray, who, believing that the Canadians suffered from a lack of cash and that the English merchants encountered consequent trading difficulties, wished that ". . . some means could be devised for obtaining a circulating medium to enable the Canadians to stock their lands, and the English merchants to dispose of their goods".[2] The governor was apparently not dissuaded from this view by the fact that paper money issues invariably got out of hand, a circumstance confirmed by the recent experience of New France and of the thirteen colonies, and one directly related to the financial emergencies with which colonial governments frequently found themselves confronted.

Under the British régime, specie gradually returned to circulation, and it represented an extremely heterogeneous means of payment, a fact which, as already noted, was largely attributable to the trade between Canada and the thirteen Atlantic colonies.[3] In 1763, the Spanish dollar had been the centre

---

[1]Adam Shortt, "The Early History of Canadian Banking", in *J.C.B.A.*, IV, p. 131.

[2]*Ibid.*, p. 133. The governor proposed a rather fanciful scheme for the issuing of paper notes, which fortunately came to naught.

[3]As in any rudimentary economy, the bulk of colonial revenues originated in customs levies. This is illustrated in the early years of the British régime by the revenues of Lower Canada in 1793: Duties, 14 Geo. III, £5692, Licenses do., £754, Casual and Territorial Revenue £389, Duties by Provincial Legislation £1613, Fines and Forfeitures £174, Miscellaneous £271. Gross revenues were therefore £8893, part obtained under provincial legislation, part being under the immediate control of the Crown. See Canadian Archives, Series E, State Book "B", Lower Canada, quoted in Innis and Lower, *op. cit.*, I, p. 379.

round which the monetary system of the New England colonies revolved. It was the famous "piece of eight" of pirate days. Following the conquest of French Canada, Spanish dollars invaded British North America, and the earliest banks (Bank of Montreal, Quebec Bank, Bank of Upper Canada) issued their first notes not in sterling denominations but in Spanish dollars. Although the Spanish dollar became the most common medium of exchange, almost anything that looked like money was used. Sterling was the legal standard of the colonies, but there were few British coins in circulation. The actual medium of exchange therefore bore little correspondence to the formal money of account. Because of the scarcity and the motley nature of the metallic currency, the British government, as had the French before the conquest, turned to the time-honoured but erroneous device of over-rating, in an effort to retain specie in the colony.

At the time of the conquest, the official rating for silver coins was still based upon the proclamation of Queen Anne of 1704. (Gold coins had received no special rating.) Under this proclamation, the Spanish dollar, with a sterling value of 4s. 6d., was officially rated in the colony at 6s. But in Massachusetts and Nova Scotia, the dollar was accepted at 5s., in New York at 8s. Both of these ratings became established in British North America. East of Quebec, and introduced by Massachusetts merchants arriving in Nova Scotia, there prevailed the 5s. rating known as "Halifax" currency. In Quebec and to the west, and introduced by New York merchants arriving in Montreal, the 8s. rating known as York currency became standard. Varying ratings were to be found throughout the country for the variety of the other silver and gold coins which commonly circulated.

Newly prescribed ratings of 1764 and of 1777 provided a basis for the legal settlement of disputed claims, but accomplished little else.[4] They illustrate a human trait which may so often be discerned in the study of economic history, the placing of unwarranted confidence in mere legislation where such legislation runs contrary to the economic interests of the individuals involved.[5] The ratings established by the ordinance of 1777 are summarized below, to indicate the major

---

[4]The ordinance of 1764 rated the Spanish dollar at 6s., but that of 1777, reflecting the influence of the Quebec merchants, altered the rating to 5s. "Halifax" currency thereby became the official standard in British North America. In a minor revision in 1795, the American dollar was rated for the first time, and as the equivalent of the Spanish dollar. See Shortt, "The History of Canadian Metallic Currency", in *Transactions of the Canadian Institute* (Toronto: University of Toronto Press), 1912.

[5]Numerous illustrations are provided by Canadian banking, currency, labour and combines legislation, as well as by international commercial policy (to name but a few), which suggest that like our American neighbours we "seem to have had a sublime faith in the efficacy of a mere law—equalled only by [our] readiness to break the law the moment it interfered with [our] particular interest". Chester W. Wright, *The Economic History of the United States* (New York: McGraw-Hill Book Company Inc.), 1941, p. 1080.

components of the contemporary circulating medium.[6] With the subsequent establishment of the new decimal currency system in the United States, its earlier polyglot specie was displaced, and many of these light-weight and defaced pieces turned up in Canada, thereby furthering the nondescript character of the circulation.

By the end of the American Revolution, during which period Canada for the first time received substantial quantities of British specie, the metallic currency of the colony had come to embody three major elements, these being the French coins remaining in the colony at the time of the British conquest, the Portuguese and Spanish coins received in trade with the seaboard colonies and the British coins which had come directly from England during the revolution. In the years between the military occupation of New France and the end of the American Revolution, the means of payment in Canada had been substantially expanded, but pleas for more hard money subsided only temporarily. During this early period, the British government paid relatively little attention to the currency difficulties of her newly acquired colonies, except for an occasional legislative pronouncement which was usually inapplicable to colonial conditions. Here the periodic "official" ratings of the coinage supply a good example, the usual effect being to cause the disappearance of particular components from circulation, because of underrating.

Before the establishment of Canadian banks, it was the large importing and exporting mercantile houses, especially in Montreal, which carried on the bulk of domestic and foreign exchange transactions, the collection of debts and the receiving and holding of deposits of money and credits. Three such houses were McTavish, Frobisher and Co., Todd, McGill and Co. and Forsyth, Richardson and Co., the last of which held the funds of the province of Upper Canada in 1800. All three were active in the fur trade of the Northwest. Because of the unsatisfactory means of payment, many of these merchants began to issue their

| [6]COINS | WEIGHT | | RATE | | |
|---|---|---|---|---|---|
| *Gold*: | dwt. | grs. | £ | s. | d. |
| The Johannes of Portugal | 18 | 6 | 4 | 0 | 0 |
| The Moidore | 6 | 28 | 1 | 10 | 0 |
| The Doubloon, or four Pistole piece | 17 | 0 | 3 | 12 | 0 |
| The Guinea | 5 | 8 | 1 | 3 | 4 |
| The Louis D'Or | 5 | 3 | 1 | 2 | 6 |
| Paying two pence one farthing for every grain of gold underweight. | | | | | |
| *Silver*: | | | | | |
| The Spanish Dollar | | | | 5 | 0 |
| The British Crown | | | | 5 | 6 |
| The French Crown, or piece of six livres tournois | | | | 5 | 6 |
| The French piece of four livres ten sols tournois | | | | 4 | 2 |
| The British shilling | | | | 1 | 1 |
| The French piece of twenty-four sols tournois | | | | 1 | 1 |
| The Pistareen | | | | 1 | 0 |
| The French piece of thirty-six sols tournois | | | | 1 | 8 |

own paper notes or "bons" to their customers, and their use became widespread. They were redeemable in goods at the store of issue, but soon passed from hand to hand. The name arose from the fact that the inscription on such notes invariably began with "Bon pour —", the amount of the note then being specified. Despite their extensive use, the prejudice of the French Canadians against any form of paper currency was still very strong, and while there were substantial accumulated savings in the province, their owners would not trust them out of their sight. The "bons" were technically illegal, but the local administration recognized them as a valuable expedient and ignored their existence.[7] However, these promises-to-pay circulated mainly on a local basis, and a uniform paper currency was still lacking. Nevertheless, the merchants continued to expand their various financial services right up to the War of 1812.

The deplorable condition of the available means of payment was emphasized by a contemporary observer who noted that "The present state of the Paper Currency of this Province is a novelty in the History of Banking and may well warrant the fears and apprehensions of persons, in the smallest degree attentive to their property.

". . . During the War with America, the Expenses of Government . . . made money more necessary, and the principal trading house at each Post, having just given ample Security for the Payment of their Bills in Montreal, furnished the necessary supply. Other Houses afterwards took a share in this, till within two years . . . everybody has become Banker. From the King's Receiver-General to the Sergeant Major of the Rangers, from the first Commercial houses to the person who retails drams, Everybody makes Money. As to security that is not now thought of. In a payment the other day of twenty five pounds I received the Bills of twelve different persons; To realize this by a draft on Montreal would require an application to as many different people, some at Detroit, some of York, some the Lord knows where."[8]

The earliest announcement of serious intention to found a commercial bank in Canada was made in 1792 by the English financial house of Phyn, Ellice and Inglis, which had been appointed agents for the United Empire Loyalists. The firm combined with Forsyth, Richardson and Co., and Todd, McGill and Co., to issue a prospectus for the "Canadian Banking Company", to be established at Montreal.

The alleged deficiencies of the existing exchange facilities were set forth, and it was stated that these merchants had experienced ". . . great inconvenience

---

[7]The ingenious attempt of a Montreal auctioneer to set himself up as a bank of issue, specializing in promissory notes for small sums, was thwarted by the authorities, this expedient apparently being regarded as beyond the bounds of toleration. This may, however, have been the first attempt to obtain a bank charter in Canada.

[8]*Simcoe Papers*, 1792, I, Book 2, pp. 323-4. See also H. A. Innis and A. R. M. Lower, *Select Documents in Canadian Economic History, 1783-1885* (Toronto: University of Toronto Press), 1933, pp. 368-9.

in Canada from the deficiency of specie, or some other medium to represent the increasing circulation of the country, as well as from the variety of money now current, and knowing the frequent loss and general difficulty and trouble attending receipts and payments, have formed the resolution of establishing a bank at Montreal".[9] The services which the bank proposed to provide at various centres in both Lower and Upper Canada included the receipt of cash deposits, the issuing of notes in exchange for such deposits, the discounting of bills of exchange and promissory notes and the keeping of cash accounts for those parties who might desire to use the bank's facilities in their receipts and disbursements.

It should be noted that all of the major functions of modern commercial banking are included here, and that the appearance of the scheme at this particular time was undoubtedly influenced by the successful operation of the First Bank of the United States, which had been founded one year earlier. A Canada Banking Company appears at least to have begun operations by issuing some notes, but there is little record of its having engaged in any other activity during its brief existence. The economic effects of the outbreak of war in Europe may have been unfavourable to its development, and most of its proposed services were already performed by the large merchants to whom banking functions reverted, following the termination of this experiment.

One frequently-voiced objection to the establishment of banks was that any issue of notes would cause specie to disappear, but such was inevitable in any case, because of the colony's adverse balance of trade. The establishing of a bank would certainly not have prevented such a drain, but it might have lessened its adverse effects upon domestic trade, through the provision of a uniform and generally accepted means of payment. In the English settlements of Upper Canada, the need for currency was almost entirely for local transactions, and economic development was not sufficiently advanced to make practicable either the discounting of bills or the introduction of a currency system based on Montreal. As already suggested, the fundamental need in Upper Canada was not so much for currency as for real capital.

In view of the rudimentary transport facilities of the time, local markets were of vital importance. The individual settler traded with the nearest merchant, and barter was very common.[10] A most important influence in these markets, apart from the needs of the settlers themselves, was the requirements of the government for servicing its military garrisons, naval forces, civil establishments and Indian posts. The economic advantage accruing from such government patronage was not as widespread as might be assumed, for ". . . in the absence of

---

[9] Canadian Archives, *Robinson Collection, Vol. 2, Doc. 52.* See also the *Larocque Papers, March 31, 1797.*

[10] In Upper Canada, agricultural activity centred round the production of wheat, flour, and peas, in addition to which lumbering and the manufacturing of potash was carried on. With the influx of settlers after the American Revolution, agriculture expanded rapidly, and by 1800 wheat was being exported to Europe.

a standard and generally available currency, there were virtually no free markets, hence government purchases benefited directly very few settlers."[11]

The lack of a medium of exchange adequate for putting settlers on a "cash" basis meant that most of the benefits from government orders accrued to the merchants. In return for grain or other articles bought from the settler, the merchant would provide him with imported articles, any balance being paid in "bons" redeemable only in October of each year, except at a 12½% discount. The government, however, paid the merchants for flour, peas, etc., in bills of exchange on Quebec or on the British Treasury. These, of course, would not have been a useful form of currency for the settlers.

An attempt to remedy this situation was made by John McGill, Governor Simcoe's chief Commissary officer, who in 1794 was appointed to the new office of Agent of Purchases. In his latter capacity, McGill began to buy his supplies on an "open market" basis from the settlers, rather than by contract with the merchants, and payment was made in transferable certificates, which, while not legal tender, did facilitate local exchange through their circulation in the purchase of other supplies and in the payment of various obligations. The certificates were redeemable at the Upper Canada seat of government, in bills of exchange drawn upon the British Treasury. This experiment was undoubtedly sound, and these promises ". . . constituted the first thoroughly reliable currency in Upper Canada. In their nature and function they quite closely anticipated the Army Bills of 1812 and subsequent years."[12] The difficulty was that, being based on actual purchases of government supplies, the volume of these certificates was inadequate to meet the needs of the expanding colonial economy. Thus the less reliable but more abundant "bons" of the merchants continued to provide the bulk of the circulating medium. Widespread barter continued to prevail, particularly in large transactions, and whiskey was apparently a common medium, for despite the shortage of currency, this pioneer country was by no means devoid of all liquid assets. Much of the specie remitted by Britain for the support of its colonial administration disappeared because of an adverse balance of trade, part to Lower Canada and part to New York.

Although the rapid expansion of trade with the United States after Jay's Treaty of 1794 caused a net outflow of specie, the relatively large purchases by the British government for the support of its colonial administration were not off-set by colonial imports from Britain. Between 1796-1800, there was a surplus of sterling bills, and since these were usually at a premium in New York and Boston, a flourishing foreign-exchange market developed, with centres in Montreal and New York, in which American currency was used to acquire sterling bills in Canada. This movement lessened the net loss of specie from Lower Canada. The exchanges were nevertheless subject to great fluctuation, and by

[11]Shortt, "Founders of Canadian Banking", in *J.C.B.A.*, XXIX, p.278.
[12]*Ibid.*, p. 286.

1803, sterling was again at a premium. J. Hale, British Pay Officer at Quebec, wrote to the home government that he had readily disposed of £50,000 in bills at 102. He ventured the further opinion that this price was attributable to "the high price of bullion in England". The high price of bullion in England was at this time giving rise to the well known "Bullionist" controversy. An explanation as plausible as that of Mr. Hale is that the colony's trade balance may have reverted to its customary unfavourable state.

In 1808, a second attempt to establish a commercial bank in Canada took the form of a petition presented to the legislature of Lower Canada by a group of merchants from Montreal and Quebec, who sought to set up a "Bank of Canada" in those centres. The movement was stimulated by the continued progress of the colony's domestic and foreign trade, by the excellent example provided by the operations of the First Bank of the United States and by the growing need for some more satisfactory means of exchange than the miscellaneous collection of "bons" and promissory notes generally in use. The supporters of the petition observed that " . . . specie is very sensibly decreasing in this province, and some safe substitute would be greatly desirable and tend to facilitate the trade of the province, particularly the export trade".[13] It was hoped that the proposed bank could meet the needs of Upper Canada by the establishment of branches in that province.

One result of the ensuing discussion of the proposal was a generally constructive exposition of the essentials of banking, and of the benefits which might be expected to accrue to Canadian trade and therefore to the general economic development of the country. Attempts were made to answer the chief popular objections to a bank, such as the continuing opposition to paper money, the belief that the availability of bank credit would lead to speculation and gambling, and the further belief that bank notes would cause specie to disappear (it was already disappearing because of the adverse trade balance). This public discussion of banking matters at least did much to prepare the way for the establishment of banks at a later date. But the petition encountered much opposition from the French Canadians, and it was not approved.

As might be expected, by no means all of the monetary and banking "theory" advanced in the contemporary discussion was free from error. In a speech before the House of Assembly, April 12, 1808, one member, a supporter of Adam Smith's views on money, quoted him as follows: "The quantity of paper or Bank notes which can circulate in any country must depend upon the quantity of exchangeable commodities therein, and will regulate itself by finding its own level. Circulation is like a sponge, which can imbibe only a certain quantity of water, and when full, any excess must immediately return to the reservoir from which it was drawn. So it is with paper. The moment the circulation is full,

[13]See the *Journal of the House of Assembly of Lower Canada*, January 29-April 14, 1808, Minutes of February 22.

the excess will return upon the Bank, and be exchanged for Specie."[14] This view surely imputes to the monetary unit an absolute value which is completely erroneous. It is apparently based on a "commodity" theory of the value of money, denying any effect of a changing quantity of money upon its value.

Despite this unfavourable outcome in Lower Canada, a group of Kingston merchants soon proposed the establishment of a similar bank in their community, but their efforts were no more successful. In the economically more advanced areas of Upper Canada, the need for a uniform currency was undoubtedly as great as in the trading centres of Lower Canada,[15] but the failure of the First Bank of the United States to obtain a renewal of its charter, and the increasingly strained relations between Canada and the United States, undoubtedly contributed much to the failure of the proposal.

It was from a somewhat unexpected direction that the first effective demonstration of the value of a well-managed paper money issue was provided. Writing to General Brock early in 1812, the Receiver-General at York had discussed the advisability of issuing some substitute for specie, in view of its scarcity and of the considerable increase in public expenditures if war were to break out.[16] Reference was made to the earlier period when merchants' "bons" provided almost the entire circulating medium, with the suggestion that another paper issue under government pledge would be generally acceptable and would avoid the high rate of exchange between Quebec and London. Brock agreed that in the event of war a paper currency should be issued, redeemable in bills on Quebec. Within a few weeks, war was declared, and an issue of Army Bills to the amount of £250,000 currency was authorized. For a period of five years they were to bear interest at 6%, payable half-yearly. They were payable, on demand, in government bills on England, at a rate to be set every two weeks, or payable in cash after five years. They were made full legal tender, and receivable in payment of all public debt. It was further ". . . made felony without benefit of clergy to forge them".[17] The issue of Army Bills was based on the Spanish dollar as the standard of value and this original issue of £250,000 (Halifax currency) was therefore the equivalent of $1 million (at 5s. = $1). The bills were actually issued on a dollar basis, the denominations including $25, $50, $100 and $400.[18]

---

[14]*Ibid.*

[15]The fur trade, about which the economic development of New France had centred, was carried on under British auspices after 1763. But the North West Company, based at Montreal, was finally forced to amalgamate with the Hudson's Bay Company in 1821, and the fur trade was then lost to the St. Lawrence basin, following the Hudson Bay route. Other forms of economic activity were supplanting the fur trade, and the timber industry expanded rapidly in the St. Lawrence area in the early years of the nineteenth century.

[16]See Canadian Archives, *C329, 1812-13, Letter from Receiver-General Selby to Brock, Dated York, April 20, 1812.*

[17]For an explanation of the origin and meaning of the phrase "without benefit of clergy", see M. Phillips, "Banking in Olden Days", in *J.C.B.A.*, XXIX, pp. 467-8.

[18]See Canadian Archives, *Upper Canada Sundries, 1812: Letter dated Quebec July 28, 1812 from Prevost (Commander of the Forces) to Brock (in Upper Canada).*

Early in 1813, the maximum issue authorized at any given time was increased to £500,000 currency, but even this limit appears to have brought objections, on the ground that wealthy individuals were locking up the bills, for the sake of interest.[19] But while the bills were entirely acceptable, and even eagerly sought, they were not able to perform their main purpose as a medium of domestic exchange because of the lack of small denominations. The Commander of the Forces was, therefore, empowered to issue up to £50,000 of the prescribed maximum in bills ranging from $1 to $20. These bore no interest, since they were payable in specie on demand. As the war progressed, it was found expedient to increase further the legally authorized maximum issue of bills to £1,500,000, although it did not prove necessary to take full advantage of this limit.[20] At the end of the war, the value of Army Bills outstanding approximated $5 million. At various times, this currency commanded a premium in specie, a remarkable accomplishment in terms of the fate of earlier paper issues.[21] At the end of 1815, the entire issue was called for redemption in cash, with no interest being paid from the end of 1815. A final proclamation had to be issued in 1818, indicating that no further redemptions would be effected after October of that year. Despite this fact, almost $36,000 in bills were still outstanding two years later.

Where the card money of New France had failed, and the issues of the Atlantic colonies had failed, the Canadian Army Bills succeeded. They were well managed, they provided the colonial administration with invaluable financial assistance in a time of emergency and they did much to restore the confidence of the population in paper money.[22] In the latter connection, they undoubtedly paved the way for the note issues of the early banks which soon were to make their appearance. It is probable, however, that the economic effects of the Army Bills were overemphasized at the time. During the war, the colony

---

[19]Canadian Archives, *Upper Canada Sundries,* March 1813: "If this disposition to hoarding should continue, which it is very likely to do, and Bills get locked up to the amount of half a Million, what is to be done?"

[20]For further details of the issue of Army Bills, see Canadian Archives, *Lower Canada Sundries,* March 29, 1813, January 24, 1814 and May 1, 1814.

[21]*Quebec Mercury,* Vol. II., November 28, 1815: Here it is noted that Army Bills for some time past, have " . . . even exceeded in value the precious metals, from 2½ to 5%, by their ability to procure Government bills of Exchange at a discount so much greater than gold and silver could affect it—What is still more striking, is that Canadian paper bore this high value at the period when the paper of the U. States was in such a state of depreciation as to create the utmost confusion in the States. Our paper aided the government, because it operated as a loan at a moment when the expenditure was of a magnitude not to be paralleled in the history of nations."

[22]See the *Quebec Gazette,* May 30, 1815: "The introduction of this paper currency—was certainly a reasonable and judicious experiment, and its unprecedented success has not only been a great pecuniary saving to Great Britain, but it has also contributed, in no small degree, to the preservation of these Provinces. The credit of this paper ought therefore to be considered as an object of the first importance and carefully supported to the last, being a most valuable resource, to be again resorted to by the Government, on future occasions, in case of need."

was prosperous, since its products could be sold at favourable prices and since cheap bills of exchange were available as a means of paying for imports.

The War of 1812 produced a surprising amount of international economic co-operation, on a strictly informal basis. Provisions were becoming very expensive for the British troops in Upper Canada in the last years of the war. These were plentiful, at high prices, in nearby United States territory, and British gold and bills of exchange were easily negotiated in that country, and in fact were in great demand. Thus, although all trade between American and Canadian citizens was strictly forbidden, " . . . it was eminently a time for not permitting the official right hand to know what the official left hand was doing. Those who knew the ropes on each side of the line kept the British Commissariat free from undue anxiety and the eastern New York and northern New England Farmers prosperous".[23]

It is not surprising that the issue of Army Bills should have been regarded as the major cause of the current prosperity, when it was in fact merely one contributing factor. Some years later, the withdrawal of the Army Bills coincided with an economic recession which enveloped the provinces following the immediate post-war boom, and there was a widespread feeling that the withdrawal of the paper bills was the basic cause of the slump, whereas external influences were again undoubtedly of major importance. One consequence of the post-war situation was that proposals for the establishment of banks received strong support in both provinces.

The appearance of this uniform paper currency had nevertheless represented an important phase in the development of Canada's means of payment, because it did demonstrate to the people the possible contributions of a well regulated paper issue. As might have been expected, the bills were viewed for a time with much suspicion by the French Canadians in Lower Canada, and a temporary hoarding of specie occurred there. The English settlements in both provinces accepted the bills from the beginning. A considerable quantity of the bills were sold in the United States when, during the period of the embargo in that country, it became necessary for American citizens to meet their foreign obligations either by shipping specie or by purchasing such European bills as might be available. The latter being safer, their purchase in Canada gave rise to a considerable inflow of specie, and specie and Army Bills circulated side by side. This could not have occurred if the paper money had originated with the colonial governments, for it would not then have been readily acceptable in foreign payments. In this particular respect, the Canadian experience with Army Bills does not provide a good example of the probable behaviour of a domestically issued currency.[24]

[23]For some interesting details of this period, see Shortt, "Founders of Canadian Banking", in *J.C.B.A.* XXX, pp. 34-7.
[24]See Shortt, "The Early History of Canadian Banking", in *J.C.B.A.*, IV, pp. 343-6.

In the period preceding the establishment of commercial banks, local attempts to expand the nondescript "hard money" supply were by no means lacking. In the Canadas, a copper coin had appeared as early as 1808, crudely made by someone in Montreal.[25] It is also recorded that in 1816, a New York merchant openly imported twelve kegs of copper money, without any apparent intention to smuggle, despite the official prohibition against such action in Lower Canada.[26] The issue of private tokens by merchants became a common practice, but the first satisfactory uniform copper coinage was later to be issued by the chartered banks. One private token issued in Upper Canada in 1821 by a wholesaler suggests that the whiskey trade was one of the first to be established in that province. It was the commodity which eventually drove rum, so popular in the Canadas, out of use.

In the Maritimes, the basic problem of retaining a metallic circulating medium was identical with that of the Canadas, and the exchange vicissitudes in Nova Scotia illustrate the trials of almost any pioneer area. Until the American Revolution, the economy of the Maritimes centred round fishing and lumbering for sale in local markets, and round subsistence agriculture. The efforts of the British government after 1783 to develop an Atlantic trade for the Maritimes, particularly with the British West Indies, were largely unsuccessful until after the United States imposed its shipping Embargo in 1807. This measure gave the Maritimes, for the first time, substantial freedom from New England competition in British West Indies markets.

The scarcity of currency of any kind had led to representations in Halifax, as early as 1766, for the establishment of a paper currency in Nova Scotia, and despite the notable lack of success with such issues elsewhere, the Provincial Treasurer had been authorized to issue treasury notes in limited amounts, in anticipation of customs revenues. These were redeemed at regular intervals, and they also enjoyed considerable use as hand-to-hand currency.

By 1787 the country had become flooded with assorted copper coins by enterprising individuals, and an Act of 1787 forbade the use " . . . of any spurious

---

[25]Paul Montgomery, *The Romance of Canada's Money* (Toronto: Macmillan Company of Canada Limited), 1933, p.14: "They had been struck by a hammer from the poorest of dies, and bore a grotesque likeness of the Governor together with the words 'Torment of the Canadians' on the face, and some caustic political advice on the reverse."

[26]Canadian Archives, *Journal of Assembly, Lower Canada*, January 24, 1817. It was apparently a very common practice for individuals to put into circulation a great deal of false or counterfeit copper money. Unless such an evil could be remedied, there was immediate loss to the poorer classes, who often possessed only this kind of money. It was also regarded as contributing to the driving of gold and silver from the province.

The pervasiveness and difficulty of the coinage problem is further illustrated in the *Quebec Mercury*, Vol. XIII, No. 8, February 25, 1817: "Another problem arises from those plain pieces of silver called English Shillings, but which are no more English Shillings than those (copper) tokens are English halfpence; these, by a preposterous condescension to the practice, not the law of the Mother country, have been admitted into circulation at thirteen pence each, altho' their intrinsic value in silver be not more perhaps than sixpence or eightpence."

half-pence or other copper coin not legally current in Great Britain". But like the coins themselves this proclamation carried little weight, for the need of small change was great. Starting about 1814, some of the leading Halifax merchants imported private coins and stamped their names on the pieces, which were then put into circulation. While such coins were not generally as popular as the private tokens in Upper Canada, these penny and half-penny pieces were current in Nova Scotia for many years, until the Canadian cent pushed them off to Prince Edward Island. To overcome the failure of the Act of 1787, it was provided in 1817 that " . . . whereas many ignorant and evil disposed persons continue to import and procure large quantities of base copper coins . . . be it enacted that immediate measures be taken to obtain a quantity of good and proper half-pence". Nova Scotia thus became the first colony to issue a regular coinage, and between 1823 and 1864, some five to six tons of penny and half-penny, cent and half-cent pieces were put into circulation.

Until 1811, each Halifax merchant had placed his own valuation on the various coins then current, but at that time, an agreement was reached as to the rates at which guineas, doubloons, crowns and dollars were to be exchanged.[27] Numerous attempts to establish legal ratings for the coins invariably failed, just as in the Canadas.

With the outbreak of war in 1812, Nova Scotia began a new era in the development of her currency system. The provincial treasury was empty, but the government was free from debt. There were three possible means of financing the wartime increase in expenditures, i.e., taxes, loans or the issue of paper money based on the provincial credit. The third method was decided upon, and the first treasury notes were issued in 1812. These, and later wartime issues, bearing 6% interest, and being easily redeemable in specie, circulated successfully, and became an acceptable addition to the current means of payment. One could scarcely improve upon a contemporary description of the Nova Scotia currency: "Our currency is now like a Scotch haggis, made up of contradictions, of things good and bad, oatmeal, onions, hog's lard, butter, crumbs of bread, salt, pepper, garlic, leeks, parsley, etc. The Haggis will burst, and scald many who are little expecting it."[28]

[27]The problems involved in currency exchange were described as follows: "Every merchant had a bank in his own office in the form of an iron chest, bound and studded with bars and rivets (some of which have not yet given place to Edward's or Milner's safes) in which the doubloons and dollars from the West Indies or Spanish Main were deposited. Scales and weights were necessary adjuncts to every office to weigh the several classes of coins, so that any sweating or filing might be guarded against, and to determine whether the money was of the standard weight. When an Irishtown merchant had to pay for a cargo of fish to an uptown dealer, his trusty clerk, bearing a heavy bag of doubloons or dollars, accompanied by a friend with a stout cudgel, trudged the crooked sidepaths of the not over safe Water Street, and duly counted and weighed the coin, which was then consigned to the custody of the iron chest." See G. A. White, *Halifax and Its Business* (Halifax: Nova Scotia Printing Co.), 1876, pp. 48-9.   [28]Quoted in Innis and Lower, *op. cit.*, I, p. 433.

The early success with treasury notes led to further issues in the post-war years, to offset the continuing scarcity of specie, and to assist in the financing of government works. As their volume increased, ways were devised to make the notes less easily redeemable. In 1828, an Act provided for the cancellation of all outstanding notes, and for the printing of £40,000 of irredeemable notes. This authorization was doubled in 1832, and a period of great financial confusion, disorder and currency depreciation ensued.[29] Order was restored in 1836, by which time the provincial debt had risen, since 1812, to £122,000. This whole experience was in marked contrast to the management of the Army Bills issues in the Canadas, but despite their shortcomings, these provincial treasury note issues should not be regarded as a complete disaster. A contemporary writer noted that: "This paper money was practically irredeemable, but though issued and kept in circulation in defiance of sound principles of finance as now understood, it rendered an important service to the city and country at various periods in their history. It helped to construct railways and public buildings, to make roads and bridge Rivers, to assist the farmers and fishermen in seasons of depression and failures of land and sea harvests, and though kicked about from Bank to Bank, though sworn at by Bank Tellers, and anathematized by those who vainly endeavoured to obtain specie for it, worn and torn to rags and at last quietly burked by the Dominion Government, yet on the principle that the end justifies the means, the old Province paper served its day and generation faithfully."[30]

[29]For a detailed exposition of this currency episode, of this ". . . slow approach to the inviting sea of inflation over a shore covered with the slippery stones of an uncertain currency", see the Bulletin of the Public Archives of Nova Scotia, *A Documentary Study of Provincial Finance and Currency, 1812-36*, Vol. II, No. 4, 1941.
[30]*Ibid.*, p. 49.

## CHAPTER III

# THE FORMATIVE PERIOD
# IN CANADIAN COMMERCIAL BANKING

### A. *The Canadas*

THE withdrawal of Army Bills from circulation in the Canadas provided both an opportunity and a need for the establishment of banking institutions. The experiment had provided a most useful addition to the inadequate means of domestic exchange, and had removed a great deal of the deep-seated prejudice against paper money issues. Its withdrawal, unfortunately timed, led to widespread demands for some form of replacement, to further the development of trade and agriculture in the provinces. The chief exports of the colony at this time were timber and furs, with ginseng, potash and grain of lesser importance. Imports were mainly dry goods, hardware, spirits, sugar and other commodities not manufactured domestically. In the absence of banks, the advancing of credit necessarily remained the prerogative of the merchants. Importing firms at Montreal extended credits to traders in both Lower and Upper Canada. These wholesalers did likewise for the local merchants, and they for their customers. The legal money of account was Halifax currency, but, as already indicated, there was no corresponding coinage. Much of the retail trade was still effected by the cumbersome process of barter, and it was mainly in terms of providing a uniform note issue that the contribution of banking institutions was first conceived.[1]

In 1817, nine Montreal merchants signed Articles of Association to conduct, without statutory authority, a banking business to be known as the Bank of Montreal, and this marked the beginning of the present Canadian chartered banking system. The widespread discussion of banking which had been carried on for a considerable period before this bank actually began operations has been explained in terms of (a) the successful operation of the First Bank of the United States (1791); (b) the shortage of currency; (c) the variety of the cur-

---

[1]See Canadian Archives, Board of Historical Publications, *Letter from Francis Gore, Lt. Governor of Upper Canada, York, May 8, 1817* (to the British government): " . . . the great scarcity of Specie having occasioned an Inundation of paper from the United States, to supply the place of Army Bills, . . . it appears to me to be reasonable, to give the preference [in establishing a bank] to such of His Majesty's Provinces as may wish to lend their Aid to remove the evil. I do not doubt but some such Establishment, either common to both provinces, or the issue of Army Bills sanctioned by His Majesty's Government, would conduce much to the Interest of Agriculture, and Commerce in this Province."

The United States paper referred to in the quotation comprised inconvertible bank notes which had depreciated greatly in terms of specie. It circulated at a discount of some 16% in New York, and its average depreciation in all states south of New York was 20%.

rency, both as to origin and condition; (d) the nuisance created by promissory notes and merchants' "bons" issued without authority; (e) the shortage of capital in the colony.[2] The publication of the bank's Articles of Association in May of that year was enthusiastically received in most quarters.[3] The bank opened its subscription books in June, elected its first directors in August and began its operations early in November. The support of a large number of American shareholders facilitated the raising of the necessary capital, and also proved of invaluable assistance in the bank's subsequent lucrative foreign exchange dealings, conducted through the United States. Although unsuccessful in its original application to the Legislature of Lower Canada for a charter, the bank persisted in its efforts, and its petition was approved in 1818. Royal assent was delayed for some time, but the charter was finally obtained in 1822.

The Bank of Montreal became the first bank of discount, deposit and issue to be established anywhere in Canada. Its Articles of Association served as the model for the banking institutions which were subsequently founded both in Lower and Upper Canada, and embodied many provisions which are characteristic of our present banking system. There is no doubt that the Articles were taken directly from the constitution of the First Bank of the United States, a document devised by Alexander Hamilton, the first Secretary of the Treasury of the new republic.[4] In their formulation, he had obviously been influenced by his knowledge of the English and Scottish banks, and by his first-hand acquaintance with the operations of the American state-banks. Thus, the idea

[2] See R. M. Breckenridge, *The History of Banking in Canada* (Washington: National Monetary Commission), 1910, Ch. I.

[3] The following editorial in the *Montreal Herald*, May 10, 1817, was typical: "By an advertisement in this paper the public will learn that a meeting of the citizens is called at the Court House on Monday morning to deliberate upon a proper plan for immediately establishing a Bank in this City, without legislative sanction. No doubt the scheme which may be proposed has been already well digested, and will be approved of . . . The utility of banking establishments, has been so generally acknowledged in every civilized country, that any argument against having them in this country, should have little or no weight. Some solitary objections might indeed be started, but those could only originate in little or prejudiced minds; or, among those whose ignorance would always be a sufficient apology, for placing them below notice. The best institutions may be perverted, and a bank conducted without most consummate prudence, might be made the instrument of many evils and even calamities. But wherever such effects have been produced, the causes have been discovered; and can easily be guarded against, by prudent men—in other establishments. Since banks were established in Scotland only two of them suspended their payments." To begin its operations, the Bank of Montreal could scarcely have hoped for a more favourable environment than that reflected by the foregoing eulogy.

[4] Except for the omission of the provisions authorizing the government to buy shares, and for the existence of a provision to organize the institution as a private rather than a quasi-public enterprise, the articles of the Bank of Montreal seem to have been identical with those of the American institution. But to say that Hamilton devised its charter need not imply, of course, that he originated all of its provisions. In this connection, see Victor Ross, *A History of the Canadian Bank of Commerce* (Toronto: Oxford University Press), 1920, V. I, p. 12: "Any institution that is built to last must be rooted in the past, be conditioned by its surroundings and should sum up the best experience of former days."

of government participation, and of the connection between the bank's capital and the national debt, came from the Bank of England. But conversely, although the Bank of Scotland had begun establishing branches in 1774, a practice which later became a basic feature of the Scottish banking system, Hamilton believed that the lessons of colonial experience indicated its undesirability in the United States.[5]

The Articles of the Bank of Montreal authorized a capital stock of £250,000, or $1 million (Halifax currency), this sum being divided into 5,000 shares each of £50. Liability was limited to the amount of one's subscribed shares, and no shareholder was entitled to more than twenty votes, regardless of his holdings. In addition to receiving deposits and discounting notes, the bank was empowered to deal in bills of exchange, in gold and silver coin and bullion, and to sell stock which had been pledged for money lent, but not redeemed. It was prohibited from lending money on mortgages and from dealing directly in real estate, although mortgages might be held as security for debts gained by the bank in the ordinary course of its business. The maximum rate of interest in all dealings was to be 6% per annum. The bank was authorized to issue promissory notes intended to circulate as money, these being payable on demand in gold or silver coin. The total in circulation was not to exceed the aggregate of the bank's paid-in capital plus its holdings of gold and silver bullion and debentures or other securities issued or guaranteed by the province. Its total debts were limited to three times the amount of capital stock actually paid-in, plus an amount equal to moneys deposited for safe-keeping. The directors were required to present an annual report to the shareholders, specifying not only the quantity of notes in circulation but also the amount of bad or doubtful debts and of profit. Additional branches were permitted in any part of Upper or Lower Canada, and the government might at any time require statements from the directors, the better to protect the public.[6] The practices of issuing notes against the general assets of the bank, of requiring a relatively large equity capital, of granting a separate charter to each bank and of establishing accountability to the government, are all typical of present Canadian commercial banking practice. The beginnings of branch banking also appeared almost immediately.

Upon commencement of its operations, the bank announced its "discount" days as Tuesday and Friday, and the practice of confining discounts to two days per week became general as subsequent banks came into operation; a "Director for the Week" was also appointed from the bank's partners, to manage its busi-

---

[5] *Ibid.*, V. II, p. 291: "It was Hamilton's merit that after some fumbling he saw clearly what the teaching of the past really was, and which of its lessons were applicable to local conditions."

[6] A complete statement of the Articles of Association of the Bank of Montreal may be found in the contemporary issues of the local newspapers. See, for example, *Montreal Herald*, May 24, 1817. The same information is available in Breckenridge, *op. cit.*, pp. 27-33.

ness for that period of time. It would appear that it obtained most of its stock of specie from the hoards of the wealthier French Canadians who, albeit with some reluctance, were persuaded to invest in the stock of the bank. For, apart from the salutary influence of the Army Bills experience, the distrust of paper money was rapidly becoming a matter, not of personal experience, but of historical conviction only.[7] The bank also embarked at once upon foreign exchange deal-ings, in which it was remarkably successful during the brief post-war boom in the colony. It soon became the largest dealer in exchange in the two provinces, and a strong and unwelcome competitor of the private dealers. The bank's sterling transactions were carried out in the New York market, and it remitted bills to England against its own imports of specie, colonial imports of goods and adverse trade balances. This plan of using New York as a market for sterling bills, as a source of specie supply and as a place for loaning at call any tempor-arily idle funds, was widely followed by the larger Canadian banks in later years. In particular, the New York market became the major outlet for the large secondary reserves of these institutions. The first investment of the bank's funds was apparently in buying Army Bills on London, " . . . to be sold in the community on the best possible terms". Some years later, the bank lent financial assistance in the construction of the Lachine Canal, which was opened in 1825. This marked its first advance for the financing of public works. Its notes were issued in dollar (Spanish) denominations and each denomination bore a dif-ferent vignette or device, " . . . so that the most illiterate can ascertain the amount by inspection without being able to read".

At the end of its first year in operation, the bank sought " . . . the right of supplying the Government in the country with such moneys as may be wanted by the different departments in Upper and Lower Canada", and this marked the beginning of a long association between the bank and the governments of the two provinces, and later the government of the dominion.[8] Agencies had been, at this time, opened at Quebec, and at Kingston and York, the principal trading centres outside of Montreal, but service in the latter two places was withdrawn in 1823 because the government of Upper Canada required that banks redeem their notes within that province.[9] In view of the great inconven-ience, cost and risk involved in the movement of specie in the early days, the Bank of Montreal, quite understandably, preferred to redeem its notes at its head office only. York was still a small community of farmers and persons trad-

---

[7]See Shortt, "The Early History of Canadian Banking", in *J.C.B.A.*, IV, p. 351. Here it is suggested that the continuing scepticism of paper money was perhaps beneficial, since the tendency of the French Canadians to convert their notes at the first opportunity tended to prevent the banks from over-issuing notes before they could correct "their first large ideas about the capacities of paper money." In this latter respect, the first banks in Upper Canada were not as fortunate.

[8]*Ibid.*, p. 20.

[9]See *Kingston Gazette*, July 28, 1818: The local agency advertised that " . . . any sum required can be obtained at the Office for good bills on Montreal and Quebec, or for Specie . . ."

ing with the Indians, and while isolated settlements were to be found to the west, Upper Canada was still mostly an unbroken forest.[10]

Two additional banks made their appearance in Lower Canada in 1818. In Quebec city, a general meeting of landholders, merchants and other inhabitants resolved to establish a bank in that community. Such an institution would be "of highest importance" to the citizens at large, since it would materially assist agriculture and afford great relief to commerce, so much depressed at that particular time. The resolution went on, inevitably, to point out that the quantity of specie in circulation was inadequate, and subject to "perpetual fluctuations".[11] A memorial was presented to the Legislature, providing that the bank should operate as a limited co-partnership until a charter of incorporation could be obtained (an arrangement similar to that adopted by the Bank of Montreal).[12]

In Montreal, the Bank of Canada began operations in 1818, having been organized to specialize in foreign exchange transactions between Canada and the United States. It was financed very largely by United States speculative capital, and it included among its owners many of the shareholders of the Bank of Montreal. Like the other two banks, it began as a "private" institution, and like them, it received a legislative charter in 1822, valid for ten years.[13] But its success was short-lived, for in the economic recession which followed the brief post-war boom, the bank's special interest, foreign-exchange dealings, became unprofitable, and many of the directors wished to liquidate the enterprise. Between 1815-25, bills of exchange on England had moved from an appreciable discount to a premium of ten per cent. The post-war depression had brought a contraction of Canadian exports to Britain, and a larger proportion of imports came from the United States. Specie thus tended to flow to the United States, while sterling bills commanded a premium. The bank did continue to operate under the guiding influence of the Bank of Montreal until 1831, at which time it was merged with that institution.

From the outset, the banks in Lower Canada appear to have presented the notes of their competitors for redemption as promptly as possible, a habit no doubt dictated in part by the scarcity of specie, in part by precautionary motives. Commenting on this practice, one writer has alleged that the self-interest of the banks " . . . thus established a check against inflation and unsound banking— No more notes than the business of the country required could remain in circu-

[10]See Canadian Archives, *Miscellaneous Documents, Canada, 1808-1825*, Vol. 8, Letter of June 4, 1868, by H. Dupuy, first cashier of the Bank of Montreal, 1817. Some interesting and illuminating sidelights on the problems involved in getting the bank ready to begin operations are recalled in this letter.

[11]See the *Quebec Mercury*, February 10, 1818.

[12]The twenty-five Articles of Association of the Quebec Bank appear in the *Quebec Gazette*, July 27, 1818. (The authorized capital was not to exceed £150,000 currency.)

[13]The twenty-three Articles of Association of the Bank of Canada appear in the *Quebec Gazette*, August 24, 1818. (The authorized capital was not to exceed £300,000 currency.)

lation."[14] This extract manages a rather neat combination of two of the more common fallacies in monetary and banking theory. First, it should be noted that when bankers are compelled to redeem their notes in cash, about all that is prevented is the expansion of the notes of any one bank at a rate much different from that of its rivals. But to say that this common rate of expansion (or contraction) will inevitably be such as to check deflation (or inflation) is completely erroneous. The second fallacy is that there is some pre-ordained quantity of money which is "required" to transact the nation's business. This view has an imposing history extending back to Adam Smith and beyond, but other things being equal, varying quantities of money will be required to transact the nation's business at varying price-levels. There are few more misleading concepts than that of the monetary "needs of business", such needs being at any time indeterminate, but such a concept has been embodied in the "commercial loan" theory of banking, long a source of comfort to the chartered banks. Alternatively known as the "real bills doctrine", it maintained that as long as commercial banks confined their lending operations to the financing of short-term, self-liquidating "real" transactions, all would be well. The community would be provided with a desirable "elasticity" in its money-supply, the banks would maintain their liquidity and excessive expansion of credit (and by implication excessive contraction) would be impossible. The theory is erroneous in all three claims.

In the case of the three Lower Canada banks, all directors were leading merchants of the colony, and a large proportion of the early advances were to these merchants.[15] This association of ownership with the British commercial element, and the identification of many partners with the Legislative Council of the province, contributed to a growing tendency to increased popular criticism of the banks' operations as time went on. In 1828 and 1829, some especially sharp attacks were directed at the banks in general, and the Bank of Montreal in particular, the latter institution being most closely associated with the country's internal and external trade.[16] It was alleged that (a) favouritism was extended to its shareholders and to larger business, discounts granted to other prospective borrowers being meagre, especially when money was unusually scarce; (b) the bank monopolized the foreign exchange markets by buying all of the large bills issued by the government and commercial interest, and selling only its own, at much higher rates; (c) the bank should be willing to redeem its notes at any of its agencies, not just at their places of issue. (It was costly to do this, but the bank had earlier redeemed all notes presented at its Quebec agency.)

[14]Victor Ross, *A History of the Canadian Bank of Commerce* (Toronto: Oxford University Press), I, 1920, pp. 13-14.

[15]The importance of notes, relative to deposits, as a form of bank credit in this early period is indicated by figures relating to the three banks at the end of 1824. Aggregate deposits approximated £135,000, notes £167,000. See *ibid.*, Ch. I.

[16]See Adam Shortt, "Founders of Canadian Banking" in *J.C.B.A.*, XXIX, pp. 277-90.

Many of these charges were well founded, but they were undoubtedly based on political as well as economic considerations.[17]

Despite the striking similarity between the charters of these first three banks in Lower Canada and that of the First Bank of the United States, it is not surprising that the modern commercial banking structures of the two nations differ so widely. Each represents the product of its particular environment, and it has been pointed out that in explaining the evolution of the Canadian banking system after 1817, three chief lines of influence may be detected.[18] The first is to be found in criticisms and problems arising from the operation of the banks in Canada, as they sought to adapt themselves to the expanding pioneer economy and to further its development. The second arises from the observation of banking experience both in the United States and in the Maritime provinces of British North America, the influence of the former being especially important. The third influence was that exerted by the British Treasury through the Colonial Office, a government department which was empowered to revise or disallow colonial legislation, especially where matters of banking and currency were involved. The degree of interest which this Office displayed in colonial legislation on such matters varied widely from time to time, but was always a reflection of the current British attitude toward their own monetary problems, rather than of the merits of the colonial legislation which might at the time be under consideration. At all times, however, this paternal interest was actively and strongly resented, both by the colonial governments and by the local banks. It is true, nevertheless, that some features of the Canadian banking system originated in instructions issued by the British government, where royal assent for some particular piece of colonial legislation required the inclusion of specific recommendations in that measure. Conversely, the Canadian banks were saved from many of the excesses which appeared in the contemporary banking development of the United States.

Because of the substantial commercial dependence of Upper Canada on Montreal, it was natural that banking developments in the latter centre were viewed with great interest, and upon the establishment of the two institutions in that city and one in Quebec, a group of Kingston merchants decided that the appropriate time had arrived for founding a bank in their own community, which was the chief commercial centre of Upper Canada. Tiring of the delay in gaining royal assent for a charter, the Bank of Upper Canada began operations in 1818 as a private organization, and its Articles of Association paralleled those of the Bank of Montreal. Its authorized capital was not to exceed £125,000, and this was payable in gold, silver or Bank of Montreal notes. Its petition for incorporation, which had been addressed to the Legislature in January, 1817,

---

[17]The bank pointed out that since beginning operations, it had imported more than £500,000 (currency) in specie, chiefly in dollars and half-dollars.

[18]Ross, *op. cit.*, pp. 390-1.

was favourably received, and the bank was granted a charter. But royal assent was delayed for almost two years, and well beyond the time prescribed for the beginning of operations. The charter therefore lapsed, failing the formal re-enactment of its provisions by the Legislature, and the bank completed its brief existence as a private organization. The Bank of Montreal and the Bank of Canada both established branch offices in Kingston in 1818, a city which then found itself called upon to support three banks where, only a short time earlier, none had existed.[19]

The new Bank of Upper Canada began its short life in an inauspicious environment of economic depression. It lacked financial strength, and was afflicted with unsatisfactory management.[20] The weight of all these unfavourable influences forced a suspension of its operations, with considerable loss to its creditors.[21]

A more enduring contribution to early banking in the province was the appearance of the Second or Chartered Bank of Upper Canada at York in 1821, the outcome of a great deal of political manoeuvring and subterfuge. The basis for its charter lay in the receipt of royal assent for the chartering of a bank at Kingston, for which, as already noted, the Kingston bank directors had long

[19]*Kingston Gazette*, June 30, 1818: This paper emphasized the urgent need for banking facilities, claiming that by collecting idle capital from different parts of the province and from the United States, the circulating medium could be increased at least fivefold. A bank would enable persons of real capital to apply it both to their private advantage and to the general improvement of the country. "No country ever grew rapidly rich (let the natural advantages be what they would) or even attained to more than a moderate degree of opulence where the enterprize of individuals was confined alone to specie capital."

[20]See the Montreal *Gazette*, March 24, 1823. Here there appears the following extract from the report of the Upper Canada Committee on Banking Institutions, investigating the failure of the Kingston bank: "The immediate failure of the said Bank appears to your Committee to have been evidently occasioned by the criminal conduct of its President, Cashier and Teller, in various acts detailed in the said examination. The conduct of the Directors of the said Institution is also reprehensible inasmuch as no enquiry appears to have been made by them into the actual state of the Bank. . . . A large deficiency appears in the funds of the said Institution, occasioned by an actual abstraction of money; of which abstraction the President, Cashier or Teller must be guilty."

The Committee emphasized ". . . the propriety of guarding against the recurrence of a similar [event] by preventing the establishment of Banking Institutions without Acts of Incorporation by the Parliament of this Province".

[21]See Canadian Archives, *Upper Canada Sundries, 1823: Letter from John Carey (creditor?) to British Government*. The complaints voiced in this letter suggest that creditors of the bank were evidently unable to secure much redress of their grievances. See also Adam Shortt, *Provinces of Canada*, IV, p. 615: " . . . in the course of years, the institution gradually vanished into an ever-expanding fog of legal arguments, commissioners' reports, questionable claims and uncollectable debts, all very carefully figured out at compound interest." See also *Upper Canada State Papers, 1832-1840*, Letter from the Executive-Council to Lt. Governor Sir John Colborne: The paper issued by this bank did for a time form a part of the circulating medium of the province, but because of "circumstances not necessary to mention, it stopped payment, and owing to certain reported abstractions, the Assembly introduced a bill to 'elucidate' the transactions of the directors and give security to the Public Creditor."

since given up hope. After a great deal of political conniving, the site of the proposed bank was shifted from Kingston to York, and its chief supporters were the government officials in Upper Canada who subsequently gained notoriety as the Family Compact.

The charter of the bank differed only slightly from those in Lower Canada. Most significant was the provision authorizing the government of Upper Canada to subscribe to the stock of the new institution. Its authorized capital amounted to £200,000, of which the government agreed to subscribe for £25,000 (2,000 shares). Public support for the venture does not appear to have been at all overwhelming, and government assistance was indispensable to its successful launching. The bank was required to obtain £50,000 in capital subscribed and £20,000 in specie paid-in, before starting operations,[22] and the latter provision proved impossible to fulfil, despite the significant government cash contribution. Some of the original supporters of the project were sufficiently impressed by this development to recommend that the whole venture be dropped.[23] But this suggestion did not gain majority support, and after having its paid-in specie requirement reduced by half, to £10,000, the bank got under way.[24] Nine of its fifteen directors were members either of the Executive or the Legislative Council of the province, and most of the others soon became likewise identified with the government. As in the lower province, the view was generally held that a paper bank-note currency would serve " . . . all the purposes of provincial trade, and yet not be likely to drain away as specie does".[25]

It is noteworthy that both the Bank of Montreal and the Bank of Upper Canada had the advantage of an alliance with the dominant political party, a circumstance that undoubtedly helps to explain the fact that for some few years, no additional banks were chartered in either province. The strength of the Bank of Montreal in these years lay principally in the fact that having got into operation first, it enjoyed considerable government patronage. The political influence of the bank gave rise to considerable resentment and jealousy on the

---

[22]See *Canadian Archives, Upper Canada Sundries 1822: Letter from the Receiver-General to the Bank of Upper Canada, June 1822.* This is a reply to a letter from the President of the bank, requesting payment of ten per cent of the capital subscribed by the government: "I am perfectly prepared to meet the Warrant you allude to for the sum of £2,500 provided that the President of the Bank will receive from me, that sum, in Notes, of the Montreal or any other Bank in Canada, or a Draft on my Agents at Montreal. As to Specie, it is impossible, I am under the absolute necessity of accepting Paper Currency, from the great scarcity of specie, and the most of the Persons, from whom the Provincial Revenue is derived, have no other means of transmitting money to me but in Paper—Whenever it happens that I receive Specie, it is always paid out towards the demands against the Public."

[23]In 1821, John McGill expressed serious doubts as to the need for any bank at York. "My own opinion is that it will be a losing business, though I have been dragged into subscribing more than was perhaps prudent."

[24]For a history of the bank's operations, see E. C. Guillet, "Pioneer Banking in Ontario: The Bank of Upper Canada, 1822-66", in *J.C.B.A.* Winter 1948.

[25]Shortt, "The Early History of Canadian Banking", in *J.C.B.A.*, V, pp. 13-14.

part of its competitors. In contrast to the prominence of the mercantile element in the early management of the Bank of Montreal, the Bank of Upper Canada was dominated by politicians, a situation which gave rise to a widespread mistrust of its management. This attitude of misgiving was not lessened as the bank made determined efforts in succeeding years to maintain its monopolistic position which it found to be exceedingly advantageous.

With the granting of charters in both Lower and Upper Canada, the first stage in the development of our modern banking system was completed, and the paper currency issues of the banks did provide the country with a much more satisfactory medium of exchange. The deplorable state of the metallic currency prompted the observation that "During the second quarter of the nineteenth century the office of a Canadian currency broker was a veritable curiosity shop, exhibiting the remnants of several national currencies in the last stages of demoralization. There, from a currency point of view, the halt, the blind and the disowned of many mints foregathered in shabby company. Their thin, worn and battered faces mutely witnessed to a long and busy life with much travel and hard usage. Only the chronic scarcity of coinage in times of peace enabled this motley crew to occupy the market-place and brazen their way into fairly respectable company."[26]

Apart from the foregoing developments in the field of commercial banking, there had also appeared an increasing need for some kind of purely savings institution, to serve the needs of the many citizens who might wish to deposit small sums at a modest rate of return.[27] A contemporary editorial notes that "the object of [such] Institution is to open to the Lower orders, a place of deposit for their small Savings, with the allowance of a reasonable monthly interest, and with full liberty of withdrawing their money at any time either in whole or in part. . . . The only effectual method of assisting the poor is to encourage industry, economy and sobriety, among them; to excite and animate their own exertions, and aid them in securing the full advantages of their success. The great source of poverty will be found in the want of economical and provident habits".[28] To further these puritanical suggestions, the Montreal Savings Bank was opened in late 1819, modelled after the Edinburgh Savings Bank, and it was followed by the Quebec Savings Bank more than a year later, these marking the beginnings of the present savings banks system peculiar to the province of Quebec.[29]

During the early 1820's, a period of readjustment and uncertainty in the

---

[26]*Ibid.*, pp. 619-20.
   [27]Interest was not as a rule allowed on deposits in the commercial banks. In the *Upper Canada Sundries*, 1822, it is noted that in a few cases of mutual consent, where a minimum deposit of £1,000 was left for a specified time, the Bank of Montreal allowed interest at 6%.    [28]*Montreal Herald*, August 24, 1819.
   [29]The Montreal Savings Bank was eventually taken over by the Bank of Montreal in 1856, at which time the latter institution established its first savings department.

economy of the Canadas, the new commercial banks were not without their difficulties. In addition to the failure of the Kingston bank (the "pretended" Bank of Upper Canada) and the termination of operations by the Bank of Canada at the end of the decade, the Bank of Montreal incurred heavy financial losses chiefly through its financing of lumber interests in Quebec and Montreal. The latter city was the financial and commercial centre for both provinces. About £80,000 were lost in 1824-5, dividends were suspended for two years and the stock of the bank was being offered for sale at 40% to 50% discount. The confidence of an uneasy public was restored when the directors, who were men of influence and wealth, pledged their resources to the safety of the bank. Reports of the counterfeiting of bank notes were becoming increasingly widespread, despite the severe penalties prescribed for such action. Occasional "specie wars" broke out among the banks, adding to the cost and inconvenience of their operations.[30]

The Bank of Upper Canada, enjoying the benefits of a monopolistic position in its own province, made steady progress during its first decade of operations, and as already indicated, strongly resisted the chartering of any other banks. The business of the bank was chiefly the discounting of promissory notes at 90 days at 6%, the negotiation of bills of exchange and the buying and selling of bullion. It engaged in no type of "speculative" activity. The bank apparently netted, after the first year, 8%-12% profit on paid-in capital. Public confidence in the institution grew steadily, and its notes circulated along the whole line of the American frontier bordering on Canada. They were at only a small discount in New York, and this was owing to the commercial relations between the two countries, not to any distrust of the institution. In 1825, the authorized capital stock of the bank had been reduced by one-half, the reason given being that the original amount was "greater than the present circumstances and commerce of the country required". After mid-1826, the bank refused to redeem its notes at Montreal, being not required to do so by charter. This brought many protests from various Montreal interests who regarded the move as a grave injustice, but the bank justified this policy, as did the Bank of Montreal, on the grounds of " . . . the great and unnecessary risk which the redeeming of the notes of our Bank at any other point but that of issue, necessarily brings upon the establish-

[30]See Canadian Archives, Miscellaneous Documents, Canada, 1805-25, Vol. VIII, *op. cit.*; "In the year 1829 I was appointed Manager of the Kingston Branch [of the Bank of Montreal] after having been nailed to the Books for 12 years. Shortly after this a specie war took place between the Bank of Montreal and the Bank of Upper Canada. Thus, Kegs and Boxes of specie would go up to Toronto, Bank of Upper Canada, in payment of balances sometimes pretty large; then if the balance happened to be on the other side, the same Boxes and Kegs would make their appearance here again, and this was continued for some months. At last peace was restored and both Banks agreed to settle their balances by Bills of Exchange or Drafts."

ment".[31] The bank stated that not more than £20,000 of its notes were circulating in Lower Canada at the time.[32]

By 1825, there were some £61,000 in Bank of Upper Canada notes in circulation, and its specie holdings had risen to £17,000. A statement forwarded by the cashier to the British government estimated the whole circulating medium of Upper Canada in mid-1825 to include some £105,000 in bank notes (including notes of the banks in Lower Canada then current in the upper province), and £30,000 in specie, for a total of £135,000.[33] The average rate of exchange on London, i.e., the average rate at which the bank had purchased private bills during the year, was 7½% premium. The cashier commented that the considerable increase in the circulation of Lower Canada bank notes in Upper Canada during the preceding two years was to be explained in terms of the Montreal capital employed in the lumber, potash and flour trade, and also by " . . . the fictitious capital set afloat by the discounts of this Bank".[34] The specie in the province was at this time derived chiefly from the issues to the troops, and from European immigrants. Spanish dollars were scarce, being bought up for export to the United States.

With the economic revival in the later 1820's, and the ensuing rapid expansion and prosperity of the 1830's, the growing need for increased banking accommodation became irresistible, despite the determined opposition waged by the politically powerful Bank of Upper Canada.[35] Substantial immigration, the opening up of frontier areas, the growth of lumbering and saw-milling, rising expenditures on public works and favourable circumstances abroad all contributed to the period of expansion which continued until the collapse in 1837. The boom was in part a stimulus to, and in part a result of, the increase in banking facilities which occurred during the period, and the confusion, typical of the pioneer economy, between the need for currency and the need for real capital is readily apparent. An application by the bank for permission to increase its authorized capital was held up by the Legislative Assembly until the Legislative Council could see its way clear to approve an application from a

---

[31]In June 1827, the bank was able to declare a 4% half-yearly dividend, plus a 6% bonus, on its paid-in capital. This rate of return was by no means uncommon in early banking.

[32]Even in this early period, present-day methods of redress were sought. See the Montreal *Gazette,* July 6, 1826: " . . . It is true that the Montreal Bank and others take these notes at a discount of one and a half *per centum,* but does not the public lose this one and a half *per cent,* and does not the whole transaction look very much like a job . . . the whole transaction merits the investigation of the legislatures of both provinces."

[33]See Canadian Archives, *Upper Canada Sundries, 1825.*

[34]*Ibid.*

[35]Montreal *Gazette,* November 26, 1831: The stock of the Bank of Upper Canada " . . . unhappily for any hope of resistance, is chiefly held by persons who have long been accustomed to direct the affairs of the Province, and rule one branch of the Legislature, so that political power, and the influence of controlling the circulating medium, as well as of crushing any establishment or individual obnoxious to the Bank, is now sought to be made perpetual, and placed in the same hands."

group of Kingston merchants who wished to establish a chartered bank in that city.[36] Both bills eventually were passed, in 1832, and the Commercial Bank of the Midland District shortly began operations.

This breaking of the monopoly of the Bank of Upper Canada stimulated further applications for charters, but success was still most difficult. The only other bank to receive legislative sanction in Upper Canada, before the union of the two provinces, was the Gore Bank at Hamilton, and it was the first bank in Upper Canada to provide for the double liability of its stockholders. It received its charter in 1836, and opened its doors on the frontier of a country " . . . with vast potential resources, but [in a] primitive state of development, and amid political unrest in a period when sound principles of banking were still to be established".[37] Following the common practice of the day, it promptly opened branches, and within a year, at least ten were in operation, extending from Dundas to Prescott.

In the session of 1836-7, nine new charters passed both Houses in Upper Canada. (Approval was also granted for increases in the capital stock of a number of the existing banks.) While none of the nine bills was disallowed in Britain, they were returned (wisely) for further consideration. Their effect would have been to increase authorized bank capital from £500,000 to £4,500,000, and potential note issues to three times the latter amount. The crisis and depression following 1837 chilled the enthusiasm of these promoters, and none of the bills was ultimately enacted.

The impatience of some of the applicants for bank charters led to the establishment of several private banks in Upper Canada in the mid-1830's, allegedly modelled on the British joint-stock principle. These were the Farmers' Bank, the Bank of the People, the Niagara Suspension Bridge Bank and the Agricultural Bank. These were comparatively small institutions whose operations were of a transitory nature. The Farmers' Bank managed to continue for some fifteen years; the Bank of the People was purchased by the Bank of Montreal, with which it had been associated in its exchange dealings. It was, incidentally, the

---

[36]Shortly before the struggle for the Kingston bank charter had succeeded, the following note appeared in the *Kingston Chronicle*, April 9, 1831: "From the general devotion of mankind to self-interest, it may be reasonably made a question, whether if a charter had been granted to Kingston, it would not have increased the obstacles to the future establishment of banks [elsewhere] . . . Each new charter will become a new obstacle to the granting of further charters."

[37]See Victor Ross, *op. cit.*, I, p. 204: "Probably the main difficulty in carrying out sound theories lay in the circumstances of the times. Had it been possible to confine banking accommodation to facilitating the movement of agricultural produce, history might have been different, but the season was short, and there was no manufacturing to provide a use for the money between seasons. Besides this, prices were low and profits, therefore, meagre. The handling of agricultural produce, alone, could not support a bank. In the undeveloped state of the country, landed property was the principal asset of most of the inhabitants, even of those reputedly wealthy. Advances were usually made on the personal security of an endorser . . . and ultimately, the security held for all slow and doubtful transactions was land."

only Canadian bank, and one of the few North American banks, which did not suspend specie payment in 1837-8. The Agricultural Bank, which failed in 1837, was responsible for the unheard-of innovation among Canadian commercial banks, of paying interest on deposits. It established a rate of 3%, a practice which earned it the lasting bitter enmity of the other banks, which reluctantly followed this lead. The Agricultural Bank had the further temerity to become involved in a specie war with the great Bank of Upper Canada (the latter institution had a practical monopoly of the specie introduced by the British and provincial governments into Upper Canada, as well as the government bills on London, which were readily saleable in the United States), and finally succumbed to its life-long attacks from its established competitors. The further development of private banking in Upper Canada was terminated by an act in 1837, which made it a misdemeanour for all private banking companies, as well as individuals, to issue bank notes.[38] There was, of course, no scarcity of self-appointed bankers in this era, and many irresponsible persons set themselves up as "private bankers" and issued notes, undoubtedly with fraudulent intent, until restrained by the legislation of 1837. Still other honestly-motivated banking enterprises would appear for a brief time, and then vanish from the scene.

In Lower Canada, the Bank of Montreal became the sole financial power in that city after its absorption of the Bank of Canada in 1831. Two years later, a charter was granted to the City Bank, which was a distinctively Montreal institution, with negligible outside resources. One private bank, the Banque du Peuple, was organized in 1835.

A distinctive feature in the history of Canadian banking was the appearance of the Bank of British North America at York in 1836. This was an institution which had earlier been incorporated in Great Britain, and whose operations were extended to Canada by royal charter, rather than by colonial legislation. It was organized as a joint-stock company with its partners and capital predominantly British. In 1837, the bank had some 600 partners in England and about 300 in the colonies, "all of whom [were] responsible to the full extent of their fortunes for the engagements of the Bank, offering therefore unlimited security to the public." When a charter sanctioning operations in British North America was granted in 1840, the liability of the partners was specifically restricted to the amount of their capital subscribed.

The peculiar advantages which this bank was deemed to afford to the public consisted of its introduction of the Scottish system of cash credit accounts, " . . . upon which a party, giving security to the Bank, can draw to a limited amount, for the occasional emergencies of his business, and is charged with interest only for the sum he has occasion for, during so many days as he shall make use of it, as the smallest amount paid in to the Bank will be received to the credit of his

---

[38]This edict brought a strong protest from some residents of Kent County, for whom the nearest recognized bank was the Gore at Hamilton.

account, and the charge of interest be diminished in proportion."[39] The bank also allowed interest on moneys deposited, a practice still novel to the other Canadian banks, and the possible contribution of the bank through augmenting the provinces' supply of specie was not overlooked. A branch of the new bank was opened in Montreal in 1838, followed by others in the various commercial centres of the provinces of British North America.

At the time of union of the two Canadian provinces, the "recognized" banks in operation included three chartered and one unchartered bank in Lower Canada, three chartered and two unchartered banks in Upper Canada, and the Bank of British North America, operating by royal charter in both provinces. Excluding the latter institution, the aggregate available banking capital in 1841 was approximately £1,486,000 (currency), note circulation £871,000, specie £341,000, deposits £626,000, discounts £2,694,000. The Bank of British North America provided a further capital of £690,000 (sterling), a note circulation of £51,000 specie £46,000, deposits £185,000 and discounts £575,000.[40]

It has already been indicated that problems of counterfeiting were encountered at an early date. Through the years, evidence of the continuation of this illegitimate form of private enterprise was abundant. In 1834, for example, the solicitor of the Bank of Upper Canada wrote in a letter to the Lieutenant-Governor of the province that " . . . forgeries upon the paper Currency of this province are at this time being carried on to an alarming extent—from information which your petitioner has every reason to believe is perfectly correct—a regular organized band of Counterfeiters are now spreading over the Country circulating forged notes upon the Bank of Upper Canada."[41]

In addition to providing the provinces with paper money issues, the banks also sought to improve, to some degree, the deplorable collection of coinage with which the country had long been afflicted. One writer in the late thirties stated that "the silver and copper coins we have in circulation are a disgrace to any civilized nation, and have more the appearance of the fifteenth than the nineteenth century. All the antiquated cast-off rubbish, in the whole world, finds its way here, and remains. This Colony is literally the Botany Bay for all the condemned coins of other countries; instead of perishing in the crucible as they ought to do, they are banished to Canada, where they are taken by the hand,

[39]*Montreal Transcript*, January 12, 1837.
[40]For a detailed breakdown of these figures by banks, see Breckenridge, *op. cit.*, p. 43. Frequent financial statements by the individual banks are to be found in the *State Papers, Upper Canada, Lower Canada Sundries,* and the *Journals of the Assembly, Lower Canada,* for this whole period.
[41]*State Papers, Upper Canada, 1828-1830.* The letter goes on to point out that " . . . in the month of October last a person calling himself John Willson of Detroit, State of Michigan, shoemaker—was detected in the act of passing forged notes of ten dollars upon the Bank of Upper Canada—and upon his apprehension forged notes to the amount of five thousand dollars were found upon his person—that since his apprehension he has voluntarily confessed . . . that he is one of a gang of Counterfeiters (most of whom reside in Lower Canada)."

however worthless in character or value they may be." Although the importation of copper coinage was illegal, the country had been subjected to a substantial influx of privately imported light-weight copper coins of doubtful antecedents.[42]

In the summer of 1832, one James Perrin, a merchant at York, ordered ten hundredweight of copper tokens from Liverpool, and these were shipped in five kegs, along with one keg of nails. All were labelled "nails", as Perrin explained, "to prevent public curiosity". When the ruse was discovered, Perrin disclaimed any intention of wrongdoing, but the solicitor for the Lieutenant-Governor stated that "I regret that in consideration of the many suspicious circumstances connected with the introduction of the coins alluded to, I cannot feel it to be consistent with my duty to recommend the prayer of petitioner."[43] Perrin was given the opportunity of reshipping the coin to England and accepted. A suspicious customs officer "found it necessary to guard with vigilance against their return to this province." His doubts were well founded, for it was not long until a second attempt to smuggle the same shipment of coins was detected. Mr. Perrin lost both the coins and £100 sterling after this episode.

Between 1837 and 1857, some of the chartered banks circulated numerous issues of well executed and full-weight copper coins and this did much to minimize the nuisance encountered with the earlier pieces.[44] But for some time there had been increasing support from the business community for a distinctively Canadian gold and silver coinage, based on the United States decimal system. The British government opposed such a suggestion, wishing to see a sterling standard prevail not only in the Canadas, but throughout the Empire. In particular, it was believed that the adoption of a decimal currency system similar to that of the United States would greatly increase the dangers of political annexation. By various legislative expedients, and the payment of the colonial militia in British silver, the British government hoped that the coinage of the colony could be brought into conformity with the nominal (sterling) standard of value. The scheme was not successful, for the silver was promptly used to purchase sterling bills, and therefore returned either to the military chest or to

---

[42]See Shortt, "A History of Canadian Metallic Currency", in *Transactions of the Canadian Institute* (Toronto: University of Toronto Press), 1912, p. 243: "About 1825 it consisted of discarded and worn British half-pence, farthings, various private tokens, native and foreign, and even brass buttons hammered smooth." In the years before the Rebellion, copper "tokens" issued by the merchants became commonly used. Also provided by the same sources were small paper "shin-plasters" of various fractional denominations.

[43]*State Papers, Upper Canada, 1828-1838.*

[44]The Bank of Montreal, the City Bank, the Quebec Bank and the Banque du Peuple, and later the Bank of Canada, obtained permission to issue these coins. The Bank of Montreal also imported $10,000 in U.S. 5- and 10-cent pieces, a most useful addition to the silver circulation. The Upper Canada banks also imported substantial quantities of British silver. See R. W. McLachlan, "The Copper Currency of the Canadian Banks 1837-1857", in *Transactions of the Royal Society of Canada*, Sec. II, 1903, see also *Canadian Archives, C.O. Records*, Q240-2, September 21, 1837.

bank vaults, in either case leaving the content of the circulating specie just as before.[45]

The ineffectiveness of over-rating, as a means of retaining specie, has already been indicated. Prices soon adjusted themselves to the over-rated coins, at which time they would again disappear from circulation. Over-rating was of course the device which seemed obvious and most sensible to the ordinary citizen unaware of the particular problem involved. The result was that this " . . . plain unsophisticated argument usually prevailed, and the colonies engaged in a lively competition, partly with outsiders, but largely among themselves, for an increased share of the available currency."[46] But among the financial interests in the two Canadas, there was a steadily growing conviction that what the colony required was a distinctively Canadian decimal coinage, not acceptable at face value in other countries, so that it could serve no other purpose than that of a domestic medium of exchange. A contemporary observer noted that the balance of trade was "enormously" against Canada, and that the country was periodically drained of specie "which is accumulated and bought up by merchants to make their remittances. Between the departure of the autumnal fleet and the return of Spring, the whole country is sacrificed to the interest, to the mercy or to the pillage of the Banks and the merchants. No separation can be made, for our bankers are our merchants, and our merchants our bankers." The efforts of England, in remitting specie for the troops, etc., were likened to "pumping water into a sieve". In Lower Canada, it was commonly observed "que l'argent est rare!" Periodic revisions of currency regulations in Upper and Lower Canada had served to complicate the problem of exchange between the two provinces, and business was suffering from the increasing monetary disorganization. Coins and ratings were becoming increasingly varied as between the provinces, with all exchanges and note redemptions being effected in the most over-rated specie available.[47] Following the union of the two provinces in 1841, the currency problem became of pressing importance, and a conflict arose between those who wished a medium of exchange in sterling denominations and those favouring the

---

[45]A detailed account of currency developments in the Canadas before union, and in the pre-Confederation period, may be found in Shortt, "History of Canadian Metallic Currency", in *Transactions of the Canadian Institute* (Toronto: University of Toronto Press), 1912, pp. 242-6.

[46]Shortt, "The History of Canadian Currency", in *J.C.B.A.*, VII, pp. 210-11.

[47]See *Lower Canada, P.S.O. 1839-40*. No. 1118: Here may be found the details of a memorial addressed to the Governor-General of British North America, urging the placing of British coins in Lower Canada on the same basis as in Upper Canada. A Lower Canada ordinance of 1839 providing for a uniform currency had been disallowed by the British government. Similar memorials were also presented in 1840 by banks in both provinces, those of Lower Canada urging the inclusion of French coins in any uniform currency ratings. One redeeming feature of the existing chaotic situation was alleged to be the deterrent to runs upon the banks from outside the provinces. Such would have been unprofitable! The Nova Scotia Assembly noted in 1850 that the same rating for coins was not to be found "in any two" of the British North American colonies.

decimal currency system, as in the United States. "In the end the dollar prevailed in Canada because of economic contiguity and the greater familiarity of the masses of the people with American coins and prices."[48] The banks in both Upper and Lower Canada had, from the beginning, issued their currency in dollar denominations, and although sterling had been the nominal standard of value, exchange had in fact been carried on in decimal units for decades.

The Currency Act of 1841 retained the Halifax standard, (5s. = $1), despite the lack of a corresponding coinage. Gold coins established as full legal tender were the American eagle and the British sovereign. Silver coins accorded the same status were the American dollar and half-dollar and the new French 5-franc piece. The old French silver coins, which had been hoarded by the habitants since before the conquest, and which had dominated the currency of Lower Canada since that time, were not rated, and were therefore valuable only as bullion. British silver was accorded the same status as it enjoyed at home, that of token currency of limited legal tender. Although the Act was accompanied by considerable protest, the value of a uniform currency soon became apparent, and ". . . nothing did more to promote economic unity, and therefore, to a considerable extent, political harmony between the naturally antagonistic sections of the new Canadian province."[49] An Act of 1850 authorized the issue of Canadian silver coins in denominations of 5s., 2s.6d., 1s., 6d., and 3d. These of course corresponded to the dollar, half-dollar, twenty-cent, ten-cent and five-cent decimal pieces (at the Halifax currency rating of 5s. = $1). Gold coins of the value of £1. 5s. (five dollars) and £1 (four dollars) were also authorized. This measure largely determined the future denomination of Canadian currency.

In 1853, transactions in decimal currency were legalized, thereby creating an additional money of account. Provision was made for a corresponding system of coinage in gold, silver and copper. British gold coinage was also made unlimited legal tender, on the bullion standard of the sovereign ($4.86 2/3 or £1. 4s. 6d. currency). Finally, in 1858, it was provided that henceforth the government accounts, as well as all accounts rendered to the government, must be kept in decimal currency. This marked the official adoption of the decimal system, and its use throughout the province soon became widespread. No further changes in Canadian coinage were made until after Confederation.

To return to the development of commercial banking, the period of rapid economic expansion following the middle twenties was brought to an abrupt halt by the international commercial crisis in 1837.[50] In the Canadas, this crisis coincided with, and was aggravated by, armed rebellion, and was as severe as anywhere on the continent. There occurred a substantial contraction of bank discounts, and a general drop in land values, which rendered worthless a great

---

[48]See Shortt, "Founders of Canadian Banking", in the *J.C.B.A.*, XXXIII, p. 31.

[49]*Ibid.*, p. 32.

[50]In the autumn of 1836, there were eleven notices in the Official Gazette in Lower Canada, all dealing with the applications of banks, either for incorporation or for extension of capital.

many loans contracted upon the pledge or possession of real estate. Imperial expenditures related to the political disorders were the one counteracting force which helped both the banks and the business community in this period.

With the general suspension of specie payments by the United States banks in the spring of 1837, the Canadian banks found themselves in an untenable position. In Lower Canada, they promptly followed the example of the American institutions and suspended without legal sanction. But the demand for specie in the neighbouring states, and its accompanying high premium, led Canadian speculators to claim specie for their notes wherever possible.[51] Thus the reserves of the Upper Canada banks were depleted, and the outflow was aggravated by the leaders of the rebellion, who sought specie for their own purposes. The banks became understandably reluctant to reissue their notes. They pointed out that in view of the widespread suspension in the United States, it would be impossible for them to reissue their notes if the maintenance of their convertibility were to continue to be required, and that the country would find itself without a circulating medium of any kind. The Lieutenant-Governor of Upper Canada was opposed to suspension, and stated that ". . . whatever may be the fluctuations in the money-market, the commercial integrity of the British Empire rests on the fixed immutable basis of faithfully liquidating, so long as it has the power to do so, whatever it has promised to pay." Despite this ringing announcement, all three chartered banks were permitted to suspend specie payments "for a limited time", and a special enactment legalized their continued operation, the inconvertibility of their note issues notwithstanding. The Commercial Bank was the first in Upper Canada to suspend, taking this action in July. It was followed next by the Gore Bank and finally by the Bank of Upper Canada in early 1838. Before this latter bank suspended, it "effected a radical contraction in its discounts and practically ceased to make new loans. It sought and found good profits in the trade in specie and exchange, its position as banker to the provincial government and to the commissary-general of the imperial government giving it exceptionally good command both of coin and of bills."

The government noted that "in the present state of the Frontier the importation of specie by the Banks is not practicable and a specie paying circulation seems therefore for the present not to be possible. The Council is of the opinion that the public will be for the time perfectly safe in the use of the notes of . . . the Chartered Banks of the Province."[52] The period of permissible suspension was ultimately extended to November 1839.

[51]See *Upper Canada Sundries*, 1837, Letter from the Bank of Upper Canada to the Lieutenant-Governor, May 16, 1837: Here the sudden rise in the value of the precious metals is noted. Notes of the Bank of Upper Canada, formerly at a 5% discount in New York, had attained a premium, being redeemable in Upper Canada in British silver. The bank feared that speculators would buy up the bank's notes circulating in the border states (and estimated at £100,000) and present them for redemption. As of the date indicated, the bank's entire note circulation was £201,000, its specie reserves £39,700.
[52]*Ibid.*

In Lower Canada, the Act permitting suspension, although such had in fact occurred in May of 1837, was not passed for almost a year, and provided that the total amount of notes issued by any bank was not to exceed its paid-in capital during the period of suspension. This restriction was somewhat more severe than in Upper Canada, where the limitation was first twice and later three times the paid-in capital of the bank. Suspension in Lower Canada was followed by a vast flood of paper money, issued as a substitute for coin, by persons insolvent ". . . and in all cases irresponsible, to the great defraudment of the public." These notes were all in fractional dollar denominations, and as had been the case in Upper Canada some time earlier, the government was compelled to legislate against the practice. None but chartered or otherwise recognized banks could henceforth issue notes for less than £5 currency.[53] The fractional notes disappeared very quickly when specie payments were resumed.

During the period of the suspension, sterling bills commanded a premium frequently in excess of ten per cent, while New York drafts were only nominally above par.[54] In Lower Canada, the general resumption of specie payments was undertaken in mid-1838, at the same time as similar action occurred in the United States. A second briefer period of suspension occurred late in 1838, and lasted for some eight months. In Upper Canada, the banks were subjected to considerable pressure with a view to having them resume payments before the legally prescribed deadline in November 1839, but objections were offered to such suggestions.[55] In spite of the financial crisis and the political uncertainty of the period, none of the chartered banks in either province failed. Many of them suffered a substantial impairment of capital, the effects of which they felt for some time to come. The basic difficulty, and one which inevitably arises from the relatively undiversified economic activity of the period, was that the banks were ". . . too prone to lend upon accommodation paper, or on real estate under a thin disguise."[56]

[53]This enactment brought a strong protest from the Molson brothers, private bankers in Montreal carrying on an extensive banking business under the name of "Molson's Bank".

[54]*Upper Canada Sundries, 1837, December 2, 1837*: Tenders received for sterling exchange by the Receiver-General of Upper Canada on December 1 ranged from 8% to 15%.

[55]See *Upper Canada State Papers 1839-40, Letter from the Executive Council to Lieutenant Governor Bond Head re resumption of specie*: In this letter, it is hoped that " . . . these institutions will submit to the inconveniences which the measure of resumption would bring upon them, rather than protract the suspension a moment longer than is made by circumstances inevitably necessary." Referring to a note addressed by Bond Head to the banks, the letter went on to say that the governor had gone as far as was advisable under the existing circumstances, as any further attempts at pressure would expose the government to the charge of causing " . . . all the distress and inconvenience to individuals which the necessary contraction of the currency would inevitably produce. The Council advise your Excellency in future not to assent to any measure of suspension which places the resumption of specie payments beyond the control of Government."

[56]See Ross, *op. cit.*, I, p. 23.

Following the union of the two provinces, and with strong opposition from the established banks, Lord Sydenham, the first governor, urged the establishment of a provincial bank of issue, to be known as the "Bank of the Province of Canada". The proposal came at a time of, and was indeed directly related to, critical provincial financial embarrassment. Its main object was to create a ready source of revenue for the government, through the proposed monopoly of note issue which it was to be accorded. Neither discount nor deposit nor other banking functions were to be undertaken. It might issue notes to the amount of £1,000,000, redeemable in specie, one-fourth of such issue to be covered by specie, the remainder by government securities. Any amount in excess of £1,000,000 would require a dollar-for-dollar specie reserve, thus conforming to the "currency school" principle of issue.

Sydenham's proposal provoked widespread discussion, but the influence of the chartered banks, which would have lost their own right to issue notes within two years, was instrumental in defeating the proposal. Typical of the discussion of the merits of the proposal was the more enthusiastic than critical statement of a supporter that ". . . in the hope of clearing the Province from a part of its heavy debt, and at the same time giving us a uniform and steady currency, he [Sydenham] has not hesitated, in spite of all opposition, to bring forward his scheme." In dissent, it was stated that "The proposed Bank of Issue, is without parallel in any age or country. Why, after what we have stated, should this be the first spot on earth, in which the experiment should be made?"[57] The opposition of the banks was of course based on the fact that with deposits still a relatively undeveloped form of bank credit, notes were the means by which the banks met the needs of the business interests, and therefore earned the greater part of their profits.[58] In view of the unfortunate outcome of numerous earlier experiments in the government issue of paper currency, and in view of the desirability of an "elastic" note issue to meet the peculiar needs of Canadian economic conditions, one is inclined to agree that the collapse of the proposed scheme was not a matter for general regret.

In summary of the period from 1841 to Confederation, it has been said that the economics of British preference (i.e., the Corn Laws and Navigation Acts) occupied the first few years, reciprocity the last few years, and that the years 1847-54 were marked by the transition from the one set of influences to the other.[59] Until 1846, the special preference accorded Canadian wheat in the British market lent a great impetus to its growing and milling in this country. The repeal of the Corn Laws, coupled with a modification of the Navigation Acts which deprived Canadian shipping of its monopoly in the Canadian-

---

[57]Montreal *Gazette*, September 4, 1841.
[58]Sydenham on one occasion referred to these banks as "unlimited paper mills".
[59]Adam Shortt, "Economic History, 1840-1867", in *Canada and Its Provinces*, V, p. 188.

British West Indies trade, contributed greatly to the depression of 1847-50.[60] The necessary general re-orientation of Canadian trade was facilitated by the 1854 Reciprocity Treaty with the United States. Quite apart from its stimulating effects through the markets provided for the sale and purchase of extractive commodities, the Canadian economy benefited from the additional demand for agricultural produce created by the Crimean War, and from the railroad construction which had already given an impetus to the boom before 1854. Although the railroads were for the most part financed by private capital, they were heavily subsidized by the provinces and municipalities, with consequent heavy increases in public debts.[61] The problems posed by these financial burdens were a most important factor in the accomplishment of Confederation in 1867.

The railroad construction and other developmental projects of the period were of course heavily dependent upon external capital, and as has continued to be the case to the present time, Canadian prosperity was at the mercy of external influences. Thus a financial crisis in Britain in 1857 soon passed to Canada, and to the United States as well, through the stoppage of heavy capital investment in those countries.

The period between 1841 and 1867 was marked by substantial advances in Canadian commercial banking, through the accomplishment of greater stability, versatility and diversification of risks. A thriving export trade in wheat and timber provided a profitable outlet for banking funds, and by the 1860's, agriculture and forest products represented 4/5 of the province's exports. These were supplemented by barley, rye and cattle. Wheat-growing was centred in the western part of the province, and exports of this commodity went both to Britain and to the United States (during the Civil War). In lumbering, the production of square timber for the British market was giving way to sawn-

[60]The Bank of Montreal established numerous branches in Canada West after 1840. With the advent of the depression at the end of the decade, the bank sustained considerable losses, " . . . the immediate cause being the unexpected but great and very sudden decline in prices of agricultural productions, timber, and colonial built ships." See *The Centenary of the Bank of Montreal* (Montreal: Bank of Montreal), 1917, p. 39. Since the entire country suffered severely, the bank found it necessary to reduce its dividend to six per cent. Twelve per cent had not been uncommon in the preceding years.

[61]The construction, both of canals and railroads, involved the governments of British North America in heavy debt. The 1840's were years of canal-building and the St. Lawrence system was completed by 1850. The project was a financial disappointment as were the newly constructed railways, designed in the beginning to supplement Great Lakes transportation. The Grand Trunk from Montreal to Toronto was completed in 1856, and to Sarnia in 1859. The long-cherished hope of the commercial interests in the provinces of Canada of channelling trade from the interior of the continent via Montreal and the St. Lawrence route had clearly failed. At the time of Confederation, government investments in transportation facilities in the province of Canada accounted for 60% of the total provincial and municipal debt, and a substantial part of the governments' current revenues was required to service this debt. The completion of the Intercolonial Railway from Halifax to Montreal in 1876 provided the first all-Canadian rail connection to a year-round Canadian port. None of these early transportation projects were paying propositions, a principal cause being the competition of the United States lines.

lumber, which supplied the rapidly developing United States market. Closely allied to lumbering was a flourishing shipbuilding industry at Quebec city, the most important manufacturing enterprise in the province. Until mid-century, most manufacturing in the province was small-scale and localized—the common examples were grist-mills, blacksmithing, carriage shops, tanneries, boot and shoe factories, breweries, distilleries and the beginnings of textile manufacturing. Other examples were saw-mills, flour-mills and cheese factories.

The technological revolution near the mid-century marked the arrival of the "steam, rail and steel" era, and manufacturing expanded rapidly in this new direction. Foundries became common, and the production of agricultural implements, railroad rolling stock, etc., was begun. Nevertheless, at the time of Confederation, the combined population of all British North America did not exceed 3½ million, of which almost 3 million was "rural" population. Montreal, the largest city, had 100,000 inhabitants, but the country was basically one of many small scattered and isolated communities, where self-sufficiency was common.

In the period preceding Confederation, the importance of deposits as a means of payment remained small, except in the cities, where banks served the wholesale, manufacturing and financial sections of the community. But particularly in Canada West, it was the note circulation which was predominant. The behaviour of chartered bank issues, typical of later years, was already developing in this early era. Thus, there was " . . . a wide and regular expansion of the note issues in the autumn to the highest volume of the twelve month; thence a rapid contraction in the early winter which persisted until the low point was reached again in May. Increased provision for borrowers' needs was furnished by the banks without other cost than paying out notes. It was a cheap currency, this issue against general assets; but without the profits of issue, borrowers in the western country would have had to pay more for their credits, or in many cases, to contrive to manage in their neighbourhood without a bank."[62]

This broad seasonal fluctuation in bank notes outstanding of course concealed numerous local variations. One local observer noted that in what had formerly been Upper Canada (Canada West), the demand for money was heaviest during and following the harvest, and in the early spring, "to gather, house and subsequently to carry to a market or stopping point, the produce of the country". In Lower Canada (Canada East), the seasonal demands were smaller, but the payment of import duties in the spring and fall of the year likewise involved increased bank accommodation. Another witness, the cashier of the Quebec Bank, observed that while the currency demands might not coincide either in timing or in magnitude as between the shipping ports and the agricultural areas, "the periods thereof are well known to practical bankers, who provide accordingly". In the ports, expansion was usually greatest in mid-December, followed by con-

[62]Breckenridge, *op. cit.*, p. 87.

tinuous contraction to mid-May, after which time expansion again began; in the agricultural areas, expansion reached its peak about mid-November, followed by contraction to mid-January, after which expansion again got under way until the opening of navigation, followed by a rapid contraction. "A slight expansion commences when the clip of wool is brought to market, and from then until the harvest begins to move, a steady contraction takes place."

In 1866 and 1867, the difference between the maximum and minimum bank-note circulation in the united province of Canada was twenty per cent in each year; the average difference for the period 1858-67 was twenty-six per cent during the year.[63]

Immediately following union, however, there was little money of any kind in circulation in Upper Canada. Barter was widespread, and the exchange of surplus agricultural products for the dry goods and groceries of the storekeeper was common practice.[64] Complaints against the general lack of banking accommodation were widespread, especially among the commercial interests, and the earlier discussion centring about the merits of a provincial bank of issue began to be revived.[65] In 1841, several changes were introduced into the charters of the banks. Double liability of shareholders became general, and a tax of one per cent per annum was imposed on the excess of bank notes in circulation beyond the amount of specie, legal tender and government securities held. This bank-note tax was protested by the Bank of Upper Canada a short time later on the ground that it would have an adverse effect upon investment in banks, since the tax claimed "the enormous proportion of one-twelfth of the whole realized profits of some of the Banks". Needless to say, the protest was of little avail. To relieve merchants from fluctuations in the value of currency between the East and West parts of the province, the Bank of Montreal, in 1843, announced that it was reducing its charges on the negotiation of all drafts, and would negotiate paper at one per cent on all parts of Canada West east of Hamilton. It would also receive deposits in the notes of Canada West banks at one-half of one per cent discount, and bank cheques on Kingston or Toronto at the same rate. The Bank of British North America announced similar rates.

In 1846, the Colonial Office despatched a letter of instructions to the government of Canada, stating the regulations and conditions which should be included in subsequent charters or legislative enactments relating to the incorporation of banking companies in that province. This letter represented just one

[63]See Dominion of Canada, First Report of the Committee on Banking and Currency (Ottawa), 1869, pp. 32-5.

[64]See Bank of Montreal, *op. cit.*, p. 37-8: "A most obliging man was the storekeeper. He gave unlimited credit. If the account was overdrawn, he took a little promissory note. When that matured, it might be renewed, with compound interest added. When that fell due, if not paid he took a little mortgage. And as a last resort, in many instances, he took a little farm."

[65]*Kingston Chronicle*, July, 1842: "Bank managers may have good reasons for their stringent policy, but their contraction of circulation has forced many persons, previously opposed, to consider the propriety of a Provincial Institution."

phase of a continuing effort exerted by Britain to restrain the most glaring abuses in the banking development of Canada. Most of the provisions of the letter were sound, and were subsequently (if not already) established.

The financial difficulties of the new government culminated in a crisis in 1848, the solution of which brought provincial paper again to the fore. It was decided to issue "debentures" for sums under £10, payable on demand at the Treasury, and receivable for all debts of the government, including customs dues. When these were returned to the Treasury, it was provided that they could be re-issued, as circumstances warranted. The banks were of course bitterly opposed to what they regarded as an insidious attack upon their prerogatives, and claimed that such a venture was illegal, a view for which they received support from the courts. This problem was overcome by appropriate legislation in the following year, and a government note issue was thus established in practice. The currency debentures were issued in the form of bank notes payable one year after date, and bearing 6% interest. With the return of normal economic conditions in 1850, and the restoration of normal channels of borrowing, the practice was discontinued. The experiment represented one of the first instances of the introduction of government paper money into the currency systems of British North America. (The episode in Nova Scotia, beginning in 1812, has already been noted, while the "Army Bills" were of a somewhat different character.)

The crisis of 1847-50 had resulted in many commercial failures in the province, and many of the banks found their capital substantially impaired, although none failed during this period. But as usual in time of crisis, the banks reduced their discounts, and the merchants tended to blame them for the greatest part of their difficulties. Coupled with the successful issue of government debentures and the existence of a "free banking" system in New York state, this led to a further revival of agitation for alternative note-issue arrangements. Specifically, it was proposed that the Canadian banking system be converted to a "free banking" system. Until this time, each bank in Canada operated under the particular set of regulations embodied in its own charter, but the terms of the Free Banking Act, passed in 1850, were to apply to banks generally. It was provided that individuals, general partners or joint-stock companies might organize banks, £25,000 being specified as the minimum capital. With the intention of achieving a greater diffusion of banking facilities, the Act sought to establish relatively small "unit" banks, which would not have the privilege of opening branches. Banks operating under the provisions of the Act were to deposit public securities with the Receiver-General and were to receive in return their own bank notes, printed under government direction.[66] Any chartered bank might partially or completely surrender its existing circulation privilege

---

[66]All parties, whether individuals or corporations, who complied with the provisions of the Act and delivered $100,000 (minimum capitalization) of public securities to the government (these to bear interest at 6%) would receive a like amount in bank notes. The government guaranteed note redemption in the event that the bank failed, notes being accorded prior claim against assets in such eventuality.

under the "unsecured" system and avail itself of the new arrangement, thereby partially or completely avoiding the one per cent tax applicable to unsecured issues. The only bank to avail itself of this opportunity was the Bank of British North America, in order that it might issue notes in the $1 (5s.) and $2 (10s.) denominations permitted by the Act. Under the terms of its imperial charter, it had previously been restricted to a minimum denomination of £1.

Very little additional use was made of the Free Banking Act. Several institutions were organized under its provisions, but the only two of these to have more than a temporary existence reverted to the conventional type of charter.[67] It was therefore not successful as a means of diffusing bank facilities. From the viewpoint of the government, the Act had promised both a "sound" basis for the issue of bank notes (the "elasticity" of the existing system of unsecured issue would have been impossible), and a most welcome demand for public securities. It would have provided a note issue similar to that which later emerged under the National Bank Act in the United States, but it was subject to one of the weaknesses of the latter Act, that the issue of notes was too expensive. The bonds deposited with government were to bear interest at 6%, but since they could generally be purchased below par, their effective yield was above this figure. Moreover, the small banks contemplated by the Act could rarely have employed profitably the minimum capital proposed. Although the proposal was unpopular, and the Canadian banks did not respond, the provisions of the Free Banking Act relating to note issue were not repealed until the Provincial Note Act of 1866,[68] and the Act itself was not repealed until the Bank Act of 1880. The Act represented the first instance of the introduction of "general" banking legislation in Canada, and of legislation which would have tied the issue of bank notes to government securities.

During the 1850's, the general economic prosperity of the province was accompanied by a great expansion in the operations of established banks and a rapid increase in the number of new banks. In the course of granting authorization for increases in the capitalization of six existing banks, the government introduced a requirement that they hold a minimum of one-tenth of their paid-up capital in provincial securities. This form of asset was yet to become substantial in chartered bank portfolios. As already indicated, lumbering, mining, the iron industry, the financing of exports and the general industrial growth of the St. Lawrence basin involved the supplying of larger amounts of capital. The government did not always investigate the new applications for charters as thoroughly as might have been desirable, and a number of fraudulent bank promotion scandals developed. The crisis of 1857, which brought panic in

---

[67]Six banks in all were incorporated under the Free Banking Act. These included the Bank of British North America, two banks which survived only from 1856 to 1858 and three others which eventually became chartered banks. Of these latter three, one had its charter repealed in 1863, one (the Niagara District Bank) merged with the Imperial Bank in 1875 and the third continued in operation as Molson's Bank.

[68]See 29-30 *Victoria*, cap. 10, sec. 16.

England, the suspension of specie payments in New York and the inevitable contraction of banking accommodation in Canada, revealed that speculation had entered the operations of the banks. Merchants with bank loans wished extensions of credit since they could not collect their own debts, but the collapse of land values rendered bank-held real estate unsaleable, and important other assets of the banks (railroad securities) had also depreciated. The banks were therefore compelled to curtail their operations, at a most inopportune time, in order to protect their note issues.

Coinciding with widespread commercial failure, the collapse of the real-estate boom, the fall in price level and two years of particularly bad harvests (1857 and 1858), this monetary stringency, while undoubtedly contributing to the general hardship, not unnaturally was assigned the major share of responsibility for the province's economic ills. One result was that discussion of an irredeemable currency became increasingly prominent. In 1859, a government Committee was appointed to investigate the banking and currency system of the province. It sent out a questionnaire which was answered in detail by various chartered banks. Some criticisms provided by the Bank of Montreal stated that (1) minimum capitalization was too small; (2) there was no obligation to hold any specie reserves; i.e., the bank believed that note issues should be governed not only by paid-up capital but by specie reserves, and that such reserves should be required for deposits as well as notes; (3) no requirement to publish names of shareholders periodically (important in connection with the double liability of shareholders and for unpaid stock). Complaint was also voiced against the 7% maximum interest rate provision: "Experience has shown that the proper adjustment of the rate of interest is the true method of regulating the credit and currency of the country, and the community as well as the Banks suffered much during the late pressure in being compelled to keep the rate of discount at an unnaturally low level."

In 1860, following the period of widespread depression, the provincial government found itself in one of its recurring periods of acute financial embarrassment, and Galt, the Minister of Finance, revived the earlier proposal for a provincial bank of issue.[69] This proposal was again opposed by the chartered banks and failed for substantially the same reasons as before. It would have provided for the establishment of a provincial treasury department with a monopoly of paper-money issue, the redemption of such money in specie to be guaranteed by the government. At least one-fifth of the authorized issue would be backed by specie reserves, and one-fifth by government securities. Any extension of issue beyond the authorized amount would be backed dollar for dollar by specie or securities. The Free Banking Act was to be repealed, and the right to issue notes denied to all banks subsequently chartered. The chartered banks

[69]The proposal was similar to that advanced by Sydenham in 1841. The influence of government debt upon the trend of early banking proposals and developments will have been readily apparent to the reader.

already issuing notes might continue to do so until the expiration of their charters, at which time the right would be withdrawn, when they might obtain a supply of the new provincial notes equal to their average note circulation. On these notes, the banks would be required to pay interest, as well as to deposit reserves with the treasury.[70]

This system obviously provided very little inducement to the chartered banks to support the proposed new basis of note issue, and the bankers, as usual, emphasized the great social loss which would be involved through the removal of the "elasticity" of the existing arrangements. The resolution was permitted to lapse temporarily, but pressure of events brought a reconsideration of the whole plan several years later. Following the suspension of specie payments by the American banks in 1862, during the Civil War, a substantial part of Canadian notes circulating below the border were returned to their issuing banks for redemption. Many of these banks, suffering from depleted specie reserves, restricted their advances, as was customary in time of crisis, and thereby prompted renewed criticism of their operations. Combined with the financial difficulties in which the government found itself in 1865, these popular and by no means unjustified outbursts led to Galt's reintroduction of the scheme for a government monopoly of note issue.[71]

To lessen the opposition of the chartered banks, Galt now proposed that upon the surrender of their note issues, they should receive five per cent interest per annum on the average amount of their circulation until the date of expiry of their charters, and that they be given until the beginning of 1868 to complete the withdrawal of their notes. In place of the chartered bank issues, government paper to the maximum amount of $8 million was to be authorized, redeemable in specie. The first $5 million of this issue was to be secured 20% by specie, the remainder by government securities; any issue in excess of $5 million, 25% by specie and the remainder by government bonds. In a further compromise, Galt agreed that if $5 million could be obtained from the banks as a government loan, use would not be made of the note-issuing powers to be incorporated in the measure. On this basis, the proposed measure was enacted, and the government, after several earlier attempts, had finally established the legal basis for issuing paper currency. Commenting on this "triumph", one sceptical observer noted that with a very large floating debt, and with its debentures listed at a 15% discount, the government "could not afford to consider the principles of finance

---

[70]Interest payable on the notes obtained by a chartered bank was to be 3% on three-fifths of the total, 4% on the remainder. Reserves deposited with the Treasury, in the form of specie and government securities, must equal two-fifths of the total note circulation.

[71]In 1864, the government account was transferred to the Bank of Montreal from the Bank of Upper Canada, because of the increasingly precarious position of the latter institution. Little cash accompanied the transfer, although the bank was indebted to the government to the amount of $1½ million. In 1865, the government was still unable to withdraw funds from the Bank of Upper Canada, and eventually lost heavily upon its failure.

too closely". This shrewd observation is of course capable of widespread application.

Upon failing to obtain the full $5 million loan which it sought, the government in 1866 arranged with its financial agent, the Bank of Montreal, for the gradual surrender of that bank's note issue, to be replaced by government paper.[72] The Bank of Montreal was by far the largest of the Canadian banks, and was a creditor of the government to the extent of some $2 million. It must also have owned a minimum of $600,000 in government securities (one-tenth of its capitalization of $6 million). It was therefore in a particularly favourable position to change the basis of its note issue, and did so, thereby becoming not only the government's financial agent but its note-issuing agent also. This increased the friction between it and its less opulent competitors, some of which reluctantly agreed to hold small quantities of the new currency, which, being legal reserve, could be substituted for specie. This marked the beginning of a gradual substitution of government paper for the specie reserve earlier held by the banks, with the responsibility of maintaining the national specie reserve shifting from the banks to the government.[73]

As a result of the rapid expansion of banking facilities in the 1850's and 1860's, there were nineteen chartered banks operating in the province of Canada at the time of Confederation. With head offices in Montreal were the Bank of Montreal, City Bank, Bank of British North America (imperial charter), La Banque du Peuple, Molson's Bank, La Banque Nationale, La Banque Jacques Cartier, Merchants' Bank and the Mechanics' Bank; in Toronto, the Bank of Toronto, Royal Canadian Bank and the Canadian Bank of Commerce; in Quebec, the Quebec Bank and the Union Bank of Lower Canada; in Kingston, the Commercial Bank (its failure was imminent); in St. Catharines, the Niagara District Bank; in Hamilton, the Gore Bank; in Bowmanville, the Ontario Bank; in Sherbrooke, the Eastern Townships Bank. The authorized capital of these banks ranged from the Bank of Montreal's $6 million to the $400,000 authorized for the Niagara District Bank and for the Eastern Townships Bank. The aggregate exceeded $37 million, of which some $28 million was paid-up. The banks' note circulation exceeded $8 million and their deposits approximated $29 million, the relative importance of the latter form of liability having increased appreciably in the preceding quarter-century. The major assets of the banks included discounts, $57 million; coin, bullion and provincial notes, $8 million;

---

[72]The Bank of Montreal found the new arrangement very lucrative, and as the government's financial agent in the issue and redemption of provincial notes, it succeeded in claiming a 1% commission on the average circulation of these notes, whether held by itself or other banks.

[73]For details of the exceptionally strong position in which the Bank of Montreal found itself at Confederation, see Shortt, "Currency and Banking, 1840-67", in *Canada and Its Provinces*, V, pp. 287-8. Envious of its new prestige, its competitors paid it " . . . the usual compliments of respect, fear, jealousy and abuse."

government securities $6 million.[74] In addition, there were four chartered banks in New Brunswick and four in Nova Scotia.[75]

While public criticism of bank operations tended to centre upon the perverse fluctuations in their note issues, there was abundant evidence that other aspects of bank activity were not beyond improvement. An illustration of this fact was provided by the failure of the Bank of Upper Canada in 1866, the first major bank disaster in that province. The fundamental cause of its insolvency was the collapse of the land speculation boom in 1857 and 1858 and the subsequent depression. The bank had extended too much accommodation based on inflated real estate values and it was estimated that at the time of its failure, it owned land in practically every county of Upper Canada.[76] It had also supported the milling industry imprudently. As the economy of Canada had expanded, shifting lines of development resulted in the bank being overshadowed by its newer and more rigorous competitors. The prestige of the government account enabled it to retain the confidence of the public for some years after its unfortunate real estate losses, but even this prop was removed in 1864, and shortly thereafter there passed from the scene the earliest chartered bank in the province of Upper Canada.

The second major bank failure, that of the Commercial Bank, in 1867, occurred for reasons similar to that of the Bank of Upper Canada, i.e., a too great discounting of "uncertain" paper, which ultimately was based on land, and served further to emphasize the risks attendant upon banking in a pioneer community. Although both of these banks had been associated with the financing of various railroad enterprises in the 1850's, the Commercial Bank did not engage in land speculation on the scale of the Bank of Upper Canada, and not having been favoured with the financial resources provided by the government deposit, it lacked the same opportunity to make so extensive and ruinous a failure as its favoured rival. The loss of confidence created by the failure of this rival undoubtedly contributed to the demise of the Commercial Bank.

As against these two notable failures at the time of Confederation, certain accomplishments of this period should be noted. In 1852, the Bank of Montreal opened an agency in Chicago to facilitate Canadian participation in the substantial produce trade of the American west. This marked the beginning of the extensive network of foreign agencies and branches subsequently developed by the chartered banks.

In 1859, an "Act Granting Additional Facilities in Commercial Transactions"

---

[74]For further details, see the *Canada Gazette*, Vol. I, No. 1 (1867), p. 52.

[75]See note, *infra*.

[76]Until this time, the bulk of bank advances were based on so-called "accommodation" paper, where the borrower tendered his own note, backed by one or more endorsers, as collateral for the loan. Borrowers endorsed paper for one another at different banks, and this procedure had led to substantial bank losses in the late 1850's. Thereafter, the bankers attempted to relate their advances more closely to "the production and distribution of commodities", i.e., to the commercial loan theory of banking.

represented the first statutory provision in Canada concerning bills of lading, warehouse receipts and the application of such to banks generally. Prior to this date, the right of any bank to acquire such documents as security for advances depended upon the terms of its particular charter, and upon general law. The Act of 1859 introduced to all chartered banks the "pledge" provisions which have since become such a distinctive feature of the Canadian banking system. These provisions furnished the basis for the extending of bank loans to certain classes of producers on special collateral arrangements adapted to their particular needs.[77] Subsequent amendments in 1861 and 1865 broadened the category of persons entitled to issue receipts eligible as collateral for bank advances, and this principle was extended to a widening range of commodities from time to time. The arrangement has remained a permanent and unique feature of Canadian banking legislation, in that it provides a list of occupations in which persons are entitled to apply for bank advances upon the security of their own goods in their own possession, upon a simple form of receipt deposited with the bank. From its inception, the legislation facilitated commercial and business transactions, by providing the banks with a form of security which promised reasonable safety for their loans.

Thus, in the Province of Canada, by the time of Confederation, the banking system, subject not only to external influences (banking developments in the United States, instructions from the British Colonial Office, the Scottish background of many Canadian bankers, etc.), but to the particular requirements of Canadian economic development, had already developed many of the features which have remained to the present day. These included the foregoing "pledge" provisions, directly related to the problem of financing the primarily extractive production of the pioneer economy; branch banking, which had definite advantages in attracting banking capital, and which in all probability made possible a wider dissemination of banking facilities than could otherwise have been accomplished;[78] the unsecured note issue, which was relatively inexpensive to

---

[77]The Act of 1859 provided that ". . . notwithstanding anything to the contrary in the charter of any bank in the Province, any bill of lading or any receipt given by a warehouseman, miller, wharfinger, master of a vessel or carrier, for cereal grains, goods, wares or merchandise, stored or deposited . . . might by endorsement thereon by the owner of, or persons entitled to receive such cereal grains, goods, wares or merchandise, be transferred to any incorporated or chartered bank as collateral security for the due payment of any bill of exchange or note discounted by such bank in the regular course of its banking business, and being so endorsed, should vest in the bank all the right and title of the endorser."

[78]Concerning the contribution of pioneer banking to the economic development of Canada, it has been stated that " . . . the history of the early banks in Canada shows that the chief reason for their existence was the service they performed by exchanging their own credit obligations in the form of bank-notes for the credit obligations of their customers, which, however good they might be, were prevented by their very form from passing current as money. As the note circulation was limited mainly by the capital, the bigger the capital the better, provided that loans could be made to a sufficient extent to utilize both capital and note circulation." See Ross, *op. cit.*, II, pp. 129-30. This latter philosophy led to periodic and disastrous over-expansion of bank advances.

provide, and which exhibited the characteristic of "elasticity" so generally lauded by the bankers. This characteristic was by no means an unmixed blessing, for in an era when the relative importance of deposits was still small and when bank accommodation was customarily extended through the note issue, the contraction of this issue in periods of economic adversity (as in 1837 and 1857) appreciably aggravated the depression. In such periods, the "inelasticity" of a government currency would have been most useful, a circumstance which suggests that the general interest might have best been served by a paper issue including both government and bank notes.

By 1867, the double liability of shareholders in the event of insolvency was applicable to all banks except the Bank of British North America, operating under an imperial charter, and La Banque du Peuple, an institution organized "en commandité", the principal partners bearing unlimited liability. In general, notes could be issued to an amount equal to the bank's paid-up capital, plus its holdings of specie and government securities, with total liabilities not to exceed three times its capitalization. Included among the powers of all banks was the right to deal in gold and silver coin or bullion and exchange, and in bills of exchange, the discounting of promissory notes, bills and negotiable securities, and to engage in any other such trade "as legitimately belonged to the business of banking". They were expressly prohibited from dealing in, buying, selling or bartering goods, wares and merchandise, or engaging in other business transactions. Lending money on the security of land was forbidden, although mortgages could be taken and held by way of additional security on advances previously established. This provision, as has already been noted, was subject to widespread contravention in the pre-Confederation period. The maximum permissible rate of interest, which could be taken in advance, had been established at seven per cent, a provision whose interpretation was to cause much controversy and discontent in later years.

In 1867, "An Act Respecting Banks" was applied to the new Dominion, and it extended the charters of the various banks incorporated in the several provinces before Confederation. In effect, it represented a consolidation of the various acts relating to banking which had been passed in the Province of Canada, and was a temporary measure to govern banking until the passage of the Bank Act of 1871, a general act relating to banks and banking in Canada. But before turning to the post-Confederation era, we shall note briefly the development of monetary and banking institutions in the Maritimes in the immediately preceding decades.

### B. *The Maritimes*

In New Brunswick, subscriptions for a proposed bank had been invited by merchants of Saint John as early as 1820.[79] The need for such a bank was viewed, as usual, in terms of its contribution to the economic development of the

[79]For details of the proposed institution, see the *Saint John Gazette*, April 19, 1820.

colony through the providing of a satisfactory domestic means of payment. Prior to this time, the circulating medium of the province was similar to that of the provinces of Canada, consisting in the main of such miscellaneous and battered coinage as could be retained in spite of a generally adverse trade balance. Prior to 1808, the province had issued a very small quantity of treasury notes principally as a financial expedient, but these had entered into circulation. Subsequent modest expansion of these interest-bearing issues suggested the desirability of a full-fledged domestic paper circulation provided by a chartered bank.[80]

The charter for the proposed bank was granted later in 1820, and the Bank of New Brunswick opened its doors at the beginning of 1821 as the first chartered bank in British North America. It will be remembered, however, that three institutions had already begun banking operations several years earlier in Lower Canada, and the provisions of their Articles of Association undoubtedly shaped the content of the charter of the Bank of New Brunswick. The success of the bank soon invited competitors, and by 1867, four chartered banks were in operation in the province.[81] The demands for banking accommodation reflected the relatively simple organization of New Brunswick's economy, based almost entirely on its forest resources. At the time of Confederation, the region was described as virtually one great lumber camp, with its forest products (excluding ships) comprising about 70% of the province's exports. Subsistence fishing and farming were common, but apart from these activities, lumbering with its allied shipbuilding and carrying trade provided the inhabitants with their livelihood.

In Prince Edward Island, the scarcity of specie had prompted experimentation in the issue of government bills from a very early date. Writing in 1786, one Islander had noted that the lack of a suitable coinage subjected people with small debts to many hardships, but that until exports could be increased, there was no way to remedy the situation, unless a law were enacted " . . . to make certain produce of the Island, such as Fish, Grain, Lumber, etc., among ourselves as legal tender under certain well guarded restrictions".[82] In the absence of an adequate means of payment, barter was of course customary. The foreign coins of various denominations which found their way to the Island were neither plentiful nor satisfactory, and the usual problems of rating the individual pieces were encountered. As in the other provinces of British North America, the

---

[80]In 1808, all treasury notes in circulation were recalled, and a new issue of some £1,500, in denominations of one, two and four dollars was introduced, bearing interest at 5% per annum to maturity, when payment might be taken in gold, silver or new notes. In 1818, the notes still in circulation were supplemented by a new issue of £10,000, this time in denominations ranging from 5s. to £5.

[81]The Bank of New Brunswick (Saint John), St. Stephen's Bank (St. Stephen), The People's Bank of New Brunswick (Fredericton) and the Commercial Bank of New Brunswick (Saint John). The paid-up capital of the banks in New Brunswick and Nova Scotia ranged from $50,000 to $60,000, being considerably smaller than those in Canada.

[82]*Colonial Office Records*, P.E.I., C., Vol. 2, November 8, 1786.

legal money of account was Halifax currency, " . . . a purely mythical and political standard, serving to screen the use of Spanish or United States coins under cover of a loyalty standard of pounds, shilling and pence."[83]

Starting with a £500 issue of its bills in 1790, the government repeated the process at intervals during the following several decades.[84] By the late 1820's, the circulating medium had been supplemented by Bank of England tokens introduced during the recent war, six-shilling, three-shilling and four-penny pieces, old smooth shillings and half-crowns, and some French silver. In 1836, a Charlottetown merchant circulated leather notes, promising to pay 10s. or one-half dollar (Spanish) for every four such notes. To reduce the difficulty of keeping Spanish dollars on the Island, the centres were punched out, to make them unacceptable elsewhere. The small centre pieces were then used as shillings, until it was discovered that they were worth more as scrap silver.

With subsequent issues of government bills, their convertibility was not maintained, and the customary unfortunate depreciation in terms of specie occurred. The government defended its policy with the now thread-bare argument that all the notes had been required for the purposes of commerce, and that their issue had therefore not been excessive. A contemporary observer was thereupon moved to comment that ". . . what ideas the learned lawyer [Solicitor-General of the province] may have of 'excess' we cannot determine, but we should presume, that when, with both hands full of paper, no man can command cash, the proportions are not very well preserved."[85]

The economy of Prince Edward Island had become well integrated with the rest of the Maritimes because, unlike the inhabitants of Nova Scotia and New Brunswick, the Islanders had turned their backs to the sea and had concentrated on farming. It had become a highly specialized agricultural area, with potatoes the chief crop, and it was able to export its surpluses to its neighbouring provinces, to help to satisfy their growing demands for foodstuffs. Nevertheless, fishing and shipbuilding (until the technological revolution in the mid-nineteenth century) were important secondary activities.

In the absence of banks, credit in this primarily agricultural area was necessarily provided by the merchants to the farmers and to the fishermen. Among the "informal" credit arrangements of the time was the self-designated "Bank of Rustico". Its capitalization was £1,000 currency, and a thrifty farmer was the president, general-manager, teller and sole stockholder. "It frequently happened that a customer had to go out to the field and bring the cashier away from the tail of the plough."[86] The Bank of Prince Edward Island was chartered in 1855, the Union Bank of Prince Edward Island in 1863. The latter institution explained that ". . . this bank is formed to supply an addition to the money

---

[83]Ross, *op. cit.*, II, p. 127.     [84]*Colonial Office Records*, P.E.I., *op. cit.*
[85]*Halifax Nova Scotian*, October 1, 1835.
[86]See *The Centenary of the Bank of Montreal, op. cit.*, p. 38.

circulation of this Island, the want of which has for some time been sensibly felt. It is the natural consequence of an increasing population, an expanding Commerce, and of the enlarged production of an industrious and energetic people.[87] It was further noted that the rival Bank of Prince Edward Island had been organized " . . . under the pressure of a similar necessity."[88] These two pioneer institutions were followed a short time later by the Summerside Bank and the Merchants Bank of Prince Edward Island. The shareholders of the latter assumed triple liability, but the charter was otherwise similar to that of the other banks on the Island and elsewhere in British North America. The chief differences between the early banks in the Maritimes and those in the Province of Canada were to be found in their smaller capitalization and their more restricted fields of operation. The Maritimes banks confined their activities pretty much to the discounting of mercantile paper, and the occasional granting of accommodation by means of cash credits. Although they originated independently, they duplicated many of the experiences of the banks in the upper province.

In Nova Scotia, efforts to obtain a charter for a bank began at least as early as 1811.[89] This, and a number of subsequent attempts, ended in failure, either because it was proposed that the notes of the institution be irredeemable or that a monopoly of note issue be granted, or because adverse effects on the outstanding volume of government treasury bills were feared. The issue of this provincial paper, which as already described, began in 1812, was not adequately controlled, and suffered severe depreciation, but its existence undoubtedly delayed the appearance of a chartered bank for some considerable time. A public meeting of Halifax merchants in 1822 had observed that the general interests of the province would be beneficially promoted by the establishment of a bank, provided that " . . . it is founded on the only principles that warrant confidence in such institutions—these are—the actual payment of its whole capital previous to its commencing business—the discharge of its engagements in specie, and the limitation of its debts and issues within a reasonable amount."[90] It was claimed that only from such an institution could the circulating capital so urgently needed by the province be furnished.[91] One merchant had pointed out a short

---

[87]*The Charlottetown Islander,* April 17, 1863.     [88]*Ibid.*

[89]See the *Quebec Mercury,* April 8, 1811. This issue quotes extracts from "a late Halifax Paper", dealing with the dissatisfactory state of the means of payment in Nova Scotia, and presenting a proposal by a group of Halifax merchants to establish a bank, the capitalization of which was to be £50,000 currency.

[90]*Halifax Nova Scotian,* February 22, 1832.

[91]The first half of the nineteenth century was a period of economic prosperity in the Maritimes, except for brief intervals, e.g., the recession following the War of 1812 and that of the late thirties. It was in such periods of economic difficulty, however, that widespread discussion of currency matters occurred. Lumbering and shipbuilding provided the basis for the expanding Maritimes economy, in a period of "wood and wind" transportation technology. See C. R. Young, H. A. Innis and J. H. Dales, *Engineering and Society* (Toronto: University of Toronto Press), 1946, p. 192.

time earlier that every business in Halifax had two great problems, the first being difficulty in selling its goods, the second in getting paid afterwards.[92] Much coin was drained off to the United States, leaving nothing as a medium of commerce. The answer to this situation was held to be good bank paper, the quantity of which (and again Adam Smith enters at his worst) "should never exceed the amount of gold and silver coin that is required for the circulation of the country. If it does this, the issuer will soon find it out by the rapid return of the surplus, to be exchanged for coin."[93] Despite these arguments designed to support the petition placed before the government, it was thought not "prudent" to undertake the experiment at that particular time.

Stemming from the reluctance of the government to sanction a chartered bank was the appearance of the Halifax Banking Company in 1825, organized as a private partnership with unlimited liability by a small group of wealthy and politically influential merchants. Its moving spirit was one Enos Collins, who had accumulated a fortune in privateering operations before the British conquest, and who subsequently set up a private lending business to afford an outlet for his surplus capital. Out of his discounting (mostly of officers' naval bills) and foreign exchange operations arose the nucleus of the new banking firm. Collins apparently had large holdings of both foreign and domestic funds, and it was said that he made money out of exchange, "both coming and going", in Boston, New York and Halifax. The firm issued its own notes, and won the absolute confidence of the business community from the very beginning. In addition to its main interest in exchange and discounting operations, it accepted deposits.[94] Until 1832, the bank held a monopoly and was comparable politically to the Bank of Upper Canada in its early years, in that five of its eight members dominated the Legislative Council of Nova Scotia. These members exerted all their influence toward the maintenance of the bank's monopoly, and several additional attempts to obtain a charter for a second bank were defeated by the Council, after having passed the House of Assembly.[95] By 1832, the Halifax Banking Company had reached a crisis in its operations. Its outstanding success and its entrenched political position had aroused enemies. It was accused of unjust discrimination among its clients, of autocratic methods, and of unfair

[92]*Halifax Free Press*, April 4, 1820. The first difficulty was alleged to be due to the universal depression of commerce "occasioned by the sudden return of the affairs of the world from an unnatural to the natural state, and . . . not therefore within the compass of our ability wholly to remedy." The latter was due to the great scarcity of the circulating medium, and to the uncertain state of credit because of the lack of a bank, "which is the touchstone of a merchant's stability." [93]*Ibid.*

[94]Breckenridge comments on the Halifax Banking Company as follows: "This Bank was a closed corporation; it had no charter; its capital was not known; the amount of its notes in circulation and its liability to the public were matters of speculation; but, notwithstanding . . . it speedily worked its way into the favour of the business community to whom it furnished the means of conducting their banking operations with comfort and safety." See Breckenridge, *op. cit.*, p. 50.

[95]See *The Bank of Nova Scotia, 1832-1932* (Toronto: Bank of Nova Scotia), 1932, pp. 24-5.

practice in redeeming its notes. It had been provided that its notes would be redeemable "in specie or provincial paper". The public thought this meant that the bank was obligated to provide both methods, but the bank's interpretation was whichever it chose. It commonly chose the latter method, paying out the depreciated treasury bills of the province. Its monopolistic position was condemned, since "the whole trade of the Town [is] at the mercy of eight men, who have the power to put a total stop to the business of every one."[96]

Finally, in 1832, after a bitter political struggle, a charter was authorized for another Halifax bank, and the Bank of Nova Scotia was founded in that year.[97] In this charter, the provision for double liability appeared for the first time in any bank in British North America, and soon became general. The bank was authorized to begin operations when one-half of its £100,000 authorized capital was paid in, and lending on real estate was prohibited. It was provided that the notes of the bank were to be payable in gold or silver.[98] Much of the capital of the new bank was subscribed in the form of Halifax Banking Company notes, which had to be converted into specie. The reluctance of the Company to co-operate led to a clash between the two institutions in their first years of competition.[99]

There were two immediate circumstances which exerted marked influence upon the charter of the Bank of Nova Scotia. The first was the widespread failure of American banks in the decade of the twenties, which prompted a renewed consideration as to the desirable provisions for a new charter. The second was the series of Colonial Office regulations issued in respect of colonial bank charters, and touching specifically on such aspects as the payment of capital, double liability of shareholders, minimum denomination of notes issued, penalties for suspending specie payment and provision for winding up any bank where capital had become seriously impaired. The charter of the Bank of Nova Scotia was designed to afford substantial protection for the public, and in this respect was probably the most advanced of its day. In the crisis of 1837, the bank suspended specie payments, as did its chief rival and practically all other banks in British North America. But in 1837, it opened agencies at both Saint John and Windsor, and these were subsequently extended to other areas in the process which was the forerunner of the present system of branch banks.

The monopoly of the Halifax Banking Company having been broken, the

[96]In a financial statement issued in 1832, the chief liabilities of the bank were the following: Capital Stock Paid In, £50,000; Notes in Circulation, £114,000; Deposits, £71,000; chief assets included: Cash £32,000; Bills discounted, £205,000.

[97]See *Bank of Nova Scotia, 1832-1932, op. cit.,* p. 24: "By and large the Bank of Nova Scotia sponsors were not the 'merchant princes' of the type who comprised for the most part the partnership of the Halifax Banking Company."

[98]*Ibid.,* pp. 37ff. The bank's notes, until after Confederation, were issued in sterling denominations. Its first issue of "dollar" bank-notes occurred in 1871.

[99]A widespread discussion of banking and currency matters, intensified by the chartering of the Bank of Nova Scotia, is to be found in the *Halifax Nova Scotian* during 1832 and 1833.

establishment of additional banks proved not so difficult, and by 1867, there were four chartered banks operating in the province. These were the Bank of Nova Scotia (1832), Union Bank of Halifax (1856), Bank of Yarmouth (1859) and the People's Bank of Halifax (1864). The Commercial Bank of Windsor (1866), had not yet opened its doors. Just as in the Province of Canada, there was a substantial seasonal variation in bank-note circulation. The cashier of the Bank of Yarmouth testified that the heaviest demands for accommodation came from August to December, being related to the harvest and the fall trade. Fishermen brought their cargoes to market and merchants and traders required advances for their winter stocks at this time. The general manager of the Bank of British North America stated that in New Brunswick, the maximum note circulation occurred in July-August, the minimum in February-March, the difference between them approximating twenty per cent. The expansion began at the opening of navigation, when large sums were required by lumberers, mill owners and boatmen. Shipyard operators and other small manufacturers added to the demands for bank accommodation.[100]

By Confederation, however, the Maritimes had passed the peak of their prosperity, and had entered what proved to be a protracted and serious economic decline, delayed only briefly by the abnormal export stimulus provided by the Civil War in the United States. What had been a highly integrated economy based on fishing, lumbering, shipbuilding and the carrying trade was now being undermined by an unfortunate combination of external circumstances. The abandonment of British colonial preference, increasing competition from New England in the British West Indies, fisheries markets and the end of reciprocity with the United States all played their part. But the death-blow was the technological revolution in transportation which ended the era of wooden sailing-ships.[101]

After 1832, the paper money of Nova Scotia included not only provincial treasury bills but the notes of the Halifax Banking Company, of the Bank of Nova Scotia and of various commercial enterprises which had issued rather substantial quantities of small-denomination bills of a negotiable character.[102] Since

[100]See Dominion of Canada, First Report of the Committee on Banking and Currency, *op. cit.*, pp. 33-5.

[101]See W. A. Mackintosh, *The Economic Background of Dominion-Provincial Relations* (Ottawa: Report on Dominion-Provincial Relations, Appendix 3, p. 12: "The colonial economy of the first half of the 19th century had been based on wood, wind and water while that of the second half was to be established on steam, rail and steel. The vast technical transformation this brought about gave rise to many problems for colonial countries, problems of new markets, new competitors, the search for new products, and of capital imports and mounting debts."

[102]See Horace A. Fleming, "Halifax Currency", Paper of the Nova Scotia Historical Society, May 1915, p. 129. (Also reprinted in *J.C.B.A.*, XXX.) Reference is made here to the paper of the well known firm of S. Cunard and Co., which even sold at a premium. This paper was payable at any of its offices in Halifax, Saint John or Charlottetown, and was consequently in demand for the transfer of funds among these cities.

bank notes were generally more acceptable than treasury bills, the government passed an Act in 1834 prohibiting the further issue, by any firm or corporation, of notes in denominations of less than £5. The way was thereby cleared for a government monopoly of the smaller denomination notes most popular in hand-to-hand payments. At the time of Confederation, the province's outstanding paper amounted to some £150,000, the obligation for redeeming which was assumed by the new government of the Dominion. A further Act in 1834 established new ratings for current coins, in terms of sterling, when hope for some uniformity with the other British provinces was abandoned.[103] In 1860, Nova Scotia (and New Brunswick) formally adopted the decimal system as the standard of value. Public accounts were to be kept in dollars and cents, but sterling equivalents were also to be designated, and this system was accompanied by still another revision of ratings.[104] On July 1, 1871, the currency ratings which had been current in the Province of Canada since 1852-3 were extended to all parts of the Dominion.[105]

[103]See Canadian Archives, *C.O. Records, Series Q.*, vol. 266, part 2, pp. 227-43. Here is found a letter from one Russell Ellice, chairman of the "North American Colonial Association", to the British government, outlining in concise and enlightened fashion the existing derangement of the currency, the reasons for the discrepancies in ratings as among the several provinces and recommending some constructive measures to reduce the chaos.

[104]The British sovereign (£1 sterling), which was £1.5s. currency, became equivalent to $5.00.

[105]As already explained, this rating was £1 sterling = $4.86 2/3, a much more awkward equation than the 1860 "Halifax" rating.

## CHAPTER IV

# THE CANADIAN MONETARY SYSTEM
# AND CHARTERED BANK EXPANSION BEFORE 1914

AT CONFEDERATION, the Bank of Montreal was the largest bank in the new Dominion. Its six million dollars of capital represented about one-fifth and its twenty million dollars of assets about one-quarter, of the respective totals for all banks.[1] The bank was also the government's fiscal agent and depository, and enjoyed special advantage as the sole issuer of provincial notes. As a temporary currency measure, the Dominion Notes Act was enacted in 1868, the effect of which was to extend to all of Canada the provisions embodied in the Provincial Notes Act of 1866.[2] During the first year of Confederation, following the receipt of a report on the contemporary banking system by a select committee of parliament, Sir John Rose, the first federal Minister of Finance, recommended that Dominion banking legislation be recast along the lines of the National Bank Act in the United States. In substance, this was another recommendation for the substitution of a bond-secured currency for the prevailing unsecured issues of the chartered banks, and it closely resembled the currency provisions of the earlier "free-banking" proposals. The recommendation would have deprived the banks of the power of issue against their general credit and would have permitted only the issue of notes prepared by the government and turned over to the banks upon the deposit of equivalent amounts of bonds. It would have permitted in each county the founding of a local bank with small capital, and to meet the recurring need for expansion of the currency it would have apparently depended to a great degree upon the periodic shifting of funds from east to west, as in the United States.

Apart from the Bank of Montreal, which favoured this proposal because of its special relationship with the government, the chartered banks were strongly opposed to the recommendation. In arguing their right to continue the issue of notes, the banks emphasized the "inelasticity", higher cost and inferior stability of the proposed alternative. Faced with widespread opposition, the Minister withdrew the resolution, and his early resignation from the government fore-

[1]Dominion of Canada, *Statistical Abstract and Record,* 1886, p. 347: As of June 30, 1868, the total paid-up capital of the chartered banks amounted to $30.3 million, total assets $77.9 million. By the beginning of World War 1, these figures had risen to approximately $115 million and $1.6 billion respectively.

[2]By the terms of the Act of 1868 (31 Vic., c. 46), the Dominion took over provincial notes in the amount of some $9 million. The specie reserve for its new issue (maximum $8 million) was 20% up to $5 million, and 25% on that part of the issue between $5-$8 million.

stalled any further efforts in this direction. His successor sponsored the Dominion Notes Act of 1870, which both confirmed the principle that the right of issue should be shared by the government and the chartered banks and prescribed the basis for such a division. The provisions of the Act of 1868 which had been designed to induce the chartered banks to accept Dominion notes in place of their own were repealed, and upon its expiration, the agreement with the Bank of Montreal relating to the issue and redemption of government notes was not renewed. This eliminated the privileged position of that institution, and made possible the subsequent participation of the other banks in government business.

The Dominion Notes Act of 1870 restricted the chartered banks to the issuing of notes of a minimum denomination of five dollars, thereby establishing for the government a monopoly of the one- and two-dollar issues. Prior to this time, all banks had issued notes in denominations as low as $1 (5s.). The authorized maximum fiduciary government issue was raised to $9 million, for which a specie reserve of 20% was to be held, while any issue in excess of $9 million was to be covered dollar for dollar by gold.[3] Between this date and the outbreak of World War I, the Act was amended on various occasions, but its basic structure remained unchanged.[4] The interval from 1853-1914 was characterized by Canada's uninterrupted adherence to the gold standard, a circumstance to which the distinctive features of the Canadian banking system contributed a great deal. This period began with the passage of the Province of Canada Currency Act and ended under the impact of wartime economic dislocations. Within these sixty years, gold was readily available at all times in exchange for other forms of circulating media.

Apart from the regulation of paper money issues, it has been noted that the Uniform Currency Act of 1871 extended decimal currency throughout the Dominion. The British sovereign, rated at $4.86 2/3, became the "standard" coin, and the United States eagle was made legal tender at $10. Authority was granted for the issue of a $5 Canadian gold coin, but no gold coins were struck in this

---

[3]The Dominion Notes Act, 1870 (33 Vic., c. 10).

[4]The following were the important amendments to the Act: 1872 (35 Vic., c. 7): the specie reserve for circulation in excess of $9 million reduced to 35%; 1875 (38 Vic., c. 5): specie reserve for circulation $9M-$12M raised to 50%, above $12 million, 100%; in 1878, the Dominion Notes Act was made applicable to Prince Edward Island, British Columbia and Manitoba; 1880 (43 Vic., c. 13): maximum issue established at $20M (in 1894, $25M), with reserve of 25% in gold and guaranteed debentures (at least 15% of the reserve to be gold); 1895 (58-59 Vic., c. 16): any amount might be issued above $20M, if the excess were secured entirely by gold; 1903 (3 Edw. VII, c. 43): maximum fiduciary issue $30M, with 25% reserve of gold and guaranteed debentures, all issues in excess of $30M to have 100% specie reserve; 1914 (5 Geo. V, c. 4): maximum fiduciary issue raised to $50M, with same 25% reserve. The Finance Act of 1914 (5 Geo. V, c. 3) marked the termination of the gold standard, and introduced a fundamental change into the structure of the Canadian monetary system. The details of this experiment are discussed at a later point.

country prior to the establishment of the mint at Ottawa in 1908, following which the earliest coins struck were sovereigns. These were followed in 1912 by Canadian $5 and $10 gold pieces. Canadian gold coinage remained small, because paper currency was preferred for domestic transactions, and in meeting external payments, bullion or British or American coins were readily available. In 1881, the provisions of this Act were applied to Prince Edward Island, British Columbia and Manitoba. This currency system remained unaltered until 1910, when the Currency Act of that year defined the Canadian dollar not in terms of the British sovereign but in terms of a specified weight and fineness of gold bullion, such that its gold content was equal to that of the United States dollar. British and American coins retained legal-tender status, based on their respective gold contents.

The state of government currency shortly following Confederation is indicated in the accompanying summary, which presents both its high and low points

### CURRENCY OF CANADA, 1872[a]
(Week of January 8, 1872)

| CENTRE | PROVINCIAL NOTES IN CIRCULATION | DOMINION NOTES IN CIRCULATION | TOTAL |
|---|---|---|---|
| Montreal | $3,209,405.63 | $3,805,926.00 | $ 7,015,331.63 |
| Toronto | 643,315.50 | 2,106,905.00 | 2,750,220.50 |
| Halifax | 80,932.72 | 433,865.00 | 514,797.72 |
| Saint John | 509,267.00 | 246,000.00 | 755,267.00 |
| Total Note Circulation | $4,442,920.85 | $6,592,696.00 | $11,035,616.85 |
| Fractional Currency Circulation | | | 486,780.15 |
| Total Circulation | | | $11,522,397.00 |

(Week of August 30, 1872)

| | | | |
|---|---|---|---|
| Montreal | $1,806,731.38 | $3,072,093.00 | $4,878,824.38 |
| Toronto | 255,955.50 | 2,562,692.00 | 2,818,647.50 |
| Halifax | 29,904.43 | 882,110.00 | 912,014.43 |
| Saint John | 482,847.00 | 260,797.00 | 743,644.00 |
| Total Note Circulation | $2,575,438.31 | $6,777,692.00 | $9,353,130.31 |
| Fractional Currency Circulation | | | 343,556.46 |
| Total Circulation | | | $9,696,686.77 |

[a]Department of Finance, *Circulation Statistics, 1872-1917.* The old provincial note issues were retired from circulation at as rapid a rate as possible, some indication of which is suggested by the sharp reduction in their total during the eight months indicated in the table. After mid-1874, no separate data on their circulation were published.

during 1872. Although the means of payment provided by the government included (1872 annual averages) $10.2 million in notes and $0.4 million in coinage, the greater part of the currency (hand-to-hand money) was represented by $25.3 million in chartered bank notes. In addition, deposits of the latter institutions amounted to $61.5 million.[5] It is therefore interesting to find that from the earliest years of the new Dominion, bank money (notes plus deposits) exceeded government money in the total means of payment, and that deposits greatly exceeded notes as forms of bank credit. By 1913, Dominion notes in the hands of the public had risen to $29.1 million,[6] coins, $19.3 million, bank notes $105.3 million, and bank deposits in Canada $1.0 billion.[7] During the intervening half-century, the increasing ratio of deposits to notes, as alternative means of payment available to the public, offers a measure not only of the development of the country's banking system but of the Canadian economy as a whole.

It was in conjunction with the foregoing monetary structure that Canadian commercial banking evolved and expanded in the decades preceding World War I, and we shall now examine the major aspects of these banking developments. It may be well to remind ourselves, however, that throughout Canadian economic development, the opportunities and occasions for "cheap-money" experiments via paper money issues have in general been much more restricted than in the United States. This is in considerable measure explained, in the pre-Confederation period, by the restraining influence of the Colonial Office, and in the latter by exclusive federal jurisdiction in matters of money and banking. The Canadian provinces would have found it much more difficult to embark upon questionable monetary ventures (viz. Alberta) than did state authorities, under the United States constitution. Likewise, the identification of banking with the financing of staples production from the early stages of Canadian economic development has encouraged or perhaps made inevitable a high degree of concentration of banking control. The conservatism of these relatively few and very large Canadian banks is in striking contrast to various phases of commercial banking development in the United States.

The British North America Act allocated to the new federal government exclusive jurisdiction over (a) currency and coinage and (b) banking, the incorporation of banks and the issue of paper money. Accordingly, in its first session, parliament passed an interim "Act Respecting Banks",[8] which provided that any act or charter incorporating any bank or banking institution in the late provinces of Canada, Nova Scotia or New Brunswick should, "until the first day of Janu-

---

[5]*Ibid.* See also Canada, *Statistical Abstract and Record*, 1886, p. 347.

[6]This figure includes only the $1, $2, $4, and $5 issues, since the large denominations were used almost entirely for bank clearings. The all-inclusive Dominion note figure was $116.4 million. With the government's specie reserves standing at $95.0 million in 1913, Dominion notes had become practically gold certificates.

[7]*Canada Year Book*, 1936, pp. 900, 906.

[8]*Statutes of Canada*, 1867, Vol. I, c. 11.

ary, 1870, and then until the end of the then next session of parliament of Canada, apply and have effect throughout the whole Dominion". The directors of such banks were also empowered to open and establish branches or offices of discount and deposit anywhere in Canada. The annual bank-note tax of one per cent, established earlier in the Province of Canada, was extended to banks "chartered, incorporated or recognized in Nova Scotia and New Brunswick", and was applied on the average amount by which their note issues exceeded the average amount of specie held. In 1870, a second interim "Act Respecting Banks and Banking"[9] was passed, providing that the banks retain their right of issue (except for one- and two-dollar denominations), that they should hold from one-third to one-half of their cash reserves in the form of Dominion notes, that the one per cent annual tax on notes be abolished, and that they be relieved of the requirement to invest ten per cent of their paid-up capital in government securities. It was further provided that any bank coming under the terms of this act might secure a renewal of its charter by letters patent until 1881. However, parliament declined a proposal that new banks be granted charters via letters patent, being unwilling to yield its immediate prerogative in this respect. The Act of 1870 included a number of additional provisions designed further to strengthen the banking system and protect the general public.

In 1871, parliament enacted legislation entitled "An Act Relating to Banks and Banking", popularly known as "The Bank Act of 1871",[10] the preamble of which states that "it is desirable that the provisions relating to the incorporation of banks and the laws relating to banking should be embraced as far as practicable in one general act". This Act represented the first permanent legislation governing banking in the new Dominion, although, by and large, its main provisions represented a consolidation of existing banking legislation. It provided that the chartering of any new bank must be authorized by a special act of parliament, the terms of which must conform with the general Bank Act. For such an institution, the minimum subscribed capital was fixed at $500,000, of which at least one-fifth must have been paid in before the commencement of operations, a further one-fifth to be paid in within another two years. The shareholders of any bank might increase its capital stock at their discretion. In extending the charters of all existing banks until 1881, the way was paved for the subsequent simultaneous renewal of all bank charters at ten-year intervals. This feature, peculiar to the Canadian banking system, was designed to provide the opportunity for a periodic widespread discussion and review of bank operations and it has developed a remarkable sensitivity to public opinion, on the part of the bankers.

The provisions of the Act of 1870 relating to note issue (minimum denomination four dollars), abolition of the annual tax on note circulation, form of reserves held and opening of branches, were all incorporated in the new legislation. It

---

[9]*Statutes of Canada*, 1870, c. 11.      [10]*Statutes of Canada*, 1871, c. 5.

was further provided that the note issue of any bank might not exceed its paid-in capital. Dividend payments were limited to eight per cent per annum until the bank had accumulated a reserve fund equal to twenty per cent of paid-in capital, and double liability was imposed upon the stockholders. The banks were required to submit detailed monthly financial statements to the government, and the earlier "pledge" provisions were somewhat extended.[11] The extension of these provisions continued in succeeding decades, in an effort to adapt the credit facilities of the chartered banks to the peculiar requirements of the agricultural economy of the West. The attempt was by no means entirely successful, as will subsequently be noted in some detail. The suspension of specie payments for a ninety-day period involved the forfeiting of the bank's charter. Such were the most important provisions of the Bank Act of 1871.

The first six years following Confederation were years of prosperity in Canada, in which trade and industry substantially expanded. Although the conception of Confederation was basically political, its consummation must be interpreted largely in terms of the serious economic difficulties which confronted the several colonies at that time. In the Maritimes and in central Canada, governments were struggling under a crushing burden of debt, incurred, in the main, in the financing of railroad and canal construction. In British Columbia, which became a province in 1871, a similar problem had arisen in connection with the government's programme of road-building into the interior, to serve the new development of placer-mining on the Fraser and Thompson Rivers, and in the Caribou area. This pressure of public debt was a powerful force lying behind the union of the separate colonies of Vancouver Island and the mainland in 1866.

Apart from the problem of government indebtedness, the country faced the necessity of substantial economic readjustment, because of the loss of preference in British markets and the termination of reciprocity arrangements with the United States. There was a steadily growing conviction that the solution to economic difficulties lay in the development of a larger domestic market and the expansion of intercolonial trade. Thus the Maritimes, whose prosperity, as we have seen, had centred upon lumbering and shipbuilding, were struck a vital blow with the advent of "steam and iron" technology in the mid-nineteenth century. With their traditional export markets declining, they viewed Confederation, and the construction of an intercolonial railway, as a means of expanding their trade

---

[11]With reference to the changes introduced in 1871 relating to the use of bills of lading and warehouse and other receipts as collateral, "Previously, such security might only be acquired at the time the debt to the bank was negotiated or contracted; it now became lawful to acquire it by virtue of an understanding entered into at such time that it would be transferred. It was also provided that the related bill, note or debt might be renewed or the time extended, without affecting the security; and the list of persons from whom security could be taken, and the list of goods which were available for such security, were enlarged to include additional industries and additional goods." See A. B. Jamieson, *Chartered Banking in Canada* (Toronto: The Ryerson Press), 1953, p. 21.

with the central provinces.[12] Similarly, the central provinces wanted the development of prairie markets, and British Columbia wanted a rail connection with the East. The accomplishment of these objectives obviously required not only co-operation among the various areas but a financial status in foreign capital markets which, in view of past difficulties, none of the provinces could have established alone. Confederation was hopefully viewed as the solution to these contemporary economic difficulties.

Accompanying Confederation were three basic decisions by the new federal government which have exerted a fundamental and continuing influence upon the entire course of Canadian economic development.[13] The first of these was the decision to acquire the western lands of the Hudson's Bay Company, to provide a frontier of settlement for the new Dominion. This purchase was effected under the terms of the Rupert's Land Act of 1869 and ". . . its economic significance lay in the design to give to the new Dominion, hemmed in between the United States boundary heavily fortified by the Civil War customs duties and the unfriendly barrier of the Pre-Cambrian shield, a region of frontier settlement capable of rapid economic development and capable in turn of stimulating development in other parts of the Dominion".[14] The second was the decision to construct a transcontinental railway via an all-Canadian route. The railway was in part conceived as an instrument of national defence, but the government also hoped ". . . to harness this great new instrument of economic expansion to the task of developing a Canadian national economy which, while still tied to world markets, would have some unified life and circulation within itself".[15] The third decision was that embodied in the "National Policy" of 1879, a policy designed to further the industrialization of the Canadian economy by means of a protective tariff. In the following decades, the government used its newly acquired western lands both to facilitate railroad construction (the cost of which was substantially increased by the decision to establish an all-Canadian route) and to encourage the rapid settlement of the West by means of its homesteading policies.

The economic prosperity of the new Dominion in the years before 1873 was based predominantly on agricultural expansion. Wheat-growing was at this time centred in Ontario, and Canadian wheat exports continued to find ready markets both in Europe and in the United States. Following the Civil War, the great era of reconstruction stimulated the demand for Canadian lumber at a time when railroad construction made possible the exploitation of additional forest

---

[12]The Intercolonial Railway to Halifax was completed in 1876, thereby linking the Maritimes with central Canada; the extension of the Canadian Pacific to Winnipeg was completed in 1883, to Vancouver in 1885.

[13]See W. A. Mackintosh, *The Economic Background of Dominion-Provincial Relations* (Ottawa: King's Printer), 1939, Ch. II.

[14]*Ibid.*, p. 15.

[15]*Ibid.*, p. 16.

resources, and when sawn lumber could be transported cheaply to the United States via canals and waterways. The growth of manufacturing at this time was associated with railroad-building, and with the expansion of the agricultural and forest industries.

This agricultural, commercial and industrial growth was accompanied by a rapid expansion of commercial banking facilities. Between 1867 and 1874, the paid-up capital of Canadian chartered banks doubled, from approximately $29 million to $60 million, as bank stocks became one of the most attractive forms of investment. Bank-note circulation more than tripled (to $28 millions) and deposits increased more than fourfold (to $77 millions), gains which reflected almost exclusively the banks' rapidly expanding lending and discounting operations.[16] During this period, a widespread but excessive optimism concerning the country's economic prospects led to increasing speculation in bank and other corporate securities, particularly those of railways, and to the general over-extension of bank credit. Prices and economic activity reached a peak in 1873, in which year, aided by external influences, severe depression occurred, lasting until 1879.

Included in the substantial number of newly established banks were several of our contemporary institutions.[17] The Bank of Commerce was founded just a few weeks before Confederation, and it shortly absorbed the Gore Bank at Hamilton. Its appearance was facilitated by the demise of the Bank of Upper Canada and the Commercial Bank, and most prominent in its organization was the Honourable William McMaster, a director of the Bank of Montreal, who objected strongly to some of the credit policies of the latter institution. The directors of the bank had announced in 1865 that they would make no further advances on accommodation paper, the basis for much of its lending in Canada West. They viewed this type of security as being unsound, and in the subsequent tightening of regulations, much of the bank's loanable funds were directed away from local enterprise, either to the support of Montreal importers or to

[16]See the *Canada Gazette,* 1873. In view of the pattern of the contemporary economic expansion, it is not surprising that all but a very small part of chartered bank accommodation was extended to borrowers in Ontario and Quebec. Of total loans and discounts amounting to some $124 million early in 1873, Nova Scotia and New Brunswick claimed less than $8 million. See also footnote 34, below.

[17]The Canadian Bank of Commerce (1867); the Dominion Bank (1871); the Imperial Bank (1875); La Banque de Hochelaga (1874), which, after absorbing La Banque Nationale in 1924, became known as La Banque Canadienne Nationale. Already established before Confederation were the Bank of Montreal (1817); the Bank of Nova Scotia (1832); the Bank of Toronto (1856); La Banque Jacques Cartier (1861), the name of which was changed to La Banque Provincial du Canada (1900); the Merchants' Bank (1864), chartered in 1869 as the Merchants' Bank of Halifax, and which subsequently became the Royal Bank of Canada (1901). Barclay's Bank (Canada), which began its Canadian operations in 1929, was absorbed by the Imperial Bank in 1956. The chartering of the Mercantile Bank of Canada and the amalgamation of the Toronto and Dominion Banks after World War II will subsequently be noted.

foreign exchange transactions in New York. This led to the Bank of Montreal acquiring a distinct unpopularity in the upper part of the province, and Mc-Master's decision to withdraw from its direction and to found a competing bank was strongly supported. He stated that "we do not oppose anyone, all we seek is the good of the country. We believe that all the floating capital which some banks get hold of is loaned out of the country. Our policy is to benefit our respective localities by employing our own, and the floating capital coming under our control, in the support of the trade and industry of the place".[18]

Although this charge of discrimination against local enterprise was directed at the Bank of Montreal, the practice of employing funds in the New York market was somewhat more general. Both it and the Bank of British North America had established New York agencies, while a number of other Canadian banks had correspondents there. The Canadian Bank of Commerce had a New York agency in operation by 1872. These institutions bought bills of exchange drawn in New York against cotton and other United States exports, and sold bills drawn on their London correspondents. Since the American unit banks did not undertake the financing of international transactions, the Canadian banks, plus a few private banking houses, shared this business. "Not only did they buy a very large proportion of the bills drawn against cotton, grain and prepared cereals, cattle and provisions, lumber and wooden wares, kerosene, steel billets and rails, agricultural and other machinery, and other exports from the United States, but the American importer had to come to them when he wished to make arrangements to pay for his purchases of foreign merchandise.[19]

Even at this early date, most of the banks held a minimum of their specie reserves at home, choosing to put as much as possible of their holdings to profitable employment in New York, where they would be available in times of emergency.[20]

The Bank of Commerce was associated in its early years with agricultural expansion in Ontario, and like its competitors, fared well in the years immediately following Confederation.[21] The depression of 1873 was severely felt by all Canadian financial institutions, and particularly by the banks, many of which

[18]Victor Ross, *op. cit.*, II, p. 21. The founder's own capital had been to a large extent acquired through his activities in the rapidly expanding wholesale business.

[19]*Ibid.*, p. 64: "The letters of credit issued by the Canadian Bank of Commerce covered jute, gunny bags, printed cottons, coffee, rubber, and many kinds of spices, essential oils and gums from India and China, hemp and sugar in large quantities from the Philippines, ebony from Madagascar, ivory from Zanzibar, and rubber, mahogany and sisal from Latin America". Many kinds of merchandise were also financed from Japan and China.

[20]See Shortt, "The Banking System of Canada", in *Canada and Its Provinces*, X, p. 636: "In times of crisis . . . when an extra supply of specie was called for, it was convenient to be able to draw upon New York, or through it upon London, for such specie as was required. The banks having regular dealings in specie and exchange with New York and London naturally enjoyed a special advantage during critical periods in Canadian credit."

[21]Dividends of 8%-10% were general in early chartered banking in the Dominion of Canada.

had become involved to an undesirable extent in the financing of the lumber industry[22] and of shipbuilding.[23] Both of these industries were particularly hard hit by a contraction of exports, the effects of which extended to those agricultural districts dependent upon them. But in general, agriculture escaped relatively lightly, a fortunate circumstance for many banks.[24] The depression bore heavily on commercial enterprises, and many failed. As customary in periods of recession, the banks effected a severe contraction of credit and thereby precipitated much criticism of their operations. Despite the considerable bankruptcy in Canadian business, the banks for the most part survived this period by resort to the use of their reserves and to substantial reductions of capital, and by amalgamations.[25] All these events ". . . resulted in sifting the wheat from the chaff among the Canadian banks, but produced an attitude of misgiving upon the part of the public towards the banking system."[26]

Despite the banking difficulties of this period, the revisions introduced in the Bank Act of 1880 were comparatively minor.[27] The recent losses by the note-

---

[22]During the depression of 1873-8, a number of banks with loans undesirably concentrated in the lumber industry were eliminated. This industry was subject to wide fluctuations in its prosperity, depending upon the state of foreign markets.

[23]In the Maritimes, the failures of the Bank of Acadia (1873) and the Bank of Liverpool (1879) were directly associated with the declining fortunes of lumbering and shipbuilding. The difficulties of the fishing industry of Prince Edward Island in 1877 and subsequent years, combined with the general economic depression, were instrumental in the failure of the Bank of Prince Edward Island (1881). This institution, like many others, suffered from the limited range of opportunities for lending its funds, and had made large advances without security. Its losses were estimated at $400,000, twice the amount of its capital. A further complication was that of an absconding cashier. The failure of the bank precipitated runs on the other banks on the Island (the Union Bank of P.E.I. and the Merchants' Bank of P.E.I.), which managed to regain public confidence. But the liquidated Bank of P.E.I. was heavily in debt to the Merchants' Bank, and this latter institution lost heavily in the outcome.

The difficulties encountered by the smaller and weaker banks in outlying centres increased with the continued decline of the Maritimes' "wood and wind" economy, and this facilitated an extension of the influence of the urban banks, and of the larger branch banks in Central Canada.

[24]During this world-wide depression, the Canadian economy fared relatively well. Its barter terms of trade improved continuously, for despite the decline in export prices, those of imports declined even more rapidly, the chief explanation being reductions in costs of transportation and of British manufactures. See Mackintosh, *op. cit.*, p. 18.

[25]See the *Report of the Royal Commission on Banking and Currency* (Ottawa: King's Printer), 1933, Table opp. p. 114. Between April 1873 and October 1879, six chartered banks went into liquidation, two in Nova Scotia, three in Montreal and one in Quebec (voluntarily). Their paid-up capital was approximately $3.5 million, and their liabilities to the public at time of suspension $2.5 million, of which notes represented $0.8 million, deposits $1.7 million. The losses incurred by these classes of creditors approximated $280,000 and were confined largely to the Bank of Acadia, Liverpool, N.S., where the creditors suffered virtually complete loss, and the Mechanics Bank, Montreal, in which the claims both of depositors and note-holders were settled at 57.5¢ on the dollar.

[26]Shortt, *op. cit.*, p. 640.

[27]*Statutes of Canada*, 1880, c. 22.

holders of certain liquidated banks raised the question of how some additional protection might be afforded to this class of creditor. The broader question of the desirability of an extension of government powers of issue (and of a corresponding restriction of bank issues) also came to the fore. In the end, the bankers seized the initiative and proposed that bank notes should be made a first charge against bank assets in the event of liquidation, arguing that in contrast to depositors, note-holders are "involuntary" creditors of a bank, hence should be accorded preferential treatment. This proposal was duly incorporated into the Bank Act. In addition, the minimum denomination of bank-note issues was set at five dollars, all larger denominations to be in multiples of five dollars; penalties were provided for any issue in excess of paid-up capital stock; the cash reserves to be held in the form of Dominion notes were specified as 40% of the bank's total reserves; no institution might assume the title of "bank" without authority; more detailed monthly financial statements were required from the banks; no advances might be made on the security of the shares of any bank (1879). The "pledge" provisions, antecedents of Section 88 of the present Bank Act, were further broadened, in that the list of persons entitled to borrow from a bank on the security of their own goods in their own possession, under the form of a warehouse receipt or bill of lading, was extended to include saw-millers, manufacturers of timber, curers or packers of meat, and tanners or purchasers of agricultural products. In 1888, distillers and manufacturers or dealers in cotton were added to the list. The evolution of Section 88 to its present status provides an interesting reflection of the gradual diversification of production in the Canadian economy, and of the attempts of the chartered banks to meet the broadening demand for accommodation.

The most serious lasting effect of the depression of 1873-8 had been the delaying of particular construction projects, e.g., the Canadian Pacific Railway, because of the closing of foreign capital markets. British capital investment in Canada was resumed on a lesser scale in subsequent years, but the high hopes that Confederation would stimulate rapid economic development in the new Dominion were doomed to disappointment until almost the turn of the century. The decade of the 1880's, and most of the 1890's, were years of economic uncertainty, attributable in substantial measure to a prolonged world-wide decline in general price levels. Although appreciable domestic expansion was accomplished over these two decades, it was nevertheless true that "in the early 1890's, neither the value nor the volume of exports per capita was higher than it had been twenty years earlier."[28] Despite improving terms of trade throughout this period, the expected rapid development of western agricultural lands did not occur. An important factor retarding Canadian expansion was the attraction of the American west, where fertile land was still freely available, and where immigrants from Europe, and from Canada, were attracted in large numbers.

[28]Mackintosh, *op. cit.*, p. 22.

It was only after 1896 that the disappearance of the American frontier, in conjunction with other favourable factors, led to the extremely rapid settlement and development of the prairies, and to a rate of economic development in Canada which exceeded by far anything hitherto experienced or envisaged.

In the period between Confederation and 1896, the two intervals of most rapid expansion of chartered bank accommodation were 1867-73, and 1880-3.[29] It will be observed from the data in the footnote below that the volume of bank business reached a peak in 1874-5 by which time the increases, since 1868, in the banks' notes, deposits and discounts had become very substantial. There followed a period of contraction which was not significantly reversed until 1880. A new phase of expansion culminated in 1882-3, at a level somewhat higher than that of the preceding peak. Following the collapse of the speculative boom in 1883, another period of retrenchment was instituted, but again the decline in banking operations was checked at a level substantially above the preceding low points. By the end of the period under consideration (1896), the banks had again achieved an unprecedented volume of business.

Underlying these periodic fluctuations there may thus be discerned a steady upward trend in chartered bank activity, despite the fact that on balance the

[29]The following data were extracted from *The Statistical Yearbook of Canada*, 1898, p. 295:

## CANADIAN CHARTERED BANKS—SELECTED DATA
(in millions of dollars)

| CALENDAR YEAR | PAID-UP CAPITAL | NOTES | DEPOSITS[a] | DISCOUNTS (To General Public) |
|---|---|---|---|---|
| 1868 | 30.5 | 9.4 | 33.7 | 52.3 |
| .... | .... | .... | .... | .... |
| 1874 | 60.4 | 27.9[H] | 77.1[H] | 131.7 |
| 1875 | 64.5 | 23.0 | 74.6 | 136.0[H] |
| 1876 | 66.8[H] | 21.2 | 72.9 | 99.6 |
| .... | .... | .... | .... | .... |
| 1878 | 63.7 | 20.5 | 70.9[L] | 119.7 |
| 1879 | 62.7 | 19.5[L] | 73.2 | 113.5 |
| 1880 | 60.1 | 22.5 | 95.3 | 102.2[L] |
| 1881 | 59.5[L] | 28.5 | 94.3 | 117.0 |
| 1882 | 59.8 | 33.6[H] | 110.1[H] | 140.1 |
| 1883 | 61.4 | 33.3 | 107.6 | 143.9[H] |
| 1884 | 61.6 | 30.4[L] | 102.4[L] | 130.5 |
| 1885 | 61.7[H] | 30.7 | 104.0 | 126.8[L] |
| .... | .... | .... | .... | .... |
| 1890 | 60.0[L] | 32.8 | 135.5 | 153.3 |
| .... | .... | .... | .... | .... |
| 1893 | 62.0 | 33.8[H] | 174.8 | 206.6 |
| 1894 | 62.1[H] | 31.2 | 181.7 | 204.1 |
| .... | .... | .... | .... | .... |
| 1896 | 62.0 | 31.5 | 193.6[H] | 213.2[H] |

[H]—high point of current cycle; [L]—low point of current cycle; [a]—Canadian deposits, public plus governments.

paid-up capital of the system was scarcely larger in 1896 than it had been twenty-five years earlier.[30]

The appreciable improvement in economic conditions which began late in 1879 was stimulated by the protection afforded by the new National Policy and by the construction of the Canadian Pacific Railway (completed in 1885). The railway construction was accompanied by a rapid expansion of commercial activity in Manitoba and by a widespread speculative land boom which collapsed in 1883. Several new banks were chartered in these years, only two of which were still in operation in 1896. A number of the established banks were extending their facilities in western Canada, and when the speculative boom broke in Winnipeg in 1883, seven agencies had already been established in that city. The operations of all of these agencies involved their respective banks in substantial losses, but no failures resulted. The losses were incurred not because of speculative activity on the part of the banks themselves, but through bad debts arising from the thoroughness ". . . with which the whole commercial community had been infected with the speculative virus."[31] Elsewhere in Canada, however, the record was much less satisfactory. Speculative activity, lack of diversification of credit risks and in a good many instances, dishonest management, were leading factors in the liquidation of nine banks between 1880 and 1896.[32] Between 1880 and 1910, it is estimated that approximately thirty per cent of Canadian banks failed.[33] In general, it was the smaller banks which encountered difficul-

[30]One evidence of this upward trend are the averages of bank discounts during successive five-year periods; 1869-73, $92.0 million; 1874-8, $143.4 million; 1879-83, $142.0 million; 1884-8, $166.1 million; 1889-93, $205.5 million; 1894-8, $228.2 million. See the *Statistical Yearbook of Canada*, 1898, pp. 299-300. These figures include discounts to municipalities, to trading corporations, to the public, and also loans on collateral and overdue debts, but exclude loans to governments.

[31]See Breckenridge, *op. cit.*, p. 125. For their faulty judgment in the matter of granting accommodation, three of the seven managers were dismissed.

[32]Of these liquidations, one was in Prince Edward Island, one in New Brunswick, one in Nova Scotia (voluntary liquidation), two in Montreal, three in Ontario (two voluntary) and one in Winnipeg. Actual losses to creditors were approximately $2 million. There were no losses to note-holders except in the case of the Bank of Prince Edward Island, where the claims of both note-holders and depositors were settled at 59.5 cents on the dollar, their aggregate losses amounting to $295,000. See *Report of Royal Commission on Banking and Currency, op. cit.* This table provides a complete list of chartered bank liquidations from Confederation to the present time.

[33]Writing in 1905, H. C. McLeod, General Manager of the Bank of Nova Scotia, observed that "in 1880, there were in existence in Canada forty-one banks; since then, seven have been incorporated and have commenced business making a total of forty-eight banks. Of this total twelve have failed and some others have saved themselves by amalgamation. The failures are therefore twenty-five percent within a period of twenty-six years, the last ten of which were years of unexampled prosperity." Shortly after this observation was made, two more banks failed, raising the percentage to almost thirty. McLeod noted further that "most, if not all, of the above mentioned failures were fraudulent, and it is now plainly evident that a few hours' examination by a skilled banker would have disclosed an insolvent condition in any one of the banks years before it collapsed." McLeod stated that during the same period, the failures among National Banks in the United States were only five per cent.

ties during this period, in which a growing concentration of population and a continuing trend to industrialization tended to strengthen the position of the larger banks. The process of amalgamation and of the establishment of branches was hastened as ". . . banking was moulded to an increasing extent to the new industrial structure".[34]

Despite the considerable number of voluntary liquidations, suspensions and amalgamations of chartered banks, the appearance of new banks was such that their numbers at the end of 1899 had increased to thirty-eight, with six hundred and forty-one branches.[35] The first clearing-house was established at Halifax in 1887, followed by that at Montreal in 1889, Toronto in 1891, Hamilton in 1891, Winnipeg in 1893, Saint John in 1896, Vancouver 1898 and Victoria 1898.[36]

The difficulties of the banking system during the 1880's were reflected to some degree in the amendments incorporated into the Bank Act in the revision of 1890.[37] One of the complaints accompanying liquidation proceedings had been that while notes might eventually be redeemed in full, the process was often prolonged, during which time the notes of the liquidating bank fell to a discount, with a consequent loss to their holders if they sought to spend them. Thus it was provided that the notes of a failed bank were to bear interest at six per cent per annum from the date of suspension until redeemed. A Bank Circulation Redemption Fund was established, to which each bank was required to pay in five per cent of its average circulation, and there has been no subsequent occasion on which the notes of a liquidated bank have not been redeemed in full, without loss to their owners. The Fund, held by the Minister of Finance and bearing interest at three per cent, was to be used to redeem the notes of any bank which failed, where the liquidator was not able to effect their redemption within sixty days. In any process of liquidation, the liquidator was obligated to pay to the Minister of Finance an amount equal to the bank's notes outstanding, before a final distribution of assets was effected. Each bank was required to establish redemption offices in the major centres, in order that its notes would circulate at par everywhere in Canada. One further provision respecting notes provided more stringent penalties for over-issue.

Reflecting the contemporary difficulties of the smaller banks, whose activities tended to be undesirably localized and specialized, the minimum paid-in capital

[34]See Ross, *op. cit.*, II, p. 659. Thus, in its annual report for 1888, the Canadian Bank of Commerce indicates that its accommodation had been extended principally to lumber merchants, to manufacturers of agricultural implements and to large-scale flour millers. Loans were also made to cattle grazers, and to assist in the production of cheese, eggs and flax. The bank was also concerned in the financing of foreign trade. (For a complete list of bank amalgamations in Canada since 1867, see the *Canada Year Book*, 1936, p. 922.)

[35]*Statistical Year Book of Canada*, 1899, p. 328: Of these branches, 306 were in Ontario, 117 in Quebec, 105 in P.E.I., and 113 in Western Canada. Between 1885 and 1903, no new banks began operations.

[36]*Ibid.*  [37]*Statutes of Canada*, 1890, c. 31.

required by any new bank was increased from $100,000 to $250,000, to be raised within one year of application. The Dominion and the provincial governments were made preferred creditors (in that order) of an insolvent bank, ranking next to note-holders. The bank's reserve fund was required to reach 30 per cent of paid-in capital before dividends in excess of eight per cent could be declared. Of the various other amendments to the Act, only one need be noted, that dealing with bills of lading and warehouse receipts. The provisions of the earlier Act were consolidated and substantially extended, so that banks might make advances, on the security of his product, to ". . . any person engaged in business as a wholesale manufacturer" and to ". . . any wholesale purchaser or shipper of the products of agriculture, the forest and mine, or the sea, lakes and rivers, or to any wholesale purchaser or shipper of livestock or dead stock, and the products thereof . . ."[38] In effect, the provisions were extended to all wholesale dealers and manufacturers, and the form of the security offered to the bank was extended to include not only a warehouse receipt (which henceforth could be tendered only by persons in possession of but not owners of the goods), but also a simple form of assignment (pledge) prescribed for owners of goods. This eliminated the practice of owners extending fictitious "warehouse receipts" to the banks. These provisions appeared for the first time as Section 88 of the Bank Act, where they have remained to the present day.[39]

Shortly after the Bank Act revision of 1890, the Canadian Bankers' Association was formed as a voluntary organization, to represent the chartered banks in matters of common interest. In 1900, it was granted the status of a public corporation by the federal government, and the objectives and functions of the Association were set forth in some detail.[40] It has represented a useful medium for the presentation of the bankers' views on issues of current interest, but its public functions have not been extensive.

[38]*Ibid.*

[39]Section 88, with its unique form of security, has been described as " . . . a typically Canadian product, adapted in the early days to assist the struggling industries of the young country and to enable the banks to aid them in many instances, where, without such preferential security, it would not have been possible to do so. . . . Because the goods forming the security are permitted to remain in the hands of the borrower and to be disposed of by him, . . . his integrity is of paramount importance". See M. D. Hamilton, "Section 88 of the Bank Act", in *J.C.B.A.*, XXXI, pp. 476-8.

[40]*Statutes of Canada*, 1900, c. 3. The Association sought "to promote generally the interests and efficiency of bank officers and the education and training of those contemplating training in banks, and for such purposes, among other means, to arrange for lectures, discussions, competitive papers and examinations on commercial law and banking and to acquire, publish and carry on the Journal of the Canadian Bankers' Association." It was also empowered to establish and supervise the operation of clearing-houses. From time to time it has assumed other administrative banking tasks, at the suggestion of the government. It very early sought to protect the common interest by opposing "the incorporation of loan companies authorized to receive deposits on current account", and it sought "to bring about uniformity in the rate of interest paid upon deposits payable after notice or in savings bank departments, and the reduction of the rate of interest paid by the post-office and government savings banks." See Breckenridge, *op. cit.*, pp. 156-8.

In contrast to the disappointingly slow growth of the Canadian economy during the three decades following Confederation, the mid-1890's marked the beginning of a twenty-five-year period of unprecedented economic expansion. To this expansion an important contribution was made by the banking system, the growth of which was directly conditioned by the financial requirements of a rapidly changing environment.

As throughout Canadian history, the basic causes of the economic changes were external. The long period of declining world prices was reversed around 1896, and a combination of rising prices for export staples (especially wheat), improving terms of trade, reduced freight costs and low interest rates provided a stimulus for unprecedented investment in the development of western Canada.[41] Down to World War I, the continuous process of economic expansion depended upon an enormous inflow of foreign capital, the bulk of which was obtained in British markets by both private and public borrowers.[42] Domestic transportation and tariff policies guided the impact of the more basic external influences, and by World War I the economy had become both substantially more diversified and substantially more dependent on world markets. It had also become a much better integrated economy, as the earlier self-sufficiency both within and among the several geographic regions disappeared. The prairies emerged as the country's great export area, while the main factor in the rising prosperity of the far west was the expanding lumber industry in British Columbia, which found the bulk of its market in the booming prairies. Manufacturing expanded rapidly in Ontario and Quebec, a process likewise dependent to a large extent on the prosperous "wheat" economy. Only the Maritimes failed to share in the rapid economic expansion of this period, as its shipbuilding, carrying trade, agriculture, fisheries and small-scale manufacturing all suffered adverse effects from technological change, national tariff and transportation policies and the decline of export markets. A high level of fixed costs had arisen in connection with the large external borrowings, and this suggested serious difficulty in adjusting to inevitable fluctuations in national income.

During this entire period of unprecedented capital inflow, the Canadian monetary system remained based on gold. In retrospect, it is remarkable that over

[41]For a comprehensive summary of Canadian economic expansion during this period, see W. A. Mackintosh, *The Economic Background of Dominion Provincial Relations, op. cit.,* Ch. III. Here it is noted that the "prospective profitableness in the exploiting industries created markets for other industries and for a time investment fed on itself."

[42]Considerable amounts of capital were also provided by the flood of immigrants to Canada in the early twentieth century. Of this whole period, the following observation may be noted: "In Canada, especially in the few years immediately preceding the first World War, the one factor, capital import, was so large as to make it possible to ignore other factors and say, with good reason, that the changes observed in all aspects of our economic life were mainly due to the import of capital." See F. A. Knox, *An Introduction to Money, Banking and International Finance.* (Queen's University: Fellows' Course in Banking) mimeographed, p. 86.

the period of some sixty years preceding the outbreak of World War I, the Canadian economy, subjected to a wide range of external disturbances, should have been able to retain a gold standard without interruption. The organization of its banking system and the availability of external capital were undoubtedly important factors in this situation.

The monetary and banking aspects of the heavy capital inflow and the rapid economic expansion between 1900 and 1913 have already provided the bases for well known intensive studies, but certain aspects of the experience require emphasis at this juncture.[43] In contrast to the absence of any appreciable net gain in Canadian exports in the two decades preceding 1896, a sudden expansion began at the latter date, and at the turn of the century their value had risen by some sixty per cent. A lag in the inevitable rise in imports permitted a "favourable" commodity balance of trade until 1900, from which time an uninterrupted and steadily increasing current account deficit prevailed through 1914.[44] During the four-year period 1896-9, the domestic note and deposit liabilities of the chartered banks increased by approximately $100 million, and the corresponding assets acquired by the banks were an increase in loans of some $85 million and net purchases of foreign exchange of $15 million. The bank's holdings of specie also increased by more than $1 million during this period.

Between 1900 and 1914, the continuously rising current account deficit was necessarily financed by the unprecedented volume of foreign capital invested in Canada. We were an immature debtor economy, characterized by a scarcity of capital (relative to our natural resources) and these foreign borrowings provided a means of acquiring real capital to facilitate the more rapid and more efficient exploitation of our productive potentialities, and also a means of acquiring a substantial range of consumers' goods which were desired for consumption but ordinarily are not produced in the primarily extractive production of the pioneer economy.

Net long-term capital imports increased substantially but at a relatively modest rate through 1904, after which heavy annual inflows occurred continuously (with only a slight tapering off during the international financial crisis of 1907) through 1914. Such an inflow was of course reflected initially in a rise in the chartered banks foreign balances and in a corresponding rise in their domestic liabilities. But this initial domestic monetary expansion was supplemented by the induced increases in commercial borrowings from the banking system as the

[43]See, for example, J. Viner, *Canada's Balance of International Indebtedness, 1900-1913* (Boston: Harvard University Press), 1923. Subsequent analyses of the problem have suggested the modification of some of Viner's conclusions as to the mechanism of adjustment of the balance of payments. See also Knox, *An Introduction to Money, Banking and International Finance, op. cit.,* part II, chapters 5, 6. The following summary is indebted to the presentation in the latter chapters.

[44]*Ibid.* Knox suggests that over the period 1890-9, Canada's commodity trade was roughly in balance, and that the relatively small net capital imports matched the invisible current account deficit.

general level of economic activity steadily rose in Canada. Rising money incomes, aided by sectional price movements, stimulated an expansion of imports, and brought about the heavy current account deficit already mentioned. By far the greatest part of these imports of capital goods and consumers' goods in the pre-War I period came from the United States (a circumstance which has changed little in subsequent years). The operation of the pre-War I international gold standard provided a ready means for converting our sterling borrowings into the American dollars required for payment of our imports. Over the whole period 1905-14, it was the increase in bank loans, rather than their net purchases of foreign exchange, which provided the main basis of the remarkable monetary expansion which occurred, for on balance, the changes in chartered bank deposits arising from net movements in their foreign balances were relatively small.[45] The banks' exchange purchases, from exporters and borrowers, roughly offset the rising demands of importers for foreign funds.[46]

During the fifteen-year-period 1900-14, the Canadian deposits of the chartered banks experienced a fourfold increase from approximately $266 million to $1,100 million; notes in circulation more than doubled, from $42 million to $105 million.[47] The major offset of this very large increase in liabilities to the public was the rapid expansion of commercial borrowing during the pre-War I years, bank loans and discounts having risen from some $250 million to $1,100 million.[48] The banks continued their earlier practice of holding a part of their cash reserves abroad, principally in New York, where they were loaned on call, and interest obtained.[49] In the event of emergency, they could be speedily converted to gold and the proceeds transferred to Canada. In those pre-war years,

---

[45]Ordinarily, monetary expansion stemming from a current account surplus induces a further expansion via an increase in bank lending stimulated by improving business conditions. This induces a rising level of imports, leading to a current account deficit. In the absence of any receipts of foreign exchange on capital account, the banks, faced with depleted foreign balances, must terminate their monetary expansion. But see the footnote immediately following.

[46]See *ibid.*, p. 102. Here Knox points out that " . . . the heavy inflow of capital thus permitted the banks to continue the domestic loan expansion despite the fact that the current balance of payments was running a deficit large enough to have wiped out the cash and foreign exchange holdings of all the banks in any one of the years of this last great boom if it had had to be met without borrowing abroad."

[47]*Canada Year Book*, 1915, pp. 577-8. During the same period, the circulation of Dominion notes ($20 and under) rose from approximately $10 million to $26 million. In the relatively simple monetary organization of the day, all but a negligible part of the country's stock of money was provided by the chartered banks, and fluctuations in this stock rested upon the decisions of the private institutions as to the profitability of expanding or contracting their assets (and liabilities). With reference to what represented the most desirable "credit" policy at any given moment, the possibility of conflict between the private and public interest was to become increasingly apparent in later years.

[48]*Ibid.*, p. 577.

[49]Thus, of total chartered bank loans and discounts of $1,100 million in 1913, some $175 million were loaned in New York. For details, see the series entitled *Report of the Chartered Banks of the Dominion of Canada*, submitted annually to the Minister of Finance.

the size of reserves held in Canada (the minimum consistent with safety) was approximately equal to the secondary reserves held abroad. Until 1914, the Canadian banks had no means of expanding their reserves from domestic sources. Additional cash could be obtained only by importing gold. Although the flow of investment funds extended to all corners of the Canadian economy, the fundamental basis of the expansion lay in the rise of western agriculture and in the development of grain and grain products, most notably wheat, as our leading exports.

To the chartered banks fell the task of financing the growing and marketing of the expanding western grain crops, and prior to World War I, this assignment was handled without major difficulty. It was only after western agriculture encountered economic adversity, first in the early post-War I period and again in the 1930's, that the inadequacy of commercial bank credit as a solution to the financial requirements of the farmer became fully apparent. Criticisms of chartered bank practices, which became violent and widespread in later years, were nevertheless apparent in this early period. It was claimed that they were reaping "fabulous" profits at the expense of the farming community, that their management by the "big" Eastern interests was not sympathetic to the needs of the farmers, that there was too much centralization in their operation, that discrimination against small customers prevailed, and that they failed to meet the pressing need for mortgage and personal credit. In its 1913 report, the Agricultural Credit Commission of Saskatchewan observed that "we desire to supplement not supplant that which exists; for it is easy in a time of stress for the Corinthian columns of the metropolis to shut out from view the rude shocks of the prairie farmers." Much of this criticism was well founded, but on the other hand, certain of the banks incurred substantial losses in the early 1920's as a result of excessive accommodation granted to western farmers during earlier prosperity.[50]

It has already been indicated that the expansion of chartered banking in Canada between Confederation and the end of the century was rather uneven, but that a steady upward trend was discernible. As one might expect, the appearance of new banks has usually coincided with periods of general economic expansion, and liquidations and mergers have occurred in times of crisis and recession. The contrast in development between 1900 and 1914 was remarkable. The paid-up capital of the banks almost doubled, and the number of branches increased fourfold, as banking services were extended over a much broader geographic area.[51] The tremendous expansion in chartered bank assets and liabilities was not, however, accompanied by any increase in the number of banks. On the contrary, seventeen mergers occurred between 1900 (following the Bank Act

---

[50]For a reasonable evaluation, see Vere Brown, *The Western Farmer and the Bank*, an address before the annual convention of the United Farmers of Alberta, January 23, 1919.

[51]Paid-up capital increased from $64 million in 1899 to $115 million in 1914; the number of branches increased from 641 to some 3,000. See *Canada Year Book*, 1915, pp. 574-8.

revision of that year) and 1913. And at the end of the latter year, there were only twenty-four banks in operation.[52] These mergers were usually between relatively small local banks and larger banks with greater diversity of operations.[53] A number of new banks did begin operations during this period, but they were either absorbed by stronger institutions or failed because of poor or dishonest management.[54] This trend toward the consolidation of ownership of banking institutions continued until the early 1930's, at which time the system had been reduced to ten banks: by 1957, as a result of two further mergers and the establishment of a new bank, the number stood at nine.

The economic expansion of Canada in the first decade of the twentieth century was accompanied and facilitated by the rapid increase in chartered bank credit indicated above. With an increasing demand for hand-to-hand currency which accompanied rising prices and incomes, the banks found themselves in a difficult position. Their note issue was restricted by statute to the amount of their paid-up capital, a limit which was being closely crowded. The financial crisis of 1907 had prompted the banks to proceed ". . . with even more than ordinary caution in extending credit."[55] and there was general fear that the accommodation required for the prompt moving of the grain crop would not be forthcoming. One head office sent out letters to its branches "like storm bulletins issued to mariners". New business was to be accepted "only when it was of a class that would lead to permanent and profitable connections". Moderate loans to farmers were sanctioned, but rates to be raised whenever possible, except on farmers' business, and borrowing not "of the highest grade" was to be cut down, to get the finances of the bank into a more comfortable position. All advances should represent "legitimate banking transactions".[56] In these years, some of the western grain companies occasionally established lines of credit with banks in St. Paul and Minneapolis.

The government provided for the emergency issue and loan of Dominion notes to the banks, to be used in financing the grain crop, and serious difficulty was

---

[52]The provisions of the Bank Act revision of 1900 were relatively unimportant (*Statutes of Canada*, 1900, c. 26). Most significant was the provision that any bank was authorized to sell the whole or any part of its assets to another bank. Prior to this time, a merger required sanction by special act of parliament. Another provision assigned certain statutory obligations to the Canadian Bankers' Association, in respect of supervising the liquidation of failed banks and the handling of bank notes.

[53]See Jamieson, *op. cit.*, p. 41: "Usually the smaller bank had reached a stage where, if it was to make further progress and to be able to retain certain of its larger customers, it would be necessary to expand its operations. Rather than incur the risk which this would entail, it preferred to negotiate with a larger bank to which its branch organization and business would prove desirable acquisitions."

[54]For the eight bank failures during 1900-14, see the *Royal Commission on Banking and Currency, op. cit.*

[55]Jamieson, *op. cit.*, p. 37. One infers, from this banker's quotation, that the restriction of banking accommodation was severe.

[56]See Ross, *op. cit.*, II, p. 235-6.

avoided. Some five million dollars of Dominion notes were borrowed and repaid by the banks between November 1907 and May 1908. But in 1908, a special amendment of the Bank Act provided that a bank might increase its note circulation, during the crop-moving season, to 115% of its paid-up capital plus reserve, the excess circulation to be taxed at a rate not exceeding 5% per annum.[57] Thus was introduced another feature peculiar to Canadian banking development, one designed to meet the problem of seasonal variation in the demand for bank credit, the degree of which is peculiar to the Canadian economy.[58]

The feature of the general revision of the Bank Act in 1913 which was of greatest monetary significance was the introduction of the Central Gold Reserves, the purpose of which was to make possible an expansion of chartered bank-note issues beyond the limits provided by the legislation of 1908.[59] The banks were authorized to issue notes beyond these limits provided any such excess was covered dollar for dollar by gold or Dominion notes deposited in the Central Gold Reserves, which were to be managed by four trustees, three appointed by the Bankers' Association and one by the government. Subsequent bank-note issues in excess of paid-up capital were in practice effected under this provision rather than by that of 1908, in order to avoid interest charges, and while the earlier difficulties of providing adequate currency to meet seasonal economic needs (especially those of crop-moving) were solved, the effect of the Central Gold Reserves was to modify the hitherto entirely "unsecured" character of bank-note issues.[60] They now became to some extent dependent on the availability of gold or government legal tender.

In response to the development of western grain-growing and to the farmer's need for financial accommodation in the harvesting of his crop, the Bank Act of 1913 extended Section 88 to authorize the chartered banks to make farm loans upon the security of threshed grain grown upon the borrower's farm.

It was at this stage in the evolution of the Canadian monetary and banking system that World War I arrived, and presented the federal government with

---

[57]*Statutes of Canada*, 1908, c. 7.

[58]The excess circulation was in fact taxed at the maximum rate, and the crop-moving season, originally interpreted as October to January inclusive, was expanded in 1912 to cover September–February.

[59]*Statutes of Canada*, 1913, c. 9. Other provisions of this legislation included the establishing of a shareholders' independent audit of bank operation (in an effort to forestall possible failures of which there had been recent notable instances, with heavy losses to shareholders), and the requirement that any proposed bank merger must henceforth be approved in writing by the Minister of Finance.

[60]See for example, C. A. Curtis, "The Evolution of Canadian Banking", in *The Annals of the American Academy of Political and Social Science*, Vol. 253, September, 1947, p. 118: " . . . it ended the elasticity of the currency, which had been possible because the issue of bank notes required no special reserve provision; it was as simple to expand the note issue as to expand deposits. This had been the great merit of the bank-note issue, permitting it to expand and contract with the seasonal needs of business, which was of great importance in the development of the country, particularly in its earlier stages."

unprecedented financial problems. The approach to these problems involved some striking changes both in the monetary and banking structure of the economy, and following a brief account of the early development of banking facilities in Western Canada, we shall turn to a consideration of these wartime and post-war developments.

## CHAPTER V

# EARLY MONETARY AND BANKING DEVELOPMENTS IN WESTERN CANADA

An important phase of Canadian banking development in the post-Confederation period was the expansion of banking facilities throughout the West. In the two centuries between 1670 and 1870, virtually all economic activity in this area had centred round the fur trade. Following its organization in 1670, the Hudson's Bay Company had established trading-posts on the shores of Hudson and James Bays, to which the Indians brought their furs and from which they obtained in exchange an assortment of products which a relatively advanced European culture could provide.[1] The Company was continually harassed in its operations by rival French traders, who in the early years frequently attacked and captured its trading-posts. By the beginning of the eighteenth century, these tactics had largely given way to economic conflict, in which the French began to penetrate the Northwest from their St. Lawrence headquarters and to seek out the Indians in order to carry on trade, thereby cutting into the Hudson's Bay Company's source of furs. Following the British conquest, this competition was carried on by English fur-trading interests centred in Montreal, and became very bitter after the founding of the North West Company in 1783.

Faced with vigorous and well organized opposition, the Hudson's Bay Company abandoned its earlier policy of awaiting the Indians at its northern posts, and as early as 1774 the Company had built Cumberland House, the first of a series of inland posts. Following several decades of life-or-death struggle with the North West Company, the latter was forced to yield, in 1821, and it became absorbed into the Hudson's Bay Company. But as time went on, and settlement progressed, the Company's monopoly gradually became undermined by individual traders and trappers, and the culmination was the transfer of the Company's western lands to the new Dominion government in 1869, on terms already indicated.

One very interesting aspect of the Hudson's Bay Company's operations was that of providing a rudimentary currency system in those areas where it traded with the Indians. The initial problem, that of the establishment of some measure of value, was solved at an early date by the concept of the "made-beaver",

---

[1]See the *Catalogue of the Hudson's Bay Company's Historical Exhibit at Winnipeg,* 1925, p. 47: "The 'outfit' of 1672 for H.B.C. trading posts was two hundred fowling pieces with powder and shot, as many brass kettles, twelve gross knives and a thousand hatchets." In these early years, the wants of the Indians were few, but gradually the stock of merchandise in the posts became more varied.

a unit equal in value to the skin of an adult male beaver in prime condition.[2] For some one hundred and fifty years, the beaver skin was the standard to which the value of all goods to be traded was related. To facilitate the actual process of exchange, the Indian trapper was given a quantity of made-beavers equal to the value of his furs. At first, these made-beavers took the form of sticks, porcupine quills, ivory discs, musket balls, or whatever else was readily available to serve as counters.[3] Beginning near 1850, the made-beaver counter was standardized in the form of a brass coin, with lesser denominations of one-half, one-quarter and one-eighth made-beavers also being issued. These tokens remained in use in some northern districts until as late as 1910, when they were valued at about fifty cents. In its operations in the Eastern Arctic, the Company still uses fox tokens across its counters; in the Western Arctic, regular money is used. The Company's trade with the Indians was really little more than barter, although modified by the use of a temporary and localized medium of exchange.

Following the arrival of the early Selkirk settlers along the Red River in 1812, the need for some form of circulating medium became apparent. During the early years of the colony's development, all its imports were sent out from Britain by the Earl of Selkirk, and sold to the settlers by his agents. Complaints of extortionate prices, etc., led to an undertaking by the Hudson's Bay Company, in 1821, to supply all merchandise needed in the colony, but dissatisfaction with the adequacy of their arrangements led to the appearance of increasing numbers of private importers in later years.[4] Meanwhile, widespread protests had arisen concerning the lack of any adequate domestic medium of exchange, metallic currency of any kind being exceedingly scarce. The Hudson's Bay Company undertook to relieve this situation when, in 1820, its head office in London sent

---

[2] In the earliest years of the Company's fur-trading, " . . . the trader examined the skins and indicated to each hunter what he was prepared to give in exchange. At one period, eight to twelve beaver skins would be taken for a gun; one beaver for a half-pound of powder, for a pound of tobacco or half-pound of beads. At first the amount of payment was left to the judgment of the factor, but in the eighteenth century the Company began to issue at London annually a 'tariff' specifying the values for H.B.C. traders to give in exchange. This ultimately developed into a nominal standard, and resulted in the 'made-beaver' system." See *ibid.*, p. 48.

[3] The Indians usually came to trade at the posts in summer, when their birch-bark canoes encountered no ice. Those natives located close to the posts frequently came in winter. Upon arrival with his furs, he would proceed to the trading-room, where his furs would be separated and valued, and the appropriate number of made-beaver counters turned over to him. He then proceeded to the store-room, where each article was prominently valued in terms of made-beaver. Almost invariably, the Indian exhausted his entire proceeds, and the counters did not leave the trading-post. He was frequently given goods on credit, and rarely defaulted on his obligations. This is explained in part, of course, because the trader knew each native individually, and acted accordingly.

[4] See *Miscellaneous Documents, Canada, 1858-86*, Vol. 11, *The Nor'Wester*, Feb. 28, 1860: The total of "recent" annual imports was quoted as being in excess of £20,000 sterling, plus freight from London to York Landing. "The Hudson's Bay Company once professed to charge £5 sterling per ton; afterwards £8 per ton. There is, however, good reason to believe that instead of £8, the settlers have paid from £10 to £20 per ton."

instructions to its officials in Rupert's Land for the issuing of one-pound and five-shilling notes in that territory.[5] They were to be issued only in payment of money due by the Company, or for sixty-day bills drawn on London, care being taken that such bills would be duly honoured. Provision was also made for the Company's notes to be received at its principal trading-posts in payment for goods sold.

The issue of these notes, and of a subsequent shipment of one-shilling notes, was delayed until 1823, apparently because of some reservations by Governor Simpson as to their effectiveness. In particular, he feared that instead of serving their main purpose as a domestic circulation medium, they would ". . . be collected by the wealthy inhabitants of the Colony, the Petty traders from Canada, or even the Traders from within the American boundaries, to whom we should be under the necessity of giving Cash for them by Drafts on England instead of passing through our hands in payment of Goods sold."[6] This view was of course not unreasonable in a pioneer colony characterized by a relatively heavy demand for imports. The notes were nevertheless issued, and they provided an acceptable medium of exchange in the colony for several decades, their retention being facilitated by the Company's policy of being careful about issuing bills on London and about issuing money to the United States.[7]

Despite this paper money issued by the Hudson's Bay Company, complaints about the inadequacy of the currency continued, and these were accompanied by the customary agitation in any economically undeveloped area for the establishment of some banking institutions.[8] While the Company sold bills of exchange on London (in the redemption of its own notes) and held money on deposit for its own employees, one of the Red River settlers wrote in 1860 that nothing which could properly be called a banking system had yet been established in that area. His statement was substantially true, because the Hudson's

---

[5]Twenty books, each containing 100 one-pound notes and 40 books, each containing 100 five-shilling notes, were shipped to York Factory in 1820, followed by a supply of one-shilling notes a year later. These notes were at first redeemable in bills on London only at York Factory, unless the note-holders paid a five-per-cent premium for such bills. This aroused considerable ill feeling, and the restriction was eventually removed, so that bills might be drawn at the Fort Garry settlement and elsewhere.

[6]See *Letter from Governor George Simpson to the Governor and Committee, Hudson's Bay Company, London,* dated York Factory, September 1, 1822.

[7]The paper notes of the Hudson's Bay Company became known as "blankets", because of their size, which was about five times that of present-day Canadian notes.

[8]See *Miscellaneous Documents, Canada, 1858-86,* Vol. 11, *The Nor'Wester,* March 28, 1860: Despite the scarcity of money, apparently much was held by the settlers "in boxes at home for months at a time". The owners lost interest income and the community lost the use of such funds, "laid up as if it were in a napkin". It was felt that the colony couldn't develop unless institutions "found to be of real advantage in other parts of the world" were introduced. These would provide greater facilities for commerce, and for the opening of savings banks which "notwithstanding the fact that this Colony has been formed for forty years, have never yet been brought into operation to form and to encourage economical habits among the poor people of this Settlement".

Bay Company performed very restricted banking functions, and the provision of full-fledged banking services in the settlement was still some few years away. The way was paved for the appearance of outside banks by the transfer of owner-ship of Rupert's Land to the federal government, at which time Canadian cur-rency became the official medium of exchange and the life of the Company's notes, even though they remained in circulation for some few years, was offi-cially terminated.

Looking briefly at the far west, it was in these years preceding Confederation that the formative influences in British Columbia's banking development first appeared. As in other parts of western Canada, the earliest economic activity in the North Pacific area was the fur trade. Originally developed on a maritime basis, this was followed by the establishment of overland trading routes by the North West Company, and after 1821, by the Hudson's Bay Company.[9] The arrival of prospectors from California after 1850, and the mass invasion during the Fraser gold-rush in 1858 greatly undermined the basis of the fur trade. At this time, the economic orientation of the British colonies on the Pacific Coast (the mainland and the island colonies) was toward their southern neighbours, rather than the eastern parts of British North America.[10] This circumstance caused serious political misgivings and was directly responsible for the con-struction of the Canadian Pacific Railway, as part of the agreement which brought British Columbia into Confederation in 1871.[11]

The development of banking facilities in that territory began with the dis-covery of gold on the Fraser in 1858, which did much to stimulate the subsequent economic development of the province.[12] Just as in Eastern Canada the earliest banking services had been provided through mercantile channels and by private banking interests, in the days before the existence of chartered banks, so in British Columbia did early banking develop. The "first rude attempts" at bank-ing were initiated by the express companies, such as Wells, Fargo and Company, Freeman's Express, etc., which came to British Columbia in the wake of the

[9]See C. R. Young, H. A. Innis and J. H. Dales, *op. cit.*, pp. 373-8.

[10]San Francisco was the centre of all trade with the British colonies on the Pacific, and the centre of all their communications with the outside world. By 1854, steamship con-nections had been established between Victoria and San Francisco.

[11]See *ibid.*, p. 384: " . . . the whole economic development of the colony during the gold era was merely an extension of similar developments south of the International Boundary."

[12]A form of banking operation, common to all the aboriginal inhabitants of British Columbia in early times, was the custom of the "potlatch". This is a Chinook word, signi-fying "gift", but the connotation was of a gift with elastic string attached, so that it would come back with interest, at rates which ranged from 100% to 200%. This system of parting with one's goods overcame the risks of fire and raiding, where large stocks might be held by one person. The system was subjected to many abuses, and was finally declared illegal by the federal government. For details of this interesting aspect of aboriginal culture, see W. M. Halliday, *Potlatch and Totem* (Toronto: J. M. Dent and Sons, Ltd.), 1935.

gold-miners in 1858.[13] Their connections with California and the eastern United States permitted the safe transport of gold-dust from the colonies. These companies were large purchasers of gold-dust on their own account, and money was received on deposit and for transmission. But their banking operations did not extend to the issuing of their own notes, and payment of the company's obligations was always made in ordinary currency or in drafts on their branches.

The first institution to undertake a full-fledged banking business was a private concern known as Macdonald's Bank, founded by Alexander D. Macdonald in Victoria in 1859.[14] This bank was not only responsible for the first issue of paper money in British Columbia and Vancouver Island, but was the first bank of issue and deposit west of the Great Lakes. Macdonald had arrived from California in 1858, and in response to an obvious need, decided to establish his bank.[15] At this time, there were no legislative enactments relating to banks, such institutions being hitherto unknown, and Macdonald was therefore able to issue notes without restriction of any kind, and without security. His bank had no charter and for some years it operated without regulation or supervision. The bank was highly successful in its early activities, for it provided useful services, and ". . . as Macdonald was not only personally popular, but also an enterprising business man, it grew and prospered".[16]

The main service which the bank provided was the purchase of gold-dust from the miners, in return for which the bank customarily paid out its own notes. For some time following the discovery of gold in British Columbia, however, gold-dust was the common circulating medium on the frontier. The urgent demand for goods in the mining areas, coupled with transportation difficulties into the interior, led to very high prices. A contemporary noted sadly that ". . . a drink of anything except water was half a dollar."[17] Each miner carried his bag of gold-dust with him, and the amount of gold required for each transaction was weighed out. While the use of gold-dust was a necessary expedient, it was uneconomical and subject to considerable abuse. Unscrupulous persons could take

[13]For an interesting account of the operations of these companies, see E. O. S. Scholefield, *British Columbia* (Vancouver: S. J. Clarke Publishing Co.), 1914, Vol. I. Other well known expresses operating at this time were the Dietz and Nelson, Barnard and Ballou Companies. About 1866, F. Garesche became the Victoria agent of Wells, Fargo, and he later became associated with A. A. Green in the firm of Garesche, Green and Co., which ultimately took over the Wells, Fargo express operations in Canada, and which developed a substantial private banking business. The banking firm later became Green, Worlock and Co., and was forced into liquidation about 1894. The depositors ultimately were paid off at about fifty cents on the dollar.

[14]See *ibid.*, also R. L. Reid, "The First Bank in Western Canada", in *Canadian Historical Review*, VII, 1926.

[15]See the *British Colonist*, March 12, 1859. The readers were informed that Macdonald had recently returned from the mining-country with samples of gold, and that "as evidence of his confidence in the country, he has opened a Banking House on Yates street." (This was indeed a curious interpretation of the need for "confidence" in banking operations.)

[16]Reid, *op. cit.*, p. 295.

[17]Scholefield, *op. cit.*

advantage of the miners, since the fineness of the dust varied, and specific sums could be merely approximated. In time, the circulation of bank notes became general, both because of growing public confidence in their reliability and because of their obvious advantages over gold-dust as a medium of exchange. The bank also accepted deposits, although these were relatively unimportant in its operations, and it sold bills of exchange on New York and London, and made advances on gold-dust which it sent, on behalf of the owners, to San Francisco for assay and coinage. In April, 1859, Macdonald became the agent for Freeman's San Francisco express.

Later in 1859, the Bank of British North America extended its operations to the far west by opening a branch in Victoria. In the beginning, it did not appear to compete vigorously in gold-buying activities, leaving this to Macdonald's and the express companies. Other lines of banking business appeared to be more attractive, and it became banker for the city of Victoria and for the government of the colony of Vancouver Island.[18] However, its operations expanded very slowly, and when its competitors opened branches in the Cariboo in 1864, the Bank of British North America followed, and as a consequence of greatly expanded purchases of gold-dust, it opened a fully equipped assay office at Victoria. Additional agencies were opened in subsequent years, but by 1877, its only British Columbia office was in Victoria.

Meanwhile, the early Cariboo discoveries had led to the revival of demands for establishing a government assay office and mint, with Victoria and New Westminster pressing their respective claims.[19] The commercial interests claimed that not only was business hampered by the lack of suitable coinage but that much trade was lost by the miners having to take their gold to San Francisco to

[18]See the *British Colonist*, Victoria, August 22, 1859: The recent establishment of the Bank of British North America was viewed as a "great acquisition" for the colony, the commercial and financial life of which had been suffering from "absolute" stagnation, for which one great reason was deemed to be the lack of banking facilities, and particularly of an adequate medium of exchange. The principal coins in circulation included American gold and silver (minted at San Francisco), sterling gold and silver coins, and a variety of French, Mexican, Scandinavian and other pieces many of which arrived via the Atlantic colonies. The usual difficulties about their ratings had arisen.

[19]See, for example, the *British Colonist*, November 5, 6, 7, 1861. Reference is also made to the existing "glut" of gold-dust and to the scarcity of coins, which commanded a five-per-cent premium over bars and dust. The governor stated in 1861 that " . . . at this moment there is an amount of gold-dust in the hands of miners from Cariboo, residing at Victoria, exceeding one-quarter of a million sterling; and so great is the present dearth of coin that it brings a premium of five per-cent and over when procurable, which is generally not the case. . . . The miners and other holders of gold-dust are naturally incensed and refuse to submit to this depreciation on the value of their property, when they know it can be converted into coin for the moderate charge of one-half of one per-cent at the United States Branch Mint in San Francisco, making an important saving to them of 4½ per-cent. They are consequently leaving Victoria by every opportunity." See R. L. Reid, *The Assay Office and the Proposed Mint at New Westminster*, Archives of British Columbia, Memoir No. VII (Victoria: King's Printer, 1926).

have it coined.[20] The government responded by setting up an assay office and refinery at New Westminster, which, however, remained in operation only until the end of 1861. The operations of its mint were even briefer, and more curious. By mid-1862 it was ready to begin coining, and a few ten- and twenty-dollar coins were struck. These were of the same diameter and gold value as those minted at San Francisco, but were struck from unrefined gold, .850 fine. These coins did not get into general circulation, and are now very rare. It is difficult to see how these coins, reduced merely to uniform fineness, could have been much more satisfactory than gold bars. The problem of a satisfactory circulating medium was actually met by the importation of coin (much by the chartered banks) and by the issue of bank notes. The governor soon issued orders, respecting the newly established mint, to "grease it and lay it away", and this having been done, it was not until early in the twentieth century that gold coinage was inaugurated in Canada.

Despite a widespread belief that continued gold discoveries would usher in a new era in the economic development of the colonies, and that the dark days of 1858 and 1859 would not be repeated, there was evidence that the expected improvement was not developing as rapidly as had been hoped. It was noted, for instance, that despite high rates of interest and good security, capital was not being attracted as was the case in Canada and Australia.[21] Mining, lumbering, fishing, real estate and trade all offered good investment opportunities, but the exploitation of these opportunities was believed to require extensive advertising and some solution to the means of payment difficulties.

In this environment of potential economic expansion the Bank of British Columbia began operations in Victoria and in New Westminster in 1862, as a competitor of the Bank of British North America and of Macdonald's Bank. Its competition with the several express companies was confined largely to gold-buying operations. It had been established by royal charter, with a capitalization of $1¼ million, and like its competitors, promptly issued notes, which were accepted without question.[22] In 1863, it opened the first bank branch in the mining area (Richfield, in the Cariboo district), preceding Macdonald's there

[20]As early as 1859, the treasurer of the colony of British Columbia had recommended to the governor that £100,000 be imported from England, to be paid for in bullion. In 1861, some £14,000 arrived, an amount which did little to ease the contemporary currency problems.

[21]See the *British Colonist*, July 9, 1862. The prevailing interest rates in the colonies were quoted at 1¼%-3% per month or 15%-36% per annum; thus, at Victoria, the rate on 30-day bills was 18%, on sixty-day bills 24% and on 60-90-day bills 36%. In England, rates ranged from 3½%-5%; in Canada, they were allegedly "seldom" over 6%. Within several years, the B.C. rates were reduced to a maximum of 18%.

[22]The founding of the Bank of British Columbia was explained in terms of (a) the recent gold discoveries on the B.C. mainland, (b) the abundance of capital in England seeking investment and (c) the success of recent banking ventures both in England and abroad. See Ross, *op. cit.*, I.

by several months, and the Bank of British Columbia by a year.[23] Since the main business of these banks was the buying of gold-dust, the establishing of a "gold-escort" was indispensable to their successful operation. In the early years, the government assumed little responsibility for the safe passage of gold from the mines, and each bank and express company was responsible for its own arrangements.[24] Although Macdonald's Bank enjoyed prosperity in its first several years of operation, it found that with its relatively limited resources, it was becoming increasingly difficult to resist the inroads made by its stronger competitors.

A further and even more serious threat to its existence came from the decision of the colonial government in 1864 to impose some restrictions on banking in the colony, particularly in respect of note issue.[25] Up to that time, the circulation

[23]Until this time, the miners had no local facilities for obtaining drafts or remittances, and Victoria was the closest point at which gold-dust could be sold. *The Colonist* (January 7, 1863) believed that the establishment of banking in the Cariboo would be of great benefit both to the miners and traders there and to the merchants, dealers and traders centred in Victoria. Following the discovery of gold in the Yukon, the chartered banks extended services practically identical with those provided in the British Columbia mining areas. The Canadian Bank of Commerce opened a branch in Dawson in 1898, and the Bank of British North America did likewise the following summer. For an interesting account of the Yukon banking scene, see Victor Ross, *op. cit.*, II. Here (p. 188) it is pointed out that in order to operate at a profit, the well-established lines of conservative banking had to be substantially modified, and "the problem was to draw a sane dividing line between courage tempered by wisdom and common sense, and courage without either". The bank's concern that its manager might have his judgment too much influenced by local problems is indicated by the following comment: "It was of course evident, as time went on, that changes in the management and personnel of the staff in Dawson were advantageous, and even necessary, in order to bring to the appraisement and conduct of the business entirely fresh points of view and opinions untrammelled by settled convictions based on several years of local experience; for the latter, although undoubtedly of great value, might well in that sanguine atmosphere have a tendency to engender undue optimism, and a consequent measure of disregard for what appears to be the 'cramping' influences of recognized methods of lending" (p. 189).

[24]*British Colonist*, June 9, 1863. Here, for example, it is stated that the Bank of British Columbia had forwarded nearly $75,000 in notes and specie to its Richfield branch, in care of its gold escort. It had begun operations in mid-June by selling drafts on Victoria, and not much gold was expected "down" before late July or early August, from which time to the end of the season remittances would be heavy. The banks and express companies shipped their purchases of gold-dust to San Francisco for assay and sale.

[25]Public opinion was divided on the propriety of bank regulation. A committee of business men studying the framing of a Bank Act concluded that such a measure would be premature, in the present undeveloped state of the colony. The *British Colonist*, January 13, 1864, observed editorially that it would be unfortunate if the banks' right to issue notes were impaired to the point of making such issue unprofitable. It did favour the establishing of some requirement as to minimum cash reserves. But " . . . the principle of a paper issue in these colonies is still in its infancy, and the value of the notes issued by our banks has hitherto been a mere bagatelle when compared with their capital and coin reserve. . . . The result of any under-restriction of a legitimate note issue, especially in these colonies, where it costs so much to maintain a metallic currency, must result in restricted banking accommodation, and at the same time depreciate the price of gold dust on the mines in the same ratio as the difference between the cost of buying with notes and buying with imported gold coin, a difference which has been calculated at 'fifteen per cent!' This is surely not an end for our legislature to aim at in framing banking laws."

of bank notes had been of exceedingly modest proportions but there was strong feeling that the government should assume some responsibility in this matter.[26] Thus, the legislature passed two measures, the first being the Bank Note Act of 1864. This prohibited all banks except those with royal charter (the Bank of British Columbia and the Bank of British North America) or those actually having issued currency before July 1, 1864 (Macdonald's Bank) from issuing notes intended to pass as money. The second measure prohibited any non-chartered bank from issuing notes after March 1, 1865. This of course meant that Macdonald's Bank must reorganize if it wished to continue in business.[27]

Before this problem could be resolved, fate dealt Macdonald a deadly blow when his bank in Victoria was robbed in September, 1864, during his absence in the Cariboo. There was apparently "a clean sweep made of everything of value on the premises", and the loot reportedly included some $15,000 in sovereigns, a few $5 pieces, $10,000 in Bank of British North America notes, small quantities of the bank's own notes, and some gold-dust, and silver coin. This money had apparently been assembled to be taken to Barkerville in the Cariboo the next day, and there were strong suspicions of an "inside" job.[28] Ingenious as the robbery may have been, its repercussions were most serious. At the Cariboo branch, Macdonald was able to meet all his obligations promptly, with the result that a run was checked and public confidence in the institution restored. He returned to Victoria several weeks later, with a substantial amount of cash, ". . . to face his creditors, who had become uneasy".[29] A committee of the bank's creditors investigated its affairs, and two days before it made its report, Macdonald departed for San Francisco, hoping to find a means of satisfying the claims against his bank.[30] He was apparently unsuccessful, for nothing further was heard from him. Thus, ". . . the Bank faded into thin air, leaving behind some treasured notes, printed on white paper, valuable only as a souvenir of the first bank of Western Canada".[31] None of these note-holders received any payment, being simply unsecured creditors of the bank. Nevertheless, this pioneer bank in British Columbia had apparently been well managed and well received by the public, and although it found the competition of its more powerful rivals increasingly troublesome, it might well have continued its useful services for

[26]For the quarter ended September 30, 1864, the Bank of British Columbia reported Notes in Circulation, $151,000; Deposits, $169,000; gold and silver coin and bullion $358,000. For the same period, the Bank of British North America reported, for its operations in Victoria Island and dependencies: Notes in Circulation $37,000, Deposits $284,000, gold and silver coin and bullion $247,000.

[27]Macdonald apparently planned to organize a joint-stock bank to take over his existing business under a royal charter. But the robbery of his bank, with its fatal consequences, intervened.

[28]See the *British Colonist*, September 24, 1864: "The absence of vigorous effort either on the part of the police authorities . . . or those personally interested in the recovery of the stolen property, elicited the most pointed expressions of astonishment."

[29]Reid, *The First Bank in Western Canada, op. cit.*, p. 301.

[30]The firm had liabilities of $80,000, assets of $31,000 at the time its operations were suspended.

[31]*Ibid.*, p. 301.

some few years, had not its career been abruptly terminated by the disastrous robbery of 1864.

Macdonald's and the other banks opened branches from time to time, some of which proved to be only temporary.[32] The Pacific colonies, despite the activity in the gold-mining industry, were in the economic doldrums between 1864 and 1866.[33] The great financial storm in the latter year had its repercussions there, and there were many business failures. A gradual recovery began in 1867, to which the prospect of Confederation lent further encouragement. Contemporary economic discussion frequently displayed a distinct "mercantilist" bias.[34]

In 1869, in response to demands for some form of savings institution which would "put more capital to work", and give small investors a chance to employ their savings profitably, the British Columbia Investment and Loan Society began operations.[35] But until the completion of the Canadian Pacific Railway to Vancouver, the entire field of commercial banking was held by the Bank of British North America, the Bank of British Columbia, and the private firm of Garesche, Green and Company, whose banking operations developed out of their express business, but which was forced to liquidate in 1894. In 1886, the Bank of British Columbia established a branch in Vancouver, and thereby provided that community with its first chartered bank. With the arrival of the railroad, the eastern banks began to appear, and the first to cross the Rockies was the Bank of Montreal, followed at an early date by eastern competitors.[36]

[32]By 1865, the Bank of British Columbia had six branches in operation, but one by one they were closed until only the Victoria and Cariboo offices remained. With the decline of placer-mining, the bank was in difficulties from 1866-8, although business at its newly opened branches in San Francisco and Portland was good. During this period, colonial finances were in a desperate state, and the colonies were borrowing in London at 12% to repay a 6% loan; they were deeply indebted to both of the chartered banks, so that they dared not deposit their meagre resources in either. In 1876, the bank closed its Cariboo branch, where gold output had fallen greatly. In 1901, it sold its assets to the Canadian Bank of Commerce, by which time its capitalization had been increased to $3 million.

[33]In 1864, gold exports ($2.8 million) represented approximately ¾ of the colonies' total exports. In 1865, gold exports declined to $2.1 million, in 1866 to $1.9 million, and in 1867 to $1.6 million. Between 1858 and 1876, the value of placer-gold mined in British Columbia was in excess of $40 million.

[34]See, for example, the *British Colonist*, January 1, 1868: An editorial points out that the colonies now have fewer but sufficient businesses and more farmers; that they produce more of their own supplies—flour, spirits, etc.; that they grow their own hops and manufacture their own beer; that they supply themselves with livestock, vegetables and cereals; that they therefore retain more of their own treasure and thus encourage their own business.

[35]On deposits of six months or less, interest paid was 6%; more than six months, 7%; more than one year, 8%; the rates paid by the chartered banks were substantially lower.

[36]The Bank of Montreal opened its branch in Vancouver in 1887 and in New Westminster in 1888; by 1897 it had seven branches in British Columbia. It had been closely associated with the financing of the Canadian Pacific Railway. Among the other eastern banks which early established offices in the province were the Canadian Bank of Commerce, the Imperial Bank, the Merchants' Bank of Halifax (which in 1901 became the Royal Bank of Canada) and Molson's Bank. These institutions, along with the Bank of Montreal, the Bank of British Columbia and the Bank of British North America, established the Vancouver clearing-house in 1898. Clearings for 1899 were $39 million, by 1906, $100 million and by 1911, $543 million. Other eastern banks arrived before World War 1.

The Bank of British North America and the Bank of British Columbia were the only two banks to operate under royal charter in Canada, and with the charter of each institution due to expire in 1885, the question of the terms of renewal and of the continuation of their peculiar position had been under active discussion in the preceding year. The banks had not at this time been made subject to the banking laws of Canada, but it was the wish of the British Treasury that " . . . not only shall these banks not violate the laws of Canada by acts contrary thereto, but also that they shall actively conform to all general laws applicable to them, and not omit to do anything required of them by such laws." The Treasury believed that the reasons for conferring special privileges by royal charter no longer existed, and that the status of these banks should be changed gradually to that of other Canadian banks. Their charters were therefore renewed for a further ten years, but with the understanding that no further modification, alteration or extension of powers would be granted by royal charter. Thus, in the revision of 1890, these banks were brought substantially within the sphere of the Canadian Bank Act.

The first branch of any chartered bank to be established west of the Great Lakes was opened at Winnipeg in 1878, and there followed a steady expansion of banking facilities to meet the needs of the West.[37] But as usual, preceding the arrival of these large institutions, valuable and extensive services had been provided by private banks, the most outstanding of which was the firm of Alloway and Champion.[38] The early dependence of other parts of Canada upon these institutions has already been noted, and it is true that throughout our history, " . . . private bankers or banking establishments were the forerunners of larger and stronger banks, and some of the chartered banks had their beginnings in private banking firms or bought out private banking firms in order to become established and enlarge their field.[39] Because of the diversity and the success of

[37]The pioneer branch was established by the Bank of Montreal, and it was followed within a year by the Merchants' Bank. Within two decades, eleven chartered banks were operating forty-six branches in Manitoba, six were in the North West Territories (i.e., Saskatchewan and Alberta) with eighteen branches, and two banks each had a branch in the Yukon. See *The Statistical Year Book of Canada*, 1898. The channels which had been developed for the mobilization of capital in Eastern Canada spread rapidly westward. These included not only the chartered banks, but life insurance companies, private bankers, mercantile houses, etc. By 1914, the chartered banks were operating some 870 branches in the three prairie provinces.

[38]Of the great many private banks which played an important part in the evolution of the Canadian banking system, Alloway and Champion was the largest and most diversified. It pursued a long and honourable career before its assets were acquired by the Canadian Bank of Commerce in 1930. In 1890, in addition to forty-one chartered banks, there were some 190 private banks in Canada. More than three-quarters of these were in Ontario and Quebec, seven in the Maritimes and thirty-one in the West. By 1920, their numbers had declined to about a dozen.

[39]See Peter Lowe, "All Western Dollars" in *Papers Read Before the Historical and Scientific Society of Manitoba, 1945-46* (Winnipeg: 1946), p. 16. This paper provided an excellent outline of the history of the firm of Alloway and Champion by a former general manager.

the operations of Alloway and Champion, it will be useful to review briefly their contribution to Canadian banking. The firm was established in 1879, and it developed a wide range of financial services particularly adapted to the needs of European immigrants. These services included the buying and selling of gold and foreign exchange, the acceptance of savings deposits, the lending of money and the sale of land to settlers. The firm also arranged for the purchase of steamship tickets and other transportation for settlers visiting their homeland and for their dependants coming to Canada.[40]

Foreign exchange operations represented an important part of the firm's business and in 1905, a "North End" Winnipeg branch was opened to accommodate the expansion of this activity. An earlier branch had been established at Portage la Prairie, but it was soon closed because of losses incurred through poor management. The bank's operations reached a peak between 1900 and 1913, as European immigrants poured into Canada. In this latter period, it was the North End branch that accumulated funds from arriving settlers, and the main office that loaned them. The latter never developed large savings deposits (being gradually surrounded by other chartered banks), but the security for loans was much better for the class of borrowers reached by the main office. Immigrant remittances were another important aspect of the firm's exchange operations. Many settlers had come from central Europe and they distrusted instruments such as bank drafts, favouring actual currency.[41] Frequently, the immigrant wished to return home in the autumn for a visit or to bring out his family, in which case he was provided with prepaid tickets and actual foreign exchange.[42] Between 1900 and 1914, there were many private exchange dealers in the West, but these were mostly of a small-scale and transitory character. For many years, all banks, including the chartered banks, depended upon Alloway and Champion for their foreign exchange services, having no departments of their own. The latter firm published a weekly "card" of rates for the benefit of all interested parties.

Concerning savings deposits, their volume in the North End branch immedi-

---

[40]The firm often sent its representatives to board immigrant trains at Halifax. En route to Winnipeg, these representatives would arrange to meet the various financial needs of the settlers. When the settlers left Winnipeg to go farther west, they were often provided with self-addressed envelopes, to mail their savings to the firm or to make requests for other services.

[41]In time they were taught to accept a post-office money order system. The immigrant would deliver his Canadian dollars, receive a receipt, and give directions as to the recipient of the foreign currency abroad. Alloway and Champion maintained accounts in banks in St. Petersburg, Dresden, Naples, Vienna, London, etc., but in the case of southern and central European remittances, the firm would instruct its foreign agents to buy post-office money orders payable to the recipient at his home post-office. In the case of the northern Europeans, who were economically more advanced and more familiar with developed exchange mechanisms, bank drafts could be used directly.

[42]In pre-War I years, the firm imported as much as 20,000 crowns ($5,000) per week in the autumn. All foreign exchange operations were carried out on a commission of ½ of 1%, based on par value.

ately following World War I approximated $2 million, a volume greater than in any other bank branch in Winnipeg, including the chartered bank branch offices. During the war, many immigrant depositors, disturbed by monetary developments in their home-lands, feared the depreciation or possible confiscation of their dollar deposits, and frequently came to get physical possession of their savings. This being provided, they were usually content to redeposit the money. The North End branch made a point of the ostentatious display of gold and paper currencies in their windows, which produced valuable psychological effects. (This never produced an attempt at robbery.) Many of the smaller private banks failed during the war because of their inability to meet the immigrants' unpredictable demands for cash.

In the making of loans, the private bankers were of course not restricted by any charter, and could take security of any kind. The only limitation was the resources at their disposal. In the earliest period of western settlement, real estate or paper based on land was about the only security available, and these loans became the chief source of revenue for the private banks. They were usually short-term (3-6 months) loans, the rate of interest varying with the security, but 12% was common on "good" loans. "The private banking firm could also make loans of a similar character to those usually handled by the chartered banks which included loans to merchants, loans to individuals against specific security or on the endorsement of one or more persons."[43] The "small loan" business in Winnipeg originated with Alloway and Champion, and was confined to that firm until the later arrival of finance companies. The chartered banks did not become interested in this outlet until a much later date. The basis of these loans was either personal endorsement by other parties or real estate security. Also accommodated were many borrowers who had reached the limits of their credit at the chartered banks.[44]

The firm's transactions in lands arose principally from its handling of scrip in tremendous volume from which substantial profits were realized.[45] The firm specialized both in land scrip and cash scrip, although the bulk of its transactions centred around the latter type. Both types of scrip appeared in connection with "Dominion Lands" policy, and provided the firm with an opportunity not only to acquire title to lands on its own account, for speculative purposes, but

[43]See Peter Lowe, *op. cit.*, p. 16.

[44]A common practice of Alloway and Champion was to buy personal notes outright, taking a percentage discount off the face, which was regarded as protection against possible loss. These amounts were transferred to profits as the notes were actually paid off. The firm itself maintained a credit of $1 million with the Bank of Commerce, which it drew upon rather sparingly.

[45]Between 1879 and 1906, the surplus capital of the banking firm was invested in well selected farm lands and municipal business properties. After the latter date, no capital risks were assumed, and the firm "reverted more closely to carrying on legitimate banking and loaning, or investments which were closely related to the banking business." See Peter Lowe, *op. cit.*, p. 22.

also to earn substantial commissions while acting as agents or middlemen between the sellers and buyers of these instruments.

In 1912, the capital and undivided profits of Alloway and Champion had risen to more than one million dollars, at which date the partnership applied for incorporation, and became a company with limited liability. Immediately following World War I, the company sold its assets to the Canadian Bank of Commerce, but the business remained intact and continued to operate as Alloway and Champion until 1930. Upon the death of its founder, William F. Alloway, at the latter date, its assets were distributed to the various branches of the purchasing bank, and thus ended the history of the private bank which in Canadian experience had been unrivalled in size and durability.[46]

Although more modest in their range of operations, there were many other private banks which provided valuable services in the early westward expansion, before the appearance of chartered banks, and many continued in operation for years after the arrival of the powerful eastern institutions. Among the prominent private bankers of this era were Brine, McDonald and Company,[47] Hitchcock and McCulloch,[48] Lafferty and Smith,[49] and Cowdry Brothers.[50] Barter between merchants and settlers was of course widespread in these early days, since "money . . . was scarce; the pioneers who eked out a scanty living on the land exchanged products, and a dollar bill entitled its owner to the distinctive name

[46]The remaining records of Alloway and Champion were kindly made available to me by the Canadian Bank of Commerce at Winnipeg. The general ledger, as of May 31, 1919, illustrates the scope of the firm's operations just before it was purchased by the chartered bank. Its total assets approximated $3 million, of which cash amounted to some $45,000, Canadian balances $31,000 and foreign balances $34,000; securities held exceeded $1 million, loans $3/4 million; holdings of real estate exceeded $1 million, farm lands representing the largest item. Among its liabilities, deposits exceeded $1.5 million; loans outstanding amounted to only $40,000; the firm's capital and reserve approximated $1.2 million.

[47]McDonald and Company, a real estate and lumber firm, began operations as a private bank in Qu'Appelle, N.W.T., in 1887, taking over an earlier banking enterprise known as Messrs. Cruthers and Company. See the *Qu'Appelle Vidette*, September 22, 1887; the firm shortly met competition from S. H. Caswell, merchant, who advertised that he had started a general banking business—sold drafts on anywhere in Canada, United States and Great Britain; received deposits on which 5% interest was paid; current accounts were solicited and collections made. See *Qu'Appelle Progress*, February 5, 1891.

[48]Hitchcock and McCulloch, with headquarters in Moose Jaw, N.W.T., provided similar services there, and continued in operation after the arrival of the Canadian Bank of Commerce in 1901.

[49]Lafferty and Smith had begun operations in Calgary as early as 1880, and in Edmonton in 1886; the firm later became known as Lafferty and Moore. At various times, their operations extended to Regina, Lethbridge, Calgary and Vancouver. They issued drafts, made collections, bought and sold domestic and foreign exchange, accepted deposits, arranged advances and dealt in scrip. See the *Edmonton Bulletin*, December 11, 1886. The first chartered bank arrived in 1891, at which time Edmonton was a town of 400-500 persons, and "the Imperial was the only [chartered] bank between Calgary and the Arctic Ocean". It had established its branch in Calgary five years earlier.

[50]Cowdry Brothers began operations about 1890, and were the leaders in early banking in Macleod. The firm was eventually taken over by the Canadian Bank of Commerce in 1905.

'capitalist'. The Hudson Bay 'traded' groceries, calico and overalls for furs; and the settlers lived almost entirely on the produce of their own soil. To establish a private bank was a dubious venture so those early bankers thought. And the settlers who were called upon to pay 24 per cent on loans thought twice before getting on the credit side of the ledger. On the best mercantile paper, the bankers loaned at 18 per cent. Through troublous times the institution survived."[51]

[51]*Edmonton Daily Capital*, September 5, 1912. This extract refers to the conditions faced by Lafferty and Moore in their operations following 1886.

## CHAPTER VI

# THE FINANCIAL ASPECTS
# OF WORLD WAR I AND ITS AFTERMATH

UNTIL World War I, the Canadian monetary system remained extremely simple, both in structure and operation. The gold standard had been adopted in the decade preceding Confederation, and for the following sixty years the preservation of the established external value of the dollar represented the sole monetary objective of the government. The possibility of pursuing any alternative monetary policy was simply not recognized, much less discussed. The government note issue was patterned after that of the Bank of England, combining a maximum fractional-reserve issue (the specified maximum varied from time to time) with a further unrestricted issue backed dollar for dollar by gold.[1]

Operating within these monetary arrangements, the chartered banks were required to maintain the convertibility of their notes (which were not legal tender) and deposits in either Dominion notes or gold, and the essential banking feature was that these institutions possessed no means of expanding their legal reserves from domestic sources. Whenever they provided gold for export, the banks necessarily reduced their cash by that amount, and the replenishment or expansion of reserves required the conversion of foreign balances (usually held in the New York market) to gold, and the importation of this gold to Canada. Call loans were regarded by the banks as their secondary reserves, part of which were held in Canada, part in New York or London. The banks which carried on a large international business held proportionately large reserves outside Canada. If money were needed at home, the calling of these loans provided cash for immediate transfer. The banks claimed that in the absence of these markets, they would need to carry substantially larger cash (non-earning) reserves, which would necessitate lower interest rates on deposits and/or higher rates on loans. After 1914, the third line of chartered bank reserves was its securities eligible for rediscount under the provisions of the Finance Act.[2] In a semi-automatic monetary and banking system, the government (Department of

---

[1]The Dominion note issue had three distinct uses: (a) the smaller denominations served as hand-to-hand currency, and were infrequently presented for redemption in gold; (b) the larger denominations were used exclusively by the banks (i) as cash reserve (forty per cent of the banks' cash reserves were to be held in such a form, and in practice the proportion was much higher), and (ii) for deposit in the Central Gold Reserves as the basis for "excess" bank-note circulation.

[2]The banks generally kept between 40%–50% of their liabilities to the public in these liquid forms (cash, call loans and securities).

Finance) exchanged gold for its own notes, and vice-versa, strictly as a routine administrative operation rather than as a matter of conscious policy.[3]

With the advent of World War I, the structure and operation of the foregoing system was fundamentally altered. The extremely rapid expansion of the Canadian economy in the early twentieth century had been based on enormous capital imports from Great Britain, and these had reached a peak in excess of five hundred million dollars in 1913. The problem of servicing the country's mounting debt had been met with ease because of a continuously rising price-level in this era of natural resource development. It was clear, however, that the Canadian economy must eventually develop a current account surplus, out of which not only could these interest payments be met but foreign indebtedness liquidated as well. This process would involve "a wholesale transfer of labour and other productive resources from employment in construction to employment in the export industries. . . . Such a transformation could not be accomplished quickly without severe dislocation.[4] As the prospect of war generated increasing financial uncertainty, the availability of foreign capital became restricted, and in the year preceding the outbreak of hostilities, the Canadian economy had already entered a period of readjustment to lower levels of both external borrowing and commodity imports. A severe curtailment of capital construction projects within Canada had generated substantial unemployment, and the decline in imports had adversely affected federal revenues. These were still based almost exclusively on customs duties and excise taxes, a fact of considerable importance in determining the broad pattern of war finance which was subsequently adopted.

The prospect of war also exerted serious repercussions on the operation of the Canadian monetary and banking system, when widespread doubts developed as to the ability of the government to maintain the convertibility of its currency into gold. Its success during the preceding sixty years had been furthered by its access to foreign capital markets, and it was feared that the circumstances of war might result in the drastic curtailment or even the termination of such external assistance. At the beginning of August, 1914, substantial runs developed at many branches of the Canadian chartered banks, as depositors sought to obtain gold for hoarding. Withdrawals of gold were especially heavy in Montreal and Toronto, and " . . . an atmosphere of incipient financial panic prevailed".[5]

After emergency consultation with the bankers, who feared a serious loss of gold reserves, the government passed an Order-in-Council on August 3 which provided for the suspension of the gold convertibility of Dominion notes and

[3]See W. A. Mackintosh in the *Evidence Presented Before the Royal Commission on Banking and Currency in Canada*, 1933, p. 3054: "In addition to its excellent record in other fields, the pre-war banking and monetary system was singularly efficient in achieving the single objective of the pre-war monetary policy, viz., the maintenance of the exchanges."

[4]J. J. Deutsch, "War Finance and the Canadian Economy, 1914-1920", in *Canadian Journal of Economics and Political Science*, VI (1940), p. 525.

[5]*Report of the Royal Commission on Banking and Currency in Canada*, 1933, p. 22.

bank notes and for the paying out of bank deposits either in Dominion notes or those of the paying bank. It will be recalled that in the Bank Act revision of 1913, provision had been made for the issue of "excess" currency by the banks, provided that such excess was covered dollar for dollar by gold or Dominion notes deposited in the Central Gold Reserves. With the suspension of gold convertibility, a substantial expansion of chartered bank note issues appeared quite likely, in which case the legal reserves of the banks, under existing arrangements, would be substantially reduced.[6] To forestall such a reduction, the Order-in-Council of August 3 further provided for advances to be made to the chartered banks by the Minister of Finance, in the form of Dominion notes, against the deposits of such securities as might be approved by the Minister. It was further provided that in place of its original limitation to crop-moving periods, "excess" circulation of bank notes might be maintained on a year-round basis.[7]

The provisions of the foregoing Order-in-Council were embodied in the Finance Act of 1914, passed at a special autumn session of parliament.[8] The effect of these provisions, which terminated the gold standard and provided for advances from the government, was to change completely the earlier semi-automatic operation of the Canadian monetary system. The Act was passed as a war measure, and it contributed substantially to the solution of the financial difficulties of that period. But having been retained in operation through a series of re-enactments until 1923, the Act was made a "permanent" part of Canada's financial mechanism at the latter date. This decision was subsequently demonstrated to be unsound, and incompatible with Canada's rather brief return to the gold standard in the late 1920's.

The foregoing measures ended the threatened crisis, and those provisions relating to the suspension of gold convertibility remained in effect until July 1, 1926. The provision concerning "excess" bank-note circulation was terminated in 1921, while that relating to bank advances was made permanent by the Finance Act of 1923, under which bank borrowings of Dominion government notes became known as rediscounting.[9]

[6]See Knox, *op. cit.*, p. 221: "As bank note holders were well protected in the case of the issuing bank, under the provisions of the Bank Act, there was not likely to be any great reluctance of Canadians to take bank notes; indeed there was a possibility that many might prefer to convert deposits into notes if they were denied conversion into gold. The banks had, therefore, to contemplate the possibility of a great increase in their note issues at a time when their freedom of note issue was limited."

[7]The banks actually issued their own promissory notes which, fully covered by the approved securities, were discounted at a specified rate of interest by the Minister of Finance.

[8]*Statutes of Canada*, 1914 (2nd session), c. 3. The Act provided that in the case of war, invasion, riot or insurrection, real or apprehended, and in the case of any real or apprehended financial crisis, the Governor-in-Council might authorize the making of advances to the banks, such as had been specified in the Order-in-Council. See also Sir Thomas White, *The Story of Canada's War Finance* (Montreal: 1921) pp. 6-9.

[9]C. A. Curtis, "The Canadian Banks and War Finance", *Contributions to Canadian Economics* (Toronto: University of Toronto Press, 1931), III, 9.

Just as in World War II, there was little realization of the duration and intensity of the impending conflict, but the military commitments undertaken by Canada in this early period presented immediate financial problems. As already indicated, it was a time of business recession, and of declining government revenues, these being closely tied to the movement of imports. For this reason, an immediate increase in revenues was not possible.[10] The remaining methods available to the government for raising funds were direct borrowing and the issuing of fiduciary notes, and direct borrowing was considered solely as a process of obtaining funds from foreign markets, since the floating of domestic securities was almost unknown.[11] Table I presents a summary, by fiscal years, of the total expenditures of the federal government during World War I and of the proportions of these cash requirements that were met from revenues and from borrowings. The substantial capital expenditures listed in the table represented commitments made before the outbreak of the war, many being designed as means of combating the depression which prevailed in the immediate pre-war period. No new public works were undertaken during the war, and in actual fact, a considerable proportion of the capital expenditures was associated with the operation of publicly owned railways.

In the fiscal year 1914-15, government revenues were insufficient to meet non-war outlays, much less to contribute to any part of the financial burden of war. The two chief methods employed to meet the deficit of $151 million were borrowing abroad and the issuing of fiduciary notes. The British government having agreed to lend to Canada sufficient funds to pay for the cost of the war, a loan of £12 million was obtained. At this early date, the Canadian government had no intention of tapping appreciable funds from the limited domestic market, and of disturbing its normal operations.[12] A second source of funds

[10]The lack of a well-developed tax system made any substantial increase in revenue both economically and politically impossible, and in any event, the government did not believe taxation even theoretically appropriate at this juncture. See Sir Thomas White, *op. cit.*, p. 11, "It has been suggested that we should have levied heavier taxation at the outbreak of the war. The effect of this would undoubtedly have been to increase the business depression and probably, through public discontent, materially affect the extent of our participation in the war."

[11]On this point, see F. A. Knox, "Canadian War Finance and the Balance of Payments, 1914-18", *Canadian Journal of Economics and Political Science*, VI (1940), 236-7: " . . . heavy reliance on Dominion Government securities in foreign borrowing was but one aspect of a general reliance on borrowing rather than taxation in war finance. Though proclaimed as a method of passing a part of the costs of war to future generations who were to benefit from the sacrifices being made, borrowing was in fact inevitable because the Dominion Government's revenues were derived mostly from customs duties. . . . So great were the total Dominion government expenditures that revenues from the sources were lamentably insufficient. The war years saw the sharpest absolute increase of the net debt of the Dominion Government that has occurred since 1900."

[12]See White, *op. cit.*, pp. 12-13. "As our military expenditure was to be mainly abroad, it would not have been wise at that time to raise a loan in Canada. Our bank deposits were fully employed in meeting commercial requirements. . . . The policy followed was the sound one, namely, to borrow for our military expenditure abroad from the British Government."

TABLE I

REVENUES AND EXPENDITURES OF THE DOMINION GOVERNMENT

1915-1920[a]

MILLIONS OF DOLLARS

|  | 1915 | 1916 | 1917 | 1918 | 1919 | 1920 |
|---|---|---|---|---|---|---|
| Ordinary Expenditures | 136 | 130 | 149 | 178 | 233 | 304 |
| Capital Expenditures and Investments | 87 | 45 | 73 | 128 | 47 | 232 |
| Total Non-War Expenditures | 223 | 175 | 222 | 306 | 280 | 536 |
| Current Revenues | 133 | 172 | 233 | 261 | 313 | 350 |
| Deficit (−) or Surplus, Excluding War | −90 | −3 | 11 | −45 | 33 | −186 |
| Expenditures on War and Demobilization: |  |  |  |  |  |  |
| Overseas | 9 | 38 | 125 | 191 | 158 | 75 |
| In Canada | 52 | 128 | 182 | 153 | 289 | 272 |
| Total | 61 | 166 | 307 | 344 | 447 | 347 |
| Total Deficit (financed by borrowing) | 151 | 169 | 296 | 389 | 414 | 533 |

[a]Compiled from the *Public Accounts* and the *Reports of the Auditor-General*. See Deutsch, *op. cit.*, p. 540. For an alternative summary of Canadian war finance, see Brown, Gibson and Plumptre, *War Finance in Canada* (Toronto: The Ryerson Press, 1940), pp. 18-19.

was the increase in the government's fiduciary note issue of $20 million (net $15 million), with a further outright issue of $26 million, part being advanced to the railways upon deposit of their securities, part being issued for general governmental purposes. In all, $41 million were issued without any gold security, which of course came into possession of the banking system, and served as the basis of a multiple credit expansion.[13] A loan of $42 million was floated in London, and $5 million was borrowed from the Canadian chartered banks.

In the following fiscal year, the British government found itself unable to continue to finance the entire cost of the Canadian war effort, but agreed to continue to meet Canadian war expenditures in Britain. At the same time, Canada began to lend assistance to Britain in financing her war purchases in Canada.[14] The fiscal year 1914-15 well illustrates the wartime objective of the Canadian government that as much as possible of its total borrowings should be obtained from abroad.

In the next year, special war taxes appeared for the first time, but the govern-

[13]Deutsch, *op. cit.*, p. 528: " . . . the fiduciary issue of Dominion notes which raised bank cash reserves in Canada by 30% opened the way for large expansion of credit, which on the basis of war orders stimulated business activity."

[14]White, *op. cit.*, p. 17. "So far as Canada's finance was concerned, what really happened throughout the war was this: Britain lent us the money in London to pay all our military expenses overseas. We repaid Britain by monies placed to her credit in Canada. She used these credits to purchase munitions, wheat, flour and other Canadian products. The sale of these products enabled Canadians to subscribe to the war loans. In a word, we paid the cost of our military operations by our production during the war."

ment's increased revenues, despite a substantial decrease in its capital expenditures, were not quite sufficient to meet all non-war outlays, hence again the entire cost of the war effort in 1915-16 was in reality financed by borrowing. As already noted, Canadian war expenditures abroad, which in this year amounted to $38 million, were financed by the British government. A loan of $45 million was floated in New York, the first in the history of the Dominion. As a residual source of funds, the government turned to the domestic market, where, amid great uncertainty and apprehension as to the outcome, the first war loan was floated in November, 1915. With a $50 million tentative objective for this pioneer "large-scale" domestic borrowing effort, the government was most favourably impressed by the $100 million which was realized. Of this total, the banking allotment was $21 million. The banks also subscribed directly to the succeeding two war loans, although receiving no formal allotment.[15] The unexpectedly large yield from the first war loan permitted some advances to Britain in connection with her war orders placed in Canada.

The 1916-17 fiscal year brought substantially increased tax revenues, attributable not only to a rising national income, but also to the introduction of a business profits tax, retroactive to the beginning of the war. However, customs duties continued to provide the major source of revenue throughout the war, and in comparison with the government's wartime cash requirements, the yields from the special tax levies were almost insignificant. It may be observed from Table I that despite the increased tax revenues in 1916-17, there was but a very small surplus over non-war expenditures, and again it was by borrowing that practically the entire cost of the year's war activity was met.

Full employment having been reached during this period, the problem of meeting the real costs of the war presented the usual choices of action, and the problem was solved "by the laissez-faire expedient of inflation".[16] With $296 million to be obtained by borrowing, a loan of $50 million was financed in the New York market, while the second and third war loans, yielding $100 million and $150 million respectively, provided the remaining funds from domestic sources. As indicated below, the existence of abnormally large profits, despite the business war tax recently introduced, was a factor of very considerable importance in contributing to the success of these loans. The banking system

[15]Curtis, *op. cit.*, p. 11. The success of the first loan was in large measure attributable to the return of war-born prosperity in Canada. For a detailed explanation of the bases of the wartime expansion of the Canadian economy, see F. A. Knox, *op. cit.*, pp. 235-9.

[16]Deutsch, *op. cit.*, pp. 530-1: "In the twelve months, the volume of money in Canada (i.e., notes and bank deposits) rose by nearly $200 million . . . prices and the national money income shot up rapidly. . . . Important groups of salaried employees, some wage-earners, and the recipients of interest and rents at contractual rates suffered a considerable reduction in real income. Consequently a greater proportion of the total national income was shifted to business profits. . . . The creation of large surpluses in the hands of one group in the community, who would lend these surpluses to the government, made available a large pool of funds for the conduct of the war. This shift in the distribution of income brought about by the inflation was perhaps the most important circumstance which made the large domestic war loans possible."

subscribed a total of $110 million to these issues, which, when contrasted with the following three issues of the war period, were relatively small in amount and of relatively narrow ownership.[17]

In 1917-18, Canadian war expenditures approximated $344 million. The magnitude of these outlays made a profound impact upon the public by virtue of the fact that the government in that year introduced a personal income tax, an instrument hitherto unknown in Canadian fiscal development. Despite this pioneer effort, and an increase in the rate of business profits tax, an "ordinary" deficit of $45 million was incurred, as shown in Table I. The total borrowings for the year thus amounted to $389 million, being almost one-third greater than in the preceding year. In addition, substantial net advances were made in Great Britain, since Canadian war expenses overseas, which were financed by the British government, were considerably less than the assistance provided by the Canadian government for British war purchases in Canada.[18] During the fiscal year, the government undertook its first intensive effort to effect a widespread ownership of war loan bonds, and in contrast to the forty thousand subscribers to the third war loan, the fourth war loan was distributed among eight hundred and twenty thousand purchasers.

Its proceeds of $398 million were in excess of those of the first three war loans combined. The remaining important source of government funds was a fiduciary note issue of $50 million, secured by British treasury bills deposited in London. The proceeds of this transaction were loaned to Britain as part of the financial assistance provided for her war purchases in Canada, the net amount of which assistance exceeded $100 million in each of the 1918 and 1919 fiscal years.

Canadian war expenditures reached a maximum in 1919, in which year they amounted to $447 million. Renewed emphasis on taxation, including increases in income tax rates, a further increase in business profits tax rates, and the imposition of further excise taxes, coupled with a decline in capital expenditures, resulted, for the second time only during the war years, in a surplus on non-war accounts. But once again, almost the entire financial outlays associated with the war effort were obtained by borrowing, and again by borrowing from domestic sources. The fifth war loan provided $690 million, and was unique among all of the war loans in that the number of subscribers exceeded one million. The sixth and final war loan was floated in October-November, 1919, in the amount of $578 million, the proceeds of which were used, not only for demobilization and continuing war charges, but also to provide for a large "non-war" deficit of almost $200 million.

[17]Curtis, *op. cit.*, p. 12.
[18]Deutsch, *op. cit.*, p. 531: "In both 1917 and 1918 . . . the extent of Canada's war effort in the financial and economic sphere depended very largely on her ability to finance her own exports. The increasing amount of the loan funds required was made possible by the highly favourable export prices and particularly by the continuation of the inflation."

The rate of interest on the first three loans was 5% and the bonds were offered at a discount. On the last three loans, the interest rate and effective yield were 5.3%.

The foregoing summary of the sources of war finance of the Canadian government indicates two basic features. The first is the fact that almost the entire costs of war activities were in effect met by borrowing. The second is that while borrowing from foreign sources was possible in the early stages of the war, changing circumstances forced increasing dependence upon the domestic market, so that in the later years, internal borrowing was almost the exclusive source of funds.

The subscriptions to the first three war loans by the chartered banks have already been mentioned. In order that the degree of monetary expansion and of inflation which occurred during the war years may be better understood, it is desirable to note briefly some of the additional wartime activities of the chartered banks.

The great expansion of Canadian chartered bank credit which occurred during World War I was occasioned by the financial needs of the Canadian government, of the British government, and of the domestic economy, both in the development of war industries and in the continued operation of ordinary commercial enterprises.[19] In the assistance supplied to the Canadian government, the banks' direct purchases of the long-term public war loans were not of great importance. The principal item in this category was the $21 million subscription to the first loan. Beginning with the third war loan, and continuing in all succeeding loans, the period of each issue was marked by a shifting of deposits from private accounts to the account of the Dominion government, a fact which would seem to indicate that the larger number of small purchasers were paying for their bonds by drawing upon accumulated savings. This tendency was particularly evident in the case of notice deposits. The banks, of course, financed to some degree the purchases of bonds by the general public through the medium of loans and by carrying bonds for customers who paid in instalments.

Direct loans were likewise an unimportant method whereby the Canadian banks provided financial assistance to the government, amounting at most to a few million dollars. The basic contribution of the banking system lay in the purchase of short-term treasury bills (four to twelve months) bearing a usual interest rate of 5½%. The bills were frequently renewed at their maturity dates, but the government's general principle was to borrow on short-term bills from the banking system in advance of floating long-term war loans to the general public. "The banks' holdings of government securities move in close relationship with the government's issue of war loans, showing plainly that a large proportion of each war loan was issued to liquidate debts already incurred."[20]

---

[19]The most comprehensive account of the contributions of the Canadian banking system to the financing of World War I is to be found in Curtis, *op. cit.*, pp. 7-40. The following sections are in considerable measure based on this work.　　[20]Curtis, *op. cit.*, p. 21.

While the issue of treasury bills by the government was not a new practice, the war greatly increased their amount, and shifted the market from London to Canada. From 1917-19, the banks' holdings of Canadian treasury bills showed a cumulative increase, and on November 1, 1919, these were in excess of $318 million.[21]

The assistance which the Canadian chartered banks provided for the British government was in the form of direct loans, on the security of treasury bills. (In 1914, the banks subscribed $5 million to a British war loan.)[22] In 1916, two loans aggregating $100 million were provided at 5% on the security of twelve-month British treasury bills. These latter securities were renewed frequently, and the loan was not repaid until 1922. During 1916, an additional short-term loan of $20 million was provided for the purchase of Canadian wheat. In the autumn of this year, a further $50 million was advanced, this time against the security of Canadian treasury bills, the banks apparently being reluctant to absorb more British bills at this time. Finally, in 1917, another $100 million loan at 6% was provided for the purchase of Canadian wheat, a loan which was completely liquidated only in 1922.

In summary, excluding the short-term $20 million loan for wheat purchases, $150 million were spent for munitions and $100 million for wheat by the British government. As the basis for these loans, the chartered banks' holdings of British treasury bills increased by $200 million, of Canadian treasury bills by $50 million. Despite the frequent renewals of the British bills, the banks achieved liquidity by rediscounting them with the Department of Finance.[23] Since the proceeds of these British loans were spent in Canada, the effects upon monetary expansion are readily apparent. These effects were multiplied by the banks' rediscounting activities, which between September 1917, and December 1919, amounted to more than a half-billion dollars. These activities appear to have been the greatest source of additional legal reserve for the banks during the war.

A highly interesting but little known episode in the evolution of Canadian banking during these years was the first serious effort to bring about the founding of a central bank. The moving spirit in this campaign was E. L. Pease,[24] President of the Canadian Bankers' Association, to whom Sir Thomas White

---

[21]*Ibid.*, p. 20.    [22]*Ibid.*, pp. 12-13.
[23]*Ibid.*, pp. 25-6: "It does not appear however, that the banks regarded as perfect securities the treasury bills of the British government, as they were, in fact, of indefinite maturity. The banks considered them a dead load, seriously affecting their reserves and lending power, and they were not at all anxious to make loans to the British government on such security. It is quite probable that the loans of the banks to Britain were not made without pressure from the Canadian government, which apparently was anxious to have the banks give all possible aid to the British government, and even went to the extent of reducing the rediscount rate on British treasury bills to three and one-half per cent."
[24]Pease was at this time Vice-President and Managing Director of the Royal Bank of Canada, and his letters from which I have quoted were kindly made available to me by S. R. Noble, of Montreal.

wrote in 1917, inquiring how the Canadian government might most effectively aid the British government in financing munitions orders placed in Canada. The banks appeared reluctant to extend further accommodation on the security of British treasury bills (see footnote 23), particularly at a time when their cash reserves were seriously affected by a large adverse balance of payments with the United States. To meet the emergencies of war finance, Pease suggested that the Bank of England might well consider establishing a rediscounting branch in Canada, at which the Canadian banks could sell their British treasury bills, and thereby achieve their desired liquidity. But apart from such a temporary arrangement, Pease stated that "a bank of rediscount in Canada is, in my opinion, an imperative necessity. You know the reluctance of the banks to avail themselves of their privilege under the Finance Act. . . . A permanent rediscounting [bank] would be an inestimable boon to Canada. It would enable us to liquefy dormant assets, thereby increasing our resources for the general benefit".[25]

Late in 1918, the Canadian Bankers' Association formed a committee to consider the question of the founding of a "bank of rediscount". Pease proposed that such a bank should take over the Dominion note issue, the Central Gold Reserves and the functions of the Finance Act, but that the chartered banks retain their note issue (a concession to his colleagues, which he thought would have to be terminated sooner or later). The proposed capitalization of $20 million was to be provided half by the government and half by the chartered banks, the share of each pro-rated to its capital. The bank would be controlled directly by the government, which would appoint directors on the nomination of the Canadian Bankers' Association.

In support of a central bank, Pease argued that the country would be confronted with serious economic dislocation at the end of the war and that " . . . in order to minimize uncertainty with regard to the difficulties which will presently confront us, and to provide . . . increased financial facilities",[26] such an institution was essential. Without it, Canada would be unable to cope with the approaching situation. While the Finance Act had been effective and useful in wartime, it should not be perpetuated, because "it is not a good principle for the government to engage permanently in the banking business".[27] Moreover, the banks borrowed only reluctantly, and were criticized when they did. A further basic defect which Pease saw in the existing arrangements was that surplus funds were customarily sent to New York, to be used in speculative markets, with little direct advantage to Canada. "The establishment of a central institution which would always control a substantial margin of our banking reserves to be available for Canadian needs . . . is what we should aim at. Any makeshift short of this would at the present juncture appear to me to be a mistake."[28]

[25]E. L. Pease to Sir Thomas White, letter of July 9, 1917.
[26]E. L. Pease, Report to the Executive Council of the Canadian Bankers' Association, November 1918.        [27]*Ibid.*
[28]E. L. Pease to Z. A. Lash, Vice-President, Canadian Bank of Commerce, letter of December 2, 1918.

Despite his reasoned arguments, Pease could obtain little support for his proposal from the bankers' committee, whose members found many grounds for resisting any change. It was undoubtedly true that some bankers believed that the provisions of the Finance Act rendered any central banking institution superfluous. The fear of losing their right of note issue and fear of competition from a new bank were other stumbling-blocks.[29] The largest and most powerful of the banks, enjoying a monopoly of the government's accounts, was strongly opposed to any new arrangement which would have assured all the banks of at least indirect participation in government affairs. The upshot of the whole discussion was that rather than support Pease's proposal, the Canadian Bankers' Association asked the government to renew the Finance Act, while it would undertake to continue its efforts to formulate a plan for a central bank that would satisfactorily take the place of the Finance Act "and be acceptable to all the banks". Thus ended the "early" Canadian central banking controversy, the content of which was destined to be repeated a few years later, when conditions proved to be much more favourable for the introduction of constructive change into Canada's banking system.[30]

In serving the needs of private business in Canada during the war years, bank loans and discounts declined from 1913, when depression appeared, until well into 1916. In the ensuing four years, loans and discounts almost doubled. Coupling this expansion in bank credit with the assistance furnished to the Canadian and British governments, the over-all increase was tremendous. "Including these items, as well as call loans in Canada and loans to provinces and municipalities, the increase in bank credit between 1916 and 1920 was not less than a hundred and twenty-five per cent."[31]

That such an expansion was possible was because of the freedom in financial operations established by the Finance Act of 1914, and in particular because of the provision establishing Dominion government notes as legal reserve, which could be obtained by the banks in practically unlimited quantities at a cost which did not vary throughout the war. The government further contributed to the inflationary situation by its issues of fiduciary notes, which, of course, came

---

[29]Pease observed in this connection that "we have to consider which is of the greater importance to the country, our note circulating privilege or a rediscount bank. The banks could exist without the former, but I can imagine circumstances when the latter might be vital to our existence". E. L. Pease to H. A. Richardson, General Manager, Bank of Nova Scotia, letter of December 6, 1918.

[30]Pease continued his efforts in support of a central bank, but the opposition of his colleagues was augmented by that of Sir Henry Drayton, who proved to be much less sympathetic to the general principle than his predecessor, Sir Thomas White. In a letter dated January 14, 1921, he inquired just what were Pease's objections to the Finance Act and what advantage a central bank could offer, "having particular regard to the basic security of the whole financial situation, and not only to facilitating the inflation which the provision of free facilities for rediscounting paper gives, but also to the question of deflation without injury to general business conditions".

[31]*Ibid.*, p. 26.

into possession of the banks, amounting in all to $96 million. The monetary situation was well summarized in the statement that:

> It would appear that there was practically no check nor limit on the ability of the banks to expand, and from the banking side this was the case. The only possible check would be the limit of desirable loans and during an inflationary period this is no check, as the "need" for loans expands indefinitely.[32]

Table II summarizes the annual changes in the quantity of money in Canada during the war years, Table III the changes in chartered bank reserves, on which the expansion of the money supply was based.

This rapid increase in money supply was primarily responsible for the sharp rise in wartime price levels, as an example of which the indexes of the wholesale price levels and of the cost of living are presented in Table IV.

In monetary terms, the national income produced rose from $2,253 in 1914 to $4,211 in 1919. It has been estimated that in 1916, the national real income rose not more than six per cent, while during the two years 1917 and 1918, the total rise was less than ten per cent.[33] The general order of these figures suggests the degree to which inflationary developments contributed to the rise in money incomes during the war.

Concerning the success of the Canadian government in raising very large

TABLE II—CANADIAN MONETARY EXPANSION IN WORLD WAR I[a]
(Means of Payment [Millions of Dollars] as of December 31)

| TYPE OF MONEY | 1913 | 1914 | 1915 | 1916 | 1917 | 1918 |
|---|---|---|---|---|---|---|
| Total Dominion Note Issue | 131.2 | 162.4 | 178.8 | 181.0 | 272.9 | 327.4 |
| Less: Chartered Bank Holdings[1] | | | | | | |
| In Central Gold Reserves | 6.4 | 5.2 | 11.2 | 31.7 | 77.6 | 122.4 |
| In Own Vaults | 104.8 | 138.1 | 145.5 | 124.8 | 167.7 | 175.7 |
| Dominion Notes in Circulation | 20.0 | 19.1 | 22.1 | 24.5 | 27.8 | 29.3 |
| Chartered Bank Notes in Circulation | 108.6 | 106.0 | 122.2 | 148.8 | 192.9 | 224.5 |
| Total Notes in Circulation | 128.6 | 125.1 | 144.3 | 173.3 | 220.7 | 253.8 |
| *Chartered Bank Deposits:* | | | | | | |
| Demand Deposits (Public) | 381.4 | 349.9 | 423.7 | 458.2 | 569.4 | 711.0 |
| Notice Deposits (Public) | 624.7 | 662.8 | 721.0 | 845.0 | 996.0 | 958.5 |
| Provincial Government Deposits | 22.8 | 20.1 | 18.7 | 18.4 | 16.8 | 14.8 |
| Federal Government Deposits[2] | 9.5 | 10.7 | 26.4 | 17.7 | 17.7 | 147.8 |
| Total Bank Deposits | 1038.4 | 1043.5 | 1189.8 | 1339.3 | 1599.9 | 1832.1 |
| TOTAL NOTES IN CIRCULATION + TOTAL BANK DEPOSITS | $1167.0 | 1168.6 | 1334.1 | 1512.6 | 1820.6 | 2085.9 |

For footnotes, see Table III.

[32]*Ibid.*, p. 29.
[33]Deutsch, *op. cit.*, pp. 530, 532.

TABLE III—CANADIAN CHARTERED BANK RESERVES—WORLD WAR I[a]
(In [Millions of Dollars] as of December 31)

| CASH ITEM | 1913 | 1914 | 1915 | 1916 | 1917 | 1918 |
|---|---|---|---|---|---|---|
| Dominion Notes Held in Canada | 104.8 | 138.0 | 145.5 | 124.7 | 167.5 | 175.7 |
| Current Gold and Subsidiary Coin Held in Canada | 25.9 | 38.7 | 42.6 | 44.5 | 55.3 | 60.9 |
| *Deposits in Central Gold Reserves:* | | | | | | |
| Dominion Notes | 6.4 | 5.2 | 11.2 | 31.7 | 77.6 | 122.4 |
| Gold Coin | 1.2 | 4.5 | 6.2 | 12.0 | 19.7 | 8.5 |
| Total Domestic Cash | 138.3 | 186.4 | 205.5 | 212.9 | 320.1 | 367.5 |
| *Net Foreign Balances:* | | | | | | |
| Net Balances Due From Banks Abroad[3] | −2.7 | 13.8 | 83.7 | 49.8 | 38.5 | 28.0 |
| Call and Short-Term Loans Abroad | 116.0 | 85.0 | 137.2 | 173.9 | 134.5 | 150.2 |
| Gold Held Abroad | 19.5 | 23.8 | 25.4 | 26.7 | 26.7 | 18.4 |
| TOTAL CASH RESERVES (DOMESTIC + FOREIGN) | $271.1 | 309.0 | 451.8 | 463.3 | 519.8 | 564.1 |

[a]Data extracted from Curtis, *Statistical Contributions to Canadian Economic History*, II.
[1]Chartered Bank Advances under the Finance Act at the respective year-ends were: NIL, $10.7, $2.0, $6.9, $48.3, and $107.1.
[2]These figures exclude liabilities to the government on account of Finance Act advances.
[3]Less "Bills Payable", i.e., time drafts drawn by Canadian banks on branches and correspondents abroad.

TABLE IV—INDEXES OF WHOLESALE PRICES AND COST-OF-LIVING
IN CANADA, 1914-1919[a]

| YEAR | WHOLESALE PRICE INDEX (1913 = 100) | COST-OF-LIVING INDEX (1913 = 100) |
|---|---|---|
| 1914 | 100.4 | 102 |
| 1915 | 109.2 | 103 |
| 1916 | 134.3 | 112 |
| 1917 | 174.9 | 136 |
| 1918 | 205.4 | 156 |
| 1919 | 216.4 | 171 |

[a]Official indices of the Dominion Bureau of Statistics. See Brown, Gibson and Plumptre, *op. cit.*, p. 24.

sums of money in the domestic market during World War I, various factors such as the increase in value of Canadian exports, the decline in private investment and increased saving through patriotic motives, must be recognized. But more significant than all these, "the role played by the inflation and the consequent expansion of profits was perhaps the most important, as is indicated by the fact that over three-fourths of the total war loans were subscribed for by business organizations, financial institutions, and persons with large incomes."[34]

[34]*Ibid.*, p. 533.

The foregoing pages have carried a brief summary of Canadian government finance in World War I. In terms of the three chief functions of war finance, i.e., to provide the government with necessary funds for carrying on its war activities, to help minimize inflation and to distribute the financial burden of war as fairly as possible, the Canadian record in World War I was unsatisfactory in a great many respects. If we consider the government's basic problem of obtaining necessary funds, it has been shown that borrowing provided an amount which was more than sufficient to cover total war expenditures. Taxation and other revenues during the war years failed to provide sufficient cash to take care of the government's non-war outlays, including capital expenditures. Of total borrowings in the fiscal years 1915-20 of approximately $2,200 million, only $200 million was obtained abroad, and $2,000 million was provided by the domestic market. In explanation of the inadequacy of tax revenues, it must again be emphasized that, at the outbreak of war, Canada had, at best, a rudimentary tax system, in which chief reliance was centred on customs duties. Some additional revenue came from a few excise duties. Under such circumstances, it is not surprising that in the early stages of the war, tax revenues were not increased appreciably. It is important to note, however, that even had such increases been possible, they were not regarded as being either economically or politically desirable. The general opinion was that the war would not be of long duration and that undue disruptions of the economy were to be avoided. Subsequent revision of this opinion resulted in some further development of the federal tax system, but the government was not disposed to cultivate this source of funds with more than "token" vigour, preferring the politically easier expedient of borrowing. In 1914, the country had not, of course, acquired any previous experience in financing a major war.

Having committed itself to such a programme of expediency, the government found, before the war was well along, that external sources of borrowing were becoming inaccessible, and it was consequently in the domestic market that the bulk of war financing was accomplished. This, as we have already seen, involved extensive use of bank credit, the responsibility for which should accordingly be attributed in large measure, not to the banks but to the government.[35] Effected at interest rates varying from 5 per cent to 6 per cent, the increase in national debt was more than three-fold during the war years, and the service costs appreciably increased the government's fixed charges, the meeting of which has constituted a particularly serious problem in the development of the Canadian economy.

The second desirable function of a programme of war finance, that of assisting in combating inflation, was not accomplished by the policies followed in World War I, and in choosing to obtain its funds by inflationary measures (the redis-

---

[35]In support of this view, see Curtis, *op. cit.*, pp. 39-40.

counting of British treasury bills for the commercial banks at a specially reduced rate is an outstanding example) the government undoubtedly increased considerably its owns costs of carrying on its war activities. The fact that the degree of inflation was less than in some of the other belligerent countries does not imply that a much sounder effort might not have been put forth.

A corollary of this policy was the inequitable distribution of the burdens of the war. One writer had stated that "it is clear that the inflation was more expedient than equitable", and that equity was of little importance when getting things done was the main consideration.[36] It is abundantly clear that the inflation did assist in getting things done, and in particular, it made possible the obtaining of very large loans in the domestic market. The effects of the inflation were such that:

> . . . industrial profits and property incomes increased, while the real income of wage-earners and individuals receiving interest payments at fixed rates declined, or rose less rapidly. It was this reduction in the real income of one section of the community, and the creation of large surpluses in the hands of other sections, willing to lend to the government, that in considerable part, at least, made possible Canada's remarkable record in mobilizing public savings through the various war and victory loan programs. The decline in the relative standard of living suffered by certain groups, the rapid increase in savings and the postponement of needed capital facilities, made possible the enormous volume of war loans and represented the sacrifices necessary for the conduct of the war.[37]

The inequities of the programme of war finance which occurred in 1914-18 were tolerable in a situation where the government's war expenditures absorbed not more than 10% of the national income. In the financing of World War II, where the financial problems were very much greater, and where the government was spending more than 50% of national income in the later years, the policies adopted in this earlier period could have led only to economic disaster. The additions to chartered bank reserves which permitted the foregoing rapid expansion of the means of payment during World War I arose both from external and internal economic influences. The stimulus of external influences is revealed by an analysis of Canada's balance of international payments during the war years, in which three distinct periods may be noted. During 1914, a heavy current account deficit was fully covered by autonomous capital imports (which by that time included loans related to war finance);[38] from 1915-17, declining capital imports were more than offset by a rising current account balance; during 1918, the reappearance of a current account deficit was ac-

---

[36]Deutsch, *op. cit.*, p. 537.

[37]J. L. Ilsley, *Budget Speech*, September 12, 1939, p. 5.

[38]In addition to substantial federal borrowings, both provincial and municipal governments continued to float foreign loans through 1916; the London market was closed to all Canadian borrowers except the federal government after 1914 and to that body after 1916. In the later stages of the war, the federal government borrowed in the United States, until this channel was closed to all foreign borrowers in 1918.

companied by an intensified decline in autonomous capital imports.[39] Thus, during 1915, the chartered banks effected a substantial increase in their foreign balances through their net purchases ($145 million) of foreign exchange from Canadian exporters and borrowers. These purchases, as in the pre-war years, provided not only an initial expansion of the means of payment and of money incomes in Canada, but also additional reserves on which a part of the subsequent wartime expansion of the banks' liabilities was based.[40]

With respect to domestic influences, the total cash reserves of the banks were increased indirectly as a result of the substantial ($90 million) wartime net increase in the issue of Dominion notes (in 1914 and 1917) and directly by the banks' discounting operations with the Department of Finance, from which advances were obtained under the provisions of the Finance Act. A rapid increase in these advances during the latter part of 1917 was followed by an even more striking expansion to a wartime peak at the end of 1918.[41]

The wartime expansion of bank credit was slight until near the end of 1915, but continued thereafter at a steady rate, and as already indicated the over-all increase during the five-year period 1914-18 was from approximately $1.2 billion to $2.1 billion. The heavy emphasis upon the chartered banks as a source of the government's domestic borrowings during World War I brought about a noticeable shift in the distribution of the banks' assets, and thereby initiated a trend which continued to the end of World War II. Between 1900 and 1913, commercial loans and discounts averaged approximately sixty per cent of total bank assets, securities less than ten per cent. As a result of the banks' participation in World War I finance, the proportion of loans and discounts to total assets at the end of 1918 had declined to roughly fifty-five per cent, despite an absolute increase in the volume of commercial accommodation during the war, and the proportion of securities to total assets had risen to seventeen per cent.[42]

[39]For a detailed discussion, see F. A. Knox, "Canadian War Finance and the Balance of Payments", in the *Canadian Journal of Economics and Political Science*, VI, 1940, pp. 226-57. See also Knox, *Money, Banking and International Finance, op. cit.*, pp. 220-36.

[40]The chartered banks' foreign balances, held in London and New York, were the most variable component of their total cash reserves. Their fluctuations largely reflected shifts in the balance of payments, although they might be deliberately reduced as a means of importing gold to Canada to increase domestic reserves, or as a means of payment for securities purchased abroad. The latter use exerted no influence on the level of bank deposits in Canada.

[41]See the *Report of the Royal Commission on Banking and Currency in Canada*, 1933, p. 39. In mid-1917, there were no advances outstanding under the Finance Act. By the end of 1918, these exceeded $100 million. The substantial rise in these advances is explained by the increasing pressure placed upon the chartered banks' cash reserves as a result of their continuing wartime loans in support of the government's fiscal programme. The necessity of covering "excess" note circulation by a 100% reserve (in the Central Gold Reserve) of gold or Dominion notes gave rise to a substantial cash drain, and the justification for any such requirement was at no time apparent.

[42]See the *Report of the Chartered Banks of the Dominion of Canada*, 1919. At the end of 1919, total chartered bank assets had risen to some $3,100 million, of which Canadian government securities represented almost $600 million, loans $1,700 million; about one-fifth of these loans were outside Canada.

The substantial increase in current loans in the early post-war period was not sufficient to restore the pre-war proportions, and one effect of the several ensuing years of deflation was that, by 1925, securities represented a new high of twenty per cent of chartered bank assets, while loans at discounts had declined to little more than thirty per cent. The later 1920's brought a substantial rise in commercial lending and a corresponding decline in security holdings, despite which the importance of the former remained much smaller than before World War I.[43]

The fiscal problems of the federal government during the early 1930's, and again during World War II sharply accentuated the general trend, some implications of which are discussed at a later point. The history of Canadian chartered banking to the present day reveals a high inverse correlation between their cyclically changing holdings of current loans and of securities, a long-term downward trend in the importance of current loans as a percentage of total assets and a corresponding long-term upward trend in the importance of government securities.[44] This long-term change in the form of bank assets is directly related to the rise of large-scale business enterprise, and to the methods whereby its operations are financed. Whereas the small business man, not having access to the capital market, may meet his needs for working capital by borrowing from his bank, the large corporation will frequently issue its own securities. This tendency, coupled with the great expansion in the federal debt in recent decades, explains in large measure the changing distribution of bank assets.

The substantial increase in chartered bank current loans, which first appeared in late 1918 and extended through 1920, contributed to a sharp but relatively brief Canadian post-war boom which was stimulated primarily by domestic influences. For despite the very heavy demands from war-damaged European countries for both consumer and capital goods in the immediate post-war years, the effect upon Canadian exports was small. The financial difficulties, and particularly the foreign exchange difficulties, of those countries caused them to turn elsewhere, and in this particular period, the relative value of exports in Canada's rising national income declined.[45]

In this early post-war period, a rising level of consumer expenditures was

---

[43]At the end of 1929, total chartered bank assets exceeded $3,500 million, of which securities holdings represented more than $400 million, loans almost $2,300 million; of the latter, external loans had risen to $500 million. See the *Report of the Chartered Banks of the Dominion of Canada*, 1929. For further details, see J. D. Gibson, "The Changing Character of Bank Assets", in the *J.C.B.A.*, XLV, pp. 145-54.

[44]This trend has on occasion presented the banks with problems having not only economic but also "political" aspects, centring about criticism of the increasingly restricted social functions which the banks are alleged to perform.

[45]See Knox, *An Introduction to Money, Banking and International Finance*, pp. 241-2. A sharp decline in exports to Britain was accompanied by an expansion of sales to the United States, especially in forest products. These offset declining overseas exports of munitions and agricultural products. In the Canadian economy, the relative importance of all primary production in national income was declining, while that of manufacturing (despite the termination of munitions manufacturing) was rising.

accompanied by a rapid expansion of domestic investment. In part, this expansion arose from the desire of business men to reconvert their productive facilities to peacetime production as rapidly as possible (the dislocation of normal productive arrangements was very much less than in World War II), but to a greater degree it represented a working capital boom. To the foregoing expansive influences were added rising expenditures of provincial and municipal governments on the backlog of public services generated during the war. The boom was financed in part by external borrowing mostly in New York (this choice being influenced by the post-war appreciation of the U.S. dollar and the depreciation of sterling in Canada), and the beginnings of American "direct" investment in Canada via the establishment of branch plants appear at this time.[46]

The peak of monetary expansion during the boom was reached near the end of 1919, by which time chartered bank notes and deposits had risen by some $400 million since the end of the preceding year. The banks' loans and investments continued to expand until late in 1920, but this expansion was more than offset by a decline in security holdings during the year. Bank reserves fluctuated little during the boom, despite the substantial rise in their notes and deposits. With Canada no longer on the gold standard, the banks were provided with practically unrestricted access to additional cash through the discounting arrangements provided under the Finance Act. During this early post-war interval, such discounting appears to have been limited to the amounts required for backing the banks' "excess" note issues, but the former restraint upon the expansion of bank credit which arose from the banks' concern for its reserve position, was no longer operative in the Canadian monetary system. The Canadian wholesale price level reached a peak of 165 in 1920 (1926=100), after which a rapid and severe decline took place within a period of eighteen months. By early 1922, a level of 100 had been reached, at which approximate stability was maintained throughout the decade. The economic recession was precipitated by a decline in Canadian exports following the collapse of the post-war boom in the United States, the effects of which decline spread throughout the

[46]The 1920's were characterized by a continuation of this process of direct investment, and in so far as Canadian securities sales abroad were concerned, by the issue of "optional payment" bonds. The first phase in the issue of such bonds had occurred between 1900 and 1913 in connection with railroad financing, borrowing by western municipalities, etc., and were payable in dollars or sterling (sometimes in sterling only); the second phase occurred in the 1920's, when, for example, the C.N.R. optional payment obligations were incurred as well as practically all provincial, municipal and corporate debt having a New York payment feature either in conjunction with Canadian funds or with both Canadian funds and sterling. The third phase began in mid-1932 when B.C. and Alberta borrowed in London, and were followed by the federal government in 1933 and 1934. These optional payment bonds were designed for greater marketability, and in periods of relative exchange stability, provided little risk. But in the 1930's, the exchange problem presented by this type of bond became serious, and the existence of these fixed obligations payable in foreign currency greatly influenced the government's interpretation of what constituted a desirable exchange rate. For details of the issue of optional-payment bonds, see W. T. G. Hackett, "Canada's Optional Payment Bonds", in *C.J.E.P.S.*, I, pp. 161-70.

economy.[47] Thus, although the value of exports declined by at least one-third in 1920-1, the general reduction in Canadian money incomes led to an even greater decline in imports, in the three-year period, 1920-2, and a large current account deficit was entirely eliminated.

During these years of post-war deflation, the volume of bank loans and discounts underwent a substantial contraction, from approximately $1.94 billion in 1920 to a low of $1.54 billion in 1925.[48] This contraction was accompanied by a considerable expansion of bank investments, a customary practice in times of recession. The serious decline in wheat prices bore heavily on prairie incomes and faced for the first time with substantial problems of economic readjustment,[49] the western farmers' criticism of chartered bank operations became widespread.[50] While many of these complaints centred about details of bank administration and of policy, a much broader issue was involved, that of the ability of a commercial banking system to provide the type of credit accommodation required by western agricultural production in an economy where fluctuations in income are both extensive and unpredictable. During the depression of the 1930's, both the financial difficulties of the western farmers and their complaints against the banks were intensified, and these will be discussed in some detail. It is unfortunately true that during this period of national disaster, the problem of meeting the distinctive credit requirements of western agriculture was not satisfactorily resolved.

The decennial revision of the Bank Act in 1923 introduced no basic changes in Canadian banking. Minor amendments dealt with the strengthening of provisions governing the shareholders' audit, with the registration of all liens acquired by the banks under Section 88 of the Bank Act and with a modification of the form in which the banks submitted their monthly financial returns to the government. The failure of the Home Bank of Canada in 1923, the first in a

[47]The greatest price decline occurred in farm products, amounting to 50% (1920-3). Within this group the price of wheat fell most, 60% (1920-2). Lumber prices fell by less than 25% and newsprint by about 33%. See Mackintosh, *The Economic Background of Dominion-Provincial Relations, op. cit.*, p. 38: "The vulnerability of the economy through the variability of the prices of its exports was clearly shown, but as yet no serious question had been raised of the competitive strength of its major exports in world markets."

[48]*Canada Year Book*, 1934-5, p. 969.

[49]The farmers' costs declined much less rapidly than the price of wheat; taxes remained high after the general decline in incomes; much farmland had been purchased at uneconomically high prices during the wartime and post-war boom; heavy fixed charges (mortgage obligations) had also been incurred during the period, and these subsequently became an unbearably heavy burden.

[50]Since these criticisms became much more extensive, both in scope and volume, in the early 1930's their consideration is deferred to the following chapter. But included in the complaints were the banks' unwillingness to extend the type of accommodation required by western agriculture, the ultra-conservative approach to the granting of credit, excessive interest charges, eastern domination of policy, their monopolistic position, etc. For a summary of the farmers' banking difficulties in this period, see D. A. MacGibbon, *Report of the Commissioner on Banking and Credit With Respect to the Industry of Agriculture in the Province of Alberta, 1922*. This report suggests that many of the farmers' complaints against the banks were entirely justified.

decade and the last in the history of Canadian chartered banking, brought a renewal of earlier demands for government inspection of banks, and appropriate provisions were subsequently enacted in 1924. The Home Bank failed, as had many banks earlier, because of unsound speculative lending by its head office, and under the 1924 enactment, the government appointed an Inspector-General of banks, who was required to inspect the affairs of each bank at least once each year, and to report his findings to the Minister of Finance.[51]

The Canadian economy entered a boom period in 1925, based in part on a relatively high level of exports and in part on an extremely rapid rise in domestic investment.[52] During the 1920's, wheat and wheat flour represented Canada's largest exports, although by the end of the decade, a new group of commodities including newsprint, woodpulp, planks and boards, and the non-ferrous metals had assumed substantial importance. These new exports reflected the post-war exploitation of the resources of the Laurentian shield, into which much domestic investment was channelled. In addition, the pre-war expansion of the prairie market, the expansion of productive facilities during World War I and the development of cheap water-power all contributed to substantial post-war investment in manufacturing, of which the rapidly developing automobile industry was a notable example. Thus the exploitation of new resources, the recovery of western agriculture and the expansion of manufacturing, represented the main channels for the record domestic investment of the period. Public and private borrowing continued in heavy volume, almost entirely in the New York market, but the net inflow of capital was reduced by the repayment of earlier issues which matured during this period.[53] As might be expected, the rapid expansion of

---

[51]Government inspection of the chartered banks is a head-office inspection, but " . . . the centralization of books and administration in the head office of the bank permits this type of inspection to be fairly effective." See C. A. Curtis, "The Evolution of Canadian Banking", in the *Annals of the American Academy of Political and Social Science*, September, 1947, p. 119.

If the Inspector-General found any bank insolvent, the Minister of Finance might, without waiting for the bank to suspend payment, request the Bankers' Association to appoint a curator to supervise the affairs of the bank until either it resumed business or a liquidator was appointed.

[52]See Mackintosh, *op. cit.*, pp. 40, 42: "For most industries price-relationships were once more conducive to investment, new resources and new techniques had started strong expansion in certain industries and world conditions were favourable to increased international trade and therefore to economic expansion in countries such as Canada. . . . [The expansion] was favoured by liberal credit, technological changes, and agricultural yields, particularly in the prairie region, much greater than average."

[53]See Knox, *op. cit.*, p. 288a. The other major long-term capital item was the trading of outstanding securities which resulted in substantial outflows of capital, apparently due to Canadian participation in the United States stock market boom of the later 1920's. On balance, the long-term capital account shows substantial inflows in the years 1922, 1923 and 1924 and in 1929, but there is no definite trend in the intervening years. The rapid rise in national income which began in 1925 generated savings in excess of domestic investment (a circumstance in part attributable to the government's cultivation of the domestic capital market during World War I), and net foreign indebtedness was reduced.

exports in the early 1920's produced current account surpluses, and these prevailed through 1926. A lag in the expansion of imports delayed the appearance of a current account deficit until 1927, which thereafter continued throughout the period.

During the period 1922-5, in the years preceding the post-war boom, the volume of chartered bank credit remained almost constant in Canada, a continuous decline in bank loans being accompanied by a rise in securities holdings. In view of a steadily improving reserve position which arose from their net purchases of foreign exchange, the banks continued the reduction of their indebtedness to the government in 1924 and 1925, by the repayment of advances under the Finance Act.[54] The disposition of the banks' acquisitions of foreign exchange arising from the favourable balance of payments situation through 1926 was immediately influenced by the prevailing exchange rate. When the Canadian dollar was rising in New York, net foreign balances were accumulated, and when the dollar fell, such balances were reduced and the proceeds used to liquidate some of the banks' advances under the Finance Act.[55] The banks had little reason to become concerned about the possibility of an inadequate reserve position at any given time, for under the prevailing automatic implementation of the provisions of the Finance Act, additional reserves could be obtained without delay.

The major change in Canadian monetary policy during this decade was the

---

[54]The maximum outstanding advances under the Finance Act had been reached in November, 1920 when these amounted to $123.7 million. The minimum figure for this decade, $2 million, was reached in February 1926. The following table indicates the maximum and minimum advances outstanding in each of the following years:

### BANK ADVANCES UNDER THE FINANCE ACT
(Millions of dollars)

| YEAR | MAXIMUM | MINIMUM | YEAR | MAXIMUM | MINIMUM |
|------|---------|---------|------|---------|---------|
| 1914 | 12.7(Nov) | 0.75(Aug) | 1924 | 37.8(Apr) | 12.7(Nov) |
| 1915 | 7.9(Jan) | 0.28(Oct) | 1925 | 21.3(Feb) | 7.0(Nov) |
| 1916 | 6.9(Dec) | Nil(Jun-J-Aug) | 1926 | 24.8(Oct) | 2.0(Feb) |
| 1917 | 56.0(Nov) | Nil(Jun) | 1927 | 32.5(Dec) | 8.7(May) |
| 1918 | 116.5(Nov) | 26.7(Mar) | 1928 | 73.6(Oct) | 23.0(Jan) |
| 1919 | 113.0(Nov) | 78.4(Mar) | 1929 | 111.4(Nov) | 71.5(Feb) |
| 1920 | 123.7(Nov) | 88.0(Jun) | 1930 | 82.7(Jan) | 0.6(Dec) |
| 1921 | 93.2(Nov) | 59.7(Oct) | 1931 | 66.5(Nov) | Nil(Mar-A-May) |
| 1922 | 61.3(Jan) | 28.6(Dec) | 1932 | 65.1(Nov) | 10.0(Sept) |
| 1923 | 31.2(Dec) | 10.1(Jul) | | | |

See Curtis, *op. cit.*, II, p. 27 and *Royal Commission on Currency and Banking in Canada, op. cit.*, pp. 41-2.

[55]Knox, *op. cit.*, pp. 294-5. The exchange operations of the banks therefore served as a stabilizing influence in the market, just as had been the case under the pre-war gold standard. Knox points out that for several years prior to the return to gold in 1926, the Dominion government had already established limited convertibility, in that it exchanged gold for its own notes, and vice-versa. The extent of exchange rate fluctuations between 1922 and 1926 emphasizes the limited nature of these operations.

formal return to the gold standard in 1926. A second and earlier noteworthy event was the Finance Act of 1923, which provided that the features of the 1914 Act, hitherto operative only in periods of proclaimed emergency, should henceforth become a permanent part of the monetary mechanism. The incompatibility of these two monetary measures was generally unrecognized because all advances under the Finance Act had to this time been effected under conditions of inconvertible currency.[56] Since 1914, the government had been under no legal obligation to redeem its notes in gold. With the resumption of the gold standard, this obligation was once more assumed (the government had informally restored partial convertibility in its transactions with the chartered banks as early as 1922), and the incompatibility of the Finance Act and gold convertibility was quickly demonstrated by the events of 1926-8.[57] The re-establishment of gold convertibility on July 1, 1926 followed similar action by the United Kingdom in the preceding year, and was part of an international return to gold during the 1920's.

Britain had restored the convertibility of sterling by adopting a gold-bullion standard in 1925. The forms of the inter-war gold standard differed greatly from those of the pre-war era, and in general the restrictions imposed upon its operation were much more severe. It was characterized by central bank management in the interests of domestic economic objectives, and in Canada, where such management of the system was absolutely indispensable to its successful operation, no central bank existed and the government declined to assume any positive responsibility in monetary affairs.

In view of this post-war emphasis toward the adaptation of monetary policy to domestic objectives, of increasing rigidities in national price structures, of increasing obstacles to the international movement of goods and services (and capital), of the decline in the international dominance of sterling, and therefore of an increasingly unfavourable environment in which a gold standard would be required to operate, the soundness of the international return to gold in the 1920's may be seriously questioned.

[56]See *Statutes of Canada,* 1923, c. 48. The Minister of Finance commented that the measure had been exceedingly useful in war, and that it likewise appeared to be essential in peacetime. The error of his views was soon to be demonstrated. The securities which the banks might pledge with the Minister of Finance as security for advances, all to mature within six months of pledging included (a) treasury bills, bonds, debentures or stocks of Canada, Great Britain, any Canadian province or any British possession; (b) public securities of the U.S. government; Canadian municipal securities; (c) promissory notes and bills of exchange secured by documentary title to wheat, oats, rye, barley, corn, buckwheat, flax or other commodity; (d) promissory notes and bills of exchange issued or drawn for agricultural, industrial or commercial purposes and which have been used or are to be used for such purposes. The rate on such advances was to be determined from time to time by the Treasury Board.

[57]See C. A. Curtis, "The Canadian Monetary Situation", in the *Journal of Political Economy,* XL, 1932, p. 319: "The Act which made this fundamental change in the Canadian monetary structure received less consideration than any other major change ever made in Canadian monetary legislation. . . . It is to be doubted if the government or the public ever adequately realized the significance of the Act."

The Canadian boom, which extended almost to the end of 1929, was accompanied by a continuous expansion of bank credit as loans and discounts rose sharply, and by a balance of payments deficit which appeared in 1927. This deficit was financed to a minor extent by a net reduction in chartered bank foreign balances but primarily by gold exports. The normal consequence of such an external drain on reserves is a restriction of bank credit, and the fact that such did not occur in Canada in these years is explained by the operation of the Finance Act. Under its provisions, the banks could and did replenish their reserves at will merely by pledging additional securities with the Minister of Finance and receiving Dominion notes, convertible into gold, in exchange. In effect, the gold drain was transferred from the chartered banks to the government, for not only did the banks' gold reserves held in Canada not decline, but their holdings of Dominion notes increased slightly during these years.[58] Although those Dominion notes issued under the provision of the Finance Act required no gold reserve, (in contrast to those issued via the Dominion Notes Act), the government was of course obliged to maintain their convertibility into gold. But with the Department of Finance not prepared to exercise discretion in the administration of the Finance Act, nor to take any steps to regulate the amount of reserves provided for the banks under its terms, the situation was clearly untenable. The traditional gold-standard restraint upon bank lending had been eliminated and no responsible public authority had been provided in its place.[59] Clearly erroneous was the chartered bank notion that "the Finance Act takes the place of the Federal Reserve System with equal efficiency, but with infinitely greater simplicity and economy".[60]

In the face of an extremely heavy gold drain at the end of 1928 (the government's reserves declined from $109 million in November to $59 million in January, 1929), and a decline in its reserve ratio (gold to Dominion notes) from 46% to 30% within a period of two months, the Department of Finance felt impelled to terminate the unrestricted convertibility of Dominion notes.[61] Thus the gold standard was rejected in practice, although such was not formally

[58]Until Nov. 1, 1924, the Department of Finance had charged interest at 5% (with one wartime exception) on advances under the Finance Act; from Nov. 1/24 to Nov. 1/27, 4½%; from Nov. 1/27 to Dec. 1/27, 4%; from Dec. 1/27 to June 8/28, 3¾%; from June 8/28 to Sept. 1/28, 5% (except 3¾% on 4% treasury notes); from Sept. 1/28 to Oct. 26/31, 4½% (with preceding exception); from Oct. 26/31 to May 2/32, 3%; from May 2/32 to May 1/33, 3½% (with certain exceptions); after May 1/33, 2½%. See *Report of Royal Commission on Banking and Currency in Canada*, 1933, p. 41. The explanation of these movements is not apparent, but it is clear that there was no attempt to restrict the volume of credit extended to the banks during the boom by means of the interest rate applied to discounts.

[59]Knox, *op. cit.*, p. 294a. The banks' total cash reserves actually increased by $49 million in 1928, as Finance Act advances reached record levels. These averaged $80 million in 1929, about double that of 1928.

[60]See the Canadian Bank of Commerce, *Annual Report*, 1927, p. 45.

[61]Dominion notes outstanding reached a peak of $237 million in November, 1928.

acknowledged until 1931, when the existing status was legally sanctioned.[62] Through 1929, Dominion gold reserves remained stationary, and although the Canadian dollar weakened surprisingly little in the New York market, it moved distinctly beyond the limits which could have prevailed under conditions of unrestricted convertibility. The alternative to the departure from the gold standard, a move which left the government free to continue its automatic dispensing of cash reserves to the chartered banks at their request, would have been to retain gold convertibility, in which case the Department of Finance would have been compelled to assume discretionary powers and to restrict its cash advances to the banks. This it steadfastly declined to do (both on and off the gold standard), and perverse fluctuations in the volume of credit proceeded without restraint, intensifying both the boom through 1929 and the depression in succeeding years.

These perverse fluctuations in the volume of credit were the inevitable outcome of a situation in which the chartered banks insisted that their volume of loans merely varied passively with the "needs of business". There was, in general, no recognition of the possible adverse effects of such variations on the general level of economic activity, and in particular, that their policies intensified rather than ameliorated periods of inflation and deflation. This lack of understanding of the broader consequences of their operations was unfortunate, but the bankers generally claimed to be much too busy with their practical problems to have any concern for "theory".[63] Even if the bankers had possessed an adequate under-

---

[62]With the heavy depreciation of the Canadian dollar which followed Britain's abandonment of gold, the government formally prohibited gold exports except under licence. The Order-in-Council was passed in October, 1931, and subsequent gold shipments were confined largely to meeting federal and provincial debt obligations in New York.

[63]The following are representative samples of the erroneous notions held by chartered bankers of the day: (a) "the fundamental thing about the Canadian bank note is that . . . it generally goes out to do something definite. After it has done that one thing, and perhaps a second or third thing, it comes back and is redeemed and disappears. It is only a temporary instrument put out to perform a service, and when it performs that service it comes back and is killed". See *Bank Act Revision Proceedings by the Select Standing Committee on Banking and Commerce*, compiled by the Canadian Bankers' Association, 1933, p. 116; (b) "I think that we have a sound currency to-day because it is practically redeemable daily; that is the reason it is a sound currency. . . . It is because our notes . . . do go out to do a real thing in response to a real credit demand, that they are, as I say, the only right kind of paper money in the world". See *ibid.*, pp. 117-18; (c) "Under the Canadian banking system there is never too much or too little, because it [the quantity of credit] falls and rises exactly as the transactions of the country fall and rise". *Ibid.*, p. 118; (d) "There can, of course, be no over-expansion of bank-note circulation that is . . . covered dollar for dollar by a deposit of gold". *Ibid.*, p. 131; (e) referring to the depression following 1929, still another banker observed that "Deflation . . . was a thing which followed a decline in prices and a decline in production. Nobody deflated anything by any intention to do so. It deflated itself by the settlement of old transactions and no transactions taking the place of the old ones". *Ibid.*, p. 525. In somewhat different vein, one is surprised to learn that the *dominant* (italics mine) motive of any banker in making a loan is to help his customer make money. Most bank managers allegedly concerned themselves little about the financial benefit to their institutions, although it is casually conceded that "they would be very foolish if they did not think incidentally about how to earn dividends for the bank". *Ibid.*, p. 504.

standing of their economic influence, this would not of course have lessened the need for some form of central bank control. It might, however, have lessened the amount of extraneous argument directed against the establishment of such an institution in the early 1930's. The Canadian monetary experience in the 1920's and the early 1930's made unmistakably clear both the need for some mechanism of control and the fact that the Department of Finance was not the agency which could reasonably be expected to function effectively in this particular area of responsibility.[64]

This was not yet the era for the appearance of the notion that some moderating economic influence might deliberately be attempted through government fiscal policy. The annually balanced budget was the avowed objective at all times, and at all levels of government. During the 1920's, when government outlays represented a relatively small proportion of the gross national expenditures, the existence of such a philosophy occasioned little serious difficulty. But in the years following the advent of the "Great Depression", when the problem of financing rapidly mounting government expenditures had to be solved, the economic consequences of the "balanced budget" tradition were most unfortunate.[65]

Following Canada's *de facto* departure from the gold standard at the beginning of 1929, chartered bank advances under the Finance Act rose very rapidly to a November peak almost fifty per cent higher than the record post-war level achieved in January. The accompanying rapid rise in commercial loans was in marked contrast to the relatively modest decline in the banks' securities holdings. Canadian national income reached a new high during the year, and stimulated by excessive bank credit designed to accommodate the steadily expanding "needs of business",[66] the boom culminated in the autumn of 1929. The rise in national income, as already pointed out, had been based on a high level of exports and a high rate of domestic investment, both in the extractive industries and in

[64]See Clifford Curtis, "Canada and the Gold Standard" in the *Queen's Quarterly*, XXXVIII, No. 1, Winter, 1931, p. 117. "The Department is primarily a civil service department, and an administrative division of the government, as efficient as any in its own field, but most emphatically its own field is not that of performing functions in the monetary system which in other countries are performed by such special institutions as the central banks". The administration of the Finance Act (in the late 1920's) clearly illustrated "the difficulties in the way of a branch of the civil service when it must choose between an 'easy money' policy, with its immediate popular appeal, and a 'dear money' policy with its immediately unpopular reactions".

[65]In the years following 1929, frequent warnings were heard that the federal government would need to raise more money to balance the budget deficits which inevitably "threaten" in time of depression.

[66]The notion that the chartered banks are merely passive agents in serving the "needs of business", and that fluctuations in bank credit in no way influence those needs, appeared to be almost universally held by the bankers. With reference to this particular period, for example, the President of the Canadian Bankers' Association, in discussing fluctuations in bank advances under the Finance Act, explained that " . . . the advances since 1923 have varied according to the business requirements of the country . . .". See the *Evidence of the Royal Commission on Banking and Currency in Canada*, 1933, I. p. 74.

manufacturing.[67]  Underlying this economic expansion were certain serious weaknesses, soon to become apparent.

Canadian exports, which were primarily extractive in character, and of which wheat and newsprint were the most important, were highly vulnerable to any change in market conditions, in view of their relatively inelastic demands.[68] The high rate of domestic investment, encouraged by the prevailing monetary expansion, could not be sustained indefinitely and it had involved " . . . the drawing of larger proportions of the population into peculiarly vulnerable occupations such as that of unskilled workers in the construction industry.[69] In addition, there had occurred a marked increase in financial rigidities, stemming from the large-scale borrowing of the decade by both private and public sources. The increase of such fixed charges in an economy of highly variable national income clearly involved the risk of subsequent financial disaster and of the necessity for painful economic readjustment. The consequences of these weaknesses became fully apparent in the impact of the world-wide depression which began late in 1929, and we now turn to a consideration of the role of Canada's monetary and fiscal policies in the solution of her unprecedented economic difficulties in this period.

[67]For income estimates in this period, see the *Bank of Nova Scotia Monthly Review*, May 1937. Here the "net available national income" is estimated to have risen from $3,789 million in 1921 to $5,445 million in 1929, and to have reached its lowest level at $2,974 million in 1933.

[68]See Mackintosh, *op. cit.*, p. 54: "The world expansion of this period was on a base rendered precarious by reason of the dislocations in world trade, the political tension amid which the expansion took place, and the inordinate expansion of credit which flowed out from the United States and other creditor countries."

[69]*Ibid.*

## CHAPTER VII

# THE GREAT DEPRESSION
# AND THE INTRODUCTION OF CENTRAL BANKING

THE collapse of world markets registered its initial and greatest impact on Canada's staple export industries. Of these, wheat and newsprint were the most important, and were already over-extended before the collapse occurred. At this stage of her economic development, Canada earned about one-third of her national income from sales abroad, and the drastic decline in export prices, coupled with the typically inelastic demand for these extractive raw materials, brought a severe contraction of export income, the repercussions of which spread throughout the economy. Apart from wheat and newsprint, proceeds from the sale of such staples as lumber, the base metals and fisheries products suffered comparable declines.[1] The initial collapse of these markets was subsequently aggravated by currency depreciations and devaluations which impaired the competitive position of Canadian exporters, and by the widespread introduction of greater tariff protection, which in the United States reached its extreme development under the Hawley-Smoot legislation of 1930.

A further circumstance of the depression, and one which influenced greatly the government's monetary thinking during this period, was the greatly increased burden of Canada's external indebtedness associated with the unprecedented decline in national income. Some forty per cent of the capital investment in Canadian non-farm business and government securities was owned externally. Half of this capital investment was in debtor form, of which two-fifths was held abroad.[2] The problem of servicing this external debt was a factor which weighed heavily in the government's decision to maintain the external value of the dollar in the early years of the depression, rather than to permit or encourage exchange

[1] The magnitudes of these price and income movements with respect to particular commodities are readily available elsewhere and need not be analysed in detail. As a general indication of the extent of deflation which occurred, it may, however, be noted that between July, 1929, and December, 1932, the price index of 17 major exports fell (from 100) to 47, that of the export prices of farm products to 30, that of all wholesale prices to 66, that of employment to 67 and that of industrial production to 52. At the latter date, the price of Winnipeg wheat had reached 38¢ per bushel, the lowest on record, and by 1933, the average of all Canadian farm prices had declined by 60% since 1929. As these price declines were usually coupled with inelastic demand, the decline in revenue was catastrophic. See the *Report of the Royal Commission on Dominion-Provincial Relations* (Ottawa: The King's Printer), 1939, Book I, Ch. 6.

[2] *Ibid.*, p. 147. In 1928-9, interest and dividends payable abroad required less than one-sixth of the proceeds of current exports; in 1933 they required one-third. More than half of the debt of all Canadian governments and more than four-fifths of the bonded debt of Canadian corporations was payable either solely or optionally in foreign currencies.

depreciation as a possible means of mitigating the deflationary pressures on the economy.

The impact of reduced export incomes was soon transmitted to the construction industry and other secondary industries, but the distribution of losses was arbitrary and uneven. Such was inevitable in an economy characterized by a high degree of functional and geographical immobility of resources and by rigidities in cost-price—selling-price relationships associated with contractual debt forms, monopolistic restrictions and tariff protection. These characteristics made the necessary economic readjustments extremely painful. It was unfortunately true that "the unequal incidence of the burden on the different groups and regions in the country was the outstanding feature and the basis of the most serious problems arising out of the depression".[3] The greatest burden was borne by the unemployed, by the producers in the major export sectors and by the owners of equity investments. Losses in the manufacturing sector were somewhat less severe both because of the government's tariff policies which diverted a greater proportion of the home market to domestic production and because of the many instances where "natural" protection was enjoyed.

In view of the decline in national income and of the large interest payments required to service the externally-held debt, both public and private, it was reasonable to expect that after having in fact been severed from gold early in 1929, the Canadian dollar would depreciate in the foreign exchange market. Such had been the experience of Australia and the Argentine, countries whose basic economic circumstances were similar to Canada's. That the Canadian dollar did not depreciate significantly in the early years of the depression was due to a net inflow of capital which reflected in part the confidence of foreign investors in the Canadian economy, in part Canadian government borrowing in New York and in part Canadian tariff policy which by curtailing imports lessened the demand for foreign exchange. There is no evidence, however, that these government measures which supported the dollar were adopted with that object in view. This result was rather of an incidental nature,[4] but entirely in accord with the government's desire to maintain "sound" money.

Until the autumn of 1931, Canadian dollar depreciation was negligible, in terms both of the U.S. dollar and of sterling. However, as world depression deepened, capital imports into Canada slowed to a trickle, and after Britain abandoned the gold standard in September, 1931, the rates of exchange among the three currencies shifted rapidly.[5] By December, the premium of the U.S.

[3]*Ibid.*, p. 147.

[4]For a carefully detailed analysis of balance-of-payments developments during this period, see F. A. Knox, *Dominion Monetary Policy, 1929-34* (Ottawa: The King's Printer), 1939.

[5]Among the factors that led to the depreciation of the Canadian dollar vis-à-vis that of the U.S. were (1) pressure on U.S. branch plants in Canada to remit their surplus funds to the U.S.; (2) a mild flight of capital from Canadian securities; (3) the speculative selling of Canadian securities, in anticipation that Canada would formally follow Britain's departure from gold; (4) suspicions of weakness arising from Canada's monetary management in 1929. See W. C. Clark, "The Flight From the Gold Standard", in *Queen's Quarterly*, 1931, Vol. XXXVIII, No. 4.

dollar exceeded 20% and the discount of sterling exceeded 16%, based on the previous gold parities. The Canadian dollar thus assumed a position roughly midway between the other two currencies, where it fluctuated until March, 1933. For some months thereafter, while sterling appreciated vis-à-vis the U.S. dollar, the Canadian dollar appreciated somewhat less rapidly, and on two occasions was at a discount in terms of each of the others. By late 1933, it had regained its intermediate position, being slightly above, and sterling appreciably above, the U.S. dollar.

In the face of the unprecedented catastrophe which engulfed the Canadian economy following 1929, our main interest is to analyse the reactions both of the chartered banks and of the Canadian government, and particularly to note the banking, monetary and fiscal policies which were deemed to be appropriate to the times.

In contrast to 1930, during which time the chartered banks had been able to increase their foreign balances, the following year brought a sharp reversal in Canada's balance of payments, and the financing of the current account deficit brought a reduction in the banks' monetary gold and external assets, despite which, as noted above, the Canadian dollar depreciated substantially. In making available foreign reserves during the depression, the banks did support the dollar, but this shifting of assets was not governed by exchange rate considerations but by ordinary commercial objectives. In the absence of government monetary leadership, it was not, of course, the responsibility of the banks to maintain "desirable" rates of foreign exchange (assuming that any agreement as to what constituted such rates could have been obtained). Nor is it surprising that during these years the restrictive lending practices of the banks aggravated deflationary pressures.

Between October, 1929, and June, 1932, the banks' Canadian deposits declined from approximately $2.4 billion to $1.9 billion, a reduction of more than twenty per cent. The sharp reduction in their Canadian loans was only in part offset by their expansion of securities holdings as they sought to maintain satisfactory earnings on their assets. These securities purchases strengthened bond prices and hence contributed to lower yields, but again the result was fortuitous, and not the motive which dictated the purchases. The chartered banks' outstanding Finance Act advances declined sharply during this period, and in the years 1929, 1930 and 1931, their maximum advances moved from $111 million to $83 million to $66 million, their minimum advances from $71 million to $0.5 million to nil.[6]

There can be no doubt that in their technical operations, the Canadian chartered banks performed with exemplary efficiency during the depression. In the words of one observer, "the policy of the commercial banks, *as commercial banks*

[6]See the monthly *Report of the Chartered Banks of the Dominion of Canada.* During 1931, the average amount of outstanding advances was $20 million, and during the first ten months of 1932, $30 million.

[italics mine], is indicated by a comparison of the records of Canadian banks during the depression with those in some other countries".[7] This policy, however, was concerned mostly with such technical problems as the choice of proper credit risks, and "Its effects on the aggregate of deposits and the complex of interest rates are unintentional and accidental."[8] It should also be noted that these effects are frequently perverse and destabilizing. By adhering to what had become accepted as proper banking practices in Canada, the banks succeeded in keeping "safe and sound . . . [a circumstance] no less necessary in bad times than in good times."[9]

The point at which the banks may be criticized is not that they were wrong in keeping safe and sound, or even that in the process of doing so they effected a highly undesirable contraction of the country's means of payment. The ultimate responsibility for this contraction must rest not with the banks but with the government, which failed to assume any responsibility for control of the total means of payment in the economy. The basic criticism of the bankers is rather that they neither understood nor were willing to learn the economic consequences of their own actions, and they consequently provided a great deal of ill-informed opposition to the subsequent formation of a central bank.[10] It should of course be emphasized that the failure to recognize the connection between monetary contraction and the aggravation of the Canadian depression was by no means confined to the bankers. It was almost universal in those early years.

In an unpublished memorandum prepared within the Canadian government by its economic advisers, it was observed that with rare exceptions, Canadian financial and industrial leaders took little part in the discussion of the country's monetary and general economic difficulties, and that the general public was quite unaware of the fact that the deflationary collapse of prices following 1929 was in any way related to the country's monetary standard or banking mechanism.

[7]G. A. Elliott, "Canadian Monetary Policy—Drift, Domestic Management and Debts", in *Proceedings of the Canadian Political Science Association*, VI, 1934, p. 252.

[8]*Ibid.*

[9]Jackson Dodds, "Banking and Currency", an address delivered before the Winnipeg Board of Trade, March 31, 1933. Mr. Dodds further observed that "lending would be the sinecure many think it is if it were not necessary to get the money back".

[10]Lest the reader object to this broad judgment of the bankers on the ground that "all generalizations are false", I would add "including that one". It is true, of course, that exceptions are almost always to be found, and in this particular instance clearly exceptional among his colleagues was S. R. Noble, who expressed the view, in a voice as from the wilderness, that "there are undoubtedly many factors which have contributed to the depression [in Canada] but I believe . . . that there is a large measure of inevitability to all of them except that of monetary deflation", and that "one of the principal reasons to doubt that proper action may be expected along [monetary] lines is the general attitude of the heads of the great commercial banks. With few exceptions, they do not understand or believe that there is anything in the theories which we are enunciating. . . . The lack of interest and, in fact, active antagonism of the commercial bankers to a central bank policy of control is due, as I have stated, to the fact that they do not understand the problem." S. R. Noble, Address to the Economics Section of the Montreal Branch, Canadian Institute of International Affairs, November 24, 1930.

By contrast, a considerable number of English financiers and industrialists had made important contributions to the theoretical discussion of such matter in that country, with the result that "the vast flood of monetary literature which has appeared since the close of the war must have dinned into at least the more intelligible public a faint comprehension of some of the problems at issue".[11]

In so far as the Canadian government may be said to have pursued a monetary policy of any kind in the early years of the depression, it was that of maintaining "sound" money, by which was meant the continued adherence to the gold standard. The government regarded this course as essential if the Canadian dollar was to be kept "honest", although this use of the term may be seriously questioned. It is true that maintenance of the gold standard ensured a stable dollar in terms of gold, but in terms of all other goods and services, i.e., of its general purchasing power, its value was altered drastically. As already noted, a *de facto* departure from gold had occurred early in 1929, but the government appeared reluctant to acknowledge this circumstance and apparently believed that the maintenance of Canada's external debt obligations constituted the maintenance of the gold standard.

The government's "orthodox" monetary policy received widespread support from the banks, the business community, most of the parliamentary opposition and from the financial press,[12] all of whom tended to regard any proposals to "tinker" with the currency as immoral. The Canadian Bankers' Association emphasized that "any attempt to raise domestic prices (whether the country is on or off the gold standard) by measures designed to increase arbitrarily the volume of commercial credit in use, is bound to disrupt the normal economic process in unpredictable direction and to cause disequilibrium difficult to eradicate later".[13] In its complete disregard for the unprecedented deflation which gripped the Canadian economy, this statement must surely rank high among those least helpful for the times. While by no means unified in their views, most Canadian economists pointed to the need for monetary reform and voiced their criticisms of contemporary government policies.

It was mainly from Western critics that the most vehement and in many respects most constructive proposals for monetary improvements arose. From various representatives of this major export region came proposals for cheap money (via the expansion of the Dominion note issue), deliberate currency depreciation, a policy of Dominion government deficit finance and revisions in

---

[11]*Memorandum on Monetary Reconstruction*, unpublished document prepared within the Department of Finance, Ottawa, 1934, Part II, p. 28.

[12]The banks took comfort in the fact that " . . . the newspapers throughout Canada, with negligible exceptions, are doing an important work in supporting the best interests of the country. While in the performance of their function of purveying news, they publish the views of exponents of monetary schemes and cure-alls, they do not endorse such views—on the contrary, in the great majority of papers, opinions expressed editorially are based on sound principles and a desire to promote public welfare". See Jackson Dodds, *op. cit.*, p. 21.

[13]Royal Commission on Banking and Currency, *Evidence*, pp. 3175-6.

the Bank Act. The government regarded all such suggestions as little short of heresy, persisted in classifying them as inflationary and defended its "sound" money mainly on the grounds that it was indispensable in retaining the confidence of foreign investors and that deliberate depreciation of the currency would increase intolerably the burden of the principal and interest payments on the country's externally held debt, both public and private.

Following Britain's abandonment of the gold standard in September, 1931, there was much speculation as to the course which Canada would follow. Despite repeated official statements insisting that Canada was still on gold and intended to remain there, that standard was legally abandoned a month later, and the *de facto* action taken more than two and one-half years earlier was thereby formally acknowledged. The Western demands for deliberate depreciation became more insistent, as one means of easing the growing competitive pressures which Canadian exporters, especially of wheat, were encountering in foreign markets as a consequence of the depreciation of foreign currencies, particularly those of Australia and the Argentine. It was pointed out that world opinion was rapidly shifting toward deliberate currency management and away from what one Western member of the House of Commons referred to as that "unmanaged accident of stupidity known as the gold basis."[14]

That the Canadian Prime Minister, the Rt. Hon. R. B. Bennett, was not being swept away in this tide of monetary enlightenment was indicated by his reaction to the British abandonment of gold. He stated that "the effect which this action by England had on Canada is difficult to exaggerate. It has resulted in a struggle to maintain the national integrity. It was necessary for us to increase Customs duties not for the purpose of protection, but to maintain the balance of our national position. We had either to face bankruptcy or restrict imports."[15] The Imperial Economic Conference, held at Ottawa in 1932, did not favour currency depreciation as a means of easing deflationary pressures but it did recognize that some monetary action aimed at stimulating a general price rise was highly desirable, and that this result could best be accomplished by the creating and maintaining "within the limits of sound finance of such conditions as will assist in the revival of enterprise and trade".[16] These conditions included low interest rates and abundant short-term money, the latter to be provided "not by the inflationary creation of additional means of payment to finance public expenditure, but by an orderly monetary policy".[17]

[14]Quoted in Knox, *op. cit.*, p. 22. Here it is pointed out that proposals to tie the Canadian dollar to sterling were rejected because of the continuing lack of general support for monetary experimentation, uncertainty as to the future of sterling, fear for Canada's credit reputation abroad and the heavy foreign debt obligations. Although not desirable, it is doubtful that such a course would have injured Canada's reputation at this juncture of world events.

[15]Imperial Economic Conference, Ottawa, 1932: *Appendices to the Summary of Proceedings* (London: H. M. Stationery Office), 1932, Cmd. 4175, p. 132.

[16]*Ibid.*, p. 30.   [17]*Ibid.*, p. 31.

During 1932, the world-wide depression reached its climax, and the exchange value of the Canadian dollar, midway between the U.S. dollar and sterling, created serious problems both for importers buying in U.S. markets and exporters selling in sterling markets. A contemporary observer noted that "when the English currency was divorced from gold the Canadian dollar was found to be not quite good enough for gold nor bad enough for sterling but hung for a year and a half like Mahomet's coffin suspended between heaven and earth, about 15 per cent below the golden heaven, no one knew how and no one knew why".[18] The government nevertheless viewed this position as a not unreasonable compromise among conflicting Canadian interests.[19] The balance of payments again became favourable in 1932 as imports were further restricted, in part by the continuing decline in national income and in part by the government's tariff measures which redirected a larger proportion of declining expenditures to domestic sources. In the early stages of its administration, the Conservative government had reluctantly adopted public works in support of the unemployed and then abandoned the programme as being both wasteful and expensive, only to revive it at a later date after a period of experimentation with the payment of direct relief.[20]

It was not until November, 1932, that the government made an initial attempt to counteract the undesirable contraction of chartered bank cash reserves, by forcing those institutions to borrow, under the provisions of the Finance Act, $35 million in Dominion notes at a cost of 3 per cent. At the same time, the banks loaned a similar sum to the government through their purchase of a two-year issue of 4 per cent treasury bills, which they pledged as collateral for their borrowings. The banks had shown no enthusiasm for expanding their Finance Act borrowings voluntarily during the depression years and in fact sought to keep them at minimum practicable levels. Because borrowings by any one bank tended to be interpreted by the others as a sign of weakness, the compulsory aspect of the government's action was essential. Forbidden to repay these advances within two years, the banks initially loaned or invested these additional cash reserves, but the measure was quite unsuccessful in inducing monetary expansion because the banks proceeded to reduce their outstanding indebtedness to the government to such an extent that during 1934 their Finance Act advances remained very little above the $35 million minimum.

This unsuccessful initial attempt by the government to increase the stock of

---

[18]Royal Commission on Banking and Currency, *Evidence*, p. 2450.
[19]See the Minister of Finance, *Budget Speech*, March 21, 1933, p. 5.
[20]See W. A. Mackintosh, "The Progress of Canada's Recovery", in *International Affairs*, XIV, 1935, p. 394. Here it is noted that until 1932, the Canadian government viewed the depression as a short-term phenomenon and adopted temporary measures while awaiting the return of better times. "It is not unfair to governments to say they dug themselves in and waited for the storm to blow over. Unemployment was so great that governments naturally decided to husband their resources. They gave up public works, and they got down to the direct distribution of relief."

money did at least provide it with newly created funds for meeting some of its expenditures, a method of finance clearly preferable to taxation or non-bank borrowing. It also caused some weakening of the Canadian bond market and a depreciation of the Canadian dollar, both of which effects were unintentional.[21] In 1934, following the World Economic Conference, the government took its second step toward deliberate monetary expansion by increasing chartered bank cash by some $53 million, this time by expanding its Dominion note issue without additional gold backing, and again thereby providing itself with "new" cash for financing public works.[22] In explaining what appeared, in the light of the government's past performance, to be "unorthodox" policy and a startling reversal of principle, the Prime Minister explained that the move should not be regarded as departing from sound monetary practice because the rules of the gold-standard game had been altered by international agreement. Such being the case, Canada could safely proceed without worrying about her financial reputation, and there would not likely be any depreciation of the dollar such as had occurred after the compulsory bank borrowings in 1932. Depreciation was apparently still regarded by the government as a disaster to be avoided at all costs.

The success of this second approach to monetary expansion lay in its conjuncture with improving world conditions and with the devaluation of the U.S. dollar. The rise in the value of sterling vis-à-vis both the Canadian and U.S. dollars did much to ease the pressure on Canadian exporters and therefore to improve the balance of payments. With expanding reserves accruing both from increased exports and from the government's domestic monetary measures, chartered bank deposits increased by some $300 million within a period of two years.[23] By 1933, following the Ottawa Conference, the Minister of Finance had been able to recognize the desirability of a fall in the general level of interest rates, an objective which the government undertook to further by its policy on conversion loans. In the case of short-term rates, the first general movement in Canada took place in May, 1933,[24] when the chartered banks reduced their rates charged on farm loans and municipal loans by 1 per cent. During the next

[21]On November 3, 1932, the day that the transaction was announced, the premium on U.S. funds was approximately 11%, but before the end of the month it had risen to 19%. Prior to the compulsory loan, the trend had been downward for some five months.

[22]While this new issue was explained in terms of providing the means of financing public works, the government was in fact persuaded to take such action because of fiscal advantage related to the public debt. Faced at the time with heavy refunding operations, the government benefited from a rapid rise in long-term bond prices in the months following its monetary action.

[23]The government's action occurred approximately five months after the United States devalued its dollar; almost immediately after the U.S. move, the Canadian dollar went to par with the U.S. dollar, and it approximated parity with sterling.

[24]See A. F. W. Plumptre, "Canadian Monetary Policy", in H. A. Innis and A. F. W. Plumptre, *The Canadian Economy and its Problems* (Toronto: University of Toronto Press), 1934.

several years, the rate paid on savings deposits declined gradually from 3 per cent to 1½ per cent.

Testifying before the Royal Commission on Banking and Currency some time later, a representative of the Canadian Bankers' Association stated that " . . . it has been the aim of the Chartered Banks to maintain rates of interest at a steady level", in order that business men could " . . . make their commitments without fear of their interest costs being subject to violent fluctuations", come inflation or depression.[25] The notion that flexible rates might perform useful monetary functions was thus entirely lacking in those circles. A serious defect arising from the concentration of Canada's financial business within a relatively few powerful banks, insurance companies and loan companies was that while this undoubtedly provided the economic "stability" for which these institutions continuously claimed credit, it " . . . resulted in a lack of open, competitive business and an emphasis upon personal banker-customer relationships; upon 'customer rates' and 'published rates' at the expense of 'market rates' in the capital markets".[26] In 1934, the government inaugurated a policy of selling treasury bills by public auction rather than by direct agreement and this brought a substantial reduction of the yield on this short-term paper.

The most fundamental criticism of Canadian monetary policy during the depression is that none existed. In its absence, various *ad hoc* measures appeared from time to time, invariably too late and too limited to be of real assistance in coping with the depression. Lacking a central bank, no conscious control of the over-all volume of money was attempted, nor indeed was the desirability of such control generally recognized until economic contraction had reached its most advanced stage. There existed "an anomalous condition of division of responsibility between the banks and the government and lack of special equipment or tradition in the Department of Finance",[27] in the light of which facts, positive monetary guidance could scarcely have been expected. The monetary system was described as being in a state of transition " . . . from the decentralized system in which the intelligent self-interest of the banks was a sufficient agency of credit control to a system in which the central institution accepts responsibility for credit control".[28]

The repeated statements of Canadian bank officials clearly indicated their failure to appreciate that the consequences of credit decisions taken according to their "intelligent self-interest" might seriously conflict with broader economic objectives. The same statements also reflected the bankers' ill-disguised antagon-

[25]Royal Commission on Banking and Currency, *Evidence, op. cit.*, p. 3281.
[26]See A. F. W. Plumptre, *Central Banking in the British Dominions* (Toronto: University of Toronto Press), 1940, pp. 10-11.
[27]W. C. Clark, *op. cit.*, p. 761.
[28]C. A. Curtis, "The Canadian Monetary Situation", in the *Journal of Political Economy*, XV, 1932, p. 334.

ism toward their critics.[29] Day-to-day lending operations were based on either or both of two conflicting notions, the first being that banks merely lend the amount of savings which the public has seen fit to deposit with them,[30] the second that banks do create credit, but only in response to the needs of business. Both of these theories are faulty, but as one writer has expressed it, they are "intensely practical; for they have been put into practice".[31] It was unfortunately true, however, that " . . . criticism of the Canadian banking system, even criticism in the sense of scientific appraisal, has always been taboo . . . but it would be passing strange if there were no room for improvement, if like all other human institutions it did not need to evolve and develop as conditions changed. All modern banking evolution has been in the direction of credit control. . . . It will be in the interests of Canadian banks and of Canada generally if our bankers give the most serious thought to this problem and determine how they can best play their part in the immediate movement to check the deadly process of world strangulation which monetary deflation (as one of the most important of several factors) is currently furthering".[32]

Unfortunately also, there is abundant evidence that sound advice of this kind was almost invariably received with hostility.[33] Much of the Canadian monetary

[29]One banker thankfully acknowledged that there were fewer banking theorists in Canada than in most countries, but that curiously enough, the bankers got along quite well without them, since they were usually too fully occupied in the practising of their profession to indulge in "theorizing". By contrast, an all-too-rare banker's view was provided by a future governor of the Bank of Canada, who stated that "I do not entirely agree however with the idea that ignorance of theory is the proper thing. Superficial knowledge of any economic theory may do harm, but a sound knowledge of the theories sponsored by the leading economists cannot do harm because with sound knowledge will go a realization of the practical limitations of each theory, and the necessary caution in regard to putting it into practice". See Graham F. Towers, "International Banking and Foreign Exchange", in *Journal of the Canadian Bankers' Association*, XXXIII, pp. 529-33.

[30]The Public Relations Adviser to the Canadian chartered banks expressed this generally accepted notion admirably in his comment that "out of the fact that banks in practice keep about ten per cent of the deposits available in cash has been developed the amazing distortion that we lend our deposits ten times over". Vernon Knowles, "The Facts About Canada's Banks", Text of Radio Speech, Sept. 14, 1937. This kind of statement served merely to confuse the issue, and its error lay in its failure to recognize the multiple expansion of credit which the system as a whole could generate when operating on a fractional-reserve basis. This process of multiple credit expansion had only recently been grasped by a few monetary economists. The general public, including the bankers, were quite unaware of the phenomenon.

[31]See A. F. W. Plumptre, "The Point of View of a Central Bank", in *The Canadian Forum*, XIII, January, 1933, p. 132.

[32]*Memorandum on Monetary Reconstruction, op. cit.*, Part II, p. 29.

[33]One banker typically observed that "in addition to the troubles that arise in the actual carrying out of [our] work [we] are subject to outside distractions nowadays, the chief of which seems to me to be the enormous flood of advice and opinion that is poured out on all of us by so-called financial experts or economists, most of which does not seem to us rough-necks to have much practical application. The written stuff we can avoid by not reading it". See the Canadian Bank of Commerce, *Annual Report*, 1931, p. 34. Apparently it was much more difficult for the harried bankers to ignore the advice which their well-wishers chose to tender verbally.

and banking discussion in the early 1930's originated from quarters which made it "suspect" with the country's conservative financial leaders, who tended to regard any criticism of existing arrangements as the product of irresponsible radicals who were seeking to promote "unsound" inflationary schemes. It was none the less true that there was an urgent need for ending the existing state of monetary "drift", a term which implied "the absence both of automatic regulation and of conscious control by a central authority toward a well defined monetary objective".[34]

The government's exchange-rate policy was merely the passive reflection of its major monetary objective, that of maintaining the gold standard, albeit in rather limited form. It was at all times opposed to positive steps toward depreciation, despite some rather forceful arguments to support such action. By its tariff measures and external borrowing operations it unwittingly supported the Canadian dollar, which depreciated significantly only after its formal departure from gold late in 1931. One of the serious problems which the Canadian economy faced during the depression was "the reduction of earnings of primary producers in relation to debts, taxes and other fixed charges, and the concomitant reduction not only in purchasing but also in borrowing power".[35] While the direct reduction of debt burdens via the scaling down of interest and principal payments offered a prospect of minor assistance, the main remedy necessarily lay in the raising of prices to levels consistent with those at which the indebtedness was contracted. To accomplish such an objective, consciously formulated monetary control was indispensable.

It is true that just as the depression had been precipitated by external events, recovery likewise had to await the revival of external markets for Canada's primary staples. But to say that recovery could not be brought about solely by domestic economic policies is far from saying that such policies are unimportant or irrelevant, and the Canadian recovery could undoubtedly have been hastened if an appropriate policy of monetary expansion had been implemented much earlier in the depression. A Royal Commission subsequently reported that " . . . the monetary and exchange policies which were followed rendered the disparities in the incidence of the depression greater than they needed to have been. The decline in national income was also probably greater. The risks and dangers connected with monetary expansion and currency depreciation were great and a mistaken or careless procedure would undoubtedly have brought the consequences which the government feared. But a skilful policy, which perhaps was not too much to expect in view of the serious problems of the time, could have avoided them. It would have been possible by any one of a number, or by a combination, of methods, such as restricting the outflow of gold, restraining the contraction of credit, avoiding an increase of protective tariffs, and

[34]G. A. Elliott, *op. cit.*, p. 251.
[35]Plumptre, *op. cit.*, p. 167.

purchasing foreign exchange, to depress the exchange value of the dollar without causing a wild flight of capital or a serious loss of foreign confidence in Canadian credit."[36]

The possible consequences of currency depreciation as an alternative monetary policy for Canada in the early years of the depression have been studied in detail elsewhere,[37] but it is nevertheless useful at this point to note the broad issues involved. Depreciation would have increased immediately the Canadian dollar prices of internationally traded goods, both exports and imports, and the justification for its adoption must rest upon the assumed expansionary income effects which such a policy would have induced. Briefly stated, the case for depreciation was that the gross proceeds from the sale of Canadian exports would increase, that because of a lag in costs exporters' net incomes would also increase and that the expansion generated in the export sector would spread throughout the economy.

In actual fact, the currency experiences of various countries which adopted depreciation to cope with depressed export industries suggest that this technique was by no means as effective in improving balance-of-payments positions as had commonly been supposed, mainly because of the relatively low elasticities of demand (in many cases less than unity) for many exported commodities. Because Canada was such an important supplier in the world wheat market, and the elasticity of foreign demand for Canadian wheat therefore low, there is real doubt as to whether Canadian wheat producers would have gained much from a policy of depreciation. It has likewise been argued that Canada's pulp and paper industry and lumber industry were not in a strong position to benefit from such a policy.[38] On the other hand, the producers of meat and dairy products and of the base metals would have gained considerably more, while gold, being sold at a fixed U.S. dollar price, was the one product which would have received maximum benefit. (The Canadian gold industry received a tremendous stimulus from the U.S. revaluation of gold in 1934, only to be confronted by a critical cost-price squeeze, equally fortuitous, during World War II and the succeeding decade.)

To the extent that imported components, e.g., raw materials, capital equipment, etc., entered into the production of Canadian exports, the possible gains in gross export income, which generally tended to be over-emphasized, would have been in part at least offset by higher costs, and the net gains which might have accrued to the sellers of particular exports would have varied widely. On balance, the net gain to exporters as a group, and the stimulus which would

---

[36]Report of the *Royal Commission on Dominion-Provincial Relations, op. cit.*, Book I, p. 156.

[37]Knox, *op. cit.* See also G. A. Elliott's review of Knox in the *Canadian Journal of Economics and Political Science*, VII, pp. 88-91.

[38]*Ibid.*

have been transmitted to other sectors of the economy, is not easy to estimate. To the extent that depreciation restricted expenditures on imports (here assuming demand to be elastic), the leakage from the domestic income stream would have been reduced, and some part of the reduction in import expenditures would presumably have been transferred to domestic production, an effect similar to that actually induced by Canadian tariff policy. Any expansion of national income would have lessened the burden of fixed charges payable in domestic currency, but as already indicated, it was the existence of such a large indebtedness payable in foreign currency that weighed so heavily in the government's decision to reject depreciation as a depression measure.

It appears reasonable to conclude that the elasticity of demand for Canadian wheat in world markets was sufficiently low that the major advocates of depreciation (the Western farmers) would have gained much less than anticipated if such a policy had been adopted. It has been further argued that any Canadian attempt at depreciation prior to Britain's abandonment of gold in the autumn of 1931 would have reacted adversely on Canadian national income because the loss of confidence by foreign investors, in a period when orthodox monetary policy was still widely accepted, would have brought a reduction of capital investment in Canada which would have outweighed the possible expansion of Canadian export incomes. It must be conceded, however, that "unmeasurable psychological considerations . . . permit differences of opinion" as to the consequences of early exchange depreciation.[39] Depreciation in these early years would also have been viewed internationally as unjustifiable, since Canada was not confronted by a balance-of-payments deficit. One can only speculate as to the possible retaliation which such action might have invited, in which event any positive effects of the Canadian action might have been purely transitional.

In place of seeking to export unemployment via depreciation, a positive approach through the use of vigorous monetary and fiscal measures to promote domestic expansion would clearly have been preferable. By 1932, however, world confidence had been so badly undermined by the events of the preceding years, and international capital movements had become so small that the factors weighing against Canadian dollar depreciation at an earlier time no longer appeared to be relevant. Furthermore, "sound" monetary policies were by this time widely questioned, especially in the light of the contrast between the depths of the depression in those countries which had remained on gold (e.g., Canada, the United States and Germany) and those which had depreciated their currencies (e.g., the sterling area). Discussing particularly the contrast between Britain and the United States, one observer concluded that their monetary experiences seemed "to justify the belief that the depression was due mainly to misguided financial policies, particularly on the part of those financially

[39]Elliott, *op. cit.*, p. 90.

powerful countries that controlled the gold supply of the world".[40] In the United States, "the financial authorities permitted continuous deflation to proceed when there can be no reasonable doubt that it could have been defeated by the policies which were put into force three years later—three years too late".[41]

It was painfully apparent by this time that the international gold standard, which had flourished under Britain's financial dominance in the nineteenth and early twentieth centuries, was no longer an appropriate mechanism in the radically altered economic environment in which it was called upon to operate. The "best" monetary system, judged in terms of the efficiency with which it performs its major function as a medium of exchange, is relative to time and place. There can be no absolutely best system, and to operate satisfactorily, either the monetary mechanism must be adapted to its environment or the environment to the mechanism. The unreality of the latter possibility was only slightly less apparent in the 1930's than at the present time, while, on the other hand, the gold standard could scarcely have been adapted to the conditions of the international post-World War I economy.

In the face of increasing economic nationalism and concentration on domestic economic objectives, with serious restrictions on the international flow of goods and services and of private capital, with the destabilizing effects of gold movements multiplied by the operation of fractional reserve banking systems and with central banks increasingly interfering with the gold standard mechanism, in order to cushion the impact of these external disturbances, the standard was rejected, in many instances reluctantly, by all but a handful of countries. Those which persisted in retaining gold, such as Germany, suffered drastic deflation from the overvaluation of their currencies. The main advantage provided by the gold standard was its relative stability of exchange rates but it became increasingly obvious during the depression that such stability could be purchased at too high a price, i.e., that of a paralysing domestic deflation. If it can be argued that the return to gold in the circumstances of the 1920's was unwise (and the unco-ordinated piecemeal return in this era undoubtedly intensified the later difficulties), it is even clearer that the proponents of the restoration of an international gold standard at the present time have learned remarkably little from the lessons of the past.

An examination of Canadian fiscal operations during the early 1930's, when the merits of counter-cyclical financing were still to be extolled by Mr. Keynes, reveals the same "orthodox" viewpoint that had characterized the monetary

---

[40]For a further discussion of this theme, see S. R. Noble, "The Monetary Experience of Canada During the Depression", in A. D. Gayer (ed.), *The Lessons of Monetary Experience* (New York: Farrar and Rinehart, Inc.), 1937. Here is found the sound observation that "Experience will have taught us nothing if, as a result of occurrences of the last seven years, we do not conclude that positive action from a monetary point of view is the first essential in controlling excesses of both boom and depression." See p. 128.        [41]*Ibid.*

developments of the period. The government found that support for, and opposition to, its fiscal views was divided along lines almost identical with that relating to its monetary views. The necessity of striving for balanced budgets was repeated endlessly by Liberal and Conservative politicians alike, by the chartered bankers, by business men[42] and by the financial press. In parliament and out, it was once again mainly from the Western "radicals" that alternative suggestions were heard, and while their economic analysis was frequently faulty, they nevertheless on occasion arrived at sound conclusions. The role of deficit financing in stimulating income and employment was of course little understood in these early years,[43] and the introduction of any public works programme was invariably accompanied by a warning of the necessity for higher taxes and more rigid governmental economy in order to balance the Dominion budget.[44] It is true that during the depression, deficit spending did occur involuntarily on a substantial scale, but in an entirely unco-ordinated fashion.[45] If these deficits had all been centralized in the Dominion government, which alone had national taxing powers and monetary authority, the borrowed funds could have been obtained more cheaply and spent as part of a positive integrated anti-depression programme. Government fiscal measures could have exerted a positive influence

[42]Typical of prevailing sentiment was the submission of the Canadian Chamber of Commerce to the Royal Commission on Dominion-Provincial Relations: " . . . the correction of the country's ills hinges in large measure upon the establishment of a sound financial position by *all* [italics mine] Canadian governing bodies. To this end, a prerequisite of sound public finance is that budgets should be balanced. The prevalence of unbalanced governmental budgets is undermining the prosperity of the country and its citizens."

[43]Surprisingly good expositions of the idea of counter-cyclical finance were nevertheless occasionally encountered. In its brief to the Royal Commission on Dominion-Provincial Relations, the Canadian Federation of Mayors and Municipalities stated that "The taxation policy of the government must be adapted to the prevailing economic conditions. High taxation during a period of business adversity serves but to place further handicaps upon potential business enterprise. A policy of low taxation should prevail in a depression period. Conversely, a policy of relatively high taxation should prevail during good times. Government income during prosperous years should be applied to the reduction of government debt. A tax policy of this nature would make it possible for governments to play their part in a planned technique aimed at the stabilization of employment opportunities." See Part III, pp. 29-30.

[44]In its limited efforts at coping with depression via public works and direct relief, the difficulties of divided jurisdiction as between the Dominion and provincial governments became apparent. Had the Dominion government attempted deliberate deficit finance, the possible constructive effects would have been materially reduced by the conflicting practices at the other levels of government. The Tax Rental Agreements, first concluded during World War II, served to eliminate the possibility of this fiscal conflict, and this objective has likewise been sought, if not entirely attained, in the post-war renewals of the Agreements.

[45]See, for example, Stewart Bates, *The Financial History of Canadian Governments* (Ottawa: King's Printer), 1939, p. 13: "Since the fiscal actions of the different governments were not co-ordinated, either with each other or with other government economic policies, fiscal policy was not envisaged as an instrument of control over economic conditions. Each government regarded its fiscal action as something determined for it by the economic conditions of the time".

and the virtual collapse of the credit of various provincial governments could have been avoided.

With monetary and fiscal theory neither well developed nor generally understood during the depression, it is scarcely surprising that attempts to cushion the impact of deflationary forces by constructive action in these areas were virtually non-existent in Canada. Moreover, even now, despite (or perhaps because of) our much more sophisticated monetary and fiscal theories, and the experience gained in their application during World War II and the post-war decade, the economist would be rash indeed who would claim that such weapons could do more than restrain for a limited time the impact of external fluctuations on the Canadian economy. The recovery which began to gather momentum in Canada during 1933 primarily reflected improving world conditions, and in particular the rising levels of employment and income in the United States, rather than domestic economic policies.

As economic depression deepened in Canada in the 1930's, and as it gradually became apparent to a larger cross-section of the community that the lack of positive monetary leadership was one of its contributing causes, monetary reform became a topic of widespread discussion. Attention was increasingly centred on the merits of a central bank, as an agency for curbing the monetary "excesses" which, in prosperity and depression, were not only possible but indeed inevitable under the existing administration of the Finance Act. The fact that the effectiveness of any monetary policy initiated within Canada might be severely circumscribed by external influences was increasingly recognized not as an argument against the employment of such a policy but rather that it should be consciously formulated and deliberately pursued in the public interest.

Testifying before the Royal Commission on Banking and Currency, a Canadian economist expressed such a view in his assertion that "we cannot turn our backs on the necessity of making decisions concerning the control of credit and monetary policy. . . . Unintelligent policies will not succeed whether we have a central bank or whether we have not. Without, however, such an institution even intelligent policies will be thwarted."[46] Up to this time, monetary conditions in Canada reflected the independent credit decisions of the chartered banks, private institutions whose lending policies were legitimately related to considerations of profitability, rather than to regulating the total volume of money and credit in accordance with any broad social objective. Indeed, far from using their lending powers to influence the general level of economic activity in Canada, the chartered bankers almost unanimously rejected the notion that they could wield any such causal influence.

To explore the desirability of establishing a central bank in Canada, the Bennett government appointed a Royal Commission in 1933, under the chairmanship

---

[46]See the Royal Commission on Banking and Currency, *Evidence*, p. 3059a.

of Lord Macmillan of London, England.[47] The Commission was further instructed, in the event that it found such an institution to be desirable, to recommend its form or structure. It was also requested to consider in what respects Canadian monetary policy should be modified. The Commission concerned itself almost entirely with the first question, merely "scratched" the second and omitted any consideration of the third and perhaps most important of all.[48] Although the Report of the Commission provides a useful summary of various aspects of Canadian financial development to 1933, it is in the briefs submitted to the Commission as it toured the country that the fascinating and illuminating observations are to be found, as Canadians from all walks of life expressed their views on monetary and banking policies and practices. Evidence was presented by such diverse groups as provincial and municipal governments, political organizations, farmers, small and large merchants, manufacturers, boards of trade, chambers of commerce, economists, banks, cranks and "helpful outsiders". The Secretary of the Commission pointed to the "distinguishable tone" that seemed to be established in the evidence from each of Canada's main economic regions, and to the fact that in many respects the most useful observations were provided by the witnesses appearing in the prairie provinces. Although their evidence was often "ill-informed and ill-presented" it was nevertheless "indigenous". Summing up the evidence submitted across the entire country, the Secretary noted that it "ranged from closely-reasoned argument actually to incoherent raving".[49]

At the outset the Commission emphasized quite correctly (and in an anticipatory vein) that the "best" monetary and banking arrangements were relative concepts and that "the circumstances in which a code was originally framed may subsequently undergo fundamental alterations, so that a system admirably adapted to serve one stage of national development may prove inadequate without fresh adjustments to meet new and unforeseen conditions".[50] More questionable was its observation that while a sound banking system was a valuable national asset, "it is not itself productive", being merely the servant of production and distribution, and that "unless a country is *running itself* [italics mine] on sound business lines, the most perfect banking system in the world cannot save it from the inevitable consequences of its breaches of economic law".[51]

To the idea of establishing a central bank in Canada, the chartered banks

---

[47]The other members of the Commission included Sir Charles Addis, also of London, Sir Thomas White, Canadian Minister of Finance during World War I, the Honourable J. E. Brownlee, premier of Alberta and Mr. Beaudry Leman, chartered banker. There is strong evidence to indicate that even before the appointing of this Commission, the Prime Minister had decided that a central bank was necessary for Canada.

[48]For an analysis of the Commission's operations, see C. A. Curtis, "The Canadian Macmillan Commission", in the *Economic Journal*, XLIV, 1934.

[49]See A. F. W. Plumptre, "The Evidence Presented to the Canadian Macmillan Commission", in the *Canadian Journal of Economics and Political Science*, II, pp. 54-67.

[50]Royal Commission on Banking and Currency, *Evidence*, I, p. 7.

[51]*Ibid.*, p. 11.

were almost solidly opposed. Business opinion in the West and in parts of the Maritimes was generally favourable, while in central Canada it was predominantly opposed. Most bankers believed that the rediscount facilities provided by the Finance Act obviated the need for any experiment in central banking, although some agreed that the administration of the Act should be improved. In actual fact, it was not "rediscounting" which took place under the Act, but rather a process of direct lending to the banks, with specified securities pledged as collateral for their advances. The appointment of the Royal Commission reflected the pronounced shift to intensified credit control and currency management elsewhere, and the question in Canada was not whether some change should be made in the existing arrangements but rather the direction and the form which the change should take.

Referring several years later to the Canadian monetary system as it existed at this time, the governor of the Bank of Canada noted that "we were then tied up in one of the most rigid monetary systems of the world, except for one factor —the Finance Act."[52] In relying upon this Act for monetary flexibility, there were three major disadvantages: (a) borrowings under the Act were intended to be temporary, so that whenever a general business improvement led to a demand for more cash, either there were undesirable deflationary consequences through the banks losing Dominion notes, or else the banks, by rediscounting under the Act, became permanently indebted to the government—in either case, the result was undesirable; (b) there was no way for the government to initiate monetary expansion when such action was desirable—the borrowing forced upon the chartered banks in 1932 was one attempt, but "the very fact that such a transaction had to take place in that form made it obvious that a central bank must be organized in Canada";[53] (c) the banks had no concerted policy with respect to Finance Act borrowings, nor was it their responsibility to develop any such policy. In view of the fact that the Department of Finance refused to assume discretionary responsibility for the administering of the Finance Act, credit was automatically available to the banks at all times. The governor noted at another point that under this monetary system "no one authority was responsible for the monetary policy of the country; and if anyone had been responsible, the inflexibility of the existing machinery would have tied the hands of that authority."[54]

It is therefore clear that the basic argument supporting the establishment of a central bank was its ability to provide intelligent and co-ordinated monetary control—i.e., to regulate currency and credit in the best interests of the Canadian economy, and that this broad objective would require measures designed to influence both the internal and external value of the dollar. Secondary objectives

[52]*Memoranda and Tables Respecting the Bank of Canada,* presented before the Standing Committee on Banking and Commerce, Ottawa, 1939, p. 23.

[53]*Ibid.,* p. 24.

[54]*Ibid.,* p. 24.

included the providing of skilled and impartial financial advice to the Canadian government, the providing of machinery for co-operation with similar institutions abroad and serving as the government's banker and fiscal agent. All these objectives received widespread support from Canadian economists who, as a group, wielded a significant influence in the struggle to establish the central bank.

The proposed bank was supported in various quarters for a variety of additional and less fundamental reasons, ranging from the desire, especially strong in the West, to "break the chartered banks' monopoly" to Prime Minister Bennett's wish to "free the Canadian dollar from American domination" and to permit the dollar to "escape from foreign domination". This latter complaint quite obviously reflected a complete lack of understanding of the workings of the foreign exchange market.

The strong opposition of the chartered banks to the establishment of a central bank rested on the following beliefs: (a) that such an institution was unnecessary, the Finance Act providing all that was needed by way of central banking machinery; this objection indicated a very narrow view of central banking operations; (b) that a central bank could not create more credit than already existed; (c) that it was dangerous to disturb the existing system with its proven efficiency and stability; (d) that the cost would be burdensome; (e) that there would be grave danger of "political" interference with the operations of the chartered banks; (f) that a central bank could not operate effectively in a debtor country like Canada which lacked a well-developed money market. It will be recalled that these were the same views which had been advanced more than a decade earlier, when the Canadian Bankers' Association declined to support E. L. Pease in his early efforts to obtain a central bank.

The bankers further emphasized that if a central bank were to be established with a monopoly of note issue, as was customary (although such was by no means essential for effective monetary control), the disappearance of chartered bank notes would eliminate one of the most distinctive and desirable features of the Canadian system. It was pointed out that these "unsecured" notes (i.e., notes secured not by special assets but by the general strength and reputation of the issuing institutions) enabled the banks to provide their various branches with till-money both economically and inexpensively, and that if the banks were denied the profit associated with the issuing of these notes, branches in many areas would necessarily be closed. The banks claimed, for example, that their facilities had been provided at many points in the West years before those local branches began to "break even" on their operations, and that without the profits arising from their note circulation, few branches could have been opened as early and many not at all.[55] The banks may have over-estimated their net return

---

[55]The banks reported that in 1932, 1,380 (42.3%) of a total of 3,262 Canadian branches operated at a loss (apart entirely from bad debt losses). In the West, the situation was worst, and in Saskatchewan more than 80% of the branches were unprofitable.

derived from the note-issuing privilege, which was claimed to be 1.5% of average circulation after payment of the 1% circulation tax imposed by the Canadian government.

In an excellent summary of the chartered banks' position published in 1933, their nearly unanimous opposition to the establishment of a central bank was clearly indicated.[56] Curiously, the author of this publication believed that one of the strongest arguments being directed against the chartered banks was that they had failed to maintain the gold standard in Canada, and he was prepared to argue that they were in no wise responsible for its demise. In both respects he erred, for one may well regret not only his implied sorrow at the departure from gold but also the particular circumstances which in fact surrounded its termination. He noted that there were those misguided persons who were "apparently under the impression that depressed business conditions, if not actually caused through the adoption by the chartered banks of a deliberate policy of credit restriction, are at least intensified and prolonged by the reluctance of the banks to lend money more freely".[57] In the belief that such was not the case, he conceded that "should this be admitted, it follows logically that the cure lies in persuading or forcing the banks to change their policy".[58] This was a fatal concession, for even if we grant his subsequent argument that it is the *voluntary* limitation and *voluntary* liquidation of loans by the borrowers themselves that contributes in major degree to the decline in bank advances during a depression, the fact remains that the decline in bank credit does occur, that this does intensify deflationary pressures and that some "external" guidance is therefore required if the conditions leading to these partially "voluntary" liquidations are to be avoided.

A basic error in the chartered bankers' arguments arose from their failure to appreciate the monetary significance of their banking operations and to acknowledge the substantial economic power which they exerted through the fluctuations in the country's means of payment which resulted from their credit policies in prosperity and depression. An all too rare exception to this lack of understanding was found in the observation by one banker that "The present depression is usually explained in terms of extravagance, over-production, excessive tariff-barriers, etc. In varying degrees these as well as other contributing factors produced situations which were essentially unsound, but speaking generally, the controlling influence has been the mismanagement of money and credit. The average price level is determined by the relation of goods and services rendered to the volume of the money supply, and the disastrous fall in the general price level would not have occurred had the supply of money been properly regulated."[59]

[56]See the pamphlet "Does Canada Need a Central Bank?" written by "A Canadian Banker", reprinted from the *Financial Post*, Toronto, 1933. Included is a verbatim report of the opinions of leading Canadian bankers respecting a central bank for Canada.
[57]*Ibid.*, p. 9.
[58]*Ibid.*, p. 9.　[59]*Royal Bank Letter*, February, 1932.

The general tenor of the chartered banks' opposition to a central bank may be gleaned from a few representative observations made by their senior officers. One observed that "without wishing to be flippant, I may fairly say that it suddenly became fashionable, after the war, for governments to create central banks just as it was fashionable some centuries ago for governments to create trading monopolies. . . . We have the power, by legislation, to create a central bank, just as (to take an absurd illustration) we could create a Canadian peerage if we cared to do so; but if we were to create a central bank in Canada, it would inevitably arouse extravagant expectations in the minds of a great many people."[60] After recording these observations, their author stated that "it is not my intention . . . to take a position on this great question at the moment."[61] Another looked upon "the agitation for a central bank in Canada as unwise, and I hope for the national good that no attempt will be made to invade the field of banking, which is one of the few business enterprises which most of our own people and all the rest of the world seem to think is on a thoroughly satisfactory basis, as it is".[62] Another claimed that "we in Canada do not suffer from inadequate credit or inadequate currency. Trade has contracted in volume and value to a degree where much less currency and credit are required for its conduct. . . . So far as our banking system is concerned, it is well to remember that not a single depositor has had to wait for a moment to get his money from a Canadian bank during the past year. . . .This fact is an argument that will appeal to most people."[63]

Perhaps somewhat wishful was the claim of another official that "reform of the banking structure is not a real issue in this as in some other countries, not only because under the Finance Act Canada already possesses through Government channels those advantages which would come from a central bank if one existed, but also because the strength of the present banking structure has been the outstanding favorable feature of the business depression through which we have been passing".[64]

Still another banker stated that he did not wish to "criticize the general principle of a central banking system. Such a system may be necessary in some countries, but I submit that every function of central banking essential for Canada is already being fulfilled through the operation of our existing banks with the auxiliary service of the Finance Act, which is regarded by the financial

---

[60]"Does Canada Need a Central Bank?" *op. cit.*, pp. 28-9.

[61]*Ibid.*, p. 29.

[62]*Ibid.*, p. 30.

[63]*Ibid.*, p. 31. See also the Royal Commission on Banking and Currency, *Evidence*, pp. 2437-9. Here one business man notes that "a great deal has been made in the Press of the fact that no Canadian bank has failed as a result of the depression, but I think that the very least that one can ask of a bank is that it should not fail." With rare insight he observed that "it is possible that in Canada we have paid a little dearly to maintain the stability of our banks. It is possible that with a properly organized system under a Central Bank of issue, stability might have been maintained at far less cost to the business community in particular and the nation at large."

[64]*Ibid.*, p. 31.

world as a model of flexibility, combined with such simple and economical operation as to be without cost either to the Government or the public. It may be noted that the Act provides for freer rediscounting than is permitted in the United States, a country with the largest central bank in the world."[65] Finally, the view was expressed that "a central bank in Canada could not increase banking resources or currency based on resources by a single dollar over what is now possible under existing legislation, nor could a central bank legitimately make available more credit than can now be supplied by the chartered banks through the elasticity of the Finance Act".[66]

In sharp contrast to the foregoing observations, the testimony of numerous witnesses before the Royal Commission revealed that the very high regard in which the chartered bankers held the existing financial system was not universally shared, particularly in the Canadian West, the country's major export region, hardest hit by the depression. The seeds of the financial difficulties which beset the prairie farmers during the depression had been sown in the earlier years of prosperity when the contracting of heavy long-term indebtedness to purchase farm lands in times of high prices had become widespread. The farmers involved became saddled with heavy fixed charges, a circumstance which in a region with a highly fluctuating income invited disaster.

Disaster struck with the unprecedented decline in farm income which began late in 1929 and which by 1932 was down 67%. All but a small proportion of long-term farm debt, which represented about three-quarters of a total farm debt estimated at $650 million in 1931, had been incurred in the purchasing of land and machinery, the funds having been supplied in the main by individual lenders[67] but to a lesser extent by Canadian life insurance companies, trust companies and loan companies. The customary security for such loans was a mortgage on the property acquired. The remaining one-quarter of total farm debt, nominally short-term, was supplied mostly on a trade basis but the chartered banks had contributed perhaps thirty per cent.[68] It is therefore evident

[65]*Ibid.*, p. 33.

[66]*Ibid.*, p. 30. Commenting on the statements of bankers that they had plenty of money available but a lack of sound borrowers, one witness noted that "this . . . is an accurate enough description of the situation from the angle of a banking company. To the general public, however, it is an exasperating and dangerous statement to make, provoking great anger and bitter comment, because they do not understand why, if money is so plentiful, the rate of interest should be so high and borrowing so difficult." See the Royal Commission on Banking and Currency, *Evidence*, p. 2439.

[67]Further details of prairie indebtedness are to be found in W. A. Mackintosh, *Economic Problems of the Prairie Provinces* (Toronto: The Macmillan Company of Canada, Ltd.), 1935, chapter XII. The "burden" of the total private farm debt in 1931 is indicated by the fact that it amounted to $26 per acre of wheat, with annual interest payments (at 8 per cent) amounting to $2 per acre. At a wheat price of 30 cents per bushel, this meant that almost 7 bushels from an average yield of 15 bushels per acre were required to service this debt.

[68]*Ibid.*

that the banks held not more than seven or eight per cent of the total farm debt, a proportion much less than commonly supposed.

As the depression deepened, the default of interest and principal payments became widespread, and each of the three provinces passed debt adjustment acts, designed to protect the debtors, but invariably criticized by the creditors, either as an unjustified impairment of their rights or as a factor which made additional lending to worthy borrowers more difficult.[69] The object of such legislation was to protect the debtor's assets from seizure, and their effect was to "freeze" farm credit. It was only in the federal legislation of 1934 that any provision was made for the scaling down of farm debts. None of this emergency legislation came to grips with the fundamental economic problem of the prairie farmer, that of providing him with credit in a form appropriate to the fluctuating income of the region.[70]

That the recognition of this problem escaped even the most enlightened of the chartered bankers was indicated in a statement by one of the Western superintendents that "the trouble . . . is not with the system, but is due to deficiencies of administration of what is recognized by financial critics as one of the best banking systems in the world—deficiencies most of which are incidental to a period of rapid agricultural development and therefore scarcely avoidable. . . . It is the same system which has served the farmers of Ontario, Quebec and the Maritime Provinces for fifty years or more, and it is not within my memory when any general complaint against the banks has been voiced by the farmers of these old-settled Provinces. How could it be successfully argued that a banking system which has so admirably served the latter is inadequate for the requirements of the Western Provinces?"[71] Once again we encounter the erroneous notion that there can be a particular banking system that can be the "best" system under all circumstances.

The depression brought serious financial difficulty not only to private but to public debtors. At the end of 1931, the combined indebtedness of the three Western prairie governments had reached some $408 million and that of the municipalities $230 million, so that the total public debt approximated that of the private sector.[72] The chartered banks' loans outstanding to these governments exceeded one-quarter of their total debt.[73]

---

[69]During the 1930's, the effect of such legislation was to curtail severely the availability of private credit to Western farmers. For an historical discussion of the inadequacy of facilities for financing Western agriculture, see W. T. Easterbrook, *Farm Credit in Canada* (Toronto: University of Toronto Press), 1938.

[70]Mackintosh points out that the "crop-payment" and "share-farming" bases of prairie finance, long regarded as makeshift devices, were in reality forms which were among the soundest and best suited for such a region.

[71]Vere Brown, "The Western Farmer and the Bank", in the *Journal of the Canadian Bankers' Association*, XXVI, 1918-19, pp. 267-8.

[72]Mackintosh, *op. cit.*

[73]See the *Return of the Chartered Banks to the Minister of Finance*, December, 1931.

Much of the criticism encountered by the chartered banks in the West arose from the fact that the short-term credit which they were equipped to provide was not the type of credit urgently required by the farmers. In particular, the latter had no adequate source of intermediate loans, ranging from two to five years, which they sought for such purposes as the purchase of stock, the maintenance and expansion of farm machinery and equipment, farm improvements, extension of cultivated acreage and the consolidation of current debts where retirement within five years appeared to be a reasonable prospect. The banks argued that they faced a serious problem when asked for advances by worthy farmers. They were not usually able to take any security for a loan, since they could not legally hypothecate real property, and all too often the prospective borrower had nothing else to offer, and so the decision was made on his general prospects. The result was that most bank advances were extended initially on the unsupported note of the farmer, and to protect themselves after assuming such a risk, the banks issued the note for three months, to make possible a frequent review of the loan and perhaps "to request additional security".[74]

A great source of irritation to the borrower was the banks' insistence on compounding interest payable at these three-month intervals, and there indeed appears to have been little justification for such a practice, which one banker dismissed lightly with the observation that "it is merely a bagatelle so far as the individual is concerned".[75] Complaints about excessive interest rates were voiced by governments, business men and farmers alike. For private borrowers, a nominal rate of 8 per cent was customary, at least to the end of 1932, with the effective rate somewhat higher. Only at the beginning of 1933 did a very slow decline get under way, despite the fact that the maximum *recoverable* rate provided by the Bank Act was 7%, payable in advance. Municipalities complained of the necessity of paying 7 per cent for short-term loans on first-class security (the proceeds from current tax levies) and of the discrepancies in rates charged for similar classes of borrowers, as between West and East. In reply, the banks claimed that their administration costs were substantially higher in the West.

Considerable agitation developed among Western debtors for the granting by the Dominion government of public credit at "cost", by which was usually meant the service costs involved in printing money. The banks were accused of granting their local managers too little discretion in their lending policies, with the result that Western borrowing requirements were deliberately sacrificed to the needs of other parts of the country. It appears very doubtful, how-

---

[74]See the Royal Commission on Banking and Currency, *Evidence,* p. 1816. Here a witness observed that "the custom of advancing loans to farmers at three months, and renewing the notes, sometimes with a compounding of the interest, until produce can be marketed, may be a necessity of a system not especially adapted to agricultural needs, but the practice simply demonstrates the need for the provision of proper facilities for the financing of agriculture".

[75]*Ibid.,* II, p. 975.

ever, that discrimination was practised against Western borrowers apart from the application of the banks' customary standards of "soundness" to their prospective customers, but it was precisely in the application of such standards that the unsuitability and inadequacy of chartered bank credit in meeting the Western farmers' requirements was clearly revealed.[76] The banks claimed that their policy was one of decentralization, and that the administration of Western operations was largely self-contained and that credit there was extended on its merits, without reference to the East. They noted that over 95 per cent of the total number of loans (not of their aggregate amount) were dealt with by their branch managers and/or regional superintendents.

Elsewhere in Canada, complaints assumed the same broad pattern, although differences in regional emphasis were to be found. In the Maritimes, the difficulties of their extractive industries, such as agriculture (fruit-growing, dairying and mixed farming), fisheries, lumbering and mining, were compared with those of wheat, and were claimed to be just as great. The levels and rigidity of bank rates were assailed by a Halifax business man who noted that "the ordinary rate for large business concerns is 6 per cent, and it has not been changed for many years so far as I know. I can say that the rate my business has been charged for the whole forty-two years I have been in business has always been 6%."[77] The average rate for agricultural loans was 6½ per cent and for municipalities 5½ per cent. The government of Prince Edward Island complained that "the farmers of this province do not enjoy the borrowing power which their assets warrant."[78] It also protested against the common three-month term of lending, the inflexibility of rates and the fact that the banks had no loans under 6 per cent "except cities and governments". This appeared to be the minimum rate regardless of the borrower's security. A ranking official of the government of New Brunswick tersely defined a chartered bank as "an institution that lends you an umbrella on a fine day and takes it away when it begins to rain".[79]

Just as in the case of most of the Westerners who appeared before the Commission to criticize Canadian monetary and banking practices during the depression, but who were opposed to any fundamental changes either in the structure or in the ownership of the chartered banks, so the Maritimes witnesses and the great majority from the other parts of the country sought improvements primarily through the modification and the adaptation of the policies of the existing institutions. By contrast, the proposals of the Co-operative Commonwealth

[76]As of December 31, 1932, the distribution of all chartered bank loans in the three prairie provinces was as follows: agricultural, $165 million; provincial governments, $10 million; municipal governments, $31 million; financial, $18 million; merchandising, $18 million; lumber and pulpwood, $5 million; other manufacturing, $5 million; miscellaneous, $22 million; total loans, $274 million. See the Royal Commission on Banking and Currency, *Evidence*, p. 1952.
[77]Royal Commission on Banking and Currency, *Evidence*, p. 2073.
[78]*Ibid.*, p. 2117.
[79]*Ibid.*, p. 2168.

Federation and of the Social Credit movement were much more radical. At the launching of the new C.C.F. movement in 1932, its leader, the late J. S. Woodsworth, observed that "while the Ottawa Conference is seeking to restore prosperity by adding a few patches to the disintegrating system of capitalism, the object of the Federation is fundamental social reconstruction".[80] Basic to this process of reconstruction was the socialization of the banking, credit and financial system of the country. Mr. Woodsworth's pragmatic belief in the wisdom of government monopoly in this area was reflected by his observation that "my own idea—and I suppose I'm as usual in a minority—is that we should centre attention on control of credit—and allow the theorists to give reasons each in his own way. The fluctuation of the Dollar is, in itself, sufficient ground for insisting on credit control."[81]

In other quarters, the central role which financial machinery must assume in a socialist economy was reflected in the demand that not only the chartered banks but likewise the new central bank should be socialized and the management of investment placed in the hands of a National Investment Board so that ". . . the State will be in a position to ensure efficiency in industrial operation, to discipline non-cooperative industries, and if necessary, dictate major lines of policy".[82] The National Investment Board would enforce the decisions of a National Planning Commission ". . . as to which trades should be developed and which cut down, by granting or withholding the necessary supplies of capital".[83] Underlying all of these views, of course, is the basic (and uncritical) assumption that the allocation of resources by a process of centralized direction will somehow be superior to that provided by an impersonal price mechanism. At the conclusion of its hearings, the Royal Commission on Banking and Currency recommended that a central bank be established.[84] It conceded that in so far as the ordinary functions of banking were concerned, the Canadian banks had provided security, efficiency and convenience,[85] but it noted that there were certain functions which were not being adequately performed by the existing system. In particular, the Commission was impressed by the lack of any single banking authority which "while linked by its activities with national finance and commerce, is nevertheless detached by its constitution and the temper of its administration from the ordinary pursuits of commercial banking."[86] Among

---

[80]Quoted from *The U.F.A.*, publication of the United Farmers of Alberta, August, 1932.
[81]Partial text of a letter from J. S. Woodsworth to G. F. Stirling, written October 25, 1929.
[82]See *Social Planning for Canada*, published by the Research Committee of the League for Social Reconstruction (Toronto: Thomas Nelson and Sons), 1935, p. 250.
[83]*Ibid.*, pp. 250-1.
[84]The inadequacy of rural credit arrangements, which had been emphasized so strongly in the evidence of many Western witnesses before the Commission, brought a recommendation that the Dominion and provincial governments make a joint study of the existing facilities, with a view to effecting necessary improvements.
[85]*Report of the Royal Commission on Banking and Currency*, p. 61.    [86]*Ibid.*, pp. 61-2.

the most urgent monetary problems found to be facing Canada were the desirable extent and the most desirable means of the control of credit and currency, the proper agency for maintaining the external stability of the currency and the proper institution from which the government of the day might receive informed and impartial financial advice. In the majority of countries, the operation of central banks provided the solution to these problems, and the establishment of a comparable institution in Canada appeared to be a desirable step. The Commission found none of the technical objections to such a move—as, for example, the absence of a well developed money market—to be of great importance, but warned that a central bank "could not cure all the economic ills of Canada", that it "would not be a source of unlimited credit for all borrowers on all occasions" and that its operations might as often be restrictive as expansionist.[87]

The Commission emphasized that the new institution must be free of narrow political interference with its operations although it was of course recognized that the State must retain ultimate sovereignty in all matters affecting credit and currency. The constitutional position of the bank thus presented something of a dilemma at the outset, one that could be resolved only gradually as the Bank gained experience from its subsequent operations.[88] The Commission recommended that the bank be privately owned and that after the first governors and directors had been appointed by the government, all ensuing appointments should be made by directors elected by the private shareholders, with government approval being confined to those chosen to serve as governor and deputy-governor. These provisions were designed to minimize the possibility of undesirable political interference in the formulation and execution of central bank policy; to eliminate any incentive to seek large profits, dividends were to be limited to 4½ per cent, with the remaining profits transferred to the government's consolidated revenue fund.

Closely following these recommendations, parliament passed the Bank of Canada Act in 1934,[89] and to protect the Bank against possible *private* pressure groups, a number of additional provisions were introduced. The size of individual holdings of Bank of Canada stock was limited, chartered bank officials were prohibited from acquiring it, and the directors, officers and employees of the banks and other financial institutions were declared ineligible for appointment as governor, deputy-governor or assistant deputy-governor of the Bank. To ensure a continuous and close liaison between the Bank of Canada and the

---

[87]*Ibid.*, p. 69.

[88]See E. P. Neufeld, *Bank of Canada Operations, 1935-54* (Toronto: The University of Toronto Press), 1955, pp. 2-3: "the concept of an ideal position has changed remarkably from the time that the project for a central bank was first seriously considered. Discussion began where the Bank was thought of as being subject only to the ultimate supremacy of parliament and developed, in fairly distinct stages, to where it was considered to be subject not only to the government of the day but to be, in fact, the instrument for implementing the policy of that government."

[89]For additional details, see the *Bank of Canada Act*, 24-25 George V, chapter 43.

government, it was further provided that the Deputy-Minister of Finance should be a member of the Bank's board of directors and of its executive committee (without vote) and that all decisions of these bodies would require the approval of the governor to become effective. Thus constituted, the Bank began its actual operations in March 1935. Its objectives were summarized in the preamble to the Bank of Canada Act which read, in part, that ". . . it is desirable to establish a central bank in Canada to regulate credit and currency in the best interests of the economic life of the nation, to control and protect the external value of the national monetary unit and to mitigate by its influence fluctuations in the general level of production, trade, prices and employment, so far as may be possible within the scope of monetary action, and generally to promote the economic and financial welfare of the Dominion. . . ."[90]

Although the Bank began its operations as a privately owned institution, the election of a Liberal government in the autumn of 1935 brought an early change. The Liberals had campaigned for public ownership of the Bank, and the change was effected in the 1936 and 1938 amendments of the Bank of Canada Act.[91]

In any country such as Canada, where all but a minor part of the country's total means of payment is supplied by privately owned commercial banks operating on a fractional reserve basis, the central bank's monetary objectives must be accomplished indirectly, through the modifications which it is able to effect in commercial bank-lending activities. More specifically, the central bank, by altering the commercial banks' cash reserves, will attempt to influence the cost and general availability of credit, in relation to changing economic circumstances.

The Bank of Canada Act provided for a monopoly of note issue by the new central bank, and from the commencement of the Bank of Canada's operations, a gradual retirement of chartered bank issues was initiated. The 1944 revision of the Bank Act prohibited the chartered banks from issuing or reissuing any notes after January 1, 1945 and from January 1, 1950, the chartered banks' liability for their notes outstanding was transferred to the Bank of Canada, in return for a like payment to that institution by the chartered banks. Accompanying these arrangements, the Bank of Canada from the outset assumed responsibility for the redemption of all Dominion notes issued and outstanding. To offset this liability of some $185 million, the Bank received from the government an equivalent amount of gold ($69 million), silver ($1 million) and Dominion securities ($115 million). The chartered banks surrendered their cash reserves, including gold ($37 million)[92] and Dominion notes ($178 mil-

---

[90]*Ibid.*, p. 493.

[91]See I Edward VIII, c. 22, p. 10 and 2 George VI, c. 42, pp. 8-9 respectively. From 1938 on, the Bank conformed in ownership as well as control to common practice elsewhere. The outstanding exception was of course the private ownership of the Federal Reserve Banks in the United States.

[92]For additional details, see the Bank of Canada, *Annual Report*, February 25, 1936, pp. 5-6.

lion) to the Bank, receiving in exchange a corresponding amount of the Bank's deposits and notes, the new forms in which chartered bank cash would subsequently be held. It had also been provided that as of the commencement of the Bank's operations, the chartered banks should liquidate all of their advances outstanding under the provisions of the Finance Act. These (amounting to $35 million, the minimum specified at the time of the "compulsory" borrowing in 1932) were repaid, and to prevent a corresponding reduction in bank cash, the government sold a corresponding amount of treasury bills to the Bank of Canada and used the entire proceeds to redeem other treasury bills held by the banks.

The effect of these initial operations was to provide the Bank of Canada with some $150 million in government securities, and gold reserves of some $106 million. The latter figure was obviously substantially in excess of the 25% minimum reserve requirement specified by the Bank of Canada Act.[93] Under the terms of the Exchange Fund Act, which took effect in July, 1935, the Bank of Canada revalued its gold (from $20.67 to $35.00 per ounce), thereby creating a profit of about $73.5 million, of which some $10.5 million was transferred to the chartered banks and the balance credited to the government's Exchange Fund.[94]

The 25% reserve requirement imposed upon the Bank was retained until May, 1940, when, following the outbreak of World War II, the Bank's holdings of gold and foreign exchange were transferred to the recently established Foreign Exchange Control Board. The reserve requirement was suspended at that time and has not been reinstated. While the establishment of some minimum cash ratio for the chartered banks is essential to the exercise of effective monetary control by the central bank, there appears to be little or no such justification for the imposition of any such minimum ratio upon the central bank itself. Such an institution is assumed to be operating at all times in the economic interest of the country, and if any situation arose where the bank's ability to effect a further desirable monetary expansion were to be threatened by inadequate reserves, the logical and inevitable outcome would be the legislative

[93]The Act provided for a reserve of not less than 25% of the Bank's total notes and deposit liabilities in Canada. In addition to gold, the reserve might include silver bullion, sterling balances held in the Bank of England, U.S. dollar balances held in the New York Federal Reserve Bank, and gold currencies held in the central banks of the gold standard countries or in the Bank for International Settlements; in addition, treasury bills of the United States or the United Kingdom maturing in not more than three months, and bills of exchange maturing in not more than three months and payable in New York, London, or in any gold-standard country.

[94]The Bank of Canada Act gave the Governor-in-Council power "to allow the chartered banks to receive the profit on gold transferred by them [to the Bank of Canada], to the extent that such gold was deemed to have been held against liabilities elsewhere than in Canada." The Governor-in-Council deemed that 40 per cent of the chartered banks' gold had been so held. The potential expansion of chartered bank cash arising from this revaluation was offset by open-market sales and by the increasing of government deposits in the Bank of Canada.

modification of existing reserve provisions. This being so, any central bank reserve requirement appears to be an anachronism, for " . . . it is necessary either to trust to your central bankers to be reasonable, or else not to trust them, and give up the idea of having a central bank at all."[95]

Among the techniques employed by central banks in exercising monetary control are the varying of commercial bank minimum reserve requirements, the varying of the rediscount rate, "moral suasion" and open-market operations. In addition, important monetary effects may be obtained, with the co-operation of the central government, by the shifting of government deposits between the central and commercial banks. The relative importance of these techniques will of course vary from country to country and from one time to another. In the case of the Bank of Canada, the power to alter the minimum cash ratio of the chartered banks was entirely lacking. This ratio was legally established at five per cent of the banks' Canadian deposit liabilities, and it remained unaltered until the Bank Act revision in 1954. The banks in practice sought to maintain their actual cash ratios at approximately ten per cent, the problem of effective central bank control being aggravated whenever the chartered banks failed to follow such a policy consistently and to react dependably to changes in their cash reserves.

At the outset, the Bank of Canada established its rediscount rate at 2½ per cent, the rate which was being charged for advances under the Finance Act just prior to the establishment of the Bank. The rate was altered only infrequently after that time, the first change occurring in 1944 when it was reduced to 1½ per cent, to indicate the Bank's intention of continuing an easy-money policy into the post-war transitional period to facilitate the reconversion of the war economy to peacetime objectives. As a monetary instrument, rate changes before 1955 exerted little *direct* effect on the cost and availability of credit, both because the chartered banks had only rarely and for brief periods sought advances from the Bank of Canada and because until even more recently there had been no customary relationship established in Canada's relatively undeveloped money market between the Bank rate and other institutional rates. Under these circumstances, the impact of a rediscount rate changes was to be found in its *indirect* effects, inasmuch as the change reflected not only the Bank's view as to what constituted appropriate interest rate and credit adjustments in any situation but also its intention to pursue actively by open-market operations the attainment of such adjustments. In the pre-war period, the rate was of no significance in the Bank's operations.

The peculiar usefulness of "moral suasion" as a technique of monetary control in Canada arises from the high concentration of ownership among the chartered banks. This circumstance has permitted the Bank of Canada to initiate informal

[95]J. D. Gibson, "Central Banking Reserves", in Innis and Plumptre, *op. cit.*

consultation and to obtain agreement concerning appropriate monetary action to a degree not possible in many other banking systems. The effectiveness of this technique depended, however, upon the gradual development of confidence and respect in the Bank of Canada, and such a reaction was by no means characteristic of the chartered banks at the time the new institution was founded. Thus, just as in the case of the rediscount rate, moral suasion was not an important feature of the Bank's pre-war monetary operations.

Prior to World War II, the Bank pursued a cheap-money policy as "the orthodox contribution of a banking system towards recovery from a depression".[96] The governor pointed out, however, that in the stimulating of business activity, "the vital matter is not the amount of money in existence; it is the size of people's incomes, in other words, the size of the national income. This can grow, and does grow, without any definite connection between such growth and a growth in bank deposits or note circulation."[97]

Open-market operations, which from the outset became one of the Bank's main instruments of monetary control, were employed extensively before the war. They were an effective means of accommodating the seasonal fluctuations in demand for bank credit as the Bank's purchases of treasury bills expanded in periods of rising demand and fell at other times. Nevertheless, for the pre-war period as a whole, the net effect of open-market operations on chartered bank cash was small,[98] the "secular" expansion of these reserves being accomplished largely through the Bank's purchases of gold and foreign currencies, the holdings of which assets reached a "pre-war" peak in December, 1940. Referring to the fact that prior to World War II, the effectiveness of the Bank's open-market operations had been in no wise handicapped by the narrowness of the Canadian money market, the governor of the Bank said that "I believe that in no country and at no time have there been bank and market responses to central bank action and central bank policies, more complete, more full and more in line with anything that a theorist might have anticipated, than have taken place in Canada".[99]

Monetary expansion during these years was also facilitated by the govern-

[96]See the Bank of Canada, *First Annual Report*, Feb. 25, 1936, p. 12.

[97]*Ibid.* The governor emphasized the importance of velocity of circulation by noting that on December 31, 1935, the chartered banks' cash reserves and deposits were almost identical with their levels of December 31, 1929, the end of a year of exceptional business activity. Despite this fact, Canada's G.N.P. in 1929 approximated $6.0 billion, in 1935, $4.3 billion.

[98]Against the Bank's open-market sales at the time of the revaluation of Canadian gold stocks must be set subsequent open-market purchases which expanded cash reserves and/or offset the continuous drain associated with the Bank of Canada's rising note circulation.

[99]*Memoranda and Tables Respecting the Bank of Canada, op. cit.*, p. 37. Between March 31, 1935 and March 31, 1939, chartered bank cash increased by slightly more than one-quarter, from $201 million to $253 million. Their Canadian deposits increased in a comparable ratio, from $2,034 million to $2,538 million. See Bank of Canada, *Statistical Summary: 1946 Supplement*, p. 14.

ment's policy of depositing a steadily rising volume of funds in the chartered banks, thereby increasing their cash reserves. Commenting on this pre-war monetary policy, one writer notes that it " . . . was not a departure from pre-Bank policy, for money had been increasing and interest rates declining before the Bank appeared. But it differed greatly . . . in the smooth, seemingly confident, and purposive manner with which it was implemented".[100]

In the semi-depressed economy in which the Bank operated during the first several years of its existence, Canada's fiscal, monetary and debt-management objectives were mutually compatible as deficit-financing, the expansion of chartered banks' reserves and falling interest rates were actively promoted. It was only when the economy became subjected to strong inflationary pressures during World War II that the reality of conflicting objectives became apparent and only in the post-war decade that the conflict between the central bank's role as debt manager and as monetary manager became so pronounced as to impair seriously the effectiveness of the Bank's operations in the latter area. If the Bank's activities preceding World War II were unspectacular, they were nevertheless valuable, for through their contribution to economic recovery they clearly demonstrated the superiority of the new arrangements over the earlier decentralized monetary and banking system and they also provided the Bank with timely experience which could be applied to the very much more difficult problems arising from wartime economic dislocations of unprecedented magnitude.

[100]E. P. Neufeld, *Bank of Canada Operations, 1935-54* (Toronto: University of Toronto Press), 1954, p. 68.

## CHAPTER VIII

# MONETARY EXPERIMENTATION:
# THE SOCIAL CREDIT VENTURE IN ALBERTA

In the history of Canadian monetary development, the Social Credit experiment in Alberta represents one of the most interesting aberrations. In contrast to the immediate objectives of the Co-operative Commonwealth Federation, Social Credit supporters claimed that their monetary proposals would avoid all necessity for the abolition of private ownership, for the destruction of the price system, for the suppression of individual initiative, for the nationalization of industry and for the imposition of any form of regimentation in the economy. This political movement in Alberta, based on monetary reform, enjoyed success during the depression because it seemed to promise higher incomes for all with no apparent cost to any group within the province.

It should be noted in passing that in no branch of economics is there as fertile a field for the flourishing of "crank" schemes as in the monetary field, and in depression it is therefore practically inevitable that cranks appear, each with his "sure cure" for the economic ills of society. These schemes receive support from a credulous and uninformed public who are persuaded either of the possibility of monetary magic or of the attainment, by monetary action, of some immediately desirable objective, but who are necessarily ignorant of the complex and less immediate consequences of such action. It is not generally recognized that in all instances "there are competing advantages [and disadvantages] from different monetary policies which cannot be appraised in precise terms" and that "for these reasons, monetary policy is a subject which requires the exercise of judgment".[1] It is obvious that the general public, lacking adequate technical knowledge and swayed by impassioned political oratory, will frequently exercise judgment which is something less than sound.

In Alberta, the supporters of Social Credit were swept into office in 1935, in a wave of "religious" fervour, having convinced the electorate that their monetary theories provided the only escape from the depths of the depression in which the province found itself. Responsibility for this depression was laid at the door of Canada's orthodox monetary and banking system, which, in failing to remedy a chronic shortage of purchasing power within the country, had made economic stagnation inevitable. To remedy this shortage, the party had promised to pay a "National Dividend" of $25 per month to all adult residents of the

---

[1]See L. W. Mints, *Monetary Policy for a Competitive Society* (New York: McGraw-Hill Book Company, Inc.), 1950, page v. Here may be found an interesting discussion of the nature and success of various crank monetary schemes.

province, lesser amounts being proposed on a sliding scale for the sixteen- to twenty-year age groups. The Social Credit administration was saved from the more serious consequences of its proposed monetary experiments by the timely federal disallowance in 1937 of its three major legislative enactments in this area, enactments which were deemed to conflict with federal jurisdiction and which were subsequently declared *ultra vires* by the Supreme Court of Canada. The party has remained in office until the present time, mainly on the strength of a competent and essentially conservative administration, unprecedented provincial prosperity associated with the development of rich oil resources and the government's judicious lack of enthusiasm for its earlier monetary proposals.

The economic theories embraced by the Alberta movement were those of Major C. H. Douglas, a British engineer and self-styled economist. Major Douglas believed, wrongly, that the pattern of income and expenditure flows in a capitalistic economy led *inevitably* to a shortage of purchasing power in the hands of consumers. In other words, for any given period, the purchasing power available for buying current output was insufficient to acquire that output at prices sufficiently high to cover its total costs of production. Thus, if "overproduction" were to be avoided, a continuous injection of new purchasing power was required.[2]

To explain his position, Major Douglas employed his celebrated "A + B" theorem, in which he divided all costs of production into two categories. The "A" costs included all payments that producers ("factories") made to individuals, such as wages, salaries and dividends, the "B" costs all payments made to organizations for such things as raw materials, machinery, maintenance of plant, bank charges, etc. Thus for any period, the total costs of production were represented by A + B, but the amount of money available to purchase the output of the period was only A, because B costs were largely in the nature of business "reserves", mere book-keeping items which, while included in total costs of production, did not represent income distributed. This view overlooks the fact that reserves are not held merely as idle balances and that even if this were so, what would be true for one firm at any given time would not be true of all taken together, since presumably the reserves would be spent some time, thereby providing purchasing power. The argument is frequently presented in slightly different form, in which it is admitted that B costs do represent purchasing power "at some time or another", but that this is not available at the right time, having been largely spent by the time that the product, for which these costs

[2]In this connection, we read that "purchasing power is not, as might be gathered from the current discussion on the subject, an emanation from the production of real commodities and services much like the scent from a rose, but on the contrary, is produced by an entirely distinct process, that is to say, the banking system. . . . There is extant in the world a common, if somewhat nebulous, idea that whoever, for instance, grows a ton of potatoes grows thereby in some mysterious way, the purchasing power equivalent to a ton of potatoes." See C. H. Douglas, *The Douglas Manual*, pp. 14-15, or C. H. Douglas, *The Monopoly of Credit*, p. 23.

are incurred, appears on the market, and therefore having returned to the banks for destruction, "as all money does".

It is further alleged that with continuing technological progress in industry, the ratio of B costs to A costs is steadily rising, so that the disparity between available purchasing power and total costs of production becomes steadily greater. This deficiency of purchasing power can be made up for a time by the expansion of bank credit, but since bank loans must be paid off, they can provide no permanent addition to the volume of available purchasing power. All money is viewed as on a short trip from and to the banks, and since interest is charged on all loans, the deficiency of purchasing power becomes greater as the granting and liquidation of bank loans proceeds. The banks are regarded as enormous mechanisms of suction, continuously withdrawing money from circulation, hence the Social Credit view that the existing "monopoly" of credit possessed by the banks must be terminated by the introduction of supplementary public issues.

To return to the alleged faulty "timing" of B expenditures, it must surely be reasonable to assume that if the B payments made yesterday in financing today's output have already been spent by their recipients, the B payments made today in financing tomorrow's output will likewise be spent by their recipients today. In other words, today's goods will be bought with today's income, which will always include payments associated with goods in process. The Douglas brand of "under-consumption" overlooks the continuity of the productive process, and would appear to prove too much, for if its analysis were valid, all production would long since have ceased, because no level of production would be profitable.

In reality, the process of production generates income sufficient to purchase the current output at prices covering total costs of production (the income payments to the owners of resources *are* the costs of production incurred by entrepreneurs), but whether this income is in fact returned to circulation as a demand for current output is by no means certain. Money is employed not only as a medium of exchange but as a store of value, and general over-production may occur, but it is by no means inevitable, and the theoretical possibility of general "over-consumption", i.e., excessive rather than insufficient money expenditures, is equally valid. It is undoubtedly true that in the Alberta environment of the 1930's, monetary expansion would have been appropriate, but the basic defect in Social Credit monetary theory is its rigidity and its alleged universal applicability, where in reality it is valid only in limited circumstances. Its defenders have been unwilling to concede the point that their doctrine, like a clock no longer running, will be "right" only once every twelve hours.[3]

In practice, the monetary experiment in Alberta did not follow Social Credit

---

[3]See W. A. Mackintosh, "Trade and Fiscal Policy", in *Canada Looks Ahead* (Ottawa: Tower Books), 1948, p. 13: "There are few of these panaceas which are not partly right at some time."

doctrine.[4] Immediately following its election in 1935, a split developed within the party as the insurgents demanded the immediate introduction of the monthly dividend. The premier, the Honourable William Aberhart, was not yet prepared to take this step, and as a compromise, the issuing of "stamp scrip" was launched in August, 1936. This step represented the adoption of quite a different plan of monetary reform which had earlier been pioneered by Silvio Gesell, a German monetary student who had lived for many years in Buenos Aires. The premier's defence of this measure was that it would show "how credit circulates" and thereby facilitate the eventual introduction of monthly dividend payments.

The dated stamp-money closely resembled Dominion one-dollar notes, and provided that "the Provincial Treasurer will pay to the bearer the sum of one dollar on the expiration of two years from the date of issue hereof upon presentation hereof, provided there are then attached to the back hereof 104 one cent certificate stamps." The scheme therefore in fact represented a tax on the holding of scrip, since a one-cent stamp had to be affixed to it weekly in order that it might retain its acceptability as a means of payment. It was hoped that scrip would be generally circulated and the government paid out some of its first issues to captive "beneficiaries", by financing unemployment relief and meeting civil service pay-rolls. Scrip received a generally poor reception and was refused as payment in many quarters, not the least surprising of which was the issuing government, which declared it unacceptable in payment of taxes. In place of the two-year redemption period originally planned, the government was forced to initiate monthly redemptions to prevent serious depreciation and within a few months the whole scheme was abandoned, less than half a million dollars having been issued in total and the most of which had been promptly redeemed.[5]

At the outset, the premier had stated that "three factors constitute this wondrously simple plan".[6] These were the payment of basic dividends, the establish-

[4]An unsympathetic critic observed that "It would be doing Major Douglas an injustice to class him among such crude sectarians as Mr. Aberhart, Mayor McGeer and Father Coughlin. The Douglas Scheme puts it all in a more sophisticated and quasi-mathematical fashion, and his proposals are more subtle. That is why they have been favorably received by intelligent people who are impressed by the use of simple algebraic equations in the elucidation of economic theories (such as Professors of English Literature and Deans of the Church of England), while any mass support which the movement may receive is due to the fact that it crystallizes and gives direction to the anti-banker complex among debtor groups." See *Social Planning for Canada, op. cit.*, p. 316.

[5]For a further analysis of the Alberta experiment, see "The Constitutionality and Economic Aspects of Social Credit", Evidence Before the Agricultural Committee of the Alberta Legislature, 1935 Session (Edmonton: King's Printer), 1935. See also V. F. Coe, "Dated Stamp Scrip in Alberta", in the *Canadian Journal of Economics and Political Science*, IV, pp. 60-91.

[6]William Aberhart, *Social Credit Manual* (Calgary), 1935, p. 17. The "plan" referred to was the Social Credit plan, not the stamp-money scheme actually introduced.

ment of automatic price-control arrangements, based on the (mediaeval?) notion of a "just" price and provision for a continuous flow of credit. Basic principles and theories were expounded at great length but discussion of technical details and problems of operation was apparently regarded as a waste of valuable time. Among the most serious flaws in the idea of a monthly dividend was the lack of any arrangement for recalling these credits from circulation if and when they became excessive. It was pointed out that if they were allowed to accumulate indefinitely, and "they will not disappear in some miraculous fashion",[7] any initial economic expansion that might be stimulated within the province would soon be choked off by the prospect of a rapid depreciation in the value of the provincial currency. If they were to be retired in appropriate amounts, the prospect of the substantial tax increases that would be necessitated would have the same discouraging effect. In the absence of some orderly regulation of the total quantity of this currency, the province would soon encounter balance of payments problems with the rest of the country, and Dominion currency would command a premium, the eventual outcome being that the provincial issues would become worthless. There was ample precedent for this predicted sequence of events, as for example in the paper money issues of New France, the issues of many of the thirteen colonies during the American Revolution, in the Southern states during the American Civil War and Germany after World War I, to name but a few.

The province could retire its currency at a rate equivalent to the periodic injections, once an "optimum" total had been put into circulation, either by taxation or by borrowing. The latter method would have been scarcely feasible for it would have led to a rapid increase in the already oppressive provincial debt. The former method would likewise have been unwise, for "to finance a government by the direct issue of circulating media and to control the amount of circulating media by taxation reverses the functions of institutions which historically have become more or less adapted to their customary functions. Taxing systems are designed to finance the government. Taxation is a slow and clumsy instrument in the control of a monetary system . . . A clear distinction should be made between financing a government and regulating the amount of circulating media to correspond with trade requirements."[8]

The chilling testimony presented by competent economists as to the undesirability of the whole scheme prompted the observation that "in periods of prosperity, economists are often regarded as idealistic weavers of fine spun theories and in depression periods they are regarded as ardent defenders of the status quo".[9] The Alberta experiment demonstrated clearly that in a federal state, monetary reform cannot be accomplished by the unilateral action of a com-

[7]"The Constitutionality and Economic Aspects of Social Credit", *op. cit.*, p. 12.
[8]*Ibid.*, p. 15.
[9]*Ibid.*

ponent part. In an economy as open as Canada's, it may indeed be extremely difficult even for the central government to accomplish its monetary objectives in the face of unfavourable external influences.

The widespread support which was accorded to one of the most interesting if least enlightening and constructive episodes in Canadian monetary experience reflected agrarian dissatisfaction with national policies in time of depression, particularly with monetary and fiscal policies, and with chartered bank policies, all of which appeared to Westerners to discriminate against the primary producers and to favour the manufacturing interests of central Canada. The particular direction which the protest assumed emphasized the traditional opposition of all debtor groups to high interest rates and sound money. The immediate appeal of the Social Credit promises was nicely summarized by a contemporary observer who explained that "Douglas . . . endowed the social credit myth with the great advantages of abstruseness and ambiguity. . . . Aberhart has given it concreteness and made it popular by appealing to one of the baser instincts in humanity, that of getting something for nothing. . . . This is the explanation of the growth of Douglas-cum-Aberhartism in Alberta".[10]

[10]See D. A. MacGibbon, "Inflation and Inflationism", in the *Canadian Journal of Economics and Political Science*, I, pp. 325-36.

## CHAPTER IX

# CANADIAN WAR FINANCE, 1939-1945

THE basic economic problems which confront a country in time of war include (1) producing the goods and services necessary for carrying on the war, (2) paying for those goods and services used for war purposes and (3) supplying the everyday needs of the civilian population. While it is with the second of these problems that wartime finance is immediately concerned, it is the first which is fundamental, and to which the others must always be subordinated. Because of the technology of modern warfare, World War II presented all three problems on a scale vastly greater than ever before.[1]

In time of war there occurs a revolution of social ends, and maintenance of the State itself becomes the clearly-defined objective. To accomplish this objective under conditions of modern warfare, it is essential that the organization and expansion of war production be accomplished with the utmost possible speed.[2] The sudden demand for an ever-increasing quantity and variety of war goods and services is likely to be highly inelastic, since the needs must be satisfied, if at all possible, regardless of price. But in the short run, supply is also relatively inelastic, and the government consequently finds itself confronted with immediate problems of procurement.[3]

Thus, within the Canadian economy, World War II occasioned the development of an unprecedented variety of direct governmental controls, i.e., measures which interfered with the price mechanism and which restricted freedom of economic choice. These controls were introduced in piecemeal fashion as the war progressed, arising from the exigencies of the immediate situation. In the early stages of the conflict, the government was able to guide the expanding war economy almost exclusively by indirect measures. Monetary expansion was the initial device adopted, but major emphasis was soon transferred to fiscal measures.[4] As wartime demands upon the economy continued to expand, monetary

---

[1] For a discussion of these problems, see Chester W. Wright, "Economic Lessons from Previous Wars" (in *Economic Problems of War and Its Aftermath,* ed. by Chester W. Wright, Chicago, 1942).

[2] This point was well illustrated by the experience in World War II, where the problem of mobilizing the required volume of resources was extremely complex, and where the economically strongest countries risked defeat before their full economic strength could be effectively mobilized.    [3] See T. O. Yntema, "Price Controls", *ibid.,* p. 112.

[4] Wartime fiscal policy must of course be determined not only in the light of its economic desirability but also in terms of its political acceptability. If fiscal measures hitherto considered drastic are to be successfully introduced, the public must first be taught to recognize their necessity. The Canadian Deputy-Minister of Finance believed that one good thing about the war was that it led to a process of general economic education.

and fiscal policy became incapable, by themselves, of effecting the adequate restriction of the civilian use of resources, and more positively, of guaranteeing the production of war materials of the kinds and quantities required. For this reason, the third stage in the transition of the Canadian economy to a war basis was marked by the greatly extended use of selective controls, in conjunction with appropriate fiscal policy.[5]

In the early months of the war, the demands upon the Canadian economy were not great, and although the prospects of a lengthy conflict were clearly seen and frequently emphasized, the necessity for the all-out economic war effort which later developed was not immediately apparent.[6] For this reason, Canada passed through two distinct periods in her economic mobilization. At the outbreak of war, the volume of unused productive capacity and of unemployed labour was substantial, a situation which prompted the government to observe that it should be possible to expand production for war purposes without causing any serious temporary reduction in civilian output.[7] No appreciable reallocation of resources was required before mid-1940, because the increased demands upon the economy were for commodities ordinarily produced in peacetime in Canada, the output of which could be expanded by the use of existing unemployed resources. A general "business-as-usual" attitude prevailed during this period, and it was not until the collapse of France in June, 1940, that the urgent necessity for an all-out war effort became apparent, whereupon the intensive development of the war economy was undertaken. The subsequent demand for various kinds of war materials necessitated a rapid expansion of Canada's productive capacity, and as full employment was approached, the need for the reallocation of resources became increasingly great. The "business-as-usual" attitude disappeared and the economy was subjected to a widening range of selective controls.[8]

The objectives of an adequate programme of war finance are threefold: (1) to provide funds for financing the enormous wartime expenditures, (2) to restrict the civilian demand for resources in order that these may be made available, as needed, for war purposes, and (3) to allocate the economic burden of the war

[5]For a summary of the failings of the competitive price system in the war economy, see Stewart Bates, "The Price System and the War Economy" (*Canadian Journal of Economics and Political Science*, vol. VII, 1941, pp. 333-4).

[6]For an explanation of the lack of industrial mobilization during the early months of the war, see R. MacG. Dawson, *Canada in World Affairs*, 1939-41 (Toronto, 1943), pp. 16-17, 116.

[7]See A. F. W. Plumptre, *Canadian War Finance*, 1939-40 (Washington, 1941), pp. 8-68.

[8]For reasons already noted, it was not possible in the early months of the war for the Canadian government to make any detailed calculation of the financial burden involved, for the turn of events after June, 1940, presented the government with financial problems whose magnitude had not originally been foreseen. Canada's wartime expenditures included not only the outlays involved in meeting its own direct wartime needs, but extended to the financing of purchases made within Canada by Great Britain and other members of the sterling bloc and by other Allied nations. The financing of these latter purchases created problems of both a quantitative and qualitative character.

as equitably as possible. While providing the necessary funds is the most obvious of these objectives, it was the view of the Canadian government that the second aspect was of basic importance. It stated that "behind the façade of dollars, the real work of war finance is to draw the resources of the country into use for war purposes and away from other uses, or from idleness. This is the initial and general economic problem; finance is the main instrument of achieving a solution . . . it is in making these resources of men, materials and machines available that the real task of finance must be found.[9] Thus, as Gladstone observed more than a century ago, "Finance is not arithmetic; finance is policy".

Almost all past conflicts have been accompanied by an undesirably large amount of inflationary financing. An important contributing factor has been the erroneous belief that, unlike taxation, domestic borrowing affords an opportunity for shifting some part of the cost of the war to future generations. While it is true that under certain circumstances, future generations may be called upon to bear some part of the real costs of a conflict, e.g., through the diminution of the productive capacity of the economy as a result of the war, this occurrence is obviously independent of the means adopted in financing the conflict. It is surely apparent that the real cost of a war is incurred by using resources for purposes of destruction which would otherwise have been available for constructive ends. The significance of the taxation-versus-borrowing controversy lies in determining how the burden of a present war will be distributed within the existing generation, and how the real income of future generations will be distributed among its own members.

The Canadian government recognized that in a war which was to be financed almost exclusively from domestic sources, the real costs would inevitably be borne by the citizens currently involved in the conflict. A fallacious argument that had so greatly influenced the financing of earlier wars was consequently avoided.[10] Discussing its programme of war finance, the government repeatedly presented the view that there were three methods of financing a war, these being taxation, borrowing, and inflation.[11] This classification can nevertheless be very misleading, for expenditure from borrowings, and even from taxes, may have inflationary consequences.

In formulating its general principles of war finance, the government discarded the third member of the "trinity", inflation (the creation of new money), as

---

[9]J. L. Ilsley, House of Commons Debates, July 30, 1940. Immediately prior to World War II, at least one American economic historian, writing in a country where the necessity of undertaking war finance had occurred more frequently than in our own, expressed the opinion that discouragingly little had been learned about such matters from past experience. See Chester W. Wright, "Economic Lessons From Previous Wars". Perhaps this view would now be modified in the light of World War II financial experience.

[10]See J. L. Ilsley, *Budget Speech*, Sept. 12, 1939, p. 3.

[11]In referring to "inflation" as one source of war finance, the government usually meant the creation of new money; this terminology at least clarifies the basis for the government's threefold division of the sources of funds—taxes, loans from current income or savings, and new money.

being certainly the most unfair and inequitable method of diverting resources to wartime ends. It consequently directed its attention to the other two sources of funds, taxation and borrowing. The Minister of Finance indicated in his first wartime budget speech that while a 100 per cent pay-as-you-go policy might seem to represent an ideal policy of war finance, being most logical, most equitable, and least likely to create disturbances and dislocations, there were certain well recognized limitations upon any programme of taxation. Accordingly, the government adopted a policy of war finance in which the pay-as-you-go objective was to be pursued to the limits of practicability; additional financial needs were to be met by a programme of borrowing from the public at the lowest possible interest rates. An equitable distribution of the economic burden of the war was to be encouraged "first by avoiding inflation, second by anti-profiteering measures, third by using taxes rather than loans as a source of war revenues, fourth by use of direct taxation the incidence of which is relatively predictable, and fifth by concentrating the burden on groups which had previously escaped relatively lightly."[12]

With reference to financial measures adopted, the government distinguished two major periods in the development of the war economy. The first was the period of expansion and preparation, the second the main period of the full war effort. In the initial period, it was announced that a short-run policy of financing would be adopted which would differ substantially from the basic policy noted above. The Minister of Finance stated that in view of the existing quantities of unemployed resources and unused productive capacity, a small and carefully regulated amount of credit expansion was desirable in promoting increased production and employment, and that such an expansion could be accomplished without inflationary consequences. The government recognized that in introducing subsequent measures of taxation and borrowing, the matter of timing would be important, in relation to their effects upon the accomplishment of the desired economic expansion. Thus, at the outbreak of the war, the immediate expansion of tax revenues was neither possible nor considered altogether desirable, and a borrowing campaign designed to attract public savings was not believed to be appropriate at that time, since it might impede expenditures by private industry and interfere with civilian consumption which the government was seeking to expand. Short-term bank borrowing was therefore adopted as the most effective means of stimulating the early development of the war programme, and of expanding employment and output. At the same time, the probability of much heavier expenditures was foreseen, and the government accordingly emphasized the need for the immediate imposition of various additional taxes, the yields from which would not appear for some considerable period of time.

Among the direct controls adopted by the government as part of its wartime

[12]A. F. W. Plumptre, *Canadian War Finance*, 1939-40 (Washington, 1941), p. 111.

168

economic mobilization programme, the Foreign Exchange Control Board's operations are of particular interest, since they represent an important aspect of wartime monetary policy. The organization and functions of the Board, conceived by the Bank of Canada, had been the subject of advance planning (a feature not associated with any of the other direct controls), and the Board could consequently be put into operation when war was declared.

The establishment of the Board on September 16, 1939, marked the first occasion on which any official restrictions had been placed on foreign exchange transactions within Canada. The Foreign Exchange Control Order gave the Board control over all financial transactions between residents of Canada and residents of other countries, the essential objective being to "maintain exchange stability and to conserve Canada's supply of United States dollars for essential war and civilian requirements by ensuring that it was not dissipated on non-essential purposes such as capital export".[13] The necessity for conserving United States dollars was directly related to the structure of the Canadian balance of payments. Following the formation of international currency blocs in the nineteen-thirties, Canada found her external trade closely tied to both the sterling area and the United States dollar area. Her substantial over-all current account surplus in the years preceding World War II was the product of a recurring net deficit with the dollar area and a recurring net credit with the sterling area. Under the existing multilateral exchange system, this situation presented no special problem, since Canada could convert her surplus sterling into United States dollars, and thereby cover her dollar deficit. With the advent of World War II, the government of the United Kingdom instituted exchange control to protect its own dollar reserves, and with sterling no longer freely convertible, Canada found her balance of payments effectively split into two parts. It therefore became necessary for her to consider her financial relationship with the United States on an independent basis.[14]

It was immediately apparent that wartime developments would accentuate the United States dollar deficit of the pre-war years, for as Canada sought to expand and diversify her capacity for war production, both on behalf of herself and of her allies, increased capital outlays in the United States would become inevitable. To conserve United States dollar reserves for these and other essential uses, foreign exchange control was introduced. At the beginning of World War II, the investment of United States capital in Canada amounted to $4.2 billions.[15] In the absence of restrictions on capital transactions, any appreciable attempt to liquidate and convert investments by non-resident holders would have

---

[13]Louis Rasminsky, "Foreign Exchange Control in Canada: Purposes and Methods" (in *Canadian War Economics*, ed. by J. F. Parkinson, Toronto, 1941, pp. 1-16).

[14]For an analysis of the wartime balance of payments, see F. A. Knox, "Canada's Balance of International Payments, 1940-45" in *The Canadian Journal of Economics and Political Science*, 1947, pp. 345-62.

[15]Foreign Exchange Control Board, *Report to the Minister of Finance* (Ottawa, 1946), p. 7.

had disastrous results upon Canadian reserves of United States dollars. Restrictions on current transactions were also inevitable if an expanding Canadian national income were not to stimulate undesirably the expansion of their domestic production. A further objective of exchange control was the elimination of the disturbing fluctuations of a "free" exchange rate, fluctuations which the currency experience of the nineteen-thirties had frequently shown to be of a disequilibrating character.

The Foreign Exchange Control Board was established as the administrative body in charge of enforcing the provisions of the Foreign Exchange Control Order. The Bank of Canada became the technical adviser to the Board, and all branches of the Canadian chartered banks became its agents. The chief provisions of the order were that (1) all foreign exchange received by Canadian residents must be sold to the Board through an authorized dealer (on April 30, 1940, it was further provided, under the terms of the Foreign Exchange Acquisition Act, that these residents must sell to the Board all foreign exchange in their possession, ownership, or control at the time); (2) Canadian residents must apply to the Board for any foreign exchange which they required; (3) transfers of Canadian dollars by residents to non-residents might be made only under permit. The Board was also authorized to establish rates of exchange for all foreign exchange transactions within Canada.

The original capital resources made available to the Board for conducting its operations were represented by a special Exchange Fund Account which had been established in 1935, the proceeds of which amounted to $84 million at the beginning of the war, held entirely in Canadian funds. The government made subsequent advances to this fund, the first being on May 1, 1940, in the amount of $325 million, to provide the Board with the means of payment for the gold and foreign exchange which it acquired under the terms of the Foreign Exchange Acquisition Order and the Exchange Fund Order. At the end of 1945, outstanding advances to the fund amounted to $1.3 billion.

Concerning Canada's relations with the sterling area, transactions could be effected either in Canadian dollars or in sterling, and no restrictions were placed upon payments to the sterling area in either currency. No import licences were required for goods originating in the sterling area. Sterling area residents wishing to sell securities in Canada were required to obtain permits which were granted without question where it could be shown that the dollar proceeds would be made available to the sterling area exchange control authorities. These authorities controlled all payments by the sterling area to Canada, and capital transactions were generally not approved.

The financing of the United Kingdom's Canadian-dollar deficit involved a variety of techniques. Among the most important were the repatriation of Canadian securities held in the United Kingdom, the accumulation of sterling balances in London which were later converted into an interest-free loan, the provision of a $1 billion "gift" and the appropriation of funds under the terms of the War Appropriation (United Nations Mutual Aid) Acts. The immediate financial burden of each of these techniques of course fell upon the Canadian taxpayer.

Despite early attempts to increase Canadian exports to the United States, to encourage increased United States investment in Canada, and despite severe restrictions upon the non-essential uses of United States dollars by Canadian citizens, Canada's exchange position vis-à-vis the United States became increasingly serious in 1941. The situation was effectively eased only after the completion of the Hyde Park Agreement in April of that year, which provided for a broader integration of war production in the two countries, and which led to a substantial expansion of Canada's net earnings of United States dollars. From that date until the end of the war, Canada's holdings of gold and United States dollars rose steadily, exceeding $1.5 billion at the end of 1945.[16]

Aside from the administrative activities of the Foreign Exchange Control Board, the principal device employed by the government to facilitate war production in the early months of the war was that of monetary expansion. The second wartime budget in June, 1940, marked the effective beginnings of fiscal control, and this was increasingly supplemented by more direct measures, of which the most outstanding was the shift from selective to over-all price control late in 1941.

Before discussing wartime financial developments, it is useful to recall that during the decade of the nineteen-twenties, the annual expenditures of the federal government were relatively stable, and amounted to less than 10 per cent of the national income. However, the advent of the depression introduced an entirely new situation, in which the national income declined rapidly at a time when the assumption of increasingly heavy obligations by the federal government was becoming unavoidable. A balanced budget was neither possible nor desirable and the national debt began to rise more rapidly than at any time in Canadian history, with the exception of the World War I years.[17] Although economic conditions had improved appreciably by the late nineteen-thirties, the government was still operating with an unbalanced budget at the beginning of World War II. As of March 1, 1939, the total unmatured funded debt including treasury bills outstanding was approximately $3,386 million, with an average rate of interest of 3.52 per cent.[18] As already suggested, the size of the debt was largely attributable to the exigencies of financing both a war and a depression, and represented a tenfold increase since 1914. In addition to this direct debt, the government had incurred various indirect obligations, chiefly

[16]*Ibid.*, p. 20.
[17]For the growth of the national debt between Confederation and World War II, see *Public Accounts*, 1939, p. 64. The only period in which the debt showed annual reductions was between 1923 and 1930. The "undesirability" of a balanced federal budget was not generally recognized in the dominant fiscal theory of the 1930's.
[18]*Ibid.*, pp. 20-1, 68.

in connection with the guarantee of the securities of various railroads which now form the Canadian National system. The total amount of these contingent liabilities, as of June, 1939, was approximately $1,085 million, an amount which was steadily reduced during the war years.[19]

In the 1939 fiscal year, the over-all cash requirements of the federal government had reached $573 million (Table VI), a figure which reflected the impact of depression expenditures upon the federal budget. Nevertheless, the annual

TABLE V—NATIONAL INCOME AND GROSS NATIONAL PRODUCT, 1939-45[a]
(in millions of dollars)

| | 1939 | 1940 | 1941 | 1942 | 1943 | 1944 | 1945 |
|---|---|---|---|---|---|---|---|
| Wages, Salaries and Supplementary Labour Income | 2575 | 2929 | 3575 | 4242 | 4783 | 4940 | 4953 |
| Military Pay and Allowances | 32 | 193 | 386 | 641 | 910 | 1068 | 1117 |
| Investment Income | 917 | 1128 | 1484 | 1761 | 1801 | 1829 | 1859 |
| Net Income of Unincorporated Business Enterprise: | | | | | | | |
| Accrued Net Income of Farm Operators from Farm Production | 385 | 492 | 490 | 988 | 805 | 1185 | 1010 |
| Net Income of Non-Farm Unincorporated Business | 464 | 521 | 628 | 705 | 744 | 804 | 901 |
| Net National Income at Factor Cost | 4373 | 5263 | 6563 | 8337 | 9043 | 9826 | 9840 |
| Indirect Taxes Less Subsidies | 733 | 830 | 1054 | 1085 | 1117 | 1111 | 1003 |
| Depreciation Allowances and Similar Business Costs | 610 | 720 | 858 | 1002 | 988 | 957 | 928 |
| Residual Error of Estimate | −9 | 59 | 42 | 115 | 35 | 60 | 79 |
| Gross National Product at Market Prices | 5707 | 6872 | 8517 | 10539 | 11183 | 11954 | 11850 |
| | (5664)[b] | (6487) | (7481) | (8941) | (9374) | (9721) | (9315) |

GROSS NATIONAL EXPENDITURE, 1939-45[a]
(in millions of dollars)

| | 1939 | 1940 | 1941 | 1942 | 1943 | 1944 | 1945 |
|---|---|---|---|---|---|---|---|
| Personal Expenditure on Consumer Goods and Services | 3904 | 4399 | 5053 | 5514 | 5727 | 6187 | 6811 |
| Government Expenditure on Goods and Services | 735 | 1165 | 1689 | 3726 | 4227 | 5022 | 3704 |
| Gross Domestic Investment: | | | | | | | |
| New Residential Construction | 185 | 200 | 233 | 194 | 174 | 225 | 272 |
| New Non-Residential Construction | 166 | 210 | 288 | 354 | 366 | 257 | 252 |
| New Machinery and Equipment | 254 | 408 | 557 | 496 | 305 | 377 | 462 |
| Changes in Inventories | 331 | 369 | 247 | 316 | −109 | −46 | −260 |
| Exports of Goods and Services | 1451 | 1808 | 2467 | 2361 | 3444 | 3561 | 3597 |
| Deduct: Imports of Goods and Services | 1328 | 1629 | 1976 | 2307 | 2917 | 3569 | 2910 |
| Residual Error of Estimate | 9 | −58 | −41 | −115 | −34 | −60 | −78 |
| Gross National Product at Market Prices | 5707 | 6872 | 8517 | 10539 | 11183 | 11954 | 11850 |
| | (5664)[b] | (6487) | (7481) | (8941) | (9374) | (9721) | (9315) |

[a]Dominion Bureau of Statistics, *National Accounts: Income and Expenditure, 1926-1950*, pp. 27-9.
[b]All figures in brackets represent constant 1935-9 dollars.

[19]Bank of Canada, *Statistical Summary*, June-July, 1939, p. 11.

Table VI—GOVERNMENT OF CANADA: CASH REQUIREMENTS, FISCAL YEARS, 1939-46[a]

(in millions of dollars)

| | 1939 | 1940 | 1941 | 1942 | 1943 | 1944 | 1945 | 1946 |
|---|---|---|---|---|---|---|---|---|
| Budgetary Expenditure | 553 | 681 | 1250 | 1885 | 4387 | 5322 | 5246 | 5136 |
| Less: Non-Cash Items | 4 | 26 | 43 | 32 | 66 | 63 | 48 | 48 |
| Budgetary Cash Requirements | 549 | 655 | 1207 | 1853 | 4321 | 5259 | 5198 | 5088 |
| Loans and Investments | 24 | 56 | 512 | 725 | 723 | 520 | 310 | 396 |
| Total Cash Requirements | 573 | 711 | 1719 | 2578 | 5044 | 5779 | 5508 | 5484 |

GOVERNMENT OF CANADA: SOURCES OF FINANCING, FISCAL YEARS 1939-46[a]

(in millions of dollars)

| | 1939 | 1940 | 1941 | 1942 | 1943 | 1944 | 1945 | 1946 |
|---|---|---|---|---|---|---|---|---|
| Budgetary Revenues | 502 | 562 | 872 | 1489 | 2250 | 2765 | 2687 | 3013 |
| Less: Non-Cash Items | 3 | 20 | 9 | 7 | 41 | 38 | 22 | 23 |
| Budgetary Cash Revenues | 499 | 542 | 863 | 1482 | 2209 | 2727 | 2665 | 2990 |
| *Borrowing:* | | | | | | | | |
|   Foreign | 24 | −106 | −100 | −179 | −81 | 13 | −97 | −207 |
|   Domestic | 18 | 267 | 907 | 1196 | 2829 | 2930 | 2744 | 2610 |
|   Open-Account | 32 | 8 | 49 | 79 | 87 | 109 | 196 | 91 |
| Total Borrowing | 74 | 169 | 856 | 1096 | 2835 | 3052 | 2843 | 2494 |
| Total Cash Requirements | 573 | 711 | 1719 | 2578 | 5044 | 5779 | 5508 | 5484 |
| Budgetary Cash Revenues / Total Cash Requirements | 87% | 76% | 50% | 57% | 44% | 47% | 48% | 54% |

[a]Computations based on Bank of Canada, *Statistical Summary: 1950 Supplement*, pp. 24-5.

deficits were by this time declining, and about 87% of the foregoing requirements were met by revenues. In this immediate pre-war year, federal expenditures represented little more than ten per cent of gross national expenditure, but the heavy financial obligations imposed by the war led to a very rapid rise in this proportion. We shall now examine the methods adopted by the government in financing its wartime expenditures and the consequences of those methods.

In his first wartime speech, the Minister of Finance indicated the desirability of undertaking monetary expansion, of introducing new taxes, and of increasing the rates of existing taxes.[20] It was not believed that these tax measures would

[20]One of the accomplishments of the federal tax measures introduced during World War II was to lessen the regressiveness of the Canadian tax system. In 1939, the combined provincial governments' revenue sources were the following: corporation taxes, personal income taxes and succession duties, 32%; commodity taxes and licences, 55%; real property taxes plus revenue from public domain, 13%. For the federal government, commodity taxes yielded 67% of tax revenues, income taxes, 33%. In view of the fact that the British North America Act restricts the provincial governments to the levying of "direct" taxes, one may well question the usefulness of the term as an economic concept.

provide immediately for any large part of the government's rapidly increasing expenditures, but that out of an anticipated rising national income, increased tax revenue would soon begin to appear. Meanwhile, to meet the inevitable deficit of this early period, short-term expansionist borrowing would be undertaken. It is clear that to the end of March, 1940, little additional tax revenue was realized from the new tax measures.[21] Nor was it intended that these measures should lead to an appreciable restriction of consumption while substantial unemployment still prevailed.

For the entire 1940 fiscal year, the increase in total tax revenues over the preceding year was only $32 million, an amount attributable to increased yields from customs duties, the sales tax and excise levies.[22] The greater part of the

TABLE VII—SELECTED FEDERAL FUNDED DEBT OPERATIONS:
WORLD WAR II[a]
(millions of dollars)

| FISCAL YEAR | 1940[b] | 1941 | 1942 | 1943 | 1944 | 1945 | 1946 |
|---|---|---|---|---|---|---|---|
| A. Sources of New (Cash) Borrowing[c] | | | | | | | |
| General Public[d] | | | | | | | |
| First War Loan | 200 | | | | | | |
| Second War Loan | | 300 | | | | | |
| First Victory Loan | | | 731 | | | | |
| Second Victory Loan | | | 843 | | | | |
| Third Victory Loan | | | | 991 | | | |
| Fourth Victory Loan | | | | | 1309 | | |
| Fifth Victory Loan | | | | | 1375 | | |
| Sixth Victory Loan | | | | | | 1405 | |
| Seventh Victory Loan | | | | | | 1512 | |
| Eighth Victory Loan | | | | | | | 1564 |
| Ninth Victory Loan | | | | | | | 2024 |
| War Savings Stamps and Certificates[e] | ........ | 52 | 82 | 59 | 47 | 29 | 10 |
| Non-Interest-Bearing Certificates[e] | ........ | 6 | 3 | | 1 | 2 | f |
| Chartered Banks | 200 | 250 | ........ | 820 | 170 | 112 | f |
| Bank of Canada | ........ | 325 | ........ | 193 | ........ | ........ | |
| Treasury Bills[e] | ........ | 75[g] | 40 | 30 | 60 | 20 | 70 |
| Total New Borrowing Within Canada | 400 | 933 | 1699 | 2093 | 2962 | 3080 | 3668 |
| New York Market | ........ | ........ | 10 | 90 | ........ | ........ | ........ |
| TOTAL NEW BORROWING | 400 | 933 | 1709 | 2183 | 2962 | 3080 | 3668 |

[21]See the *Public Accounts*, 1939, pp. xii-xiii; *Public Accounts*, 1940. The chief features of the tax programme introduced in the first wartime budget were a new excess profits tax, a flat-rate increase of 20% in the personal income tax, an increase of 3% in the corporate income tax, sharp increases in excise taxes and a widening of the base of the sales tax. For details of these tax measures, see J. L. Ilsley, *Budget Speech*, Sept. 12, 1939, pp. 6-11.

[22]See *Public Accounts*, 1939, 1940.

| | | | | | | | |
|---|---|---|---|---|---|---|---|
| B. Retirements | | | | | | | |
| New York | ........ | ........ | 20 | 110 | 106 | ........ | 155 |
| London | 84 | 147 | 160 | 3 | h | ........ | ........ |
| Canada | 100 | 110 | 36 | 42 | 60 | 252 | 761 |
| TOTAL RETIREMENTS | 184 | 257 | 216 | 155 | 166 | 252 | 916 |
| C. Increase in Direct Funded Debt | | | | | | | |
| Net Borrowing | 216 | 676 | 1493 | 2028 | 2796 | 2828 | 2752 |
| Refundable Tax Liability[i] | ........ | ........ | ........ | 70 | 155 | 219 | 71 |
| Accounting Adjustment[j] | ........ | ........ | ........ | 23 | ........ | ........ | ........ |
| TOTAL INCREASE IN FUNDED DEBT | 216 | 676 | 1493 | 2121 | 2951 | 3047 | 2823 |
| D. Direct Unmatured Funded Debt, at March 31 | 3696 | 4372 | 5865 | 7986 | 10937 | 13984 | 16807 |
| E. Average Interest Rate Payable on Debt | 3.40 | 3.06 | 2.90 | 2.60 | 2.55 | 2.51 | 2.49 |

[a]The data in the above table are based on Dominion of Canada, *Public Accounts,* for the several wartime fiscal years; *Budget Speeches,* for the several fiscal years; National War Finance Committee, *Statistics and Information on Dominion Government Public Borrowing Operations from September 1939 to December 1945* (Ottawa, 1946).

[b]From September 1, 1939 to March 31, 1940 only.

[c]Excludes renewals, and the conversion of maturing issues.

[d]Excludes the chartered banks and the Bank of Canada. The direct cash purchases of public issues by the banking system were of negligible amount.

[e]Net increase during the fiscal year.

[f]Net retirement during the fiscal year, which in the case of the non-interest-bearing certificates amounted to $6 million, and of the chartered banks to $260 million.

[g]Included in the purchase of $325 million by the Bank of Canada.

[h]In 1944 and succeeding fiscal years, the repatriation from Britain of the direct funded debt was of negligible proportions.

[i]Arising from personal income tax and excess profits tax revenues.

[j]This adjustment represents the inclusion in the debt, for the first time, of the premium at which certain of the funded debt issues were redeemable. Previous to this adjustment, the debt, as of March 31, 1943, had been determined as $7,893 million. Beginning with the 1944 fiscal year, these redemption bonuses were added to the figure representing the debt outstanding. On this revised basis, the 1943 figure would read $7,916 million. A further modification of accounting practice in 1944 was the inclusion of the refundable portion of income tax revenues in the debt figure. This portion amounted to $70 million in 1943, providing an over-all debt figure of $7,986 million as of March 31 of that year.

government's increase in cash requirements was therefore financed by borrowing.[23] The increase in the unmatured funded debt between the outbreak of the war and the end of fiscal 1940 may be seen from Table VII. The issue to the chartered banks reflected the policy of deliberate monetary expansion which was pursued in the early stages of the war. It will be observed that in no wartime fiscal period was net borrowing effected abroad, for on the two occasions on which new funds were obtained in the New York market, the proceeds were used to assist in retiring maturing issues of substantially greater amount. Through

[23]For fiscal 1940, 76% of total cash requirements (811 million) was covered by revenues, and the government's rising expenditures still represented only 11%-12% of gross national income.

175

the process of repatriation, the direct funded debt payable in London was virtually eliminated, and as a result of the net retirements effected during the war years, approximately 99 per cent of Canada's direct debt was domestically held, as of March 31, 1946.

The Bank of Canada determined its wartime monetary policies in close relationship to the government's changing fiscal needs, and throughout the war, one of its main tasks was the managing of chartered bank cash, first with a view to enabling those institutions to accommodate the government with necessary loans, and second to maintain stability, at lower yields, in the bond market, in order to provide a continuing favourable reception for successive issues of government bonds. The Bank employed open-market operations as its chief means of control, supplemented by certain other monetary techniques. In addition, the organization of the chartered banks made the device of informal suggestion particularly effective. One of the immediate objectives of the Bank's monetary policy following the outbreak of the war was therefore to provide the chartered banks with additional reserves to permit their purchase of an issue of government securities, in accordance with the monetary views expressed in the budget. In so doing, the Bank was merely continuing its earlier fundamental policy of credit expansion.[24] Since the chartered banks traditionally sought to maintain a 10 per cent reserve against their Canadian deposit liabilities, open-market operations served as an effective technique whereby the central bank might influence the supply of money. The effects of the Bank of Canada's wartime operations upon the cash reserves of the chartered banks are summarized in Table VIII.

During the early months of the war, the Bank of Canada's active note circulation began to expand rapidly. Apart from normal seasonal increases and the continuing replacement of chartered bank notes, underlying factors included the rising national income, its changing distribution, changing methods of income payments and the disappearance of United States dollars from circulation. This rapid expansion of the Bank's note liability continued throughout the war.[25] With respect to its assets, the Bank, through its open-market purchases and through its direct purchases of securities from the government, both of which served to expand chartered bank cash and to support the bond market, held an overwhelming proportion of its total assets in the form of securities by the end of the war. The impact of war finance upon the Bank of Canada and upon the chartered banks is summarized in Tables IX and X.

The most striking effect upon the accounts of the chartered banks was the

[24]In this instance, the Bank's action took the form of the open-market purchase of short-term securities. In the case of the 1941 purchase of $250 million of new bonds (Table VII), the chartered banks required no additional cash.

[25]The expansion of notes relative to deposits was a striking feature of the Canadian wartime monetary structure. Between March 1940 and March 1946, bank notes held by the general public increased from $256 million to $1,002 million, while chartered bank deposits increased from $2,734 million to $5,586 million. See Table VII for further details of the Canadian money supply.

## TABLE VIII—EFFECTS OF BANK OF CANADA OPERATIONS ON CHARTERED BANK CASH RESERVES, 1939-45a

(in millions of dollars)

| Type of Asset or Liability: | Changes Producing a Decrease in Chartered Bank Reserves | | | | | | | Changes Producing an Increase in Chartered Bank Reserves | | | | | | |
|---|---|---|---|---|---|---|---|---|---|---|---|---|---|---|
| | 1939 | 1940 | 1941 | 1942 | 1943 | 1944 | 1945 | 1939 | 1940 | 1941 | 1942 | 1943 | 1944 | 1945 |
| Gold Coin and Bullion | | −225.7 | | | | | −15.4 | 39.8 | | | | | 171.7 | |
| Sterling and U.S. Dollars | | −25.9 | | −200.4 | | | | 36.0 | | 162.4 | | | 220.5 | |
| Dominion and Provincial Securities | | | | | | | | 46.3 | 344.0 | 32.7 | 407.9 | 244.0 | | 364.8 |
| Other Assets | | | −2.2 | | | | | | 7.0 | 21.1 | | | 10.0 | |
| Rest Fund | 0.5 | 1.3 | 1.9 | 0.9 | 1.6 | 2.0 | | | | | | | | |
| Liabilities Payable in Sterling, U.S. and Foreign Gold Currencies | | | | | | 172.3 | | | | | | | | −15.4 |
| Active Note Circulation | 43.8 | 99.4 | 118.0 | 192.9 | 179.0 | 145.1 | 69.6 | | | | | | | |
| Dominion Government Balances | 29.6 | 64.1 | | | | | 144.8 | | −33.9 | | −18.0 | −25.0 | | |
| Other Deposits | 14.8 | | 13.1 | | | | | | −8.3 | −3.5 | −16.1 | | | |
| All Other Liabilities (net) | 3.3 | 12.4 | 3.5 | | 6.4 | 4.8 | 7.4 | | | | | | | |
| | 92.0 | 364.7 | 187.5 | 409.5 | 187.0 | 324.2 | 237.2 | 122.1 | 393.2 | 219.7 | 442.0 | 269.0 | 402.2 | 380.2 |
| DEDUCT | | | | | | | | 92.0 | 364.7 | 187.5 | 409.5 | 187.0 | 324.2 | 237.2 |
| Change in Chartered Bank Cash Reserves | | | | | | | | 30.1 | 28.5 | 32.2 | 32.5 | 82.0 | 78.0 | 143.0 |

aSee Bank of Canada, *Annual Reports*, for the several years above.

TABLE IX—BANK OF CANADA: WARTI

(milli

MONTH-END (MARCH A

## LIABILITIES

| As of March 31 and Dec. 31 | CHARTERED BANK CASH | | | | | | GOV'T DEPOSITS | | OTHER DEPOSITS | | SPECIAL FOREIGN DEPOSITS b | | ACTIVE B. OF C. NOTE CIRCULATION | | ALL OTHER ACCOUN' | |
| | NOTES IN TILLS | | DEPOSITS AT B. OF C. | | TOTAL | | | | | | | | | | | |
| | M | D | M | D | M | D | M | D | M | D | M | D | M | D | M | |
| 1940 | 57.3 | 98.3 | 202.3 | 217.7 | 259.7 | 316.0 | 48.0 | 10.9 | 10.6 | 9.5 | .... | .... | 163.8 | 261.6 | 11.9 | 2. |
| 1941 | 80.6 | 116.3 | 208.0 | 232.0 | 288.6 | 348.4 | 17.1 | 73.8 | 8.3 | 6.0 | .... | .... | 284.7 | 379.6 | 13.4 | 3 |
| 1942 | 99.1 | 121.1 | 241.9 | 259.9 | 341.1 | 381.1 | 118.8 | 51.6 | 6.1 | 19.1 | .... | .... | 409.8 | 572.5 | 16.3 | 2. |
| 1943 | 108.7 | 122.9 | 261.0 | 340.2 | 369.7 | 463.1 | 21.2 | 20.5 | 24.7 | 17.8 | .... | .... | 610.4 | 751.5 | 19.4 | 5 |
| 1944 | 100.3 | 139.4 | 359.2 | 401.7 | 459.5 | 541.1 | 65.8 | 12.9 | 22.8 | 27.7 | .... | 172.3 | 797.6 | 896.6 | 44.5 | 3' |
| 1945 | 113.4 | 162.9 | 422.0 | 521.2 | 535.4 | 684.1 | 18.7 | 153.3 | 52.7 | 29.8 | 177.1 | 156.8 | 935.4 | 966.2 | 26.3 | 4 |
| 1946 | 124.7 | 176.9 | 518.1 | 565.5 | 642.9 | 742.3 | 149.2 | 60.5 | 89.1 | 93.8 | 95.2 | 1.0 | 977.5 | 1009.3 | 36.9 | 4 |

aThe data in Table IX are gathered from the Bank of Canada, Statistical Summary, 1946 Supplement, pp. 6
bDeposits payable in sterling, U.S. dollars, and foreign gold currencies, held on account of foreign clients
cIncludes foreign exchange held on account of foreign clients.
dIncludes "other securities".
eUnder the Foreign Exchange Acquisition Order and the Exchange Fund Order, the Bank's gold and forei

TABLE X—CHARTERED BANKS: WARTI

(milli

MONTH-END (MARCH A

## LIABILITIES

| As of March 31 and Dec. 31 | | | DEPOSITS | | | | | | | | | | | |
| | NOTES | | DEMAND | | NOTICE | | DOMINION AND PROVINCIAL | | CANADIAN DEPOSITS b | | FOREIGN | | TOTAL DEPOSIT c |
| | M | D | M | D | M | D | M | D | M | D | M | D | M | D |
| 1940 | 92 | 84 | 750 | 1031 | 1661 | 1641 | 313 | 133 | 2734 | 2805 | 467 | 405 | 3262 | 32 |
| 1941 | 83 | 73 | 1050 | 1268 | 1703 | 1669 | 219 | 167 | 2958 | 3108 | 411 | 462 | 3447 | 36 |
| 1942 | 74 | 62 | 1144 | 1499 | 1550 | 1673 | 611 | 485 | 3302 | 3608 | 473 | 545 | 3843 | 42 |
| 1943 | 55 | 43 | 1659 | 1697 | 1890 | 1948 | 268 | 750 | 3750 | 4356 | 550 | 655 | 4443 | 51 |
| 1944 | 40 | 34 | 1892 | 1862 | 2225 | 2423 | 251 | 852 | 4340 | 5149 | 666 | 746 | 5140 | 59 |
| 1945 | 31 | 26 | 1935 | 2063 | 2725 | 2865 | 279 | 1013 | 4938 | 5949 | 739 | 812 | 5792 | 68 |
| 1946 | 24 | 21 | 1985 | 2291 | 3170 | 3469 | 626 | 492 | 5786 | 6295 | 800 | 813 | 6712 | 72 |

aThe data in Table X are gathered from Bank of Canada, Statistical Summary, 1946 Supplement, pp. 16-
bEstimated month-end deposits payable in Canadian currency.
cIncludes inter-bank deposits.
dUntil March, 1935, this included gold and coin in Canada, Dominion notes and "free" Central Gold

## ASSETS

| | | | | c RESERVE FOREIGN CURRENCY | | d TOTAL RESERVE | | SECURITIES | | | | | | | |
|---|---|---|---|---|---|---|---|---|---|---|---|---|---|---|---|
| TOTAL ASSETS OR LIABILITIES | | GOLD | | | | | | DOM.-PROV. UNDER 2 YEARS | | DOM.-PROV. OVER 2 YEARS | | d TOTAL | | ALL OTHER ASSETS | |
| M | D | M | D | M | D | M | D | M | D | M | D | M | D | M | D |
| ?4.0 | 626.6 | 225.8 | .... | 60.7 | 38.4 | 286.5 | 38.4 | 93.4 | 448.4 | 104.7 | 127.3 | 198.0 | 575.8 | 9.5 | 12.4 |
| 12.1 | 842.9 | e | .... | 69.5 | 200.9 | 69.5 | 200.9 | 411.1 | 391.8 | 114.5 | 216.7 | 525.6 | 608.5 | 17.0 | 33.5 |
| ?2.0 | 1048.2 | .... | .... | 276.3 | 0.5 | 276.3 | 0.5 | 866.3 | 807.2 | 209.4 | 209.2 | 596.0 | 1016.4 | 18.7 | 30.1 |
| ?5.4 | 1308.3 | .... | .... | 0.3 | 0.6 | 0.3 | 0.6 | 752.5 | 787.6 | 276.4 | 472.8 | 1028.9 | 1260.4 | 16.2 | 47.3 |
| ?0.1 | 1687.4 | .... | .... | 0.3 | 172.3 | 0.3 | 172.3 | 788.9 | 906.9 | 557.0 | 573.9 | 1345.9 | 1490.8 | 44.0 | 24.3 |
| ?5.5 | 2031.9 | .... | .... | 177.1 | 156.8 | 177.1 | 156.8 | 926.5 | 1157.3 | 608.7 | 688.3 | 1545.2 | 1855.6 | 23.2 | 19.5 |
| ?0.8 | 1948.6 | .... | .... | 95.2 | 1.0 | 95.2 | 1.0 | 1296.2 | 1197.4 | 559.9 | 708.2 | 1866.1 | 1920.6 | 29.4 | 27.1 |

Statistical Summary, Apr.-May, 1947, pp. 33-4.

hange holdings were sold to the Foreign Exchange Control Board.

## ASSETS

| | SECURITIES | | | | | | | | | LOANS CANADA | | | | | | | |
|---|---|---|---|---|---|---|---|---|---|---|---|---|---|---|---|---|---|
| d ASH IN NADA | UNDER TWO YEARS | | OVER TWO YEARS | | OTHER | | TOTAL | | CALL | | CURRENT | | ABROAD | | TOTAL ASSETS | |
| D | M | D | M | D | M | D | M | D | M | D | M | D | M | D | M | D |
| 316 | 606 | 691 | 704 | 597 | 289 | 242 | 1599 | 1531 | 52 | 40 | 1115 | 1108 | 199 | 173 | 3715 | 3731 |
| 348 | 740 | 793 | 787 | 723 | 240 | 243 | 1766 | 1759 | 35 | 32 | 1114 | 1170 | 182 | 184 | 3910 | 4137 |
| 381 | 724 | 1262 | 920 | 739 | 237 | 292 | 1881 | 2293 | 34 | 31 | 1300 | 1168 | 191 | 187 | 4352 | 4767 |
| 463 | 1657 | 1664 | 715 | 963 | 317 | 312 | 2689 | 2940 | 24 | 48 | 1003 | 1157 | 193 | 196 | 4914 | 5609 |
| 541 | 1796 | 1941 | 1010 | 1288 | 349 | 382 | 3156 | 3611 | 41 | 92 | 982 | 1211 | 206 | 226 | 5589 | 6459 |
| 684 | 1878 | 1415 | 1326 | 2171 | 402 | 452 | 3606 | 4038 | 78 | 251 | 1094 | 1274 | 211 | 271 | 6249 | 7353 |
| 742 | 1671 | 1308 | 2028 | 2325 | 497 | 599 | 4197 | 4232 | 148 | 135 | 1181 | 1507 | 255 | 255 | 7193 | 7799 |

Statistical Summary, Apr.-May, 1947, pp. 35-6.

ve deposits; after that date, Bank of Canada notes and deposits.

TABLE XI–THE MONEY SUPPLY OF CANADA, 1940-1946[a]

(Month-end figures [March and December] in millions of dollars)

VOLUME OF CANADIAN MONEY

| | 1940 | | 1941 | | 1942 | | 1943 | | 1944 | | 1945 | | 1946 |
| --- | --- | --- | --- | --- | --- | --- | --- | --- | --- | --- | --- | --- | --- |
| | M | D | M | D | M | D | M | D | M | D | M | D | M |
| Notes Held by General Public: | | | | | | | | | | | | | |
| Bank of Canada | 164 | 262 | 285 | 380 | 410 | 573 | 610 | 751 | 798 | 897 | 945 | 966 | 978 |
| Chartered Banks | 92 | 80 | 83 | 71 | 74 | 60 | 55 | 42 | 40 | 33 | 31 | 25 | 24 |
| Total Notes | 256 | 342 | 368 | 451 | 484 | 633 | 665 | 893 | 838 | 930 | 966 | 991 | 1002 |
| Coinage[b] | 35 | 38 | 39 | 42 | 44 | 49 | 51 | 55 | 57 | 60 | 61 | 63 | 64 |
| Deposits with Chartered Banks: | | | | | | | | | | | | | |
| Public Demand | 750 | 1031 | 1050 | 1268 | 1144 | 1499 | 1659 | 1697 | 1892 | 1862 | 1935 | 2063 | 1985 |
| Public Notice | 1661 | 1641 | 1703 | 1669 | 1550 | 1673 | 1890 | 1948 | 2225 | 2423 | 2735 | 2865 | 3170 |
| Other Canadian[c] | 323 | 133 | 205 | 171 | 608 | 435 | 201 | 711 | 223 | 860 | 278 | 1021 | 431 |
| Total | 2734 | 2805 | 2958 | 3108 | 3302 | 3607 | 3750 | 4356 | 4340 | 5145 | 4938 | 5949 | 5586 |
| Deposits with Bank of Canada: Dominion Government and Other[d] | 59 | 23 | 25 | 84 | 125 | 79 | 46 | 52 | 88 | 59 | 71 | 206 | 238 |
| Total Volume of Money | 3084 | 3208 | 3390 | 3685 | 3955 | 4368 | 4512 | 5256 | 5323 | 6194 | 6036 | 7209 | 6890 |

[a]Data compiled from Bank of Canada, *Statistical Summary: 1946 Supplement.*

[b]March figures are approximations only.

[c]Variations in this item are accounted for mainly by variations in Dominion government deposits.

[d]Excludes chartered bank deposits with Bank of Canada, and deposits in foreign currencies.

## Changes in Volume of Canadian Money

| | 1940 F[a] | 1940 C[b] | 1941 F | 1941 C | 1942 F | 1942 C | 1943 F | 1943 C | 1944 F | 1944 C | 1945 F | 1945 C | 1946 F |
|---|---|---|---|---|---|---|---|---|---|---|---|---|---|
| **Notes Held by General Public:** | | | | | | | | | | | | | |
| Bank of Canada | 51 | 99 | 121 | 118 | 125 | 193 | 200 | 179 | 188 | 145 | 137 | 70 | 43 |
| Chartered Banks | -5 | -5 | -9 | -9 | -9 | -10 | -19 | -18 | -15 | -9 | -9 | -8 | -7 |
| Total Notes | 46 | 94 | 112 | 109 | 116 | 183 | 181 | 161 | 173 | 136 | 128 | 62 | 36 |
| Coinage | 3 | 4 | 4 | 4 | 5 | 7 | 7 | 6 | 6 | 5 | 4 | 3 | 3 |
| **Deposits with Chartered Banks:** | | | | | | | | | | | | | |
| Public Demand | 45 | 178 | 300 | 238 | 94 | 231 | 515 | 197 | 233 | 166 | 43 | 201 | 50 |
| Public Notice | -39 | -100 | 42 | 28 | -153 | 4 | 340 | 275 | 335 | 475 | 500 | 442 | 445 |
| Other Canadian | 190 | -123 | -118 | 38 | 403 | 264 | -407 | 276 | 22 | 149 | 55 | 161 | 153 |
| Total | 196 | -45 | 224 | 304 | 344 | 499 | 448 | 748 | 590 | 790 | 598 | 804 | 648 |
| **Deposits with Bank of Canada:** | | | | | | | | | | | | | |
| Dominion Government and Other | 32 | -42 | -34 | 61 | 100 | -5 | -79 | -26 | 42 | 6 | -17 | 147 | 167 |
| Total Volume of Money | 277 | 11 | 306 | 477 | 565 | 684 | 557 | 889 | 811 | 937 | 713 | 1016 | 854 |

[a] F indicates change during the fiscal year.

[b] C indicates change during the calendar year.

181

expansion of deposits based upon their purchases, both direct and indirect, of government securities. The demand for bank credit originated primarily with the government, the volume of commercial loans rising relatively little during World War II.[26] By the end of the war, the structure of Canadian bank deposits was closely related to the federal debt, a situation important in terms of its effects upon the future economic stability of the country.[27] Table XI summarizes the wartime increase in the supply of money in Canada.

The increase in the quantity of money during the early part of the war was attributable almost entirely to the government's adoption of a deliberately expansionist policy. Speaking early in the 1941 fiscal year, the Minister of Finance stated that with considerable unemployment still prevalent, the object of financial policy would be to ensure the diversion of as large a proportion as possible of the increasing national income to wartime ends, while at the same time, leaving sufficient stimulus to bring the country to full employment at the earliest possible time.[28] The monetary expansion was continued, since it was felt that under the existing circumstances inflationary results would not appear. The increase in real income up to this time had been such as to prevent inflationary pressures and it was felt that these results could be maintained for some little time longer.[29] As indicated in Table VII, both the Bank of Canada and the chartered banks made substantial cash purchases of new government securities. In addition, the banking system bought a small amount of the Second War Loan, the Bank of Canada providing about $19 million and the chartered banks $1 million. The sale of War Savings Certificates and Stamps and of non-interest-bearing certificates was introduced during this year. The last-mentioned security was made available for those persons who wished to provide funds without cost to the government for prosecuting the war. The government was anxious to tap even the smallest sources of savings effectively and regularly, since such funds represented, in large measure, allocations from current income. The sale of treasury bills to the Bank of Canada represented the net increase in their account outstanding, and was the first of only two occasions during the entire war when these securities were sold directly to the central bank.

The chief purpose of the $325 million subscribed by the Bank of Canada was to provide a loan to the Foreign Exchange Control Board, in order that it might purchase the gold reserves of the Bank of Canada, in accordance with the terms

---

[26]The chartered banks' current Canadian loans rose by approximately 20%, while their total assets almost doubled. The financing of private enterprise engaged in war production was accomplished in considerable measure through the use of internally accumulated reserves, and much additional financing of war industry was effected by the establishing of Crown corporations. The loaning of funds by government agencies to private business was adopted as a further means of financing war production.

[27]See Chapter X.    [28]See J. L. Ralston, *Budget Speech*, June 24, 1940, p. 5.

[29]This view did not pass unchallenged. For a summary of the economic objections voiced against a continuation of this policy see J. F. Parkinson, "Some Problems of War Finance in Canada" (*Canadian Journal of Economics and Political Science*). Vol. VI, 1940, 403-21.

of the Exchange Fund Order of April 13, 1940, and also that it might purchase the foreign exchange required to be sold to the Board by Canadian residents in accordance with the terms of the Foreign Exchange Acquisition Order of the same date.[30] Under the terms of the Exchange Fund Order, the Bank of Canada sold to the Foreign Exchange Control Board its gold holdings valued at $226 million. The minimum gold reserve requirements of the Bank were then temporarily suspended. Under the Foreign Exchange Acquisition Order, the Board also bought foreign exchange from the Bank to a Canadian dollar value of $27.7 million. Following the enactment of this latter order, the Bank of Canada's holdings of foreign exchange consisted almost entirely of sterling held for the account, either of the federal government or of the Foreign Exchange Control Board, in connection with its programme of repatriating securities from Britain. Such holdings represented in effect a short-term loan to the government, and their accumulation tended to expand chartered bank cash. To the extent that such a result was regarded as undesirable, it was forestalled either by the Bank's open-market sales or by a rise in government balances in the Bank. Reductions in the Bank's exchange holdings of course produced opposite effects.

The rapid rise in the government's cash requirements in fiscal 1941 related both to expenditures involved in furthering Canada's own direct war effort and to the financial assistance accorded to Allied countries.[31] This latter category included not only the repatriation of British-held securities but also substantial loans to the Foreign Exchange Control Board.[32] Non-war expenditures were substantially decreased during the year. Many of the new tax proposals did not involve immediate payment, but they reflected the intention of the government to place its chief reliance upon direct taxation as the source of increased revenues and to concentrate the burden upon the lower and middle income

[30]The original Canadian dollar resources of the Board consisted of the profit arising from the revaluation of the gold stock of the Bank of Canada in 1935, this profit being credited to an Exchange Fund. The Fund was not operative until its proceeds were transferred to the Foreign Exchange Control Board at the time of its inception.

[31]See Table VI. Total cash requirements were $1,719 million, of which one-half was covered by revenue, one-half by borrowing. These requirements now represented about one-quarter of Canada's rapidly expanding gross national expenditure, thereby reflecting the increased tempo of the war effort after mid-1940, when for the first time the real dimensions of World War II were becoming apparent.

[32]British government expenditures within Canada contributed appreciably to the financial needs of the latter country. From the outbreak of the war to the end of February, 1942, the sterling area's net deficit of Canadian dollars had risen to $1,770 million and had been financed in three ways. In increasing order of importance, these were gold payments from the United Kingdom to Canada, repatriation of Canadian securities held in the United Kingdom and the accumulation of sterling balances in the Foreign Exchange Board in London. This last method was by far the most important of the three, and the accumulated sterling balances had reached $1,100 million by March 31, 1942. Canada's other major balance of payments problem, that of maintaining an adequate stock of United States dollars, became extremely difficult in the first one and one-half years of the war, and this in fact would have become impossible except for arrangements under the Hyde Park agreement of April, 1941, after which the urgency of this exchange problem began to recede.

groups. For reasons both of equity and expediency the increases in direct commodity taxes were to be minimized.[33]

Deliberate monetary expansion was desirable only as an interim technique, and as the level of employment continued to rise, the government soon resorted to increasingly restrictive fiscal measures as its major weapon for attacking insistent inflationary pressures. The pay-as-you-go policy was introduced, in that to the extent that tax revenues fell short of meeting the government's increasing financial needs, public borrowing from the current income of the moderate and lower income groups was to be the main objective. The commercial banks were viewed as a secondary source of borrowing, with the Bank of Canada to be approached as a last resort in meeting the residual needs of war finance.

Considering the entire period from the outbreak of war to March 31, 1941, price rises were irregular and of moderate proportions. The index of wholesale prices rose from 100 (September, 1939) to 118.9, the cost-of-living index from 100 to 107.3.[34] It was because of the appearance of a much more inflationary trend in the months immediately following that the government introduced an "over-all" price ceiling in December, 1941, and discarded expansionist finance as a deliberate policy.[35] The desired increases in employment had been substantially effected and given the government's decision to reject the use of monetary policy as a weapon against inflation, increasingly restrictive fiscal measures became essential, and the pay-as-you-go policy was pushed to the limits of its practicability. From this time forward, the growing demands of the war effort necessitated an increasing reallocation of resources from civilian to military uses. Until this time, civilian consumption had shown a substantial increase as war production expanded. Late in 1941, the Minister of Finance noted that "we too have now come to the stage where the choice between guns and butter must affect the average man and woman in Canada. We must accept a temporary reduction in our average standard of living if we are to achieve the necessary standard of fighting. We cannot hope to live as well as most of us are used to living and fight a total war at the same time."[36]

The continued expansion of the Canadian war economy was reflected by the

[33]See J. L. Ralston, *Budget Speech*, June 24, 1940. The chief tax measures included a 10 per cent war-exchange tax on all imports from non-Empire countries, a major objective being the conservation of exchange, and to restrict civilian production in that industry, a new excess profits tax on industry, being 12 per cent of total profits or 75 per cent of excess profits, whichever was the greater; sharp increases in personal income taxes through a general upward revision of rates and a lowering of exemptions; a new flat-rate national defence tax of 2 per cent or 3 per cent, according to one's status and income; substantial increases in excise levies on various "luxuries". The only significant tariff changes were those designed to offset the additional excise taxes.
For the changing wartime distribution of tax collections, see the Bank of Canada, *Statistical Summary*, April-May, 1947, p. 45.
[34]Report to the Wartime Prices and Trade Board (Ottawa: 1943), p. 68.
[35]For a discussion of the developments of wartime price controls, see K. W. Taylor "Canadian Wartime Price Controls, 1941-46" (*Canadian Journal of Economics and Political Science*, Vol. XIII, 1947, pp. 81-8).   [36]See J. L. Ilsley, *Halifax Speech*, Oct. 6, 1941.

tremendous increase in the government's cash requirements in successive fiscal years, these requirements reaching a peak of $5,779 million (Table VI) in fiscal 1944. By this latter period, approximately one-half of gross national expenditure was being channelled to war production, with not quite one-half of the required funds being obtained from taxation (Table VI). In seeking to establish higher levels of taxation, serious difficulties soon arose from the lack of uniformity among the tax systems employed by the several provinces. The federal government sought to replace the great variety of provincial income taxes, both corporate and personal, with a few, clear-cut heavy federal levies, and a temporary agreement was reached with the provinces in 1942 whereby, in consideration of a pre-determined basis of remuneration, they agreed to vacate the personal and corporate income tax fields for the duration of the war.[37] The federal authorities thereby gained exclusive jurisdiction in these fields, and the pay-as-you-go policy of war finance was soon pushed to what was regarded as the limits of its practicability.[38] Wartime tax yields were rapidly expended, as noted earlier, both by the introduction of new taxes and by sharp increases in the rates of existing taxes.[39]

Beginning in fiscal 1942, funded borrowing operations reflected the decision of the government to abandon deliberate monetary expansion (Table VII). Henceforth, the major appeals for borrowed funds were directed to the general public (i.e., to non-banking sources), in an effort to channel a steadily increasing proportion of the rising national income to war purposes.[40] The instruments employed in these appeals were the periodic War and Victory Loans, War Savings Certificates and War Savings Stamps. It was at this time that the semi-annual Victory Loan appeals were launched (Table VII), and the use of il-

[37]See J. L. Ilsley, *Budget Speech*, June 23, 1942, p. 3.
[38]See J. L. Ilsley, *London Speech*, August 26, 1942.
[39]For a discussion of the tax measures introduced in the successive wartime budgets, see R. Craig McIvor, "Canadian Wartime Fiscal Policy, 1939-1946", *Canadian Journal of Economics and Political Science*, XIV, 1948, pp. 62-93. In fiscal 1942, substantial increases occurred in the personal and excess profits taxes, and federal succession duties appeared for the first time. In the 1943 budget, the personal income tax was again the chief instrument employed in gaining additional revenue, when a refundable "compulsory savings" feature was introduced for the first time. Wartime income taxation, both personal and corporate, reached its highest level in this budget, and in subsequent years, tax proposals were aimed largely at improving administration and removing inequities.
[40]The only cash obtained directly from the banking system in fiscal 1942 was a small $7 million subscription to the First Victory Loan by the chartered banks. But in fiscal 1943, despite the floating of the largest (Third) wartime Victory Loan to date, the rapid rise in cash requirements necessitated heavy reliance upon the banks. Direct borrowing from the chartered banks was confined to a new type of instrument, the Deposit Certificate, issued periodically with a twenty-six weeks' maturity, and bearing interest at ¾ of 1 per cent. This instrument provided the government with funds in the intervals between its periodic public loan campaigns, and became the major instrument in bank borrowing after this time. Coupled with cash sales to the Bank of Canada, the government's borrowing from the banking system exceeded $1 billion (Table VII). In the following year when the Fourth and Fifth Victory Loans were sold to the general public, direct borrowing from the banks was relatively small. This was also substantially true in 1944-5.

liquid Deposit Certificates introduced to minimize the inflationary consequences of the government's increasing need for short-term funds. The combined effect of these developments was to create semi-annual "peaks" in the volume of chartered bank loans. The Bank of Canada regularly accommodated the increase in deposits by open-market purchases, but the need for later compensating action was obviated by the steady expansion of the Bank's note circulation, as explained above, which drained reserves from the chartered banks.

The Bank of Canada's holdings of foreign currency, principally sterling balances, increased by $207 million (Table IX). This asset represented purchases from the Foreign Exchange Control Board on a temporary basis, in order to assist the Board in financing its sterling balances. These purchases tended to increase the cash reserves of the chartered banks, but in each instance the Bank of Canada moved to reduce the expansionist effects by appropriate open-market operations.[41] The money supply increased by $560 million, or by approximately 17 per cent during the 1942 fiscal year, the most important bases being the continued expansion of the Bank of Canada's active note circulation, and a very substantial rise in federal government balances, particularly with the Bank of Canada. The official index of the physical volume of business showed an increase of 33 per cent during 1941. This index was of course heavily influenced by the output of goods not available for civilian consumption. The index of wholesale prices had risen from 118.9 to 129.5, and that of the cost of living from 107.3 to 114.9 during the last nine months of 1942.[42] It was evident that not only must fiscal measures become more restrictive but also that a new system of price control was needed to provide greater support than that afforded by the earlier selective approach, if inflation were to be kept within bounds in subsequent periods when shifts in production, rather than over-all increases, would become increasingly important.

Cash requirements in fiscal 1943 had increased by 60 per cent from the preceding period, and amounted to $4,745 million. This increase was attributable principally to a billion-dollar gift to the United Kingdom and to greatly increased expenditures by the Canadian army. Confronted by the necessity for raising an ever-increasing volume of funds, the Minister of Finance stated that he had inevitably come to the clear decision that "proposals in this budget must include measures to increase our revenues within the fiscal year substantially, at least to the point where our dependence on borrowing will be more nearly within the limits of our current saving; they must provide for increased saving, both corporate and personal; they must also include measures to ensure that the task of contributing to the required increase in current saving is more widely and equitably distributed."[43] The year's financing was such that taxation and other

---

[41]See the Bank of Canada, *Annual Report*, 1942, pp. 6-7.
[42]*Report of the Wartime Prices and Trade Board*, pp. 112-15.
[43]J. L. Ilsley, *Budget Speech*, June 23, 1942, p. 8.

## Table XII—General Public Holdings of Certain Liquid Assets[a]
(in millions of dollars)

| | CURRENCY OUTSIDE BANKS | ACTIVE CHARTERED BANK DEPOSITS | TOTAL CURRENCY PLUS ACTIVE BANK DEPOSITS | INACTIVE BANK DEPOSITS | TOTAL CURRENCY PLUS TOTAL BANK DEPOSITS | CANADIAN GOVERNMENT SECURITIES—DIRECT AND GUARANTEED | TOTAL OF CERTAIN LIQUID ASSETS |
|---|---|---|---|---|---|---|---|
| 1939 | 281 | 1089 | 1370 | 1544 | 2914 | 3279 | 6193 |
| 1940 | 380 | 1184 | 1564 | 1438 | 3002 | 3670 | 6672 |
| 1941 | 493 | 1409 | 1902 | 1433 | 3335 | 4162 | 7497 |
| 1942 | 682 | 1667 | 2349 | 1436 | 3785 | 5344 | 9129 |
| 1943 | 848 | 1877 | 2725 | 1654 | 4379 | 7184 | 11563 |
| 1944 | 990 | 2163 | 3153 | 2060 | 5213 | 9131 | 14344 |
| 1945 | 1054 | 2459 | 3513 | 2391 | 5904 | 11310 | 17214 |
| 1946 | 1096 | 2900 | 3996 | 2856 | 6852 | 11175 | 18027 |

## General Public Holdings of Certain Liquid Assets—Related Factors[a]

| | CHARTERED BANKS' CANADIAN LOANS AND NON-GOVERNMENT SECURITIES | | | BANK OF CANADA GOLD AND EXCHANGE HOLDINGS | ALL OTHER (NET) | TOTAL | CANADIAN GOVERNMENT DEBT (LESS GOVERNMENT DEPOSITS & HOLDINGS OF GOVERNMENT ACCOUNTS) | | | TOTAL OF RELATED FACTORS |
|---|---|---|---|---|---|---|---|---|---|---|
| | | | | | | | Held by | | |
| | Canadian Loans | Other Securities | Total | | | | Net Total | General Public | Banks | |
| 1939 | 1141 | 626 | 1767 | 290 | —176 | 1881 | 4312 | 3279 | 1033 | 6193 |
| 1940 | 1148 | 572 | 1720 | 38 | —205 | 1553 | 5118 | 3670 | 1448 | 6672 |
| 1941 | 1201 | 518 | 1719 | 201 | —209 | 1711 | 5785 | 4162 | 1623 | 7497 |
| 1942 | 1084 | 487 | 1570 | 1 | —213 | 1357 | 7772 | 5344 | 2428 | 9129 |
| 1943 | 1015 | 443 | 1459 | ...... | —247 | 1213 | 10350 | 7184 | 3167 | 11563 |
| 1944 | 1118 | 465 | 1583 | ...... | —248 | 1335 | 13009 | 9131 | 3878 | 14344 |
| 1945 | 1292 | 525 | 1817 | ...... | —258 | 1559 | 15656 | 11310 | 4346 | 17214 |
| 1946 | 1643 | 639 | 2282 | ...... | —285 | 1997 | 16030 | 11175 | 4855 | 18027 |

[a]Data based on Bank of Canada Research Memorandum, General Public Holdings of Certain Liquid Assets, March, 1953.

revenues provided only 44 per cent of the greatly expanded cash requirements, despite the fact that the pay-as-you-go policy was being pushed to the limits of practicability. Renewed emphasis was placed upon the fact that fiscal policy constituted just one phase of the battle against inflation, others being the price-ceiling, the control and rationing of supplies and the direction of man-power, all four of which were complementary rather than alternative measures.

At the end of the fiscal year, the direct unmatured funded debt was more than twice as great as at the beginning of the war, but the proportion payable in foreign markets had steadily declined. Repatriation of direct debt was actually a short-lived means of providing the sterling area with appreciable quantities of Canadian dollars, and for obvious reasons, the receipt of British gold was likewise unimportant. The accumulation of sterling balances was the major technique, subsequently supplemented by outright gifts. During fiscal 1943, an interest-free loan of $700 million represented the means by which the Foreign Exchange Control Board disposed of the bulk of the sterling balances which it had accumulated up to that time.[44] Reviewing the year's fiscal operations, the Minister of Finance pointed to the undesirability of such heavy bank borrowing, and to the corresponding need for greater loans from current savings in succeeding periods.[45]

In connection with the interest-free loan to Britain, the Bank of Canada sold to the Foreign Exchange Control Board exchange which it had purchased earlier on a temporary basis. To counteract the consequent reduction in chartered bank reserves, and also to provide for the increase in chartered bank liabilities arising from their purchases of Deposit Certificates after the beginning of July, the Bank engaged in open-market buying, and its net security holdings increased substantially during the fiscal year (Table IX). The increase in the chartered banks' investments was likewise largely attributable to their purchases of these Deposit Certificates. By contrast, the volume of their Canadian loans showed a marked decline for the first time since the beginning of the war (Table X). The supply of money increased by approximately 14 per cent, while the index of the physical volume of production rose by 22 per cent in calendar year 1942. In contrast to the preceding year, the wholesale price index rose relatively little in 1942, from 129.5 to 134.2, while that of the cost of living rose from 114.9 to 117.9.[46] It was therefore apparent that despite the much greater dependence upon bank borrowing during fiscal year 1943, the anti-inflation programme had been somewhat more successful than in the preceding period. There is little doubt that much of the explanation is to be found in the increased support derived from the over-all price control policy which had been introduced in December, 1941.

The government's cash requirements reached a peak of $5,633 million in fiscal 1944. Noting that this figure was 19 per cent greater than that of the

[44]See Foreign Exchange Control Board, *Report to the Minister of Finance*, p. 34.
[45]See J. L. Ilsley, *Budget Speech*, Mar. 2, 1943, p. 6, and Bank of Canada, *Annual Report*, Feb. 9, 1943, p. 10.   [46]*Report of the Wartime Prices and Trade Board*, pp. 112-15.

preceding period, and recalling the recent substantial dependence upon bank borrowing, the Minister of Finance observed that inflationary forces could be held in check "only by the rigour of our existing taxation, by the willingness of Canadians to save on an unprecedented scale, and by our price control and wage control".[47] By this time, government expenditures involved a diversion of one-half of the gross national expenditure, but despite this high proportion taxation provided 47 per cent of the year's funds.[48] The unmatured funded debt rose by almost $3 billion as wartime financial needs reached a peak but, in contrast to the preceding period, the amount of new funds required from the banking system was small. The major method adopted in financing the sterling area's deficit of Canadian dollars was the establishment of the Canadian Mutual Aid Board, under whose jurisdiction an appropriation of $1 billion was made available to the United Nations, in order to supply them with materials needed for the effective prosecution of the war.[49] By the end of the fiscal year, more than nine-tenths of the appropriation had been used. The British government reduced slightly the unpaid balance of its $700 million loan from Canada by providing the Canadian government with United States dollars in the amount of $40 million Canadian.

For the first time since the establishment of the Bank of Canada, its rediscount rate was changed, in February, 1944, being reduced from 2½ per cent to 1½ per cent. Since rediscount facilities were seldom used by the chartered banks, the reduction was not of immediate consequence, and its main object was to indicate the Bank's intention of continuing after the war its easy-money policy which had brought about the existing levels of interest rates.[50]

[47]J. L. Ilsley, *Budget Speech*, March 2, 1943, p. 1. Factors contributing to the inflationary pressure, other than monetary expansion, included a state of full employment, a continuing decline in the output of consumers' goods, fewer and higher-cost imports, and widespread cost-price selling-price squeezes.

[48]In the course of discussing his various sources of revenue, the following comment by the Minister of Finance was of interest: "The customs tariff has fallen from the high position it has previously held as an instrument of fiscal and economic policy. Under the circumstances of war, the tariff has little effect except as a producer of revenue. The scope and direction of trade are now governed by the considerations of supply, transportation and enemy action and not by the tariff. . . . There will again, however, be a time when the tariff will be an important instrument of policy and when this country will have to decide whether it will play its part with other countries which are prepared to help in freeing the world's trade, in enlarging markets, and in promoting the full and effective use of the world's resources".

[49]See The War Appropriation (United Nations Mutual Aid) Act, May 20, 1943.

[50]Bank of Canada, *Annual Report*, Feb. 10, 1944, pp. 5-6. Following this move, the Bank launched an open-market buying programme which enabled the chartered banks, through expanded cash reserves, likewise to purchase securities on a substantial scale. In conformity with the reduction of the Bank's rediscount rate, effective bond yields declined. The soundness of this policy is questioned at a later point, its main effect being that of adding to the already serious inflationary pressures in the economy.

In connection with this attempt of the Bank to stabilize yields at lower than wartime levels, a recent observer expresses similar misgivings, in the comment that "Even granting that neither the actually smooth transition nor the subsequent inflation could possibly have been foreseen, it seems that the Bank erred on the side of too great monetary expansion". See E. P. Neufeld, *Bank of Canada Operations, 1935-1954* (Toronto: University of Toronto Press), 1955, p. 98.

Despite the relatively small amount of cash obtained from the banking system through the sale of new issues, the increase in the supply of money, approximately 18%, was one of the greatest of any wartime fiscal year. This is explained by the banking system's substantial acquisitions of outstanding securities in the intervals between the periodic public loan campaigns. A rough measure of these re-purchases may be obtained from Table IX and Table X, if from the increase in the banks' holdings of government securities their direct purchases at time of issue (Table VII) are deducted. An alternative indication of their volume is furnished by the fact that whereas the banking system's direct purchases represented approximately 13 per cent of the wartime increase in the funded debt, the National War Finance Committee estimated that when consideration was given to securities transactions *after* their original marketing, the banking system held almost 30 per cent of the wartime increase in this debt. Despite continuing monetary expansion in conjunction with a growing scarcity of civilian goods and services, the wholesale price index moved only from 134.2 to 141.8, and the cost-of-living index from 117.9 to 118.4 in the 1943 calendar year.[51] Reviewing the economic developments during this period, the government again stressed the contribution which price- and wage-control, in supplementing fiscal policy, had made to the minimizing of inflation in a period when the financial requirements of the government had reached a maximum.

When introducing his budget for the fiscal year 1945, the Minister of Finance noted that the period of the most extensive Allied military action had already begun, a fact which prevented any immediate appreciable reduction in the outlays of the Canadian government. In fact, it was stated that there was a strong possibility that the budgetary deficit for the fiscal year would be greater than for the year just past.[52] The total cash requirements of $5.6 billion were only 1 per cent lower than those of the preceding year, and taxes and other revenues provided 48 per cent of the total. The 1944 gross national product had reached a wartime peak of $11.9 billion, of which the government's cash requirements represented about 48%.[53]

The year's fiscal measures were guided by four basic considerations. These included the magnitude of cash requirements, the urgent need for encouraging a supreme productive effort in view of the scope of military operations which were approaching their climax, the desire to remove certain anomalies and

---

[51]*Report of the Wartime Prices and Trade Board*, pp. 68-70.

[52]The term "budgetary deficit" is used to indicate the increase in net debt, hence does not represent the amount of the government's borrowing needs. This latter amount is equal to total cash requirements less total revenues, and is known as the "cash deficiency". In the 1944 fiscal year, the cash deficiency was 10 per cent higher than the budgetary deficit, but in three of the earlier years, when repatriation and the accumulation of sterling balances was proceeding on a large scale, the cash deficiency was more than double the budgetary deficit. For the war period to the end of fiscal year 1944, the cash deficiency was 50 per cent greater than the budgetary deficit.

[53]Bank of Canada, *Statistical Summary, 1946 Supplement*, p. 64. See Table V and VI.

cases of particular hardship arising from the high levels of taxation, and finally the wish to clarify post-war fiscal policy in order that business might have some measure of certainty in planning reconversion.

The increase in the supply of money, although appreciably smaller than in the preceding fiscal year (Table XI) nevertheless exceeded 13 per cent. That the economy had reached the limits of its productive capacity was indicated by the fact that the index of the physical volume of business rose only one point from 236 to 237 in the 1944 calendar year. The cost-of-living index showed a fractional decline, and that of wholesale prices was unchanged.[54] The government offered a very optimistic interpretation of its success in combating inflation as it reviewed the events of 1944, and not without some reason, although there was little doubt that increased difficulties would present themselves in the succeeding period, when some of the unusually favourable circumstances which had prevailed in 1944 might not again be present, and when other inflationary pressures would be increasingly severe.[55]

Although the military operations of World War II ended in August, 1945, the budget for the 1946 fiscal year was essentially a war measure, and for that reason, its effects upon monetary expansion are included in this survey of Canada's wartime fiscal policy. At the same time, it was a peacetime measure, inasmuch as ". . . its effects on employment and income must be accepted as of major importance".[56] Its measures were therefore designed not only to meet the year's financial requirements, but also to facilitate an orderly process of reconversion, and the government therefore believed it appropriate to ease the burden of wartime taxation.[57] The basic feature of the budget was therefore the first appreciable decline from the highest levels of wartime taxation, leaving a somewhat larger deficit to be financed by borrowing. The government's cash requirements fell by only 7 per cent and of a total of some $5.3 billion, taxation provided 54 per cent.[58] The government was now spending 46 per cent of national income which had declined slightly to $11.4 billion in 1945.[59]

The Eighth and Ninth Victory Loans provided more than $3½ billion from the general public (Table VII), an amount which considerably exceeded that which was obtained in any other fiscal year. Not only was no direct borrowing

[54]*Report of the Wartime Prices and Trade Board* (Ottawa, 1945), pp. 68-80.
[55]*Ibid.*, pp. 3-4.
[56]J. L. Ilsley, *Budget Speech*, Oct. 12, 1945, pp. 3-4.
[57]See *ibid.*, pp. 6, 13.
[58]Bank of Canada, *Statistical Summary*, June-July, 1946, pp. 51-2. See Table VI.
[59]The principal tax modifications included the removal of the 10 per cent war exchange tax on all imports from non-Empire countries; the removal of the sales tax from machinery and apparatus which was to be used "directly" in the process of manufacture or production; the abolition of the refundable portion of the excess profits tax, and reduction of the tax rate to 60 per cent; an increase in the minimum "standard" profit of all firms from $5,000 to $15,000; a flat-rate reduction of 16 per cent in the personal income tax; the modification of the taxation of annuities and pensions, and the reduction of duties in the event of "quick" succession.

effected from the banking system but a substantial decrease occurred in the chartered banks' holdings of deposit certificates (Table VII).[60] However, the banks continued indirectly to absorb government securities on a substantial scale (Tables IX, X), and the increase in the supply of money was the greatest that occurred during the war. The index of the physical volume of business declined, falling from 237 to 213 during 1945. The wholesale price index rose from 141.8 to 143.5, and that of the cost of living from 117.6 to 119.1 in the same interval. This latter increase was the greatest indicated by official sources since 1942.[61] The Minister of Finance warned against the continuing inflationary pressures, the presence of which was indicated by these price trends, and pointed to the undiminished need for sound fiscal policy supported by continued direct controls, if these pressures were not to inflict serious damage upon the post-war economy in the very critical period of reconversion.

We may now summarize briefly the borrowing operations of the Canadian government between September, 1939, and March 31, 1946. The total amount of new cash (total borrowings less conversions and renewals) raised within Canada amounted to $14,832 million. Of this total, the general public, i.e., sources other than the chartered banks and the Bank of Canada, provided $12,541 million. Excluding the purchase of treasury bills, the Bank of Canada provided $444 million, and the chartered banks $1,551 million. The net increase in treasury bills outstanding was $296 million.[62] In terms of percentages, the general public provided 85 per cent of all new funds, the Bank of Canada 3 per cent and the chartered banks 10 per cent. The sale of treasury bills by public tender, of whose ownership no detailed figures are available, provided the remaining 2 per cent. Such was the distribution of original purchases.[63] On only two occasions was borrowing undertaken in the New York market, and in each case the proceeds were used there to assist in retiring larger maturing issues. The total of these borrowings was small, and there were no funded borrowing operations in the London market.

It should be recognized that while the general public provided 85 per cent of all new funds at the time of original sales of securities, the chartered banks were indirectly responsible for a considerable part of those subscriptions. Bank credit was particularly important in the temporary financing of bond purchases by various investors, both in connection with official instalment plans and with

[60]The rate on these obligations was reduced to five-eighths of 1 per cent on March 4, 1946. At the same time, the government reached an agreement with the chartered banks which limited their holdings of government securities, other than very short-term securities, to 90 per cent of Canadian savings deposits. See the *Canadian Banker*, 1946, p. 32.

[61]The difficulties associated with maintaining a realistic cost-of-living index in wartime were generally recognized. Few persons accepted the official figures as indicating the realities of the situation.

[62]*Public Accounts*, 1945, p. lii. See also J. L. Ilsley, *Appendix to the Budget*, 1946-7, p. 41.

[63]For the estimated distribution of Canada's direct and guaranteed funded debt at the end of each wartime year, see Table XIII.

TABLE XIII–SIZE AND ESTIMATED DISTRIBUTION OF THE CANADIAN
DIRECT AND GUARANTEED FUNDED DEBT[a]
(in millions of dollars, as of December 31)

| | 1939 | 1940 | 1941 | 1942 | 1943 | 1944 | 1945 |
|---|---|---|---|---|---|---|---|
| *Outstanding Debt* | | | | | | | |
| 1. Direct Funded Debt | | | | | | | |
| (a) Unmatured: | | | | | | | |
|     Special Banking Issues | 470 | 785 | 1075 | 1708 | 2243 | 2491 | 1796 |
|     Other Issues | 2984 | 3352 | 3924 | 5771 | 8382 | 11277 | 15044 |
| (b) Matured and Out- | | | | | | | |
|     standing | 4 | 7 | 14 | 4 | 27 | 22 | 15 |
| 2. Guaranteed Funded Debt | 1085 | 1031 | 971 | 772 | 715 | 608 | 556 |
| 3. Total Debt Outstanding | 4543 | 5175 | 5984 | 8255 | 11367 | 14398 | 17411 |
| 4. Exchange Rate Adjustment | 52 | 64 | 82 | 93 | 80 | 73 | 68 |
| 5. Adjusted Total Debt Out- | | | | | | | |
|     standing | 4595 | 5239 | 6066 | 8348 | 11447 | 14471 | 17479 |
| *Estimated Distribution* | | | | | | | |
| 1. Bank of Canada | 229 | 572 | 605 | 1012 | 1256 | 1477 | 1842 |
| 2. Chartered Banks | 949 | 908 | 1166 | 1782[b] | 2508[b] | 3121[b] | 3506[b] |
|     Total Bank-Owned Debt | 1178 | 1480 | 1771 | 2794 | 3764 | 4598 | 5348 |
| 3. Government Accounts | 138 | 89 | 133 | 210 | 499 | 742 | 821 |
| 4. General Public: | | | | | | | |
|     Non-Resident | 1398 | 1276 | 1109 | 995 | 1003 | 1035 | 1144 |
|     *Resident Corporate:* | | | | | | | |
|       Refundable Tax | ........ | ........ | ........ | ........ | 20 | 60 | 184 |
|       Financial Institutions | 587 | 667 | 823 | 1073 | 1424 | 1818 | 2232 |
|       Non-Financial Cor- | | | | | | | |
|       porations | 202 | 360 | 455 | 602 | 932 | 1240 | 1195 |
|       Governments: | | | | | | | |
|         Provincial | 68 | 72 | 88 | 123 | 172 | 243 | 312 |
|         Municipal | 62 | 62 | 67 | 72 | 96 | 96 | 124 |
|     Total Resident Corporate | 919 | 1161 | 1433 | 1870 | 2644 | 3457 | 4047 |
|     Resident Non-Corporate | 962 | 1233 | 1620 | 2479 | 3537 | 4639 | 6119 |
|     Total General Public- | | | | | | | |
|       Owned Debt | 3279 | 3670 | 4162 | 5344[b] | 7184[b] | 9131[b] | 13310[b] |
| 5. Total Debt Outstanding | 4595 | 5239 | 6066 | 8348 | 11447 | 14471 | 17479 |

[a]Data based on Bank of Canada Research Memorandum, "General Public Holdings of Certain Liquid Assets".

[b]Chartered bank temporary advances to the general public in connection with Victory Loan issues are included in chartered bank holdings of government securities, and deducted from holdings of the general public.

deferred deliveries and other arrangements. Of the total known credit provided for the public's purchases of bonds, the amount supplied by the commercial banks represented perhaps 95 per cent.[64] The known credit averaged approxi-

[64]National War Finance Committee, *Dominion Government Public Borrowing*, p. 16.

mately one-quarter of the purchase price of the various wartime issues, but in all cases, was liquidated before a succeeding issue was floated.

In terms of the functions of war finance, it is instructive to compare the accomplishments of the Canadian government in two world wars.[65] With regard to raising the necessary funds, the sources employed in World War II represent a marked contrast to those of the earlier period. On that occasion, almost the entire costs of the war were met by borrowing, since taxation and other revenues failed to provide sufficient cash to take care of the government's non-war outlays, including capital expenditures. Furthermore, borrowing from foreign sources was possible in the early stages of the war, although changing circumstances operated to necessitate increasing dependence upon the domestic market until it finally became almost the sole source of funds, and by far the more important source over the war period as a whole. The inadequacy of tax revenues can be explained partly by the undeveloped state of the Canadian tax system in 1914, in which customs duties, the major source of revenue, were supplemented by excise revenues. Under such circumstances, any rapid expansion of revenues would have been impossible, but it is important to note that the government's philosophy was such that tax increases were considered neither economically nor politically desirable, even if they had been possible.

The entire programme of war finance was developed from essentially faulty premises, a criticism which can scarcely be maintained with reference to the approach in World War II. Finding itself forced back upon a hitherto untried domestic market, the government's World War I borrowing involved the extensive use of bank credit, a circumstance directly related to another function of war finance, that of assisting in the efficient allocation of resources to war production. The value of national income produced about doubled between 1914 and 1919, but the increase in real output produced during that period was almost certainly less than 10 per cent.[66] The general order of these figures suggests the degree to which inflationary developments contributed to the rise in money incomes, and to which the money costs of carrying on the war were increased. It has been shown, however, that it was this inflation which made possible the large-scale domestic public borrowing which was effected in the later stages of the war, prompting the comment that the financial programme was "more expedient than equitable".[67] Touching upon the third function of war finance, it is clear that considerations of equity were notably absent in the earlier period. In World War II, where government expenditures rose to one-half of the national

---

[65]For a concise account of the early experience, see J. J. Deutsch, "War Finance and the Canadian Economy, 1914-1920" (*Canadian Journal of Economics and Political Science*, Vol. VI. 1940). The contributions of the banking system to war finance are best described by C. A. Curtis, "The Canadian Banks of War Finance" (in *Contributions to Canadian Economics*, Toronto, 1931), III. See also F. A. Knox, "Canadian War Finance and the Balance of Payments, 1914-18" (*Canadian Journal of Economics and Political Science*, vol. VI, 1940).
[66]Deutsch, "War Finance and the Canadian Economy", especially pp. 530, 532.
[67]*Ibid.*

income, the adoption of policies pursued in the earlier period would have been intolerable.

As a consequence of the World War I experience, the Canadian government in 1939 was determined to avoid such heavy reliance upon borrowing as a means of financing the recent conflict. To this end, it took active steps to condition the public to the possibility of a long and costly war. In general, it may be said that the whole economic approach to the problem of financing World War II was sounder than in the earlier period, and that the monetary-fiscal techniques available for implementing the programme were much better developed.

It has already been emphasized that in determining the particular policies of war finance that are to be adopted, the government necessarily becomes involved not only in considerations of economics but also of politics. While the Minister of Finance may have little doubt as to the technically desirable course of action under given circumstances, his actions will be modified in varying degrees by considerations of political expediency and public acceptability. One important function of wartime propaganda thus becomes that of educating the public to accept and support, in as large measure as possible, the economic programme which past experience has indicated as being essential to the most effective prosecution of the war. The success of the Canadian experience was in no small measure a result of the persistent campaign which presented to the great majority of the citizens, in clear and simple terms, the need for the stringent measures which were enacted, and which were generally supported, as the war effort developed.

With the early and continued insistence of the government upon a basic pay-as-you-go policy which was to be pursued to the limits of its practicability, there will be general agreement. In the early months of the war, this policy was held in abeyance while a deliberate programme of monetary expansion was undertaken, in order to absorb the slack which was present in the Canadian economy at the outbreak of the war. While this programme was also undoubtedly justified, there is evidence that it was not without its inflationary effects, despite government predictions to the contrary. Relatively rapid rises in price levels occurred during the first two years of the war, suggesting that the expansionist policy had been pursued somewhat beyond desirable limits. While full employment was the objective, such an area is impossible to define, and the inflationary effects of bottle-necks which developed in various segments of the economy were undoubtedly underestimated. The cessation of deliberate monetary expansion and the adoption of an over-all price ceiling late in 1941 coincided with a pronounced check to the price increases, a check which cannot be explained, however, completely in terms of these two factors.[68]

In its efforts to derive the greatest possible proportion of its cash requirements

[68]See Benjamin H. Higgins, *Canada's Financial System in War* (New York, 1944). The introduction of consumer rationing, the increased use of subsidies and the introduction of higher income taxes were additional factors to be considered.

from taxation, the government effected a substantial expansion and improvement of the federal tax system. The magnitude of the increase in tax revenues may be explained in terms of the increase in the national income, the increase in the rates of existing taxes, and the addition of new taxes to the system. The wartime emphasis upon direct taxation served to lessen the regressiveness of the system as a whole. An additional effect of the programme of war finance was to redistribute the national income in favour of the wage-earning and agricultural classes.[69]

The expansion of tax revenues was consistently based upon the ability-to-pay principle, a matter of basic importance in a situation where such a large part of the national income was required in financing the war effort. The difficulties of administering the tax programme on such a basis were increased by the fact that Canada has a high proportion of small incomes, and that in her primarily agricultural economy a substantial amount of income is received in kind, rendering the calculation of the net income of the farming population next to impossible.[70] The additional problem presented by the particular allocation of taxing powers between the federal and the provincial governments was resolved for the duration of the war when the provinces agreed to vacate the fields of personal and corporate income taxation, in return for fixed payments from the federal government. However, the Canadian tax system as a whole, having been developed in large measure through fiscal and political expediency, left much to be desired as a weapon of wartime fiscal policy. In expanding the system to provide for enormously expanded wartime financial requirements, the government wisely concentrated its efforts upon the greater use of direct taxation, since the system was already seriously regressive. The major sources of wartime tax revenues were the yields from personal income, corporation income and excess profits taxes, and succession duties.

In attempting to finance as large a part of its war expenditures as possible on a pay-as-you-go basis, the government can scarcely be charged with failing to utilize the foregoing sources of revenue to the limits of their practicability. For the entire war period, the personal income tax and the corporation income tax including excess profits tax yielded approximately equal revenue. In both instances, the highest rates of taxation were introduced in the 1942 budget, and were continued substantially unchanged through 1945. The government's self-

[69]See Bank of Canada, *Statistical Summary, 1946 Supplement*, pp. 102-3, 107. The index of the farm price of agricultural products rose from 91.8 in 1939 to 176.5 in 1945 (1935-9=100). Using the same base, farm operating costs rose from 99.5 to 123.5 in the same interval. The index of average wage rates in ten major groups of industries rose from 105.3 to 147.8, and the cost-of-living index from 101.5 to 119.5. See also J. L. Ilsley, *Budget Speech*, Mar. 2, 1943, pp. 5-6.

[70]The relative unimportance of agricultural income as a source of tax revenue is indicated by the fact that in the taxation year 1941, for example, the total tax levied amounted to only $1.6 million, on an assessed income of $18.2 million. On this point, see Department of National Revenue, *Taxation Statistics* (Ottawa, 1946), p. 115.

determined criteria of the desirable limits of taxation were expressed in terms of the need to maintain initiative, to prevent the wasteful use of productive resources and to adhere to the ability-to-pay principle. However difficult it may be to translate the last criterion into practice, there is little doubt that as a result of the emphasis upon direct taxes, regressiveness was substantially lessened, as already noted, during the war years.

With reference to the other criteria of tax policy, it seems clear that the government frequently exceeded its announced intentions. This is perhaps not surprising in a situation where the Minister of Finance continually found that "fiscal necessity and the rude facts of war press us hard."[71] In particular, considerable discouragement of individual initiative was encountered because of the high rates of personal income taxation, although this discouragement arose in some degree because of a misunderstanding, particularly on the part of labour, of how graduated tax reductions at the source actually affected the ultimate tax payable. However, it was only in relatively few instances that the very heavy combined levies on business enterprise extended to an actual impairment of capital, and the severity of the wartime measures for the limitation of business profits was not such as to precipitate the serious post-war transitional difficulties which had frequently been predicted by industry.[72] It is not to be denied, however, that the role of taxation in the over-all war effort was adequately understood, and, on the whole, effectively implemented. In both respects, Canadian tax policy in World War II was very much superior to that in World War I, and in obtaining from taxation approximately one-half of its total wartime cash requirements, the accomplishment of the government was one which compares very favourably with the records established by any of the other major belligerents.

While all taxation may not be categorically designated as a non-inflationary means of war finance, nor all borrowing designated as inflationary, such a generalization has rough validity. Accordingly, in the borrowing of that part of its war requirements which could not be met from tax revenues, the Canadian government, with World War I experience as a notable object-lesson, recognized the importance of minimizing the inflationary potentialities of its financial programme.[73] In this it was effectively supported by the Bank of Canada, a comparatively recent addition to the Canadian banking structure. The three sources of borrowing available to the government were the general public, including financial institutions other than banks, the commercial banking system, and the

---

[71]J. L. Ilsley, *Budget Speech*, June 23, 1942, p. 9.

[72]For an analysis of the wartime profits statistics of selected groups of business enterprise in Canada, see the Bank of Canada, *Statistical Summary, 1946 Supplement*, pp. 52-62.

[73]Where taxation is paid out of past savings rather than current income, the economy's aggregate demand for goods and services of course rises. The same result applies in the government's public borrowing operations. The relevant distinction here, in terms of inflationary effects, is therefore not that between taxation and borrowing, but between taxation *or* borrowing from current income and taxation *or* borrowing from past savings.

Bank of Canada. The relative importance of these three sources of wartime funds has already been indicated. The bulk of borrowing from the central bank was effected in the early stages of the war when the government's monetary policy was one of deliberate expansion. Thereafter, direct borrowing was confined almost exclusively to the general public and to the commercial banks. The campaign for borrowing from the general public was very ably conducted by the National War Finance Committee, established in January, 1942, and disbanded in December, 1945. To the extent that such public borrowing fell short of meeting its financial needs, the government turned to the commercial banks as a residual source of funds.

In comparing the extent to which the government was able to restrict inflation in the two wars, it is clear that the relative success attained during World War II cannot be explained in terms of differences in the degree of monetary expansion which took place during the two conflicts. From the end of fiscal year 1939 to that of 1946, the total quantity of money increased, in round figures, from $3 billion to $7 billion, or by approximately 133 per cent (Table XI). In World War I, from the end of 1913 to that of 1918, the increase was from $1.2 billion to $2.1 billion, amounting to only 75 per cent.[74] But as already noted, the wartime expansion of real income was very much greater during World War II, as was the proportion which was diverted to war purposes. A much sounder conception and implementation of fiscal policy during World War II confined monetary expansion within its limits which, with less vigorous leadership and less public support, might have been substantially exceeded. Any attempt to have financed the recent war effort through the approach adopted after 1914 would undoubtedly have led to chaos. While a proportionately greater monetary expansion occurred during World War II, the restriction of inflation was facilitated by the tremendous increase in Canadian productive capacity and by the government's programme of direct economic control which effectively supplemented its fiscal policies.

To the degree that the government was successful in controlling inflation, it also contributed to its third objective of war finance, that of the equitable allocation of the financial costs of the war. The effects of inflation were recognized as constituting a thinly disguised process of taxation of the most arbitrary, unjust, and undesirable type. By minimizing this enforced reduction of purchasing power and by concentrating upon direct (income) taxation, the government probably distributed the wartime financial burden in a manner as satisfactory as the complexities of the Canadian tax system and as the very heavy financial requirements would permit.

In referring to one of the basic objectives of war finance, that of assisting in combating inflation, the Minister of Finance indicated that the government's reliance upon the commercial banking system, and the consequent monetary

---

[74]Deutsch, "War Finance and the Canadian Economy", p. 540.

expansion which took place during the war years, was considerably greater than he had hoped would have been necessary. An accompanying feature of this monetizing of the public debt was the marked alteration in the relative importance of the earning assets of the commercial banks, with government securities supplanting loans as the asset of major importance. This unprecedented liquidity of chartered bank assets, stemming from Canada's wartime fiscal policy, was accompanied by a comparable increase in liquidity of assets held by the general public, the extent of which is indicated in Table XII. As of the end of 1945, the Canadian chartered banks had arrived at the point where:

> Security holdings now represent more than 55% of the total assets of the banking system while loans in Canada are less than 20% of the total. Just before the war, securities accounted for slightly more than 40% of bank assets while loans were in the neighbourhood of 30%. If we go back to the late 'twenties, we find that loans comprise a much larger proportion of bank assets than did securities and if we look back before the First World War, we see that over 60% of bank assets were in the form of loans and that securities were comparatively unimportant. The truth is that the war accelerated a trend which has already been in evidence for a generation not only in Canada but in the United States and Great Britain. . . . This radical change reflects fundamental alterations in the business structure, in the role of government in economic life, and in international relationships and conditions. It is unlikely that loans will regain their former preponderance over securities in banking assets."[75]

The high proportion of earning assets held by the banks in the form of public debt tied the future of the banking system very closely to the market for federal government securities, a market in which the Bank of Canada would necessarily occupy a position of great importance.

The intention of the Bank to maintain a pattern of low interest rates in the post-war period has already been noted. That such an easy-money policy could be maintained without serious danger of further inflation was not a view that was universally shared. The low-interest-rate policy in Canada was a legacy from the depression following 1929, many of the effects of which were still present a decade later when war was declared. The continuation of the policy throughout the war years facilitated the government's programme of war finance, restricting interest payments on the mounting national debt to as low a level as possible. Among the difficulties of maintaining the low level of rates was the fact that the central bank must at all times be prepared to support the market through its open-market purchases, a process which provides the commercial banks with additional reserves, and facilitates credit expansion. The Bank of Canada's decision to maintain low interest rates was of course arrived at, and was understandable, in the light of the early post-war recession which was almost universally

---

[75]H. L. Enman, "Annual Report of the General Manager of the Bank of Nova Scotia" (*Canadian Finance*, Dec. 19, 1945, p. 16).

anticipated, but its ability to maintain such a policy for an indefinite period, without at the same time risking seriously inflationary consequences, appeared doubtful, and the justification for such doubts was demonstrated by subsequent Canadian post-war monetary experience, when the growing conflict between debt policy and monetary policy confronted the Bank with problems not previously encountered during its comparatively brief existence.

Despite the continuous reduction in the average rate of interest payable on the national debt during the war years, the total service cost at the end of the war was as great as the amount of the government's pre-war budget. To lessen the problems associated with this fixed transfer expenditure, the government encouraged the widest possible distribution of the ownership of the debt, a policy in which it was fairly successful. However, to the extent that the taxes necessary for meeeting these expenditures contribute to general levels which discourage initiative, reduce production, and result in a lower real income, some part of the real cost of the war will have been passed to succeeding generations.[76]

In the history of the Canadian economy, where the national income has been notoriously variable, the problem posed by the existence of substantial fixed charges has been one of recurring difficulty. The exigencies of the recent programme of war finance, despite the very creditable manner in which that programme was developed, accentuated this general problem. For the maintenance of a high level of employment in Canada, and for her continued economic expansion, it was extremely important, and in fact indispensable, that a substantial measure of freedom in post-war international trading should be developed, in order to permit the expansion of foreign markets on which the Canadian economy is peculiarly dependent. A substantial volume of international trade, developed on a normal basis, is the *sine qua non* for maintaining a relatively high and expanding Canadian national income. With such an income, the burden of fixed charges is effectively eased. Discussing this problem in 1946, it was this writer's opinion that "the problem may also be attacked and should be attacked from the standpoint of reducing the amount of these fixed charges. This approach is particularly attractive at the present time. For the immediate future, it seems fairly certain that inflation is the general condition which must be

---

[76]The question of how great was the real cost of the war (the amount of real income actually sacrificed) is of considerable interest, in view of the amount of unemployment prevailing in Canada in 1939. Despite the substantial diversion of resources to war purposes, the level of civilian consumption may not have declined by a very considerable amount. On the basis of figures supplied by the Dominion Bureau of Statistics, an interesting investigation might be pursued along these lines. It is a matter for speculation as to how the actual output of civilian goods during the war (under conditions approximating full employment) would compare with the output that would have been produced had the war not occurred, in which case unemployment would almost certainly have continued on some appreciable scale. While such an investigation would perhaps not justify the conclusion that the war was economically "costless", it may well be that the real cost might be found to be considerably less than commonly supposed.

combated in Canada, as in the United States. In view of this situation, an obviously desirable step is that of balancing the federal budget, and of accumulating a surplus to be used to initiate a programme of debt retirement. The surplus should be used to retire bank-held debt, and no further bank borrowing should be undertaken. It is to be hoped that the continued sale of post-war Canada Savings Bonds, through absorbing the savings of individual citizens, will permit a continued demonetizing of the debt, with consequent reduction in the money supply. Such a reduction will at best be a slow and difficult process, and with continued insistence by the government upon maintenance of the present levels of interest rates, the process may well be impossible. Under currently prevailing conditions, debt reduction is not only economically desirable but politically practicable. Coupled with the present uncertainty as to the financial implications of Canada's international commitments, the strongest argument may be advanced against further *ad hoc* tax reductions. The effective easing of the burdens of the Canadian taxpayer will best be accomplished through arriving at a more satisfactory basis for the allocation of taxing powers between the federal and the provincial governments, thereby permitting improvements in the tax system".[77]

It was noted further that in the period from Confederation to the end of World War II, the years in which national debt was reduced were very few, and were concentrated almost exclusively in the nineteen-twenties. The secular rise was punctuated by sharp increases in periods of war and depression. The immediate post-war years provided the urgent opportunity for the initiation of a fiscal policy which, while lessening the fixed charges upon the economy, would contribute at the same time to the current and future economic stability of Canada. The extent to which this opportunity was utilized will now be examined.

[77]See R. Craig McIvor, "Canadian Wartime Fiscal Policy, 1939-1946", *op. cit.*, pp. 32-3.

## CHAPTER X

# POST-WAR MONETARY AND FISCAL POLICY[1]

THE purpose of this chapter is to analyse and evaluate Canadian post-war monetary and fiscal policy, in the light of the recurring inflationary pressures to which
the economy was subjected. In the evaluation of past events, even the least per-
ceptive critic possesses two great advantages, that is, published statistical data
and the revelations of hindsight. When rightly used, hindsight is a valuable
guide, but the critic must be careful to distinguish two significant questions:
(1) In the light of the relevant contemporary circumstances, what alternatives
were available to policy-makers at the time decisions were made? (2) What
were the merits or demerits of the policies adopted, when viewed in the light of
subsequent events—that is, given the same problem again, would different
policies be adopted?

Any analysis, to be useful, must guard against over-simplification and unrealistic abstraction, and it is therefore impossible to evaluate Canadian post-war
monetary experience fairly unless the analysis moves beyond the consideration
of primarily domestic influences to an adequate recognition of the economic
difficulties posed by violent shifts in our balance of payments. The following
criticism of specific aspects of Canadian policy does not imply any over-all con-
demnation,[2] for although we may deplore the damage which inflation has
wrought, it must be admitted that its post-war development in this country has
been relatively moderate, despite the substantial limitations imposed upon Canadian monetary policy by our open economy.

Before considering the details of post-war economic developments, we shall
review briefly the techniques of monetary control available to the Canadian
authorities, and the general attitude of the authorities toward the implementation
of these techniques. Of the four "traditional" instruments of central banking
policy (minimum reserve ratios, the rediscount rate, open-market operations, and
what has been euphemistically called "moral suasion"), the Bank of Canada until
recently possessed only the latter three, one of which (the rediscount rate) was
largely ineffective except as a method of applying psychological pressure to the

---

[1]The early sections of this chapter represent a revision of an article published in the
*Canadian Journal of Economics and Political Science.* See R. Craig McIvor and John
H. Panabaker, "Canadian Post-War Monetary Policy, 1946-1952", May, 1954, pp. 207-26.

[2]Since any critic should be charitable as well as just, there are few economists who, in
the appraisal of Canadian post-war monetary policy, could not benefit by heeding the
injunction of John viii. 7: "He that is without sin among you, let him first cast a stone."

chartered banks and the bond market. When the Bank of Canada opened its doors in 1935, the regulation of currency and credit "in the best interests of the economic life of the nation" involved the establishing of an appropriate anti-depression monetary policy, that is, the securing of "easy-money" conditions, and open-market operations provided a useful tool. In the radically different inflationary environment of the early post-war economy, where, because of the Bank of Canada's importance in the total securities market, its purchases and sales exerted undesirably large "price" repercussions, open-market operations were unfortunately circumscribed.[3]

Apart from any bias toward inflation that may have developed from the circumstances of the Bank's founding, one senses that there was a sort of grim inevitability about the post-war inflation, rooted in the general fear of a recurrence of the economic depression of the 1930's. The basic and understandable miscalculation in Canadian post-war monetary (and fiscal) policy was the delayed recognition of the persistence of inflationary forces as the fundamental economic problem to be combated. There was a strong belief in government circles that any post-war inflation, if such occurred, would follow the general pattern of 1918-21, that is, a sharp upward flurry, quickly terminating in crisis and unemployment. The decline in government military expenditure would eventually break the inflationary boom,[4] and, as the Deputy-Minister of Finance pointed out, the situation at the end of the war looked anything but bright. The war had been fought at a tremendous cost in blood and treasure and had left Canada with serious problems of reconversion and a vastly increased national debt. Foreign trade, on which the Canadian economy remained vitally dependent, was completely disorganized and the economies of important customers shattered. In this situation, and fearful of the social and political upheaval which any return to pre-war depressed conditions would entail, the government committed itself to the objective of a high and stable level of employment and income. Its vigorous preparations toward achieving this end included the introduction of new social services such as family allowances, veterans' benefits, more liberal housing legislation, agricultural price supports, etc. In the monetary-fiscal area, it established the Industrial Development Bank to fill a gap in the capital market, and,

---

[3]See G. S. Dorrance, "The Bank of Canada," in R. S. Sayers (ed.), *Banking in the British Commonwealth* (Oxford, 1952), 122. "It is not satisfactory if every significant group of transactions by the central bank leads to a considerable alteration in the prices of the relevant securities. Therefore if the central bank is to engage successfully in 'open market operations' there must be a well-developed capital market in which the activities of the central bank play only a minor role."

[4]See *Economic Controls* (Reference Book for the Dominion-Provincial Conference on Reconstruction), 1945, 8. "It is . . . clear that the curtailment of war contracts could be relied upon *eventually* to break an inflationary boom. The difficulty is that it probably would not prevent an initial inflation of prices. Such an inflation, however short-lived, would be followed by an abrupt deflation which would gravely delay reconversion and produce wide-spread unemployment."

## Table XIVa—ANALYSIS OF CHANGES IN RESIDENTS' ESTIMATED ACTIVE MONEY SUPPLY, 1946-56

($ million)

| YEAR | CHANGE IN TOTAL LIQUID ASSETS | FACTORS RELATED TO CHANGE IN TOTAL LIQUID ASSETS | | DISTRIBUTION OF CHANGE IN TOTAL LIQUID ASSETS | | | | |
| | | CHANGE IN BANK CREDIT OUTSTANDING | OVER-ALL GOVERNMENT SURPLUS (−) OR DEFICIT (+) | NON-RESIDENT | RESIDENT | | | |
| | | | | | ACTIVE ASSETS (MONEY SUPPLY) | INACTIVE ASSETS | | |
| | | | | | | DEBT HOLDINGS | INACTIVE BANK DEPOSITS | TOTAL |
|---|---|---|---|---|---|---|---|---|
| 1946 | 812+ | 438+ | 374+ | 58+ | 382+ | 82− | 454+ | 372+ |
| 1947 | 177− | 833+ | 1010− | 72− | 24− | 374− | 293+ | 81− |
| 1948 | 142+ | 261+ | 119− | 88+ | 391+ | 619− | 282+ | 337− |
| 1949 | 83+ | 142+ | 59− | 115+ | 53− | 429− | 344+ | 85− |
| 1950 | 703+ | 725+ | 22− | 316+ | 263+ | 38+ | 86+ | 114+ |
| 1951 | 653− | 2+ | 655− | 390− | 178+ | 480− | 39+ | 441− |
| 1952 | 239+ | 382+ | 143− | 281− | 369+ | 113− | 264+ | 151+ |
| 1953 | 264+ | 484+ | 220− | 120− | 40− | 341+ | 83− | 424+ |
| 1954 | 253+ | 26+ | 227+ | 92− | 291+ | 449− | 503+ | 54+ |
| 1955 | 1115+ | 1226+ | 111− | 101− | 275+ | 533+ | 408+ | 941+ |
| 1956b | 113+ | 565+ | 452− | 79− | 115+ | 260− | 337+ | 77+ |

NOTE: The change in total liquid assets is determined by the changes in bank credit outstanding (as measured by bank assets other than government of Canada securities) and by the government's over-all cash surplus or deficit (as measured by changes in the government debt outstanding less government deposits and holdings of government accounts). No adjustment has been made here for the effect of changes in the exchange rate on the effective debt of the government and consequently on the government's cash surplus. For further details, see the sources cited below.

aCompiled from Bank of Canada, *Statistical Summary: Financial Supplement 1954*, pp. 33-4, and *Statistical Summary*, November, 1956, pp. 330-1.

bTo end of third quarter (preliminary).

in its White Paper, set forth such policies as cyclical budgeting and the mainten- ance of low interest rates to encourage capital investments.[5]

The fact that the expected recession did not occur is widely taken as proof that the government completely misjudged the situation, although it might at least be argued that because of the various measures introduced to forestall reces- sion, the government influenced in some degree the prevailing economic climate.

Although the Canadian cost-of-living index rose from roughly 77 to 122 (1949=100) between June, 1946 and June, 1957, it would be a serious error to suppose that this post-war decade was one of continuous and relatively con- stant inflationary pressures. On the contrary, there have been three clearly dis- tinguishable inflationary periods, the first extending from July, 1946, to Decem- ber, 1948, the second from June, 1950, to December, 1951, and the third from mid-1955 to the present time of writing (mid-1957). In the intervening years, i.e., from January, 1949, to June, 1950, and from January, 1952, to June, 1955, the Canadian economy has enjoyed comparative price stability.

During World War II, the Canadian government financed slightly less than one-half of its total cash requirements from tax revenues, and the remainder by borrowing.[6] An inevitable consequence of this fiscal policy was that by 1946 the economy had achieved an unprecedented state of "liquidity", providing an ominous inflationary potential for the post-war period. It was against this in- ternal situation that the two periods of most severe inflationary pressure were sparked by external developments which marked drastic changes in the world economic situation and which made a reconsideration of domestic economic policy, including monetary policy, imperative. In the early post-war inflation, the immediate stimulus was the abrupt abandonment of wartime price controls by the United States in mid-1946. In the next inflationary period, the precipitating factor was the outbreak of the Korean War in mid-1950. Morever, the evolu- tion of Canada's post-war monetary policy was conditioned by a succession of external disturbances, in the light of which contemporary policy decisions were necessarily made.[7]

[5]See W. C. Clark, "Canada's Post-War Finance", in *Canadian Tax Journal*, I, No. 1. Jan.-Feb., 1943, 6 ff.; also the White Paper on *Employment and Income* (Ottawa, 1945), 11, 21.

[6]See R. Craig McIvor, "Canadian Wartime Fiscal Policy, 1939-46", *Canadian Journal of Economics and Political Science*, XIV, No. 1. Feb., 1948, 62-93.

[7]Thus, for example, the post-war plans of the government indicated a belief that the Japanese war would continue for some considerable time after the end of the fighting in Europe. The atomic bomb upset this assumption, and there was no "twilight" war period during which the removal of wartime controls could be accomplished on an orderly and gradual basis with the patriotic co-operation of the public. Again, the severe balance-of- payments crisis which emerged in 1947, resulting in part from substantially more severe dislocations in Europe than had been supposed, provided problems of urgent priority, the solution of which involved awkward internal monetary repercussions. In the post-Korean period, the 1950 speculation in the Canadian dollar complicated the problem of dealing quickly with the inflationary upsurge associated with the outbreak of that conflict.

## TABLE XV—GENERAL PUBLICᵃ HOLDINGS OF CERTAIN LIQUID ASSETSᵇ

(millions of dollars)

| | CURRENCY OUTSIDE BANKS | ACTIVE CHARTERED BANK DEPOSITS | TOTAL CURRENCY PLUS ACTIVE BANK DEPOSITS | INACTIVE BANK DEPOSITS | CANADIAN GOVERNMENT SECURITIES—DIRECT AND GUARANTEED | | TOTAL OF CERTAIN LIQUID ASSETS |
|---|---|---|---|---|---|---|---|
| | | | | | NON-MARKETABLE | MARKETABLE | |
| June 30/46 | 1075 | 2777 | 3852 | 2811 | 765 | 10484 | 17912 |
| Dec. 31/48 | 1185 | 3150 | 4335 | 3408 | 1410 | 8839 | 17992 |
| Net change | 110 | 373 | 483 | 597 | 645 | −1645 | 80 |
| Dec. 31/48 | 1185 | 3150 | 4335 | 3408 | 1410 | 8839 | 17992 |
| June 30/50 | 1196 | 3329 | 4525 | 3839 | 1077 | 8789 | 18230 |
| Net change | 11 | 179 | 190 | 431 | −333 | −50 | 238 |
| June 30/50 | 1196 | 3329 | 4525 | 3839 | 1077 | 8789 | 18230 |
| Dec. 31/51 | 1275 | 3568 | 4843 | 3894 | 1194 | 8194 | 18125 |
| Net change | 79 | 239 | 318 | 55 | 117 | −595 | −105 |
| Dec. 31/51 | 1275 | 3568 | 4843 | 3894 | 1194 | 8194 | 18125 |
| June 30/55 | 1518 | 4201 | 5719 | 5220 | 1960 | 6345 | 19244 |
| Net change | 243 | 633 | 876 | 1326 | 766 | −1849 | 1119 |
| June 30/55 | 1518 | 4201 | 5719 | 5220 | 1960 | 6345 | 19244 |
| June 30/56 | 1604 | 4236 | 5840 | 5323 | 2293 | 6708 | 20164 |
| Dec. 31/56 | 1605 | 4206 | 5811 | 5412 | 2541 | 6353ᶜ | 20117 |
| Net change: | | | | | | | |
| Mid-'55–Mid-'56 | 86 | 35 | 121 | 103 | 333 | 363 | 920 |
| Mid-'56–End-'56 | 1 | −30 | −29 | 89 | 248 | −355 | −107 |
| Mid-'55–End-'56 | 87 | 5 | 92 | 192 | 581 | 8 | 873 |

ᵃIncluding non-resident holdings.

ᵇCompiled from Bank of Canada, Research Memorandum, "General Public Holdings of Certain Liquid Assets", March, 1953, and Statistical Summary, various months.

ᶜAs of December 31, 1956, the Bank of Canada altered the basis for valuing its securities from "not exceeding market value" to amor-

In the adaptation (or lack of adaptation) of Canadian monetary policy to changing post-war circumstances, several phases may be discerned. The first phase, characterized by a generally "expansionist" policy, extended from February, 1944, to February, 1948, that is, from the lowering of the Bank of Canada's rediscount rate to 1½ per cent until the undertaking of mildly restrictive measures, as indicated by the first appreciable break in bond prices. The second, or "neutral", phase continued from February, 1948, until October, 1950, at which time the bank rate was raised to 2 per cent. The third phase, one of monetary restriction, extended from October, 1950, to September, 1953. This was followed by a policy of monetary ease which lasted into late 1955, prompted by the moderate economic recession which began to gather momentum near the end of 1953. This stage culminated in the lowering of the bank rate to 1½ per cent. The last phase to be considered is one of increasing and sustained monetary restraint, in the face of a very rapidly expanding and persistent demand for back credit. With the government's fiscal policies no longer regarded as the prime instrument of control, it was the Bank of Canada which was accorded the major role in the attempt to forestall inflationary pressures in the buoyant fully-employed Canadian economy.

We now turn to a more detailed consideration of the first period of post-war inflation, from June, 1946, to December, 1948.[8] This period was one of apparent contradiction and inconsistency in government policy, in which substantial budgetary surpluses were accompanied by the continuation of cheap money. This anomaly can best be explained on the basis of the miscalculations noted above, for if the post-war inflation had fallen into the anticipated pattern, the temporary inflationary complications presented by cheap money would, it was hoped, have been more than offset by the maintenance of stability in the capital market. Such stability would have helped to maintain confidence during the ensuing recession, and to ease the government's debt management problems.

Moreover, there appear to have been "theoretical" as well as institutional and psychological considerations underlying the reluctance of the government to reconstruct its monetary policy. Monetary restriction, as a means of control, had fallen into general disrepute, having come to be regarded in many quarters as ineffective, and therefore unimportant. Current fashion concentrated attention on fiscal policy, and in the early post-war years, it is in this area alone that any government restrictive influences must be sought. Monetary restriction was conceived, officially, as being useful only in the improbable post-war circumstance

---

[8]Although it is immediately apparent that this period was historically unique, its analysis provides valuable lessons which might usefully be applied to periods of less rapid economic change. The unique features of this period—pent-up domestic demand, unprecedented liquidity, and abnormal export pressures (based on foreign reconstruction and rehabilitation needs, and maintained by extraordinary financial arrangements)—are unlikely to recur, unless at the end of another war (in which event we must leave formulation of post-atomic-war monetary policy to some *ad hoc* committee).

TABLE XVI—NATIONAL INCOME AND GROSS NATIONAL PRODUCT, 1946-1956[a]

(In millions of dollars)

| | 1946 | 1947 | 1948 | 1949 | 1950 | 1951 | 1952 | 1953 | 1954 | 1955 | 1956 |
|---|---|---|---|---|---|---|---|---|---|---|---|
| Wages, Salaries and Supplementary Labour Income | 5323 | 6221 | 7170 | 7761 | 8311 | 9716 | 10868 | 11715 | 11994 | 12810 | 14284 |
| Military Pay and Allowances | 340 | 83 | 82 | 115 | 137 | 201 | 270 | 309 | 367 | 394 | 424 |
| Investment Income | 1975 | 2269 | 2464 | 2445 | 3155 | 3642 | 3763 | 3782 | 3661 | 4339 | 4782 |
| Net Investment from Unincorporated Business: Accrued Net Income of Farm Operators | 1112 | 1223 | 1518 | 1504 | 1503 | 2072 | 1851 | 1652 | 1147 | 1404 | 1608 |
| Net Income of Non-Farm Business | 1071 | 1189 | 1326 | 1369 | 1444 | 1507 | 1574 | 1675 | 1625 | 1793 | 1951 |
| Net National Income at Factor Cost | 9821 | 10985 | 12560 | 13194 | 14550 | 17138 | 18326 | 19133 | 18794 | 20740 | 23049 |
| Indirect Taxes Less Subsidies | 1269 | 1604 | 1772 | 1830 | 2018 | 2478 | 2714 | 2907 | 2947 | 3238 | 3601 |
| Depreciation Allowances and Similar Costs | 903 | 1118 | 1276 | 1437 | 1636 | 1910 | 2120 | 2418 | 2673 | 2878 | 3151 |
| Residual Error of Estimate | 33 | 61 | 5 | 1 | −1 | −52 | 95 | 15 | −78 | 60 | 65 |
| Gross National Product at Market Prices | 12026 | 13768 | 15613 | 16462 | 18203 | 21474 | 23255 | 24473 | 24336 | 26916 | 29866 |

## GROSS NATIONAL EXPENDITURES, 1946-1956
### (In millions of dollars)

| | 1946 | 1947 | 1948 | 1949 | 1950 | 1951 | 1952 | 1953 | 1954 | 1955 | 1956 |
|---|---|---|---|---|---|---|---|---|---|---|---|
| Personal Expenditures on Consumer Goods and Services | 7977 | 9173 | 10112 | 10963 | 12029 | 13273 | 14366 | 15112 | 15881 | 17139 | 18556 |
| Government Expenditure on Goods and Services | 1832 | 1570 | 1798 | 2128 | 2326 | 3243 | 4245 | 4388 | 4413 | 4728 | 5209 |
| Gross Domestic Investment: | | | | | | | | | | | |
| New Residential Construction | 371 | 506 | 637 | 742 | 801 | 781 | 786 | 1061 | 1166 | 1481 | 1556 |
| New Non-Residential Construction | 443 | 599 | 818 | 903 | 1026 | 1260 | 1554 | 1706 | 1659 | 1847 | 2549 |
| New Machinery and Equipment | 584 | 1016 | 1230 | 1323 | 1389 | 1769 | 1916 | 2073 | 1841 | 1947 | 2512 |
| Changes in Inventories | 519 | 947 | 605 | 231 | 960 | 1620 | 310 | 591 | −275 | 510 | 939 |
| Exports of Goods and Services | 3210 | 3638 | 4054 | 4011 | 4183 | 5089 | 5573 | 5400 | 5147 | 5753 | 6310 |
| Deduct: Imports of Goods and Services | −2878 | −3621 | −3636 | −3837 | −4513 | −5613 | −5400 | −5843 | −5574 | −6430 | −7699 |
| Residual Error of Estimate | −32 | −60 | −5 | −2 | 2 | 52 | −95 | −15 | 78 | −59 | −66 |
| Gross National Expenditure at Market Prices | 12026 | 13768 | 15613 | 16462 | 18203 | 21474 | 23255 | 24473 | 24336 | 26916 | 29866 |
| | (9045) | (9165) | (9438) | (9722) | (10330) | (10935) | (11677) | (12121) | (11844) | (12907) | (13831) |

aData based on D.B.S., *National Accounts: Income and Expenditure*, 1926-1950, pp. 27-9; *ibid.*, 1949-52, pp. 16-17, 50; *ibid.*, 1950-56, pp. 18-19, 54. Figures in brackets are constant dollar (1935-39 = 100) figures.

that "after war shortages are over, consumers' expenditures and capital development were to proceed at a rate which would overstrain our productive capacity."[9] The bank saw "no prospect of such a situation arising in a form which would call for a policy of raising interest rates."[10]

With the burden of economic control falling to fiscal measures, an interesting question is whether the "mopping-up" effect of the surpluses in the first period was deliberate, or whether the government was the passive beneficiary of the expansion (and inflation) which occurred. The evidence on this point is not entirely clear. Comparing the 1946 budget forecast with subsequent results, it would appear that the budgetary surplus in the fiscal year 1946-7 was unanticipated.[11] In the 1947 Budget Speech, the Minister still appeared to be hoping for the best and expecting the worst. Acknowledging that the recent surplus reflected unexpected economic strength, he stated that "our surplus is a real one and one from which we can find encouragement, but it has been obtained at high levels of revenue and expenditure which do not necessarily give an accurate indication of the shape of things to come."[12] Thus although the desirability of debt reduction was emphasized and the need for curbing inflationary pressures was strong, tax relief measures were again introduced, to encourage production and to counter public resentment. A comparison of budgetary prediction and

[9]Bank of Canada, *Annual Report*, 1944, 5. This quotation appears to reject monetary restriction not on grounds of ineffectiveness but rather as being inappropriate to the contemporary economic environment. But when the economic conditions to which the governor of the Bank referred did in fact develop, monetary restriction continued to be rejected, largely, one suspects, because of awkward repercussions for debt management. This point is discussed later.

[10]*Ibid.* The relative neglect of monetary policy as an instrument of control in the early post-war years was not confined to Canada, being quite evident in the United Kingdom and the United States. This neglect is frequently explained in terms of the "Keynesian" influence. It might be objected that Keynes would not have all but ignored the possibilities of monetary control in the inflationary post-war environment. Some support for this argument may be found in *The General Theory*: "If we are precluded from making large changes in our present methods, I should agree that to raise the rate of interest during a boom may be, in conceivable circumstances, the lesser evil" (p. 322). However, in reply to this objection, Keynes's main position on this point remains the opposite: "the remedy for the boom is not a higher rate of interest but a lower rate of interest! For that may enable the so-called boom to last. The right remedy for the trade cycle is not to be found in abolishing booms . . . but in abolishing slumps and thus keeping us permanently in a quasi-boom." (p. 322).

[11]In this first budget designed for peacetime conditions, the Minister of Finance introduced various tax reductions which were calculated to produce a budgetary deficit of some $300 million for the fiscal year 1946-7. See J. L. Ilsley, *Budget Speech*, June 27, 1946, 28. The actual result was a surplus, in part arising from large "special" receipts which it was not possible to estimate in advance of the order of $375 million. The Minister also stated that "if only immediate economic considerations were involved, one could make a case for temporary higher taxes in order to curb the excess of spending in some directions that is tending to pull prices up" (p. 8).

[12]D. C. Abbott, *Budget Speech*, April 29, 1947, 7. At this time, the Minister planned for a budgetary surplus of some $190 million, a figure which was more than tripled in the event.

performance again suggests that the magnitude of the surplus ($676 million) was substantially beyond the expectations for the fiscal year 1947-8.

It was not until the 1948 Budget Speech that fiscal policy, which had loomed so large in government planning documents, was examined and defended in detail. The Minister advanced the case for the continuation of "surplus" budgeting both ably and at length. He emphasized the fact that there was still a great need to prepare for less prosperous times, and that international tensions rendered the government's financial requirements uncertain, and that in view of its over-riding responsibility to influence economic trends, the government could not justify the release of additional purchasing power through tax reductions. Considering the continuing high level of employment such releases would necessarily intensify inflationary pressures. Moreover, it was necessary to build up an export surplus before the economy could be freed from the emergency import controls necessitated by the 1947 exchange crisis, and this could not be done if additional domestic purchasing power were released.

Thus "the general policy for this year [fiscal year 1948-9] should be to use our surplus to reduce our debt and thereby to fight inflation in the manner most suited to our type of government and our way of life."[13] This policy had definite political advantages at the time, for while it afforded the Opposition the immediate cry of "over-taxation", it also afforded the government the prospect (if prices became stabilized) of going to the country in 1949 with inflation no longer an issue, and with substantial tax reductions possible. There was a useful correspondence between political and economic objectives which the government exploited to its advantage.

Concerning the fiscal policy of the earliest post-war years, it appears reasonable to conclude that at least the magnitude, and on occasion the mere existence, of budgetary surpluses was fortuitous, for there were repeated warnings of a recession which in fact did not develop. If this conclusion is correct, then there was no serious conflict at this time between the monetary and fiscal *policies* of the government, although these policies were conditioned by what in retrospect proved to be essentially false premises. At the time of the 1948 Budget Speech, the continuing insistent inflationary pressures rendered non-restrictive policies much less justifiable, and a fair inference from the Speech is that the continuation of budgetary surpluses was regarded as a feasible means of overcoming the inflationary consequences of the relatively easy-money policy which the government was extremely reluctant to terminate.

[13]D. C. Abbott, *Budget Speech*, May 18, 1948, 13. In contrast to the forecast surplus of $489 million, the realized surplus for the fiscal year 1948-9 was $596 million. Underlying each of the budget speeches was the wholly unwarranted assumption that the existence of a budgetary surplus was *ipso facto* a restrictionist influence. As indicated below, the manner of disposition of the surplus is of fundamental importance. A somewhat different source of misunderstanding as to the economic effects of Canada's post-war fiscal policy arises from undue preoccupation with the government's "budgetary" position, rather than its "cash" position. The latter is a considerably broader and therefore more relevant concept.

During the first six months of 1948 the first phase of post-war monetary policy came to an end. During January and February, the first significant break in bond prices occurred, with yields on the longest-term Victory Loan bonds rising from 2.60 per cent to 2.93 per cent. At the same time, the Bank of Canada suggested that circumstances "made it undesirable for capital expenditures to be financed through expansion of bank credit."[14] It must be conceded that at least a suggestion of monetary restraint had appeared, thus providing some support for a fiscal policy which was now becoming increasingly restrictionist by design. But despite these developments, statements by the Minister of Finance and by the governor of the Bank of Canada left much doubt as to the further use to be made of monetary policy. The Minister pointed out that there was little or no discernible correlation between the interest rate and the volume of current saving, that an increase in such saving (in contrast to a mere transfer from inactive deposits) could be achieved only by a drastic policy which would lead to "chaotic" conditions and seriously embarrass both institutional and individual investors. Moreover, the government did not believe that a further "reasonable" rise in rates would discourage borrowing.[15]

In his testimony before the Special Committee on Prices, the governor in effect admitted the poverty of central banking policy in the existing situation by his reported statement that "when the general public was not a net buyer of government bonds it was not feasible for the Bank of Canada to increase 'open market' security sales with a view to restraining the increases in chartered banks of loans and non-government investments."[16] This was indeed a disquieting position to be taken by a central banker, particularly in the Canadian situation where the normal instrument of control is through the securities market.

During the first period of inflation, the Canadian dollar was restored to parity in an attempt to reduce the upward pressure on the Canadian price structure originating from inflationary forces abroad, particularly in the United States, but the soundness of this move cannot be fully assessed.[17] Its effect on internal prices was quickly swallowed up in the continuing inflation and it was followed by a reversal of capital-flows, that is, by a loss of exchange reserves, primarily associated with the unexpectedly rapid drawing-down of advances extended to foreign governments. The most important feature of the balance of

[14]Bank of Canada, *Annual Report*, 1948, 7.
[15]See *Report of the Royal Commission on Prices* (Ottawa, 1949), II, 164. Here are quoted some excerpts from an address by the Minister to the American Academy of Political and Social Sciences, April 1, 1948. See also the Budget Speech, May 18, 1948, 6. Here the Minister admits the existence of the situation which the governor of the Bank of Canada could not foresee in 1944. "What we need is a slowing down, not a sudden cessation, of the capital development which has been taking place at a pace which has been straining our resources."     [16]*Ibid.*, 165.
[17]Events subsequent to this 1946 appreciation were evidently not sufficiently encouraging to persuade the government that a satisfactory solution to the 1950 exchange problem could be provided by a repetition of this earlier action of appreciating to a new fixed rate.

payments in these years was a large and insistent demand for United States goods and a shortage of convertible exchange to be used in payment. The 1947 balance-of-payments crisis necessitated the introduction of temporary direct import controls, special taxes, and severe exchange restrictions on travel expenditures. These (and the coming of the Marshall Plan) served to check the current balance-of-payments deterioration, but their consequences were by no means entirely desirable.[18]

In the light of the balance-of-payments situation at the time of the 1946 appreciation, almost any exchange rate policy would appear, from some point of view, to have been the wrong one.[19] The loss of foreign exchange reserves might have suggested depreciation, but Canada was enjoying large over-all current account surpluses, $460 in 1946, $85 million in 1947, and $471 million in 1948. Moreover, in view of the relatively low price elasticities of demand for Canadian exports and imports vis-à-vis the United States in the early post-war years, it is highly doubtful whether any practicable measure of depreciation would have appreciably benefited the current account balance.[20]

The adoption of a free rate in 1946 might have lessened the subsequent pressure which developed against our exchange reserves, although this, of course, cannot be demonstrated. Whatever the advantages which a free rate might have provided, such a course was impracticable in view of the commitments just assumed by Canada as a member of the International Monetary Fund.

The integration of Canada's external and internal policies does not appear to have been effectively accomplished during this period. On the one hand, there was the attempt to restrain the impact of external inflationary developments by means of currency appreciation, while, on the other, the cash accruing to the Canadian government through the loss of exchange reserves failed to provide

[18]W. C. Clark, "Canada's Post-War Finance", 14. The Deputy-Minister of Finance referred to the "distortions and rigidities", "uneconomic production", and "vested interests" which subsequently arose, in direct contradiction to Canada's official encouragement of more liberal trade policies.

[19]The government has three broad exchange rate possibilities: (a) fixed rates (which provide a relatively small degree of autonomy for domestic economic policy); (b) fluctuating rates (which provide much greater domestic autonomy); or (c) some compromise such as "floating" rates, which are permitted to fluctuate without interference between certain limits. It may be fairly assumed that the present Canadian "free" rate is really of the "floating" variety, in the sense that our monetary authorities would not be prepared to accept an unlimited range of fluctuations. Thus, for example, the politically feasible limits to the permitted shifts in the external value of the Canadian dollar might be, say, from $1.10 U.S. to $ .90 U.S. Appreciation is more disturbing politically, since it brings serious repercussions for our major export industries, particularly those whose products must be sold at relatively fixed foreign currency prices. On the other hand, substantial depreciation exerts undesirable inflationary effects under prevailing post-war economic circumstances.

[20]For a dissenting view, and a criticism of that view, see Harry C. Eastman, "Canadian Post-War Monetary Policy: A Comment", in the *Canadian Journal of Economics and Political Science*, August, 1955, pp. 363-4, and R. Craig McIvor, "Canadian Post-War Monetary Policy: A Rejoinder", in *ibid.*, November, 1955, pp. 534-7.

an effective means for restraining internal credit expansion, and the potentially anti-inflationary effect of allowing demand to spill over into the United States market by living on the reserves was lost.

The Minister of Finance contended that the fact that the quantity of money in Canada had not increased since October 1946, reflected the soundness of the government's post-war fiscal policy. Particular reference was made to the restrictive effects of the repayment of debt held by the banking system.[21] The government's cash surplus in 1947 was of record size (about one billion dollars) to which a significant contribution had been made by the repayment of previous advances extended to the Foreign Exchange Control Board, as the reserves of the Board steadily declined. However, while the use of the government's cash surplus to repay bank-held debt did *in itself* exert a restrictionist effect, through the accompanying cancellation of bank deposits, the chartered banks' reserves were not reduced by this operation. The net result, in the absence of central bank action to absorb the excess reserves, was a mere shift in the ownership of chartered bank credit from government to private holders, as the latter category was rapidly expanded.

Between mid-1946 and the end of that year, chartered bank cash reserves actually increased by something more than $100 million, largely as a result of purchases of bonds by the Bank of Canada. These purchases, at a time when the longest Victory Loan bonds were yielding about 2.55 per cent and when the chartered banks' cash ratio was over 11 per cent, helped to provide the basis for the billion-dollar credit expansion which developed during the period. Thereafter, between December, 1946, and the end of 1948, the Bank of Canada succeeded in preventing a further net increase in bank cash; in fact, a decline of $4 million occurred. However, the banking system continued to expand credit to restore its customary 10 per cent cash ratio. Thus from an average of 11.2 per cent in December, 1946, the cash ratio fell to an average of 10.4 per cent in December, 1948. So liquid were the banks during this period that they became increasingly aggressive buyers of "investments",[22] and these purchases, combined with the heavy flow of institutionalized savings, would appear to have been sufficient (in the face of little net activity in the bond market in 1946 and 1947) to drive interest rates to new low levels.[23]

---

[21]See D. C. Abbott, *Budget Speech*, May 18, 1948, 5.

[22]See Bank of Canada Research Memorandum, "General Public Holdings of Certain Liquid Assets", March, 1953, Table III-A; also Bank of Canada, *Annual Report*, 1949, 7. In 1945, the banks held approximately $100 million less in non-government securities than in 1939. In 1946 such holdings rose by $114 million, in 1947 by $317 million, and in 1948 by $111 million. In fact, from 1945 to 1947, total chartered bank purchases of provincial, municipal, and corporate securities exceeded the Bank of Canada's estimates of the net new issues of such securities.

[23]The Bank of Canada did not "cause" the appearance of premium prices on Canada bonds, and technically, it did not actively support the market during the post-war period. The important point is that it did not sell in sufficient volume to offset net private buying which was tending to depress yields.

During 1947, residents' active money supply declined only slightly ($24 million) despite the government's debt retirement operations, while in 1948 it increased by $391 million.[24] The most important factor in this latter rise was the shift from government bonds to other forms of liquid assets on the part of the resident general public, whose holdings declined by some $619 million.[25] These shifts in the ownership of the public debt merely emphasize the general futility of central banking operations in this early inflationary period. In the face of the Bank of Canada's disapproval (February, 1948) of direct chartered bank financing of private capital expenditures through securities purchases, but with still a comfortable cash position (which averaged 10.9 per cent during 1948)[26] the banks turned to buying government bonds, increasing their holdings by $311 million during the year. Thus, the government's rather pious hope that borrowers would obtain funds without an expansion of bank credit was without foundation, although the mechanism was slightly disguised.[27]

In view of the steadily increasing restrictionist "intent" of fiscal policy, one may well ask why the government did not initiate some positive monetary control, without which the domestic attack upon inflation could scarcely hope to be effective. The apparent answer to this question raised grave problems of the ability of the Bank of Canada to deal effectively with any inflationary situation, given the institutional organization of the Canadian capital market.

It is an economic commonplace that central bank operations designed to effect monetary restriction have a more dependable influence than those directed toward expansion, since the banks and the business community cannot be forced to utilize the credit made available when confidence is low. But whereas debt management policy, interest rate policy, and open-market operations are likely to involve no conflicting objectives where the problem is to encourage economic expansion, early Canadian post-war monetary experience revealed the unfortunate fact that where inflation was the problem, the conflict between monetary restraint and considerations of debt management could be so serious as to render any effective central bank action impossible.

One must not minimize the importance of debt management considerations in seeking to attain effective monetary control. As a result of the fiscal policy in World War II, the Canadian public debt assumed a vastly more important place

---

[24]See Table XIV.

[25]There had been a similar shift in 1947, implemented largely by non-financial corporations as they began to finance their early programmes of post-war capital expansion. In that year, sales by the life insurance companies (which later became very important) were negligible. The effects of the shift in 1947 were obscured by the government's huge cash surplus and the fact that the great part of the debt was kept out of the active money supply by a corresponding increase in inactive deposits. In 1948, the disposals of government securities originated largely with the non-corporate public ($332 million) and the life insurance companies ($169 million).

[26]Bank of Canada, *Annual Report,* 1948, 10.

[27]*Ibid.,* 7.

in the structure of the economy, and the government was committed (at the very least) to maintaining an orderly and stable market. With substantial amounts of this debt in the hands of individuals, particularly unsophisticated investors,[28] it was neither socially just nor politically feasible to pursue a policy of open-market monetary restriction regardless of the consequences for debt management. Moreover, in the light of the deteriorating international situation, and the need for large-scale appeals to the market in the event of war, the necessity for maintaining confidence within the bond market could not be ignored. But if it is correct to assume that the Bank of Canada regarded debt management as the dominant factor in the determination of its monetary policy in this first inflationary period, and that its freedom to make open-market sales was severely limited because of this, then it must be admitted that its ability to initiate monetary restraint had been lost, since, under prevailing institutional arrangements, open-market operations are the Bank's only permanent technique of credit control.

Given the expansionist bias of these institutional arrangements, and the very real requirements of debt management, a policy involving the positive curbing of chartered bank reserves between mid-1946 and the end of 1948 was probably impossible to expect. It is not clear, however, that a tighter control of reserves would have been inconsistent with the Bank of Canada's responsibilities in debt management (among which need not have been included an acquiescence in the development of premium bond prices).[29]

Despite the increase which occurred in the active money supply in 1948, the first post-war surge of inflationary pressure appeared to have exhausted itself

[28]Too often, in discussions of the "responsibility" of the monetary authorities toward the unsophisticated but patriotic investor, the argument turns on the loss which he may suffer as a result of a decline in the money price of the securities. Thus "Congressman Patman . . . expressed the view that it was 'a shame and a disgrace' and a violation of a 'sacred obligation' that the Federal Reserve had allowed government bonds to decline below par" (National City Bank of New York, *Monthly Letter*, Nov., 1951, 131). Actually, of course, such arguments may stem from lack of understanding, or from a cynical exploitation of the money veil for political purposes. The bondholder can be "done in" more effectively by maintenance of the money price of his securities at the expense of a decline in their real value. Moreover, in this case, the damage is done to all the bondholders, not just to those who want to sell their bonds prior to maturity. In addition to concern for the unsophisticated investor and for maintaining widespread confidence in the bond market, debt management must recognize such considerations as the necessity for refunding, the desirability of minimizing interest rates as an "economy" measure, etc. Not all of these considerations are compatible with one another.

[29]The Minister of Finance consistently denied that the Bank of Canada had ever "attempted to maintain an artificial support for government bonds". See, for example, *House of Commons Debates*, June 20, 1951, where the Minister further stated that "the Bank of Canada invests in government bonds, but they are purchased at prevailing market prices." Such disingenuous statements merely obscure the significance of the Bank's open-market operations. In reply to a charge that the Bank had (in 1948) instituted a policy of, in this instance, higher interest rates, the Minister admitted that "the Bank of Canada was simply recognizing what had taken place elsewhere". Whenever questioned as to the effects exerted by the participation of the Bank of Canada in the bond market, the Minister was invariably evasive.

by the end of that year, and from the last quarter of 1948 to the second quarter of 1950 there were few significant changes in the Canadian monetary system.[30] Debt holdings of residents decreased substantially, but this movement was offset by increases in inactive deposits. In its cash operations, the government sector was approximately in balance, and the increase in private bank credit was largely offset by increases in non-resident holdings of Canadian liquid assets.

In June, 1950, with the outbreak of war in Korea, a serious inflationary problem returned to plague Canadian monetary authorities. In contrast to the immediate post-war years, the second inflationary period was characterized by conditions which might well recur, notably the superimposing of a very large defence effort on a substantial capital boom because of the sudden deteriorioration of the international scene. But while both periods of inflation were essentially periods of transition, the first from wartime conditions to the peacetime "normal" of 1949, and the second from an encouraging prosperity in the first half of 1950 to a state of "cold-war" preparedness, substantial economic differences should nevertheless be noted.

Immediately following World War II, Canada's foreign trade position was, as already indicated, uncertain, but with the advent of the Korean War, there was every prospect that the organization of defence economies in the United States and elsewhere would require enormous quantities of Canadian raw materials, and strong export markets were assured for many months to come. In the consumers' and capital goods markets, the first inflation had begun with serious shortages but with the prospect of rapidly increasing output, and in fact by 1950, the most important shortages had either been eliminated or reduced to manageable proportions. By contrast, the Korean outbreak was accompanied in Canada by a fear of the renewal of severe wartime shortages. The problem of reconversion and demobilization had been acute in 1946, but with the coming of the post-Korean defence economy, the prospect was for labour shortages rather than possible widespread unemployment. In 1946, there remained in operation the structure of wartime direct economic controls, with the expectation that these could be abandoned by an orderly and gradual process. The Korean situation began with the economy unshackled, and with the government determined to keep it as untrammelled as possible in spite of the necessity for specific restrictions, notably in allocation of materials. Finally, the liquidity resulting from war finance had reached its peak in 1946. By 1950, much of this liquidity had been squeezed out through the subsequent expansion of real income and the effect of the first inflation.

The second inflationary period was accompanied by an enormous speculative inflow of capital in anticipation of a revaluation of the Canadian dollar to parity. During 1950, the current account deficit in Canada's balance of payments amounted to $329 million, but despite this, investors and speculators both at home and abroad became convinced that the existing foreign exchange rate

[30]The resident active money supply increased by about $68 million during this time.

could not be held, and that a return to parity was inevitable.[31] Thus Canada experienced an unprecedented short-term capital inflow, and "In ten weeks in the third quarter . . . our exchange reserves increased by over 500 million dollars."[32]

Due credit must be given to the monetary authorities for their handling of the second inflationary crisis, for, freed from much of the economic uncertainty which contributed to monetary paralysis in the earlier years, the Bank acted vigorously. In October, 1950, it moved to obtain relief from the inflationary pressure arising from the financing of the embarrassingly large capital inflows by freeing the dollar. But there do not seem to have been any real alternatives to this action. To have restored the rate to parity would have justified the expectations of speculators, and would have led to large-scale withdrawals of foreign capital.[33] To have continued the 10 per cent depreciation vis-à-vis the United States dollar would have involved the licensing of capital imports, an entirely unrealistic alternative since the prevailing climate favoured the loosening of economic controls.

Post-war fluctuations in Canadian foreign exchange reserves exerted important repercussions on the volume of domestic credit. Thus in 1947, the decline in reserves contributed to the government's cash surplus, part of which was employed in reducing bank-held public debt.[34] In 1950, the financing of the extraordinarily large increase in reserves was accomplished partly by the sale of Deposit Certificates ($200 million) to the chartered banks, and partly by the Bank of Canada's direct acquisition of foreign exchange assets (up to $393 million). For a time, the Bank was able to offset much of the potential monetary expansion by open-market sales of securities. Later, as the Bank's extraordinary foreign exchange assets declined, it absorbed substantial amounts of securities, and the net effect of the Bank's operations was an increase in chartered banks' reserves of $56.4 million in 1950. Thus the violent movements of external factors impeded any swift response to the internal inflationary upsurge. Since the cash position of the government was severely strained by the deficit associated with

---

[31]The depreciation which had been carried out in September, 1949, can be justified only as a competitive adjustment in the face of the much more drastic simultaneous reductions in the value of the pound sterling and many other currencies. On any other grounds, the Canadian depreciation can scarcely be defended. Canada had both a current account surplus in 1949 ($187 million) and reasonable stability in her foreign exchange reserves (a loss of $11 million between the end of 1948 and August, 1949). In contrast, the pressure on sterling reserves was tremendous.

[32]See W. C. Clark, "Canada's Post-War Finance", 15.

[33]Since the end of the war, our foreign exchange reserve position had been dominated by the effects of short-term capital movements. Under fixed exchange rates, such movements exerted a destabilizing influence, in the belief that the fixed rate could not be held. With the free or floating rate since 1950, the short-term capital movements have worked in our interest, as a stabilizing force, and as a means of simplifying the problem of financing exchange reserves.

[34]The failure of this policy to accomplish a tightening of credit has already been noted above.

the financing of rising exchange reserves, it would not have been feasible to have applied strong pressure on the banks at this particular period.[35]

On October 16, the immediate problem of the exchange rate and the capital inflows having been resolved by the freeing of the dollar, the Bank of Canada announced an increase in the rediscount rate from $1\frac{1}{2}$ per cent to 2 per cent, and officially abandoned its 1944 policy in which it had indicated that post-war conditions were not likely to be such as to require higher interest rates. This reversal of policy was accompanied by more restrictive fiscal measures in which taxes were increased, and in such a manner as to discourage the consumption of commodities for which materials were likely to be in short supply. In practice, the higher rate meant that the Bank of Canada, in its open-market operations, would permit the changing forces of demand and supply to be reflected more readily in fluctuations in securities prices.[36]

The entry of the Chinese Communists into the war coincided with an intensification of inflationary pressures within Canada, the latter facilitated by the rapid expansion of bank credit during the second half of 1950.[37] In February, 1951, there occurred an event unprecedented in Canadian banking when a so-called "credit-ceiling" was imposed upon the chartered banks.[38] As indicated by Table XVII, the credit ceiling worked very well. It enabled the Bank of Canada to take another important step toward a more flexible monetary policy by permitting declines in long-term bond prices to well below par, without excessive disorganization of the market. With the credit ceiling to prevent the banks from using the additional cash, the Bank could continue to "cushion" the market by absorbing bonds as required.

As a transitional measure, considerable justification may therefore be claimed for resorting to this ceiling, but as a precedent for future action, the use of this form of "direct" control has little to commend it as a substitute for the more gradual and orthodox application of pressure by customary techniques as infla-

---

[35]The importance for monetary control of the maintenance of substantial government deposits in the chartered banks should be noted. Shifts in deposits from the chartered banks to the Bank of Canada can have as important restrictionist effects as open-market operations, without any *direct* effect on the securities markets. This device might have been employed more vigorously in 1947.

[36]The market, unaccustomed to this sort of behaviour by the Bank, did not appear to have appreciated what was occurring. In November, interest rates did weaken, but the magic of "par" was still strong, and at the end of December the longest Victory Loan was quoted to yield 2.97 per cent.

[37]At the end of 1950, the cash ratio of the chartered banks had been reduced to 10.1 per cent. The banks had no "excess" reserves to utilize, although these might be obtained by the sale of bonds. See Bank of Canada, *Annual Report*, 1950.

[38]Bank of Canada, *Annual Report*, 1951, 9. The governor of the Bank of Canada noted that: "In view of the degree of inflationary pressure and the strength of the demand for more credit, the Bank felt that the situation called for action over and above further tightening of the chartered banks' cash reserve position. Meetings with representatives of the chartered banks during February, 1951 to discuss the situation found the banks in agreement with the suggestion that further expansion of total bank credit was undesirable under existing conditions."

tionary pressure develops. It seems quite unfair to burden the chartered banks with the responsibility for control of the credit structure and in effect to penalize those banks which, prior to the instituting of the ceiling, had behaved with relative restraint in expanding loans. Pressure should be borne, rather, by those banks most fully extended. The reluctance of the monetary authorities to

TABLE XVII—CANADIAN DEPOSITS OF THE CHARTERED BANKS[a]
(Actual Volume and "Customary" Volume)

|  | 1950 | | 1951 | | 1952 | |
|---|---|---|---|---|---|---|
|  | CANADIAN DEPOSITS | 10 × CASH RESERVES | CANADIAN DEPOSITS | 10 × CASH RESERVES | CANADIAN DEPOSITS | 10 × CASH RESERVES |
| January |  |  | 7,890 | 8,020 | 7,830 | 8,770 |
| February |  |  | 7,766[b] | 7,280 | 7,754 | 8,390 |
| March |  |  | 7,655 | 7,480 | 7,851 | 8,460 |
| April |  |  | 7,734 | 7,700 | 7,989 | 8,480 |
| May |  |  | 7,731 | 7,560 | 8,063[c] | 8,340 |
| June | 7,419 | 7,240 | 7,702 | 7,680 | 8,096 | 7,890 |
| July | 7,433 | 7,550 | 7,761 | 8,070 | 8,208 | 8,480 |
| August | 7,369 | 7,810 | 7,686 | 7,950 | 8,200 | 8,480 |
| September | 7,557 | 7,340 | 7,680 | 8,050 | 8,183 | 8,550 |
| October | 7,786 | 8,120 | 7,743 | 8,040 | 8,393 | 8,680 |
| November | 7,881 | 7,790 | 7,874 | 8,670 | 8,443 | 8,480 |
| December | 7,847 | 7,920 | 7,890 | 8,600 | 8,314 | 8,400 |

[a]Monthly averages in millions of dollars, as reported in Bank of Canada, *Statistical Summary*, various issues.

[b]Imposition of credit ceiling.     [c]Removal of credit restrictions.

assume full responsibility for monetary restriction in such a crisis appears to be unjustifiable.[39]

In late 1951, the parliamentary assistant to the Minister of Finance, in response to complaints about the general decline in bond prices, provided some interesting but equivocal statements on debt policy.[40] Along this same line, the governor

[39]In his 1951 Budget Speech, the Minister of Finance stressed the "voluntary" cooperation of the banking system in the public interest. In the 1951 *Annual Report* of the Bank of Canada, the governor observed that "It was evident that there was a desire on the part of banks to maintain a higher cash ratio than they had during the first half of 1951." It is true that in the second half of 1951 the cash reserves of the chartered banks rose by some $124 million, but this was largely a result of a decline in the Bank of Canada's "Other Deposits" which was not offset elsewhere in the Bank's accounts. With the credit ceiling effective, it would appear that the cash ratios of the chartered banks would inevitably rise, regardless of their wishes in the matter.

[40]See *House of Commons Debates*, Nov. 19, 1951, p. 1131: "it is not the policy of the government, or of the Bank of Canada, to cause a fall—or, for that matter, a rise—in the market price of government bonds." It was further pointed out that between issue and maturity, the price of a marketable bond "is a reflection of varying conditions which affect the desire of bondholders to sell and of other persons to buy." The validity of the first quotation rests upon an apparently calculated ambiguity as to the interpretation of the Bank's "causal" influence in the market. But however interpreted, it represents a substantial change in the government's thinking since the appearance of the 1945 White Paper, in which the avowed purpose of monetary policy was the continuation of low interest rates to encourage investment in productive capital, thereby contributing to employment.

of the Bank of Canada stressed the "limited buying interest in Government of Canada bonds" which prevailed at the time.[41] These references appear to confirm a continuation of the government's unwillingness to admit the importance of the influence exerted by the monetary authorities in the market.[42]

Despite the more flexible monetary policy of the post-Korean period, the movements of chartered bank cash reserves and the need for the credit ceiling indicated that the Bank of Canada still preferred to minimize disturbances in the capital market by supplementing modest rate-increases by informal controls. The credit ceiling was a makeshift device which might well have been avoided had the Bank been willing to employ its newly-found monetary freedom more vigorously with a view to greater rises in bond yields.[43]

An interesting feature of the monetary situation during the second period of inflation was the heavy selling of bonds by the life insurance companies.[44] The only effective way of restraining the net sales of such institutions in such a period of inflation is through the flexible long-term bond market. This in turn suggests that the monetary authorities may be correct in attempting to separate the individual and the institutional investor by the device of the non-marketable Canada Savings Bond, inasmuch as the Bank's reluctance to make effective use of open-market operations in curbing credit in the post-Korean period was based on the adverse repercussions upon debt management. If the unsophisticated "individual" bond purchaser can be provided with a non-marketable bond, free from adverse capital fluctuations, the stultifying influence of "moral" commitments to bondholders is greatly reduced, since presumably the corporate investors will not expect immunity from the possibility of adverse fluctuations in bond prices before maturity.

An objection to this arrangement is that as the proportion of the national debt held in the form of non-marketable bonds increases, the potential inflationary danger becomes more serious. The monetization of this kind of debt is not sub-

[41]Bank of Canada, *Annual Report*, 1951, 12.

[42]During 1951, the Bank of Canada added $249 million to its holdings of government debt, and the government accounts added $162 million. Retirements amounted to some $592 million.

[43]Like most *ad hoc* measures, the credit ceiling had severe limitations. In this connection, see Mabel F. Timlin, "Recent Developments in Canadian Monetary Policy", *American Economic Review*, XLIII, No. 3, May, 1953, 46-7. Here it is observed that a credit ceiling is likely to be concocted "only after a trend has been well established and when it may be difficult to arrest. Moreover, political pressures may dictate the removal of these substitute arrangements at a relatively early date." It is a singular coincidence that the credit ceiling was imposed in February, 1951, at about the time that wholesale prices in the United States reached their post-Korean peak.

[44]See Bank of Canada, *Statistical Summary*, Sept., 1952, 145-6. Changes in the insurance companies' net holdings of direct and guaranteed Canadian government debt were as follows: 1946, +$107 million; 1947, −$12 million; 1948, −$169 million; 1949, −$171 million; 1950, −$185 million; 1951, −$149 million. The insurance companies' sales in 1948 and 1949 were readily absorbed by the monetary system since the chartered banks were net purchasers ($311 million and $153 million). In 1950 and 1951, the banks were net sellers, and the insurance companies provided an additional large and persistent supply of bonds to the market.

ject to any form of direct control (except repudiation) other than "moral suasion". In any period of a widespread flight from securities to money, the monetization of non-marketable debt would present serious problems.

Allowing for the monetary expansion which occurred as a result of the capital inflow in the last half of 1950, it is significant that, in the face of a very large surplus in the government sector, and of the credit ceiling, the total active money supply was reduced by only $8 million during 1951. Indeed, active money in the hands of residents rose by $178 million. With the current relatively high levels of taxation and government spending, the restraint of any renewal of serious inflationary pressure (especially in the absence of wartime public co-operation) via fiscal weapons appeared subject to serious political limitations, and it thus appeared that the major burden must rest upon monetary policy. The effectiveness of such policy both during the early post-war inflation and after "Korea" left much to be desired. Beginning before mid-1955, bank credit expanded rapidly and continuously to mid-1956, and amid much stronger inflationary pressures, it was still to be demonstrated that the Bank of Canada, pursuing policies no longer captive to considerations of debt management, nor seriously impaired by unfavourable external influences, could exercise a powerful and pervasive restraining influence throughout the economy.

In view of the fact that between the end of 1945 and 1951 the total stock of money in Canada increased by almost 50 per cent, while the constant-dollar gross national expenditure rose by only 15 per cent, it has been suggested that monetary policy "would have been more rational if increases in bank reserves and bank deposits in response to rising external prices or increases in output had been deferred until the wartime inflation had worked itself out."[45] Viewed in retrospect, it is certainly arguable that the much earlier use of monetary restriction, for example in the immediate post-war period, was highly desirable as an anti-inflationary weapon; but in view of the contemporary circumstances, it appears unduly harsh to suggest that the failure to implement such a policy involved irrationality. The Bank could not realistically have been expected to ignore completely the implications of such restrictions for the management of

---

[45]Timlin, "Recent Developments in Canadian Monetary Policy", 52. No indication is offered here of the anticipated process by which the anti-inflationary effects of a restrictive monetary policy would become effective, that is, whether by operating directly on the general price level through the immediate effects upon the active money supply or indirectly via the consequences of rising interest rates. Post-war experience suggests that the latter might have been more important than mere changes in the active money supply. As against the inequities stemming from the two periods of major inflation, the lasting benefit has been the substantial increase in Canadian productive capacity associated with the unprecedented level of post-war capital investment. Against this gain must be set the possibility of serious cyclical disturbances arising from the stickiness of the inflated post-war costs of production. One might argue (as Miss Timlin undoubtedly would) that the same capital expansion could have been obtained at lower price levels; if this premise is granted, the remaining grounds for a retrospective defence of actual monetary policy to late 1950 is severely limited.

the public debt, and in view of the general economic uncertainty the Bank may well have viewed any substantial dislocation of the capital market as undesirable. However, the severity of these limitations on open-market action does appear to have been over-emphasized, particularly in the immediate post-war years, when the priority attached to considerations of debt management was apparently so great that monetary policy was prevented from taking as much as a first step in the direction of economic restraint.

From the beginning of 1952 until mid-1956, the Canadian economy enjoyed general price stability,[46] but significant changes have occurred in the general level of economic activity during this period, thereby providing an opportunity for testing the effectiveness of a flexible monetary policy under a variety of circumstances.

During most of 1952 and 1953, the Canadian economy approximated that happy condition of full employment without inflation, but with the threat of the latter always present, the Bank of Canada practised moderate monetary restraint in an effort to contain the expansion of aggregate demand within the limits of the rise in real output. Record levels of capital investment were financed in part from domestic sources and in part from abroad.[47] During 1952, Canada's current account balance became favourable, the only such occurrence during the entire post-war period, but the huge net inflow of U.S. capital, amounting to some $850 million, was primarily responsible for the Canadian dollar rising to a premium of more than 4 per cent during the year.

As already indicated in Table XVII, the direct credit restrictions imposed upon the chartered banks early in 1951 were removed in May, 1952, as were those on consumer credit, leaving "normal" methods of central bank action to control chartered bank lending.[48] The rise in bank loans during the year ($308 million) reflected in substantial measure a renewed upsurge in the volume of consumer credit outstanding, and because of official monetary restraint (chartered bank cash having increased by only $7 million in 1952) the banks not merely reduced their cash ratio but became net sellers of short-term securities.

[46]This "over-all" stability has frequently concealed substantial and offsetting relative price changes, notably as between the "agricultural" and "non-agricultural" sectors of the economy.

[47]During 1952, Canada's G.N.P. rose from $21.4 billion to $23.0 billion, and in 1953 to $24.2 billion. These represented real increases of 6 per cent and 3½ per cent respectively. During 1952, rising defence expenditures, personal consumption expenditures and capital investment related primarily to resource development, to defence and to housing all contributed to the rising G.N.P. In 1953, defence expenditures tapered off, but personal consumption expenditures and capital investment continued their gains, the latter shifting somewhat in character as outlays on social capital—schools and roads—became increasingly important. A substantial inventory accumulation also occurred in 1953, while beginning with 1951, the successive bumper harvests helped to swell real output (and to provide serious marketing difficulties for the Canadian government and the Western wheat producers).

[48]See Bank of Canada, *Annual Report*, 1952, p. 8.

In the face of relatively stable long-term yields, the gap betwen long- and short-term yields became narrower than at any time during the preceding twenty years.[49] Table XIV shows that substantial increases occurred both in the active money supply and in residents' inactive assets during the year.

Canada's continuous post-war economic expansion continued through most of 1953 but by the last quarter there were indications that the long-anticipated recession might be at hand, and despite higher levels of output and employment for the year as a whole, unemployment was significantly greater at the year's end than twelve months earlier. Employment opportunities were no longer increasing as rapidly as the labour force. Another record volume of capital expenditures was financed in part by a net capital inflow of some $450 million, the counterpart of which was a current deficit based on a lower physical volume of exports and continuously rising imports. The rate of exchange between the Canadian and U.S. dollars remained stable throughout the year.[50] Until the autumn of 1953, the Bank of Canada continued its policy of restraint, but with the decline in business activity in the final quarter the Bank became a net purchaser of securities. The year's rise in chartered bank loans ($607 million) again reflected the continued expansion of consumer credit[51] and also the financing of inventory accumulation. Chartered bank cash declined by some $11.4 million, and to support their loan expansion, a further reduction of their cash ratio and of their holdings of government and non-government securities occurred.[52] Despite a firming of short-term yields during the first three quarters, there was little change in interest rates over the whole year.[53]

Table XIV indicates that the total liquid assets of the general public rose by $264 million, as the effect of monetary expansion was appreciably modified by substantial government debt reduction. In contrast to 1952, the active money supply declined slightly and most of the increase in residents' inactive assets reflected increased holdings of government debt and in particular, of Canada Savings Bonds.

During 1953, several important steps designed to broaden the short-term securi-

---

[49]*Ibid.*, p. 9.

[50]At year end, the Canadian price of the U.S. dollar was .971; a year later it was .974.

[51]During 1952, the total of selected items of consumer credit outstanding rose by $414 million, and in 1953 by $326 million.

[52]As of December 31, the banks' cash ratio moved from 11.0 per cent (1951) to 10.4 per cent (1952) to 9.7 per cent (1953).

[53]The notable exception was the yield on 91-day treasury bills, which rose from 1.349 to 1.890 during the year. From the outbreak of World War II until Korea, the interest-rate structure remained inflexible as fiscal requirements dominated the market. Differences in yields were directly related to differences in maturities, being lowest on the shortest-term debt and highest on the longest-term debt. When monetary flexibility appeared after Korea, short-term yields rose more rapidly than those on long-terms (just as in the U.S.), and by late 1953 had in certain instances moved above the latter. With the general decline which began toward the end of the year, short-term yields again moved relatively more rapidly and the anomaly disappeared.

ties market were introduced. Until the establishment of the Bank of Canada in 1935, Canadian money market[54] funds were supplied almost exclusively by the chartered banks, which dominated the financial scene. "Call" loans were granted to investment bankers, stock brokers and individuals, on the security of stocks and bonds, while to finance the "needs" of domestic business the banks bought short-term commercial paper. The purchase and sale of foreign bills was likewise centred in the chartered banks, the only dealers in the foreign exchange market. Each bank operated a foreign exchange department in which buying and selling orders were matched as closely as possible, and net positions in sterling or U.S. dollars were eliminated by appropriate transactions either in the Canadian or, if necessary, the wider New York and London exchange markets.[55] It was only in the banks' foreign exchange and government securities dealings that "open" markets could be said to exist, and here the markets were extremely narrow.

In 1934, the Canadian government instituted a competitive tender basis for the sale of its fortnightly issues of 91-day treasury bills, in part to lower the cost of this short-term accommodation and in part to facilitate the operations of the Bank of Canada, the establishment of which was imminent. The Bank became an important purchaser of these securities, as did the chartered banks, whose rising investments reflected the prevailing conditions of economic depression. Treasury bills were customarily held to maturity, except where utilized by the banks to adjust their cash position, and their ownership outside the banking system was negligible.[56]

Until the advent of the Bank of Canada, the chartered banks as a group possessed no domestic source of ultimate liquidity, and no reliable external source. In times of financial emergency, the liquidation of foreign assets or recourse to foreign borrowing became necessary, but such accommodation was by no means dependable, and the monetary consequences were frequently perverse. Without a central bank, the prime prerequisite for a "safe, steady and liquid money market" was lacking.[57] Since its inception, the Bank has frequently stressed the desirability of developing such a market, where temporarily idle funds could be loaned and borrowed, but only within the past several years has significant progress been made in this direction. Recent developments in the Canadian money

---

[54]While usage varies from time to time and place to place, the term "money-market" generally includes only those capital market transactions which relate to the exchange of short-term securities, i.e., where temporary funds are bought and sold.

[55]See the Royal Commission on Banking and Currency, *op. cit.*, p. 34.

[56]Before 1935, the chartered banks loaned most of their temporarily idle balances in New York and London. Following this date, these investments were shifted to Canada, as a result of which the banks' investment decisions became more closely related to domestic economic conditions and their operations more subject to central bank influences. In this connection, see G. S. Dorrance, "The Bank of Canada" in R. S. Sayers, *Banking in the British Commonwealth* (Oxford University Press), 1952.

[57]See A. F. W. Plumptre, "Central Banking Machinery and Monetary Policy" in H. A. Innis and A. F. W. Plumptre, *The Canadian Economy and Its Problems, op. cit.*, p. 198.

market[58] have attracted the interest of some of the larger non-financial corporations and of municipalities, and a broader ownership of short-term government debt has been effected. In time, it is possible that the market for non-government short-term instruments may likewise be broadened.

The first of these measures designed to broaden the money market appeared in 1953 when the Canadian government introduced a weekly rather than fortnightly offering of treasury bills and diversified the offering by making available 273-day bills to supplement the 91-day maturities, "both of which developments found favour with the market and increased the demand for and turnover of such securities."[59] In addition, the Bank of Canada instituted what are known as "purchase and resale" agreements with thirteen approved securities dealers operating as jobbers or merchandisers in treasury bills and short-term Canadian government securities. The object of such agreements was to assist these dealers in the financing of larger inventories in order to diversify the ownership and broaden the market for those forms of debt. Within specified limits, the Bank undertook to buy this paper from the dealers, with an undertaking to sell it back at a specified price, i.e., at a yield to itself equivalent to the Bank (rediscount) rate.[60]

The Canadian recession which extended from late 1953 through the first half of 1954 was shorter and its impact less severe than that which had appeared somewhat earlier in the United States. It was also highly "selective", inasmuch as the adversity encountered in some sectors of the economy was accompanied by continuous expansion in others. The contributing factors were both external and domestic, including the U.S. recession, increased competition in export markets and from imports, reduced defence expenditures both in Canada and the U.S., declining demand for particular durable consumers' goods and a substantial reduction in farm cash income. This reduction in income arose not directly from the poor crop but from marketing and "delivery" difficulties. Inventory reductions contributed to lower capital expenditures and to a slight decline in non-farm output, the latter regaining its previous peak by the end of 1954. Farm output declined by some 25 per cent during the year as a consequence of the poor wheat crop. Despite these difficulties in agriculture, textiles, electrical appliances, automobiles and other "metals-using" industries, expansion continued without interruption in the pulp and paper, oil, chemicals and many of the base-metals industries. The G.N.P. declined in 1954, the only such instance

[58]See Chapter X, below, for details of central bank "purchase and resale" agreements, the expansion and diversification of treasury bill offerings, the introduction of chartered bank "day-to-day" loans, the alteration in chartered bank minimum cash ratios, the changing significance of the Bank rate, etc.

[59]Bank of Canada, *Annual Report*, 1953, p. 8. During 1954, the total of treasury bills outstanding was increased by $130 million, and the proportion of the total held by non-bank sources rose from approximately 5 per cent to more than 30 per cent.

[60]Between January 1953 and June 1954, the total of such funds provided by the Bank reached a maximum of $73 million. See *ibid.*, p. 11.

during the post-war years, despite which personal income remained at the level of 1953 and personal consumption expenditures actually increased.

Although chartered bank loans began to decline in 1954, there was little net change for the year as a whole, but the incidence of the recession was reflected in decreased industrial, merchandising and finance company borrowings. A further step in the evolution of the Canadian money market was the introduction of chartered bank day-to-day loans. These provide the securities dealers holding purchase and resale agreements with the Bank of Canada with funds for financing their inventories and, except in emergencies, have replaced the comparable facilities which from January 1953 to June 1954 were provided by the Bank of Canada. The central bank has now become their lender of last resort to which the dealers may turn for funds at a penalty rate (the rate paid customarily being above the day-to-day loan rate) if the desired accommodation is not available from the chartered banks.

The day-to-day loan market operates on an entirely impersonal basis, and these loans, being callable in fact at any time, provide the banks with a highly liquid asset, ranking in this respect between cash and treasury bills, and therefore with an additional effective means of adjusting their cash position.[61] The loan rate,[62] customarily below that on 91-day treasury bills, enables the securities dealer to finance his inventory without loss,[63] and if his day-to-day loan is called, his normal procedure is to seek to replace it at some other bank. If chartered bank cash is tight, he may be forced into the Bank of Canada where, like that of the chartered banking system, his ultimate source of liquidity will be found.

At the end of 1954, outstanding day-to-day loans amounted to $81 million, in addition to which, because of an easy cash position, the chartered banks had during the year substantially increased their holdings of treasury bills ($116 million) and other government securities ($449 million), most of these increases having been effected during the latter part of the year. In part, the banks' surplus cash arose from an alteration in their legal reserve requirement.

The 1954 revision of the Bank Act introduced a number of basic changes into Canadian banking practice, one of the most important of which was the provi-

---

[61]See the Bank of Canada, *Annual Report*, 1954, p. 12. If, for example, a bank chooses to call day-to-day loans, this will provide the bank with cash on the following day. If it sells treasury bills, Canadian government securities maturing in less than five years or longer-term securities, cash is obtained on the second, third and fourth day following, respectively. If the bank needs cash on a "same day" basis, it must borrow from the Bank of Canada. Before the advent of day-to-day loans, unexpected demands for cash were usually met by the sale of treasury bills.

[62]Day-to-day loans were launched in June, 1954, at an agreed rate of 1½ per cent. The rate declined to 1 per cent in July and stood at ¾ of 1 per cent at the end of the year. From this low, it had risen to 2¾ per cent by May, 1956.

[63]Before day-to-day loans were available, securities dealers financed their inventories via "call" loans, at rates from 2½-3½ per cent. These were not in fact "call" loans, because the personal relationship between banker and customer operated to restrain the withdrawing of such credit on short notice.

sion of a variable minimum cash ratio for the chartered banks and a change in the manner of its calculation. In place of the fixed minimum 5 per cent cash ratio (in practice the banks worked to 10 per cent), calculated on a daily basis, the new minimum was set at 8 per cent and the Bank of Canada was empowered to vary this ratio between 8 and 12 per cent. The maximum rate of increase may not exceed one per cent per month and the banks must be provided with one month's notice of any change in the ratio.[64] The calculation of the ratio on a monthly basis (average weekly figures for the month) permits the banks to adjust their reserve position more finely and to minimize their holdings of idle cash. As a consequence, the banks have in recent times been working very close to the new minimum, and have thereby become much more sensitive to official monetary policies.

The lowering of the minimum cash ratio in mid-1954 freed some $200 million of chartered bank cash, less than half of which was "mopped up" by the Bank of Canada.[65] Under these circumstances, the banks, as already indicated, became net buyers of government securities, despite which they were still able to end the year with an 8.7 per cent cash ratio. Nevertheless, from September 1953 to mid-1954, easy-money policies were pursued much more vigorously in the United States than in Canada, with the result that the spread between U.S. and Canadian yields widened. This stimulated an inflow of both short-term and long-term funds, the latter provided by the purchase of new Canadian securities floated in the relatively attractive U.S. market. Declining yields on all Canadian maturities (a trend which was actively supported after mid-year by domestic monetary policy)[66] were accompanied by a further strengthening of the Canadian dollar at a time when widespread complaints about the exchange rate were being heard from both Canadian exporters and other domestic producers subject to import competition.

Thus, in view of U.S. monetary policy in late 1953, it would scarcely have been feasible (even if desirable) for Canada to have continued its monetary restraint. The general nature of the type of external limitation on Canadian monetary policy is summarized in the statement that "as long as economic activity stays at a high level, Canadian monetary policy can differ appreciably from that of the United States, as it has in fact done in the last few years . . . [but] should the economic climate become less favourable, Canadian monetary developments are likely to parallel more closely those in the United States."[67]

[64]The minimum 8 per cent ratio has not been changed to date. The chartered banks' deposits in the Bank of Canada continue to be calculated on a daily average basis but their notes and Canadian deposit liabilities are calculated as the average of four consecutive Wednesdays, ending with the next-to-last Wednesday in the preceding month.

[65]Chartered bank cash declined by some $91 million during 1954.

[66]By the end of 1954, the yields on treasury bills, short-term and medium-term securities had fallen to levels approximating those in the United States, while the spread in long-terms had become much narrower.

[67]See the Bank of Nova Scotia, *Monthly Review,* February-March, 1954, p. 4.

Another major modification in chartered bank practice, introduced in the 1954 revision of the Bank Act, was the authority for the banks to finance housing construction by investing in mortgages insured by the government under the National Housing Act.[68] The banks appear neither to have sought this authority nor to have received it with any great enthusiasm, and their venture into such an unfamiliar field reflected the desire of the government to ease the financing problems of the housing industry. During World War II the Canadian insurance companies, a leading source of residential mortgage funds, had increased their securities holdings to a much larger than normal proportion of their total assets. Thus in the early post-war years as residential building expanded, the insurance companies' gradual liquidation of securities holdings provided a ready source of mortgage funds. By the end of 1952, however, the holdings of mortgage investments had risen to approximately 30 per cent, a level which they regarded as appropriate in the light of their liabilities. Thereafter, with a much smaller flow of insurance funds into mortgages, the financing of residential construction required additional sources of money. By the end of 1954, the chartered banks' residential mortgage commitments stood at $74 million, and the Bank of Canada noted that their participation in this new field " . . . has enlarged their role in the financing of investment in Canada and improved the general structure and flexibility of the capital market."[69]

During 1954 the total liquid assets of the general public rose by some $253 million (Table XIV), a figure roughly comparable to that of 1953. However, the 1953 increase was brought about mainly by a large increase in bank credit outstanding which was offset only in part by the government's cash surplus, and the bulk of the additional liquidity was embodied in residents' inactive assets. By contrast, the 1954 increase arose mainly from a substantial government deficit, the expansion of bank credit outstanding being very small, and the increase in liquidity took the form of a very large rise in the active money supply.

During the first quarter of 1955 there was little indication of the sustained economic expansion which was to develop later in the year and, by Canadian post-war standards, unemployment was serious during the winter and early spring. With their commercial loans rising very little, the chartered banks continued to acquire securities and to further the general decline in yields. Current

---

[68]This provision was first incorporated into the revised National Housing Act which took effect in March, 1954, and it was subsequently transferred to the Bank Act as revised in 1954.

[69]Bank of Canada, *Annual Report*, 1954, p. 13. The Bank indicated that some part of the chartered banks' mortgage lending represented a net addition to the total institutional lending for such purposes, and part merely displaced loans that would have been made by other institutions. In the latter case, these institutions would be able to lend equivalent funds in other parts of the capital market. An advantage claimed for chartered bank participation was that through their branches they could make funds available in many areas which previously were beyond the reach of the insurance companies and other lending institutions.

short-term yields had moved far out of touch with the Bank rate, which had remained unchanged at 2 per cent since October 1950. The Bank felt that a closer relationship was desirable and by way of putting its rate "into commission for active service", a reduction to 1½ per cent was announced on February 14. The Bank observed that "In the past, Bank Rate has been changed infrequently in Canada and little use has been made of the Banks' facilities. The growth in the breadth and scale of activity in the short-term money market over the past two years has made it desirable that the Bank Rate be made more flexible and bear a closer (though not fixed) relation to other short-term interest rates. The present adjustment will help to make Bank Rate a more significant factor in the money market and facilitate its more flexible use in the future as circumstances may require."[70] The adjustment was not intended as an announcement of still greater monetary ease and in actual fact the long decline in yields came to an end very shortly after the Bank had lowered its rate.

As economic expansion gathered momentum during the second quarter of 1955 the chartered banks' commercial loans expanded rapidly, their net securities purchases declined sharply and by mid-year their cash ratio had fallen to 8.3 per cent. Rising levels of employment and income in the United States exerted a strong influence on the Canadian economy not only through their psychological effects but more tangibly through the strengthening of Canadian exports and the renewed growth of capital investment expenditures. Canada's G.N.P. rose to $26.8 billion in 1955, a 10 per cent increase over the preceding year and almost entirely a "real" gain. Physical expansion was made possible by the progressive utilization of unemployed resources which at the beginning of the year had been large, by post-war standards. By the end of 1955, the slack had been completely absorbed, as the declining rate of real expansion clearly indicated, and the dangers of renewed inflation had once again become serious.

Almost half of the 1955 rise in gross national expenditures arose from higher personal consumption expenditures but gains in all categories of capital investment were an important factor. As indicated below, this record rise in expenditure was supported to a considerable degree by a record post-war expansion of bank credit. The Bank of Canada described its monetary policy during the last half of the year as that of "offering increasing resistance to further expansion." Chartered bank lending nevertheless continued to expand, and at an increasing rate, in spite of which fact a growing scarcity of credit was reflected in rising interest rates as the banks first liquidated treasury bills and day-to-day loans, then other securities, in order to accommodate the growing demand for loans.

[70]Bank of Canada, *Annual Report*, 1955, p. 7. Here it was further explained that while under the conditions of monetary ease which had prevailed since the introduction of day-to-day loans in mid-1954, the securities dealers had not been "in the Bank" nor had the chartered banks required advances, such accommodation might well be sought under tighter monetary conditions, hence the desirability of a more flexible rate to meet such contingencies. Such accommodation was in fact provided in late 1955, in 1956 and in 1957.

Here the accelerated expansion of consumer credit was one of the main influences, augmented by increases in personal loans and loans to construction contractors, public utilities and provincial and municipal governments.[71]

Both the chartered banks and the "approved" securities dealers had frequent recourse to Bank of Canada advances during these months, and in an unprecedented series of moves, the Bank raised its rate on three different occasions before the end of the year, but apparently only *after* short-term market rates had registered comparable advances.[72] These rising market yields appear to have been the main outcome of official monetary policy in 1955, for it seems clear that bank borrowing was not noticeably discouraged by the degree of monetary pressure which the Bank was able to effect. Its operations permitted chartered bank cash to rise by $5 million, $20 million and $45 million in the second, third and fourth quarters respectively, and the greatest expansion of bank loans occurred during the last quarter when with the return of full employment and a declining growth in real output, the risks involved in continuing rapid credit expansion were abundantly clear.

To strengthen its monetary control in the coming months, the Bank succeeded in supplementing its open-market and rediscount rate techniques with certain other measures. In the autumn of 1955, meetings with the chartered banks produced some decisions which may well affect permanently the operations of the chartered banks. The Bank pointed out that the rate of credit expansion had become "well in excess" of the physically possible rate of growth in real output, and it was suggested to the chartered banks that "requests for new and increased credits should be examined very carefully, and existing credit limits surveyed with a view to maintaining control over future growth."[73] Unlike 1951, no over-all ceilings were proposed, and the need for some additional credit expansion was recognized, but the necessity for a sharp curtailment of its current rate of growth was obvious. In particular, the banks were asked to avoid any new commitments for "term" lending,[74] since it was apparent that bank funds were

---

[71]*Ibid.*, p. 11. Over the year, total chartered bank loans rose by 19 per cent. The rise in consumer credit outstanding amounted to $350 million, more than three times its increase in 1954 and greater than in 1953.

[72]The rate was raised to 2 per cent on August 5, to 2¼ per cent on October 12 and to 2¾ per cent on November 18. [73]See Bank of Canada, *Annual Report*, 1955, pp. 10-11.

[74]*Ibid.*, p. 17. The Canadian banks have not generally provided term loans to borrowers, i.e., loans where the term of repayment extends beyond that of ordinary commercial loans, or loans effected by a process of direct placement, in which the banks buy securities directly from their customers rather than in the capital market. The Bank pointed out that the appearance of term lending in Canada had been largely confined to three different occasions, i.e., between January 1948 and February 1949, February 1951 and May 1952 and in 1955, and on each occasion the Bank had "felt it necessary to propose and the banks have agreed to a cessation of most forms of term lending."

As a technique of monetary control, the value of moral suasion may be seriously questioned. In support of other central bank operations it may be temporarily effective in coping with some selective monetary problem, but it is invariably instituted after a crisis has developed and will owe its success, as with any other "direct" control, to an interference with the freedom of the market.

being used to finance long-term business requirements in economic circumstances where recourse to equity financing or non-bank borrowing was clearly more appropriate.

A somewhat different approach to more effective monetary control was the Bank of Canada's request that the chartered banks adopt a standard practice concerning the maintenance of a minimum "liquid asset" ratio rather than merely a minimum cash ratio. Specifically, the banks were asked to achieve, by the end of May, 1956, a minimum 15 per cent ratio of liquid assets (cash, day-to-day loans and treasury bills) to deposits, and thereafter to maintain this minimum on a monthly average basis. This measure was clearly intended to render the banks much more sensitive to official measures of monetary restraint and consequently to enable the central bank to influence interest rates and securities markets earlier, more gradually and with greater certainty than would otherwise be possible. If the banks' liquid asset ratio is near or at the minimum at a time of strong demand for loans, the liquidation of securities will be essential for meeting this demand but the losses involved in this process will tend to restrain the dimensions of the loan expansion that will actually take place.[75] In the 1955 credit expansion, the chartered banks obtained additional cash by reducing their liquid assets and the necessity of selling longer-term securities was postponed for an undesirably long time. The Bank of Canada conceded that whenever such action is open to the banks, "monetary restraint, unless of an extreme character, may therefore be temporarily ineffective."[76] This observation was based upon its own immediate experience for there is no doubt that the existence of some conventional minimum liquid asset ratio would have permitted a somewhat more effective control of credit expansion late in 1955.

The basic difficulty of course lay in the excessive liquidity of the Canadian banks which originated in the unprecedented expansion of the national debt during World War II. Moreover when, as in the post-war years, the Canadian government has managed its debt so as to shorten the average maturity of its outstanding issues[77] in order to lessen interest charges, it at the same time risks impairing the effectiveness of monetary policy. Thus, during 1955, in addition

---

[75]*Ibid.*, p. 16. "The loss of interest earnings on the bonds sold and the capital losses usually incurred on such sales at a time of monetary restraint will lessen the bank's incentive to expand loans; and at the same time the bank's sales of bonds will have their restraining effect in the bond market and through it on the securities market generally."

[76]*Ibid.*

[77]Canada Savings Bonds are long-term issues in name only, for they may be redeemed without capital loss at the option of the holders at any time. The government's very limited long-term funding operations since World War II occurred during 1954 and 1956. For details of the former issues see the Bank of Canada, *Annual Report*, 1954, p. 24. In August, 1956, the government made available a conversion issue of $35.0 million 3¾% bonds, due March 15, 1996-8, at a price of 97, to yield 3.90%. Its reception by the financial community was disappointing, and $100 million of the issue was withdrawn from the market, while the bulk of the remainder was purchased by the Bank of Canada and various government accounts.

to their maturing issues, the chartered banks switched short-term maturities to loans with little loss, while the loss incurred in liquidating "longer" holdings was not an effective deterrent to such action. From the viewpoint of monetary management there is a great deal to be said for lengthening the maturity of the national debt[78] and particularly that part held by the chartered banks, with the short-term holdings of the latter institutions confined to levels essential in meeting minimum liquidity requirements.

When the chartered banks have depleted their liquid assets, these must sooner or later be replenished by the sale of securities, and it was the Bank of Canada's view that where the banks could operate in this way, the end result of the process might well be "more drastic and disturbing adjustments in the securities markets and a more abrupt change in lending policy than would have been necessary if, through adherence to a firm convention regarding minimum liquid asset ratios, lending policy were more immediately responsive to monetary restraint.[79] Between late 1955 and the end of May 1956, the Canadian banks steadily built up their liquid asset ratio through their sales of bonds and purchases of treasury bills, the total issue of which was expanded rapidly from roughly $1.2 billion at year end to almost $1.7 billion as of the end of May.[80] The developing market for treasury bills was indicated by the fact that at the end of 1955 almost 44 per cent ($526 million) of the total outstanding was held by non-banking sources.[81]

The dimensions of the monetary expansion effected during that year are reflected in the growth of the general public's total liquid assets by no less than $1,115 million, an increase unmatched and rarely approached in any post-war year. Moreover, this increase occurred despite a government cash surplus of some $111 million, (Table XIV). Most of this additional liquidity assumed inactive forms, a fact in part explained by substantial public buying of securities (Canada Savings Bonds) in the latter part of the year. The expansion of the active money supply was confined to the general magnitude of that of the preceding year.

---

[78]For an interesting elaboration of this theme, see H. C. Simons, "Debt Policy and Banking Policy", in *Economic Policy for a Free Society* (Chicago: The University of Chicago Press), 1948, pp. 231-9. Simons points out that the problem is "that of preventing banks from feeding inflation . . . on the basis of liquid 'governments' as virtual excess reserves. Still more broadly, it is that of removing obstacles, real and illusory, to an anti-inflationary debt policy of borrowing from the public at the substantial interest cost that long maturities or consols would involve, that is, of funding our debt into illiquid, unsupported and firmly held bonds or, if you please, of paying interest on real debt instead of paying merely hoarding premiums on money in the nominal form of bonds."

[79]See Bank of Canada, *Annual Report*, 1955, pp. 16-17.

[80]The government assisted the banks in effecting this adjustment both by the expansion of its outstanding treasury-bill issues and by the use of the proceeds from their sale to acquire substantial holdings of its own outstanding short-term debt.

[81]By late May, this percentage had declined because of the continuous expansion of chartered bank holdings as they moved toward the new minimum liquid asset ratio.

Until mid-1956, the total of chartered bank loans continued to grow very rapidly, in response to the demands of an extremely buoyant economy,[82] and rising inflationary pressures reflected the need for more effective monetary restraint.[83] The Bank rate, having been raised a fourth time to 3% on April 4, was subsequently increased to 3¼% on August 9 and to 3½ on October 17. The governor of the Bank on each occasion insisted that the objective was not to push interest rates up, but merely to "keep in line with the market". This emphasis can be misleading however, for the Bank's influence on market rates as it seeks to regulate the total supply of money by open-market transactions is clearly decisive. In a basic change of policy as of November, 1956, the Bank abandoned its life-long practice of "fixing" a rediscount rate in favour of a more flexible arrangement which provides that the rate shall at all times be ¼ of 1% above the weekly average tender rate on 91-day treasury bills.[84] Having frequently been interpreted in the past as a signal of central bank intentions, rate changes will no longer be so regarded, but the Bank's "conditioning" of the market, if less obvious, will be no less real.

In its efforts to forestall the development of serious inflationary pressures in an economy of substantially full employment, the Bank supplemented its much-publicized rate changes and its open-market dealings by less formal but more selective methods. Consultations were held with various non-banking sources of credit, such as the instalment finance companies and the major department and chain stores, with a view to achieving voluntary credit restraint.[85] In view of the unsuccessful outcome of these consultations, the Bank obtained an agreement from the chartered banks late in 1956 to limit their credit provided to each

[82]An indication of the underlying strength of the economy was provided by the government's mid-year estimates of Canadian capital investment. Private new capital expenditures were estimated at $6.9 billion, and with the addition of repair expenditures, total private outlays amounted to $8.9 billion. Total government capital outlays were estimated at $1.4 billion. The over-all total of $10.3 billion exceeded 1955 figures by 20 per cent, and it was not certain that a real increase of such magnitude could be accomplished.

[83]The very substantial rise in the active money supply and in the general public's holding of liquid assets is summarized in Table XV.

[84]This represented a change from the view expressed by the Bank in its 1955 Annual Report (p. 7) that the Bank Rate should bear a close "but not fixed" relation to other short-term interest rates. The move appeared to represent an effort by the Bank to de-emphasize the significance of rate changes and to shift attention to the impact of the changing demand for funds which, coupled with a less rapid adjustment in their supply (for which the Bank does bear responsibility) had led to the steady increase in the cost of money through the preceding year.

[85]In the late autumn, the governor of the Bank stated that he thought that the substantial rise in the volume of consumer credit outstanding was not yet "excessive" and that there was no "blame" to be attached to anyone, but that if the volume kept on growing it could become dangerous. He therefore "hoped" that the companies operating in this area would ease up on expansion. Representatives of the leading sales finance companies agreed to take certain voluntary measures, including possibly a ceiling on the total volume of their loans and higher minimum down-payments, but no effective arrangement for curbing the rapid expansion of consumer credit was concluded.

instalment finance company to the maximum amount utilized during the preceding year.

By the end of 1956, the cumulative effects of official monetary restraint had become quite apparent, and were spreading to all sectors of the Canadian economy, amid numerous complaints about the rising costs and decreasing availability of credit.[86] The excessive liquidity of the chartered banks, which had for many months forestalled the impact of tighter money, had been virtually eliminated, as those institutions were no longer willing to reduce significantly their holdings of securities.

[86]An interesting phase of the continuing development of the Canadian money market since 1954 was the introduction of "prime commercial notes" as an instrument of corporate finance. These are issued mainly by large Canadian non-financial corporations in need of temporary funds and are secured by the general credit of the issuing firm. Their maturities range from three to twelve months and they are bought by firms having temporarily idle balances, usually with the investment dealers as intermediaries. With a thin and less organized market, these notes are less liquid than other short-term instruments such as treasury bills, and their yield is therefore higher, being based on the yield on finance company paper.

## CHAPTER XI

# SOME PROBLEMS OF MONETARY-FISCAL "CONTROL" IN THE CANADIAN ECONOMY

THE concept of fiscal policy as an instrument of economic stabilization is relatively new, having evolved from the theoretical analysis developed by Lord Keynes in the late 1930's. In Canada, the formal acceptance of the principle of counter-cyclical finance by the federal government was most clearly set forth with the publication of its White Paper on Employment and Income in 1945.

By contrast, the theory and practice of monetary control has enjoyed a very much longer development in many countries, although in Canada the government's assumption of responsibility for conscious monetary management dates only from the establishment of the Bank of Canada in 1935. For some sixty years, between 1853 and 1914, Canada had adhered to the gold currency standard without interruption, and her monetary "policy" comprehended nothing more than maintaining the convertibility of her dollar. With the suspension of gold convertibility at the outbreak of World War I, and the passage of the Finance Act, which with some modifications remained in force for some two decades, fundamental changes were introduced into the Canadian monetary system. These changes were incompatible with Canada's return to gold (on a bullion basis) in 1926, and after only two and a half years the *de facto* suspension of gold convertibility was forced upon the government. The subsequent agitation for the establishment of a central bank in Canada grew not only from the excessive monetary expansion which the Finance Act had made possible in the late 1920's but also from the excessive contraction which occurred in the early years of the depression and which the government attacked belatedly, clumsily and ineffectively under the provisions of the same Act. The clearly demonstrated inadequacies of a monetary system lacking central direction led finally to the establishment of the Bank of Canada and to the introduction of a consciously formulated Canadian monetary policy aimed at influencing the general level of economic activity within the country.

The appearance of a central bank had been strongly opposed by almost all of the chartered banks, which as already noted, had effectively discouraged an earlier effort to introduce such an institution at the end of World War I. From its earliest beginnings, the development of chartered banking in Canada had been closely related to the financing of export staples, and the relative scarcity of capital characteristic of the pioneer economy had dictated a high degree of banking centralization. The branch banking system was admirably suited to this purpose and to providing banking facilities in the frontier areas of the economy which otherwise would have been either not forthcoming or long delayed. As in all phases of Canadian economic growth, external influences conditioned the pattern of banking development, and the relatively narrow scope for banking "experimentation" during the pre-Confederation period is to be explained by the restraining influence of the British Colonial Office. In later years it stemmed from the strongly entrenched position of the banks which rendered them immune to the demands for "reform" which originated mainly on the prairies. There, the conventional lending facilities of the chartered banks were almost totally inadequate to provide for the peculiar credit requirements of the wheat farmers.

As a result of a concentration movement which had been in evidence for some decades, Canadian banking ownership in the early 1930's was highly centralized in a relatively few powerful institutions, soundly and conservatively managed, commanding unquestioned public confidence, and claiming that a central bank was completely unnecessary because it could provide no service not already within the scope of the existing institutions. While this view, as noted earlier, fails completely to appreciate the functions of a central bank, and fortunately did not prevail, it did possess a certain plausibility and undoubtedly helped to explain the relatively late appearance of central banking in Canada. Having already analysed the broad objectives and the techniques of Canadian monetary and fiscal policy in the late 1930's and in World War II, it is of some interest at this point to review and attempt to assess our experience with more than a decade of post-war monetary and fiscal controls.

A sound evaluation of Canadian post-war monetary policy must of course recognize the fact that inflation has been a world-wide phenomenon, the impact of which was unavoidable in this country. The potential contribution of monetary action in the immediate post-war years and following Korea lay in the mitigation of external influences and in the restraint of inflationary pressures of domestic origin. Granted that the effectiveness of Canadian monetary action left much to be desired, how are the shortcomings to be explained?

Until 1950, the serious use of monetary policy as a weapon of inflationary control was deliberately rejected. This attitude of the Bank appears to have been fostered in part by the prevailing emphasis on fiscal policy, for example in the United States and the United Kingdom, which had arisen in part from a lack of faith in the effectiveness of monetary action. The Bank's attitude was further conditioned by the fact that whether effective or not, monetary restriction could be instituted only at the cost of substantial disorder in the capital market, and this was too high a price to pay for the possible damping of an inflation which was expected to be a temporary problem. When the anticipated substantial post-war recession failed to develop, the government in these early years relied almost exclusively upon fiscal policy as a deliberate and much tidier approach to the restraint of inflation. The experience of 1950 strongly suggests that for any restraining attempt to be successful, both monetary *and* fiscal measures must be co-ordinated in the attack.

In view of the error in the government's major post-war premise, that is, the imminent necessity of coping with recession, hindsight suggests the desirability of much earlier monetary restriction than in fact occurred. Here, of course, the relevance of debt management considerations must be recognized. Because of the dominant position of the Bank in the capital market, it would have been impossible for the Bank to undertake effective (in terms of chartered bank cash) open-market sales without significant declines in security prices. Since, before 1950, the Bank was unwilling either to institute or to tolerate such declines, its open-market weapon was immobilized. The wisdom of a monetary policy which appears to have been based almost exclusively on its consequences for debt management, as against some "compromise" policy which could have provided a greater measure of flexibility, must be seriously questioned. With the outbreak of the Korean War, Canadian monetary policy was belatedly and abruptly reversed, but this monetary action was severely handicapped by the operation of external influences and by a reduction of the chartered banks' "excess" cash. Fiscal measures thus continued as the main instrument of economic stabilization, for despite the "reactivation" of monetary controls, more positive open-market activity (and therefore more flexible bond prices) would have been essential to a successful policy of restraint in this period.

In the comparatively brief interval between late 1953 and mid-1954, the Canadian economy experienced a relatively mild recession, in which agricultural difficulties and inventory reductions were immediately relevant. The incidence of the recession varied greatly from sector to sector, but the over-all decline in economic activity was not great. The Bank provided an appropriate policy of moderate monetary ease, and stimulated by United States recovery, Canadian expansion had again gained momentum by mid-year.

The period of easy money provided a particularly favourable background for the introduction of the chartered banks' day-to-day loans, a highly liquid type of asset which allows the banks to reduce their idle cash to minimum requirements. Moreover, the revised basis of calculating the minimum legal cash ratio has enabled the banks to judge their monthly cash requirements more accurately. Working with little excess cash and observing a minimum liquidity ratio designed to immobilize their shortest-term assets, the banks have consequently become much more sensitive to official monetary policy. The strong tradition against borrowing from the Bank of Canada[1] was notably weakened by the

---

[1]In January, 1954, the Bank of Canada had recorded an advance of $10 million to the Royal Bank. This rare occurrence was particularly interesting because of the explanation provided by the borrower in its 1953 *Annual Report*: "If the chartered banks become accustomed to temporary borrowing from the Bank of Canada to take care of temporary adverse swings in their cash position they will also be more willing to purchase treasury bills and other short-term securities when they experience a temporary favourable swing in their cash position. In doing so, the chartered banks will tend to broaden the market for these securities". This and several other early advances were gestures clearly not dictated by need, as were the later borrowings in 1955, 1956 and 1957.

pressure of the credit "squeeze" which began late in 1955, for in the last quarter of that year and in 1956 and 1957 the chartered banks frequently obtained advances from the Bank.[2] The approved securities dealers also received central bank accommodation in these years through the operation of purchase and resale agreements, a further indication of the growing credit "squeeze" in the Canadian economy.[3]

The foregoing developments suggest that the Bank rate may assume an importance much greater than formerly. With both the banks and the security dealers facing the occasional prospect of being forced into the Bank at a penalty rate, one important consequence of the continuing development of the Canadian capital market has been that the influence of rate changes has shifted from a "psychological" to a more direct basis, associated with the recent linking of the Bank rate with the treasury-bill yield. On the other hand, as long as a rate change could be regarded as a clear indication of central bank intentions, the impact of the change could presumably be spread over a broader section of the capital market than has been possible with open-market operations. Under the new method of calculating the Bank rate, the "announcement" effect is no longer obtained.

It is of course true that a continuing increase in the proportion of short-term debt held by non-bank sources will broaden the impact of the Bank of Canada's open-market transactions, but the most important consequence of such a trend will be the additional monetary flexibility which the Bank will gain. It has already been pointed out that when central bank open-market activity causes significant price changes in securities markets, the scope of its activities (sales) is likely to be undesirably circumscribed. Assuming that the Bank's objective is to influence particular yields, a narrow market might seem to be ideal, but the practical ("political") limitations to extensive operations of this kind are important. On the other hand, a broad market, by lessening price fluctuations stemming from central bank securities transactions, will provide a much more satisfactory medium for controlling chartered bank reserves, since the institutional restrictions on the Bank's operations will be relatively slight. Only where the breadth of the market permits the central bank some freedom of action, freedom to back away from purchasing securities offered and freedom to initiate sales of its own, can effective monetary restraint be exercised.

The rapid monetary expansion which occurred in Canada between mid-1955 and mid-1956 raised serious doubts that the recently increased sensitivity of the

---

[2]The chartered banks have "automatic" access to central bank advances at the penalty (rediscount) rate in limited amounts and for seven days only. Larger borrowings are subject to negotiation.

[3]The purchase and resale agreements are at present applicable to government and government-guaranteed securities with maturities not exceeding three years. The accommodation granted by the Bank may extend to thirty days, but the average term has been two and one-half days. Dealers, like the banks, must observe established borrowing limits.

chartered banks to official monetary policy had in fact resulted in a more effective control of their lending operations. While there were legitimate differences of opinion as to just how serious the inflationary pressures had become and hence as to what degree of central bank restraint was most appropriate, it was perfectly clear, as the Bank of Canada pointed out in late 1955, that the current rate of credit expansion could not be permitted to continue. Nevertheless, it was not until after mid-1956 that the Bank effectively curbed this undesirably rapid and sustained monetary expansion. By the last quarter of that year, the chartered banks had virtually discontinued their "switching" activities (from governments to loans) which had played such an important role in thwarting the objectives of the Bank of Canada, and with their general and other loans no longer rising significantly, the Canadian money supply was finally stabilized. As of late 1956, the Bank's continuous application of restrictive monetary measures had intensified the general credit "squeeze" and had undoubtedly restrained the expansion of aggregate demands upon the economy to a rate generally consistent with its growth in productive capacity. It may fairly be claimed that in its first major test as the central agency for combating inflation, the Bank of Canada provided a somewhat belated demonstration of the invaluable and indeed indispensable role which a genuinely flexible monetary policy must assume if inflationary pressures are to be combated effectively. It must also be noted, however, that this same experiment pointed up quite clearly some of the inherent limitations of monetary controls, particularly when applied in an open economy in close proximity to the United States. During the post-War II decade, Canada had shifted its emphasis in combating inflation from an almost exclusive reliance upon fiscal measures in the early years to a comparable dependence upon monetary techniques after mid-1955. The inherent limitations of the latter approach, as revealed by Canadian experience, are discussed below, and they emphasize the shortcomings of an anti-inflationary policy which has shifted from one "extreme" to another, in the sense that fiscal and monetary instruments have been utilized mainly as alternative rather than complementary techniques of control.

The rejection of fiscal policy as the prime approach to economic stabilization appears to have rested upon several grounds. While it is both a powerful and essential component of any successful attack upon severe inflationary pressures, the problem of educating the public as to the objectives and implications of counter-cyclical budgets is difficult, particularly where the government's efforts are likely to be misrepresented by its opposition, both inside and outside parliament. The existence of a budget surplus leads, *ipso facto*, to charges of over-taxation, and also encourages wasteful and excessive government expenditures. Particular fiscal measures designed to affect resource allocation in the economy, being in some sense discriminatory, arouse violent and, from the viewpoint of the sectors affected, legitimate complaints. Even if counter-cyclical policy is assumed to be feasible at the federal level, there is the very real problem in Canada of maintaining its effectiveness in the face of possibly conflicting fiscal measures adopted by the provincial and municipal governments. The Royal Commission on Dominion Provincial Relations addressed itself to this problem shortly before World War II, but its recommendations were never implemented. The current technique of Tax Rental Agreements, originated in 1941, and designed to provide a broad area of fiscal freedom for the federal government, at present fall far short of ensuring continuing harmony between federal and provincial fiscal programmes.

On a somewhat different level, the Canadian recession of 1953-4 which developed mainly from problems encountered in agriculture and in the textile and electrical goods industries, revealed clearly the difficulties of applying fiscal measures to what were highly selective weak spots rather than parts of a general economic recession. With expansion continuing at an undiminished rate in many industries, a policy of deficit financing would not only have failed to meet the problems of the lagging sectors but would undoubtedly have provided an unwelcome inflationary impetus.

A review of Canada's post-war fiscal policy indicates that the lags which are inevitable in the democratic process of government render such policy insufficiently adaptable for tactical use, while on the other hand, the broad outlines of the fiscal programme may be conditioned not so much by internal economic conditions as by changing social philosophies (e.g., as to the role of welfare expenditures) or by random external disturbances. The government's rejection of fiscal measures as the prime instruments of economic control, and the lesser role which they would henceforth be assigned, was indicated in the 1955 Budget Speech, where the Minister of Finance advocated "a tax policy and a tax structure that would produce a balanced budget under conditions which represent a high level of output and employment".[4] Observing that fiscal policy was just one instrument of economic stabilization, he further noted that monetary and other policies might in certain contexts have considerably greater influence and the events following mid-1955 left little doubt of the prime importance assigned to monetary control.

Apart from these particular features which impede effective fiscal control, many technical problems remain to be solved. Although it will be generally conceded that much has been learned about fiscal techniques since the 1930's, there is a great need for further study of the particular reactions of given economic units to specific fiscal measures in order that policies may be more intelligently conceived. Moreover, effective action requires not only a knowledge of what to do but when to do it, and the problem of timing is one of crucial importance. The more effective timing of fiscal (and of monetary) policy requires the continuing development and the earlier availability of a broader range of relevant

[4]Minister of Finance, *Budget Speech*, April 1955, p. 2733.

economic data in order that basic trends may be promptly determined and evaluated.[5]

Granted that the foregoing difficulties help to explain the absence of a rigorous anti-inflationary fiscal policy in Canada between mid-1955 and mid-1957, it is useful to consider briefly the consequences of the continuous policy of monetary restraint pursued during that period. Although the instruments of monetary control are generally regarded as being more flexible than fiscal techniques, their effectiveness, as explained earlier, was severely impaired for many months by the chartered banks' massive liquidation of government securities and their corresponding expansion of loans.[6] For much too long a time, the capital loss involved in this "switching" process provided no effective deterrent to the banks, which had available a very large volume of relatively short-term bonds. While the introduction of the fifteen-per cent "liquidity" ratio immobilized some resources that would otherwise have been available for switching, and therefore lessened the magnitude of the problem at that time, it really has done little to solve it, for given another period of recession, with a declining demand for bank loans and a consequent growth of bank investment in short-term governments, the general problem posed by excessive chartered-bank liquidity will reappear. It is by no means clear that a stationary minimum liquidity ratio represents a useful addition to the Bank of Canada's instruments of monetary control, nor does such a device seem likely to further the broadening of the money market, for if the banks must hold a larger volume of treasury bills to conform to the new ratio, these resources will be immobilized and therefore not available for market dealings.

It may well be true that in effecting such a rapid run-off of securities in 1955-6, the chartered banks acted unwisely. As an alternative to such a policy which, while yielding short-run gains to the banks, incurred the severe displeasure of the Bank of Canada, the banks might have held their securities portfolios relatively stable, in the knowledge that the continuing expansion of the Canadian economy would soon have restored their securities to a suitable proportion of total assets, as loans and total assets continued to expand.

On the other hand, the banks had made little secret of their own displeasure at the circumstances accompanying the announcement by the Bank of Canada of its minimum "liquidity" ratio requirement late in 1955. While such a concept was by no means novel, and had long been observed voluntarily by the British banks, it was made mandatory for the Canadian banks, and lacking any statutory basis, it appears to have been a heavy-handed approach, subject to the usual shortcomings of all direct controls. In particular, it interfered with the

[5]See J. Harvey Perry, "Some Aspects of Recent Fiscal Policy", in *The Canadian Tax Journal*, V, July-August, 1957, pp. 285-98.

[6]There is of course always some lag in the curbing of bank loans which arises from the banks' existing commitments to their customers. In 1955-6 this applied not only to the banks' "general" business loans, but also to their provincial and municipal loans, to their N.H.A. commitments and to the lines of credit established by instalment finance companies.

freedom of the capital market, in that the banks were thereby required to maintain a distribution of assets different from what they would voluntarily have chosen, and it was of course introduced only after certain undesirable trends in the economy had become well established.

Closely related to the difficulties encountered by the Bank of Canada in establishing effective monetary control in this period was a suggestion made in the governor's 1956 *Annual Report* that serious study should be given to the possibility of a gradual segregation of the chartered banks' savings deposits from its commercial lending activities. By allocating such funds to the kinds of investment "naturally" associated with long-term savings—e.g., to the financing of N.H.A. mortgages on new housing and to other long-term uses, it was implied that the re-emergence of excessive bank liquidity would be forestalled, and with the scope of the banks' possible "switching" activity correspondingly reduced, their operations would be much more responsive to official monetary policy.[7] The validity of such a view is not self-evident, and the banks, although subjected to considerable criticism for a substantial cut-back in their mortgage lending during the growing credit squeeze, received the suggestion with little apparent enthusiasm and with the observation that before they could arrive at any decision, very careful and presumably very extended study would be necessary.[8]

As noted below, the Bank has employed open-market dealings as its chief instrument of monetary control during the 1955-7 period. It has not made use of its authority, granted in the 1954 revision of the Bank Act, to raise the minimum cash ratio of the banks above the eight per cent level established at the outset, and the circumstances in which it would be inclined to take such action now appear remote.[9] Conversely, the Bank has introduced certain practices for

[7]The governor suggested that as a transitional measure, the banks might consider investing one-half of the annual increase in their savings deposits in the manner suggested. This proposal was grossly misrepresented in the press as an unjustified attempt to alter the traditional conduct of chartered banking in a way that would inevitably jeopardize the safety of depositors' funds. It was also generally regarded as a politically inspired suggestion designed to ease the mounting pressure on the government arising from severe cut-backs in residential housing construction attributed to the particularly severe credit squeeze in that industry. Such an interpretation was by no means discredited when early in 1957, the Bank of Canada agreed, in the midst of its continuing emphasis upon tight money, to provide the banks with enough additional cash to permit them to expand their housing commitments by $150 million during that year.

[8]The "political" hazards inherent in the chartered banks' entry into residential mortgage financing (1954) were of course apparent from the outset, for they could scarcely have hoped to escape eventual criticism when the sooner-or-later inevitable contraction of lending in this area occurred.

[9]The financing of the embarrassingly large capital inflow after September 1949 caused a substantial rise in bank cash, with serious inflationary implications, and an increase in the banks' minimum cash ratio would have been most useful. However, the capital inflow occurred largely because of a "fixed" rate of exchange (at a level regarded as untenable) and a repetition of such a crisis is scarcely likely with flexible rates. Recent experience suggests that the Bank may have acquired the "wrong" kind of additional powers in the 1954 revision of the Bank Act.

which no statutory authority exists. The agreements with the banks concerning the cessation of term lending, the limitation of loans to instalment finance companies, the maintenance of a minimum liquidity ratio, etc., all represent forms of what is rather poorly termed "moral suasion". This approach has been much more colourfully designated as "ear-stroking", the establishing of an informal code "by means of which the animal becomes aware of what is expected of him and behaves accordingly".[10] While the Bank of Canada has been a persistent devotee of ear-stroking, there are strong grounds, both moral and practical, for confining such arbitrary activity to demonstrable emergencies, because the banks are being requested, in the absence of legal sanction, to pursue some course of action other than that which they conceive to be in their own best interests. Moreover, if the technique is used too often, the desired co-operation may not be achieved, for "if the standard of the done thing is set too far apart from what the enlightened self-interest of the persons concerned dictates, the done thing will not in the end be done".[11] What is required is an adequate monetary framework such that the necessity for persuasion will be minimized, and where its occasional use will be confined to feasible objectives which are not properly the responsibility of the more formally established monetary techniques.[12]

In the two-year interval between late 1955 and late 1957, the Canadian economy operated virtually at full employment, and the continuous strain on the country's physical productive capacity was, as in earlier post-war years, centred in capital investment expenditures. While the bulk of these expenditures were related to the rapid development of natural resources, investment in secondary and service industries was also substantial. In addition to this sustained high level of demand from the business sector, consumer and government expenditures rose appreciably, and despite a continuously expanding real output and a rapidly growing net import of goods and services, the general price level rose throughout the period. The need for continuous monetary restraint under such circumstances was emphasized by the fact that these pressures on the price level were primarily domestic in origin, and had developed in spite of offsetting influences such as the growing Canadian dollar premium and a decline in the world prices of several of Canada's primary exports.

The Bank pointed out that in view of its statutory responsibilities, it had no alternative to attempting monetary restraint, and by mid-1956 this objective had been effectively attained. From mid-1956 to mid-1957, the Canadian money supply showed no significant net increase, and the continuously growing de-

---

[10]See Sir Dennis H. Robertson, "The Role of Persuasion in Economic Affairs", in *Economic Commentaries* (London: The Staples Press, Ltd.), 1956, p. 155.  [11]*Ibid.*, p. 158.
[12]A review of Canadian monetary policy from mid-1955 to mid-1957 suggests that the Bank of Canada has preferred to combine informal controls with "lesser" rate increases (and thereby minimize disturbances in the capital market) than would otherwise have been required to achieve given ends. The Bank's *Annual Report, 1956*, clearly implies that monetary policy should have been more restrictive, if such had been considered feasible by the authorities.

mand for funds, reflecting the buoyant state of the economy, was accompanied by an exceedingly modest expansion of chartered bank loans.[13] More important as sources of additional capital were foreign borrowing (mainly in the United States capital market), rising levels of personal savings and the existence of a federal cash surplus which permitted substantial debt retirement, with a consequent release of funds which became available for financing private investment. Despite an impressive rise in the aggregate of loanable funds in the Canadian capital market during 1956, the relative scarcity of credit continued to grow, a circumstance which was reflected by a sustained general rise in interest rates and by a cumulative pressure on corporate liquidity.

By mid-1957, government bond yields had, on all maturities, reached "new" highs, with the 1920's representing the most recent period in which comparable rates had prevailed. Within a two-year interval, the yield on selected issues of short-term Canadian government bonds had risen from 2.7% to 4.6%, on medium terms from 2.9% to 4.7% and on long terms from 3.2% to 4.2%. It will be observed that in mid-1955, the "customary" pattern of rates prevailed, with "short" yields lower than "medium" and "medium" lower than "long". By the end of 1956, the relatively greater pressure on short- and medium-term bonds had raised their yields above the long-term level, and this pattern was maintained to mid-1957.[14] The most striking movement had occurred in the yield on three-month treasury bills, which during the same two years rose from approximately 1.4% to a high of 4.08%.[15] As noted earlier, the Bank of Canada's rediscount rate is now determined "automatically" by the weekly yield on these bills (at a level one-quarter of one per cent higher).

Having for the first time completed a two-year period in which continuous monetary restraint assumed the major role in combating inflation in the Canadian economy, it is now possible to assess, at least tentatively, both its accomplishments and its limitations. There can be little doubt that through its progressive shrinking of bank liquidity and the consequent moderation of the growth in bank lending, such a policy has restrained potentially serious domestic pressures. If Canadian monetary expansion had long been permitted to continue at the rate attained in the few months following mid-1955, a disastrous spiral of rising prices and costs would appear to have been inevitable. Effected primarily through the operation of a flexible capital market, the gradual but cumulative influence of the

[13]Between mid-1955 and mid-1956, the "general" loans of the chartered banks rose from $3.5 billion to $4.5 billion; at mid-1957, these loans stood at slightly above $4.6 billion.

[14]The initial impact of the chartered banks' "switching" of assets was reflected mainly in the rapid price declines (increase in yields) of treasury bills and short-term governments. By mid-1956, short-term yields had risen above mediums, a relationship which showed some indication of being reversed only after mid-1957.

[15]This yield was established in the weekly auction of August 22, 1957. During 1956, the rising treasury bill yield had been furthered by the growth of finance company financing via the medium of the short-term note. This occurrence was in part responsible for the decline in the general public's holdings of treasury bills.

credit "squeeze" limited the demands on the Canadian economy without incurring the rigidity, inefficiency and loss of freedom which inevitably accompany the use of direct controls.

The essential manifestations of a successful policy of central bank restraint are the rising cost and the decreasing availability (increasing scarcity) of credit, and by virtue of its success, such a policy will inevitably be criticized by unsatisfied borrowers. The traditional function of rising rates is to discourage marginal borrowers of capital and to encourage greater savings, and the market decides "who gets how much at what cost". It is readily conceded, of course, that in this process, "the actual distribution of loanable funds may not seem to be the most desirable one from the point of view of society as a whole, or of large groups within it".[16] If a different distribution is deemed to be socially desirable, it can be effectively accomplished only through the legislating of direct controls, thereby removing the problem from the area of central bank responsibility.[17] While the objections of unsatisfied borrowers to a policy of "tight" money are to be expected, a much more widespread criticism of high interest rates appears to have developed among Canadian business men. As defenders of a free enterprise economy, their criticism is ill-founded, in the light of the certain alternative of disastrous inflation, and appears to be based on a misconception of the function of interest rates.

It is frequently alleged that by increasing costs, higher rates lead to higher prices and therefore "cause" or aggravate inflation. This claim neglects the fact that in the aggregate, interest costs are a very small component of total costs and that the causal influence is therefore weak. The basic explanation of rising interest rates is the growing relative scarcity of credit in the economy, which in turn reflects excessive demand frequently swollen by inflation. Canadian post-war experience clearly suggests that when an attempt is made to forestall an upward adjustment of rates under such circumstances, the spiral of rising costs and prices is likely to be very much more serious than where monetary flexibility permits a market adjustment to take place.

The broad objectives of Canadian post-war monetary policy have been to promote sustained economic growth and monetary stability, twin goals which, in the event, have proved incompatible. While a quite remarkable post-war expansion of Canadian productive capacity, based on a continuously high level of investment expenditures, has been recorded, so, unfortunately, has a serious decline in the value of the dollar. The two phenomena are closely related, inasmuch as investment outlays have been the most dynamic and important factor in sustaining full employment throughout the post-war years. The real counterpart of these outlays has been the allocating of a record proportion of available resources

---

[16]See the Bank of Canada, *Annual Report*, 1956, p. 31.

[17]It is nevertheless true that some of the Bank of Canada's informal "agreements" with the chartered banks and, on occasion, with other financial institutions, operate as "qualitative" monetary controls.

to the production of capital goods, a development which has been mainly responsible for generating, at various times, excessive aggregate demands upon available productive capacity. The inevitable result has been the intensification of inflationary pressures which has been reflected in an accelerated if uneven decline in the value of money. While within generally determinable limits growth is consistent with economic stability, the pace of Canadian development since World War II has brought frequent conflict between these goals, with stability the objective sacrificed. The assertion that the same rate of growth could have been accomplished with less inflation (by the earlier use of more restrictive monetary measures) cannot, of course, be conclusively demonstrated or refuted. Criticism of Canadian post-war monetary policy may rest on this particular premise but it may also reflect the belief that it would have been "better" to seek greater stability even at the cost of slower growth. Here a difficult judgment of social values is involved, and there is obviously room for a wide range of views as to the merits of the alternatives.

Although Canadian experience during the past two years has demonstrated the indispensable role of effective monetary restraint in minimizing economic instability, the practical limitations on the timing and scope of monetary measures have also been clarified. Concerning the difficulties of timing, it must be recognized that "no one, particularly in the early stages of a boom, can choose some particular moment at which to decide that inflationary dangers are present without doubt and in dangerous degree—The question at issue is always one of degree and of the probable continuation as well as direction of discernible trends".[18] Here, as with fiscal techniques, sound judgment will obviously be furthered by the continuing development of a broader and more timely range of relevant economic data. The difficulties of timing monetary changes were pointed up by the appearance of numerous "soft" spots in the Canadian economy late in 1957. With weakening export markets and falling prices in basic exports such as pulpwood, newsprint, lumber and base metals, as well as in some secondary industries, demands for the relaxation of tight money were increasingly heard. Capital investment expenditures nevertheless continued very strong and these, in conjunction with undiminished consumption expenditures, sustained the basic strength of the economy. A mixture of cross-currents was in evidence, and the lack of any clearly discernible trend supported the holding action adopted by the Bank. Justifiable fears were nevertheless expressed that whenever the conditions appropriate to easier money arrived, the lag in recognizing such a need might seriously weaken the effects of the action, particularly in an economy deprived of a great deal of its earlier liquidity.

Apart from the difficulties in timing, the effectiveness of recent Canadian monetary policy has been limited by other factors. Some of these, as with timing, represent weaknesses in the technical aspects of monetary control, inasmuch as

[18]See Bank of Canada, *Annual Report,* 1956, p. 23.

they affect the promptness or the degree of restraint attained. Others arise *because* of the technical efficiency of monetary instruments and reflect the consequences of their successful operation.

The problems presented by the excessive liquidity of the chartered banks through 1955 clearly fall in the former category and require no additional discussion. They nevertheless raise the question of what might constitute the most appropriate policy of Canadian debt management, especially in the arrangement of maturities. The liquidity of the banks during 1955 rested primarily upon the large volume of relatively short-term government securities which could be sold with little capital loss, and a strong argument can be made in favour of a longer-term average debt, in the interests of more effective monetary control. While it is particularly desirable that the term of bank-held maturities be lengthened, a similar lengthening of holdings by the general public would reduce the cash demands upon the government in periods of tight money and minimize the necessity for new borrowings at high rates in order to finance redemptions. The argument that a longer-term debt would involve prohibitive interest costs is not sound, and the additional cost might well be a small price to pay for the greater monetary stability attained in the future.[19] Had long-term funding, a rare occurrence in Canadian post-war debt management, been undertaken at the end of the War, much of the additional interest costs would of course have been avoided.

Another difficulty was the fact that various sources of credit other than the chartered banks were available to Canadian borrowers. Funds were provided domestically by finance companies, other corporate lenders both financial and non-financial, and by individuals. In addition, the volume of external borrowing reached unprecedented levels, but with respect to the problem of minimizing inflation, the inflow of foreign capital (mostly from the United States) was advantageous. With no net acquisition of foreign exchange by the banking system, the inflow involved no monetary expansion and the real cost of a significant part of the Canadian investment programme was borne externally, as reflected in a very large current account deficit. The continuously rising discount on United States funds through 1956-7 provided an additional buffer against the transmission of inflationary pressures through imports, but it also added to the "political" difficulties of maintaining tight money as the protests of important export interests gathered strength.

Assuming that monetary policy has been successful in stabilizing the volume of bank credit (as was substantially true in Canada by mid-1956), a continuing rise in the rate of money expenditure necessarily reflects a more rapid turnover of money, an "activation" of idle deposits. This process is likely to continue for some time because of the general pressure on liquidity, but as borrowers continue

---

[19]In 1946, the average rate of interest on the Canadian national debt stood at 2.59%, and the annual interest payments represented approximately 3.79% of the gross national product. In 1956, the average rate had risen to 2.86% but annual payments represented only 1.65% of the gross national product, the lowest ratio in many years.

to seek out and tap available pools of idle savings, the scope for such action is steadily narrowed.[20] Meanwhile, the effectiveness of monetary policy may be seriously delayed. The Bank of Canada found the instalment finance companies and small-loan companies particularly troublesome in this respect, and described them as amounting to "a rival banking system, competing for deposits and short-term funds in order to make short-term loans to finance consumption—and out of step with the trend of credit policy in the regular banking system".[21] These companies had effectively diverted a large volume of savings to the financing of a rapidly rising level of consumer credit, for which the borrowers appeared to be remarkably insensitive to interest charges, by acquiring funds through the sale of short-term notes and of securities in the capital market. For a considerable time, their lending activities were affected relatively little by official monetary action, but here as elsewhere, tight money became increasingly effective as the pressure of the continuing squeeze on liquidity mounted.

The degree of monetary restraint which can be maintained in Canada is at all times conditioned by her very close economic ties with the United States, and it is not by accident that the broad shifts in monetary policy in the two countries have generally coincided. When, at certain times, greater restraint in Canada has produced a significant differential in interest rates, the result has been an accelerated inflow of capital, stimulated both domestically and abroad. This was true in 1956 and 1957, particularly with reference to longer-term securities,[22] and the growing strength of the Canadian dollar, reinforced by a growing rate of direct investment, created serious problems for many of Canada's leading export industries and for those domestic industries which were subjected to stronger import competition. Given the prevailing social philosophy which requires national governments to seek continuous full employment at whatever cost, and given a serious short-run immobility of resources which precludes their effective re-allocation, the external limitations on Canadian monetary "autonomy", except for brief intervals, are quite apparent.

[20]In general anticipation of the growing effectiveness of monetary control, i.e., of higher rates and scarcer credit, there may be a significant amount of current borrowing to provide not for present but future use. There is some evidence that such borrowing occurred in Canada in 1956-7, thereby aggravating the immediate difficulties of slowing the rise in the rate of money expenditure.

[21]*Ibid.*, p. 27. The Bank emphasized the destabilizing influence of large fluctuations in consumer credit, and further claimed that the diversion of an increasing amount of savings to finance consumption was an anomaly in a situation where "all the saving that can be accomplished is needed to provide resources for the capital investment program". This unqualified priority accorded to the continuation of investment expenditures which had already reached unprecedented proportions might, of course, be reasonably questioned.

[22]During 1955, the net capital outflow arising from transactions in Canadian securities (securities outstanding, new issues and retirements) amounted to $45 million. By contrast, these transactions provided a net capital inflow of some $748 million in 1956 and of $552 million in the first half of 1957, due mainly to a greatly expanded volume of new flotations in the U.S. market, but also in part to higher U.S. purchases of outstanding issues. See the Bank of Canada, *Statistical Summary, Financial Supplement*, 1956, p. 91.

A different sort of problem is that of maintaining the broad general acceptability of a policy of tight money. Inherent in the operation of monetary restraint is the fact that the greater the degree of success achieved, the greater and more vocal is the opposition provided by the increasing numbers of unsatisfied borrowers who allege discrimination. This claim is in a sense true, for the allocation of the relatively scarce "commodity" via the market mechanism will inevitably eliminate some potential borrowers. To avoid such an outcome by rejecting monetary restraint is inconsistent with the objective of containing inflation, where the basic problem is not "whether" to curb excess demand, but "how". The justification for major reliance on the market process is that its impersonal allocation of available funds will involve less discrimination than will any alternative method. Recent Canadian monetary experience has nevertheless revealed some serious inequities.

The impact of a credit squeeze on the capital market is inevitably uneven, but its initial pressure is directed at chartered bank cash, with a view to restraining monetary expansion and thereby affecting the cost and availability of credit. The liquidity of the economy is continuously reduced and eventually the consequences of the squeeze are reflected "in the spending and savings decisions of income receivers and of holders of cash balances and other assets".[23] In Canada, central bank pressure had succeeded in stabilizing the volume of the banks' general loans[24] by mid-1956, and the earliest and most serious casualties of the credit squeeze were borrowers entirely dependent on this source of credit. These, in the main, were relatively small business enterprises and to a lesser extent, small municipalities, all lacking the financial status essential for direct borrowing in the capital market via securities issues. Particularly hard hit was residential construction, an industry typified by small-scale organization, when after mid-1956 the banks severely cut back their new commitments for financing housing under N.H.A. mortgage provisions. On the other hand, the banks' largest and long-established customers appear to have continued to receive increased accommodation between mid-1956 and mid-1957, reflecting in part a modest rise in total general loans but primarily the result of a redistribution of the banks' loanable funds.[25] For these borrowers, to whom bank loans frequently represent

[23]For an extensive elaboration of this proposition, see the *Federal Reserve Bulletin*, March, 1953, pp. 1-16.

[24]A category which includes personal, farm, industrial, merchandising, financial, construction, utilities and miscellaneous loans, amounting in the aggregate to approximately four-fifths of total loans. The "other" loans include those to provincial and municipal governments, stockbrokers, investment dealers, grain dealers and to persons for financing the sale of Canada Savings Bonds.

[25]In this period, industrial loans to forest products, iron and steel products, mining and mine products, transportation equipment and public utilities borrowers increased by some $290 million, while the total of general loans rose by less than half this amount. Farm loans showed no net change, but personal, merchandising, petroleum and construction contractors loans showed the greatest declines, aggregating some $170 million.

only a secondary source of funds, and for other borrowers only marginally dependent on the banks, the impact of the credit squeeze is relatively long delayed and in many instances may not be very burdensome.[26] Discrimination against small business is therefore inherent in the nature of continuing monetary restraint, and the sharp rise in Canadian business bankruptcies during the foregoing period emphasized the adverse effects of such a policy on initiative and enterprise, and provided some support for the view that it was "a magnificent instrument for promoting [economic] centralization".[27]

It is sometimes alleged that monetary control is an ineffective instrument for combating inflation, not because of technical deficiencies affecting the promptness or degree of restraint attained nor because of any difficulties in maintaining its general acceptability, but because it fails to come to grips with the phenomenon of the wage-price spiral, and more generally with those forces which represent "cost-push" inflationary pressures. On closer analysis, however, this criticism really amounts to asserting the obvious fact that monetary restraint cannot, by itself, prevent inflation. Indeed, it is painfully clear that in the Canadian economy, no combination of domestic policies, however soundly conceived, can accomplish this result when inflation is a more or less world-wide phenomenon. The events of the 1946-8 and 1950-1 periods provide excellent illustrations of the difficulties involved. With reference to 1955-7, inflation appears to have been, to a much greater extent than in the previous periods, generated domestically,[28] and here it is reasonably clear that monetary restraint, although operating directly to moderate "demand-pull" pressures, has at the same time indirectly minimized cost pressures.

It is of course a mistake to regard these two sets of forces as independent. Basic to the development of inflation is the mutual interaction of rising costs and rising prices, with cumulative effects. The effective curbing of excess demand has not only, through its easing of pressures on the general price level, moderated the dimensions of wage demands but has also restricted the magnitude of such increases which the economy could support. Rising wages are *per se* not inflationary, for unless monetary conditions are such as to permit a compensating rise in prices, i.e., unless demand is sufficiently strong to permit an inflationary

[26]The contrast here is between the non-availability of additional credit, the situation encountered by the relatively small bank borrower, and the higher cost of additional credit for those borrowers having access to the domestic and/or foreign capital markets. A rapid increase in interest rates may of course cause serious difficulties, as for example, in the case of municipal and provincial governments, many of which resorted to the borrowing of U.S. funds in the face of an increasingly unfavourable exchange rate.

[27]See John K. Galbraith, "Are Living Costs Out of Control?", in *The Atlantic Monthly*, April, 1957, pp. 37-41.

[28]In contrast to their movement in the two earlier periods of severe inflation in Canada since World War II, import prices (in Canadian dollars) rose relatively little during 1956-7, in part because of the continuous depreciation of the United States dollar. The existence of the huge current account deficit in 1956 was in itself a strong anti-inflationary force.

spiral to develop, then wage increases, by making some production unprofitable, lead instead to unemployment. The real problem here is once again that of public acceptability or the extent to which monetary control may be curbed by "political" pressures, i.e., by the unwillingness of the government to accept a measure of unemployment as the price of accomplishing a greater degree of economic stability. This is a fundamental and continuing problem, and its importance can scarcely be exaggerated.

Canada's post-war experience has clearly indicated that the complementary use of monetary and fiscal instruments is essential if economic instability is to be minimized. Within a decade a striking shift in emphasis has occurred, from the latter to the former approach, and the inherent limitations of a policy of continuing monetary restraint have thereby been recently emphasized. It nevertheless remains true that despite the difficult problems encountered, there is no alternative, painless or otherwise, for a society seriously committed to coping with inflation and to the preservation of economic freedom.

# SUGGESTIONS FOR FURTHER READING

The following short list of references is recommended to those students who may wish to extend their reading, and to make the selection most useful, it has been confined to readily available interpretive material. This limitation precludes any reference to a great deal of invaluable information which may be gleaned from a study of the public archives and it likewise explains the absence of purely statistical and statutory sources, without which a sound interpretation of events is obviously impossible. The reader seeking further guidance along these lines may consult the numerous references to be found in the footnotes of the text. Although the readings below are grouped by chapters, it will be apparent that in some instances their relevance extends beyond the chapters in which they are listed.

## CHAPTER I

Board of Historical Publications, Canadian Archives, *Documents Relating to Canadian Currency, Exchange and Finance During the French Period* (Ottawa: King's Printer), 1925.

Board of Historical Publications, Canadian Archives, *Documents Relating to Currency, Exchange and Finance in Nova Scotia, 1675-1758* (Ottawa: King's Printer), 1933.

Breckenridge, R. M., "The Paper Currencies of New France", *Journal of Political Economy* (Chicago: The University of Chicago Press), I.

Shortt, Adam, "Canadian Currency and Exchange Under French Rule", *Journal of the Canadian Bankers' Association*, V, VI.

## CHAPTER II

Innis, H. A. and Lower, A. R. M., *Select Documents in Canadian Economic History, 1783-1885* (Toronto: University of Toronto Press), 1933.

Nova Scotia Archives, *A Documentary Study of Provincial Finance and Currency, 1812-1836*, II, 1941.

Shortt, Adam, "The Early History of Canadian Banking", *Journal of the Canadian Bankers' Association*, IV, V, VII.

—————— , "The History of Canadian Metallic Currency", *Transactions of the Canadian Institute* (Toronto: University of Toronto Press), 1912.

—————— , "Founders of Canadian Banking", *Journal of the Canadian Bankers' Association*, XXIX, XXX, XXXIII.

253

## Chapter III

Bank of Montreal, *The Centenary of the Bank of Montreal* (Montreal), 1917.
Bank of Nova Scotia, *The Bank of Nova Scotia, 1832-1932* (Toronto), 1932.
Breckenridge, R. M., *The History of Banking in Canada* (Washington: National Monetary Commission), 1910.
Canada, *First Report of the Committee on Banking and Currency* (Ottawa), 1869.
Fleming, Horace A., "Halifax Currency", *Journal of the Canadian Bankers' Association*, XXX.
McLachlan, R. W., "The Copper Currency of the Canadian Banks, 1837-1857", *Transactions of the Royal Society of Canada*, Section II, 1903.
Ross, V., *A History of the Canadian Bank of Commerce* (Toronto: Oxford University Press), I, II, 1920.
Shortt, Adam, "The History of Canadian Currency", *Journal of the Canadian Bankers' Association*, VII.

## Chapter IV

Curtis, Clifford A., "The Evolution of Canadian Banking", *Annals of the American Academy of Political and Social Science*, 1947.
Hamilton, M. D., "Section 88 of the Bank Act", *Journal of the Canadian Bankers' Association*, XXXI.
Jamieson, A. B., *Chartered Banking in Canada* (Toronto: The Ryerson Press), 1953.
Knox, Frank A., *An Introduction to Money, Banking and International Finance* (Queen's University, Fellows' Course in Banking), mimeographed text.

## Chapter V

*Catalogue of the Hudson's Bay Company's Historical Exhibit at Winnipeg, 1925* (Winnipeg: Hudson's Bay Company).
Lowe, Peter, "All Western Dollars", *Papers Read Before the Historical and Scientific Society of Manitoba, 1945-46* (Winnipeg), 1946.
Reid, R. L., "The First Bank in Western Canada", *Canadian Historical Review*, VII.
Scholefield, E. O. S., *British Columbia* (Vancouver: S. J. Clarke Publishing Company), 1914.

## Chapter VI

*Bank Act Revision Proceedings by the Select Standing Committee on Banking and Commerce* (Canadian Bankers' Association), 1933.
Curtis, Clifford A, "The Canadian Banks and War Finance", *Contributions to Canadian Economics* (Toronto: University of Toronto Press), III, 1931.
————, "Canada and the Gold Standard", *Queen's Quarterly*, XXXVIII.
————, "The Canadian Monetary Situation", *Journal of Political Economy*, XL.

Deutsch, John J., "War Finance and the Canadian Economy, 1914-1920", *Canadian Journal of Economics and Political Science*, VI.

Knox, Frank A., "Canadian War Finance and the Balance of Payments, 1914-18", *Canadian Journal of Economics and Political Science*, VI.

MacGibbon, Duncan A., *Report of the Commissioner on Banking and Credit With Respect to the Industry of Agriculture in the Province of Alberta, 1922* (Edmonton), 1923.

White, Sir Thomas, *The Story of Canada's War Finance* (Montreal), 1921.

## Chapter VII

Canada, *Report of the Royal Commission on Banking and Currency in Canada* (Ottawa: King's Printer), 1933. (See also the mimeographed *Evidence* presented to this Commission).

Canada, House of Commons, Session 1939, *Memoranda and Tables Respecting the Bank of Canada* (Evidence Given Before the Standing Committee on Banking and Commerce).

Canada, House of Commons, *Evidence and Proceedings of the Standing Committee on Banking and Commerce* (Annual).

Canada, Minister of Finance, *Budget Speech* (Annual).

Clark, W. Clifford, "The Flight From the Gold Standard", *Queen's Quarterly*, XXXVIII.

Elliott, G. Alex, "Canadian Monetary Policy-Drift, Domestic Management and Debts", *Proceedings of the Canadian Political Science Association*, VI.

Knox, Frank A., *Dominion Monetary Policy, 1929-34* (Ottawa: The King's Printer), 1939.

Neufeld, E. P., *Bank of Canada Operations, 1935-1954* (Toronto: The University of Toronto Press), 1955.

Noble, S. R., "The Monetary Experience of Canada During the Depression", in Arthur D. Gayer, *The Lessons of Monetary Experience* (New York: Farrar and Rinehart, Inc.), 1937.

Plumptre, A. F. Wynne, *Central Banking in the British Dominions* (Toronto: University of Toronto Press), 1940.

## Chapter VIII

Aberhart, Wm. A., *Social Credit Manual* (Calgary), 1935.

Coe, V. F., "Dated Stamp Scrip in Alberta", *Canadian Journal of Economics and Political Science*, IV.

*The Constitutionality and Economic Aspects of Social Credit*. Evidence Before the Agricultural Committee of the Alberta Legislature, 1935 Session (Edmonton: King's Printer), 1935.

## Chapter IX

Bank of Canada, *Annual Report*.

Canada, Minister of Finance, *Budget Speech* (Annual).

Knox, Frank A., "Canada's Balance of International Payments, 1940-45", Canadian Journal of Economics and Political Science, XIII.

McIvor, R. Craig, "Canadian Wartime Fiscal Policy, 1939-46", *Canadian Journal of Economics and Political Science*, XIV.

Parkinson, J. F., "Some Problems of War Finance in Canada", *Canadian Journal of Economics and Political Science*, VI.

Rasminsky, Louis, "Foreign Exchange Control in Canada: Purposes and Methods", in J. F. Parkinson, ed., *Canadian War Economics* (Toronto), 1941.

## Chapter X

Bank of Canada, *Annual Report*.

Barber, Clarence L., "Canada's Post-War Monetary Policy, 1945-54", *Canadian Journal of Economics and Political Science*, XXIII.

Canada, Minister of Finance, *Budget Speech* (Annual).

Clark, W. Clifford, "Canada's Post-War Finance", *Canadian Tax Journal*, I.

Dorrance, G. S., "The Bank of Canada", in R. S. Sayers, ed., *Banking in the British Commonwealth* (Oxford), 1952.

Eastman, Harry C., "Canadian Post-War Monetary Policy: A Comment", *Canadian Journal of Economics and Political Science*, XXI.

McIvor, R. Craig, "Canadian Post-War Monetary Policy: A Rejoinder", *Canadian Journal of Economics and Political Science*, XXI.

McIvor, R. Craig and Panabaker, John H., "Canadian Post-War Monetary Policy, 1946-52", *Canadian Journal of Economics and Political Science*, XX.

Timlin, Mabel F., "Recent Developments in Canadian Monetary Policy", *American Economic Review*, XLIII.

## Chapter XI

Bank of Canada, *Annual Report*, 1955, 1956, 1957.

Canada, Minister of Finance, *Budget Speech* (Annual).

Galbraith, J. Kenneth, "Are Living Costs Out of Control?", *The Atlantic Monthly*, April, 1957.

Perry, J. Harvey, "Some Aspects of Recent Fiscal Policy," *Canadian Tax Journal*, V.

Robertson, Sir Dennis H., "The Role of Persuasion in Economic Affairs" in *Economic Commentaries* (London: The Staples Press, Ltd.), 1956.

# INDEX